Nutshell Series
Hornbook Series
and
Black Letter Series
of
WEST PUBLISHING
P.O. Box 64526
St. Paul, Minnesota 55164–0526

Accounting

FARIS' ACCOUNTING AND LAW IN A NUTSHELL, 377 pages, 1984. Softcover. (Text)

Administrative Law

AMAN AND MAYTON'S HORNBOOK ON ADMINISTRATIVE LAW, 917 pages, 1993. (Text)

GELLHORN AND LEVIN'S ADMINISTRATIVE LAW AND PROCESS IN A NUTSHELL, Third Edition, 479 pages, 1990. Softcover. (Text)

Admiralty

MARAIST'S ADMIRALTY IN A NUTSHELL, Second Edition, 379 pages, 1988. Softcover. (Text)

SCHOENBAUM'S HORNBOOK ON ADMIRALTY AND MARITIME LAW, Student Edition, 692 pages, 1987 with 1992 pocket part. (Text)

Agency—Partnership

REUSCHLEIN AND GREGORY'S HORNBOOK ON THE LAW OF AGENCY AND PARTNERSHIP, Second Edition, 683 pages, 1990. (Text)

STEFFEN'S AGENCY–PARTNERSHIP IN A NUTSHELL, 364 pages, 1977. Softcover. (Text)

Alternative Dispute Resolution

NOLAN–HALEY'S ALTERNATIVE DISPUTE RESOLUTION IN A NUTSHELL, 298 pages, 1992. Softcover. (Text)

RISKIN'S DISPUTE RESOLUTION FOR LAWYERS VIDEO TAPES, 1992. (Available for purchase by schools and libraries.)

American Indian Law

CANBY'S AMERICAN INDIAN LAW IN A NUTSHELL, Second Edition,

American Indian Law—Continued
336 pages, 1988. Softcover. (Text)

Antitrust—see also Regulated Industries, Trade Regulation

GELLHORN AND KOVACIC'S ANTITRUST LAW AND ECONOMICS IN A NUTSHELL, Fourth Edition, approximately 475 pages, 1993. Softcover. (Text)

HOVENKAMP'S BLACK LETTER ON ANTITRUST, Second Edition, 347 pages, 1993. Softcover. (Review)

HOVENKAMP'S HORNBOOK ON ECONOMICS AND FEDERAL ANTITRUST LAW, Student Edition, 414 pages, 1985. (Text)

SULLIVAN'S HORNBOOK OF THE LAW OF ANTITRUST, 886 pages, 1977. (Text)

Appellate Advocacy—see Trial and Appellate Advocacy

Art Law

DUBOFF'S ART LAW IN A NUTSHELL, Second Edition, 350 pages, 1993. Softcover. (Text)

Banking Law

LOVETT'S BANKING AND FINANCIAL INSTITUTIONS LAW IN A NUTSHELL, Third Edition, 470 pages, 1992. Softcover. (Text)

Civil Procedure—see also Federal Jurisdiction and Procedure

CLERMONT'S BLACK LETTER ON CIVIL PROCEDURE, Third Edition, 318 pages, 1993. Softcover. (Review)

FRIEDENTHAL, KANE AND MILLER'S HORNBOOK ON CIVIL PROCEDURE, Second Edition, approximately 1000 pages, 1993. (Text)

KANE'S CIVIL PROCEDURE IN A NUTSHELL, Third Edition, 303 pages, 1991. Softcover. (Text)

SIEGEL'S HORNBOOK ON NEW YORK PRACTICE, Second Edition, Student Edition, 1068 pages, 1991. Softcover. (Text) 1993–94 Supplement.

SLOMANSON AND WINGATE'S CALIFORNIA CIVIL PROCEDURE IN A NUTSHELL, 230 pages, 1992. Softcover. (Text)

Commercial Law

BAILEY AND HAGEDORN'S SECURED TRANSACTIONS IN A NUTSHELL, Third Edition, 390 pages, 1988. Softcover. (Text)

HENSON'S HORNBOOK ON SECURED TRANSACTIONS UNDER THE U.C.C., Second Edition, 504 pages, 1979, with 1979 pocket part. (Text)

MEYER AND SPEIDEL'S BLACK LETTER ON SALES AND LEASES OF GOODS, 317 pages, 1993. Softcover. (Review)

NICKLES' BLACK LETTER ON NEGOTIABLE INSTRUMENTS (AND OTHER RELATED COMMERCIAL PA-

Commercial Law—Continued

PER), Second Edition, 574 pages, 1993. Softcover. (Review)

SPEIDEL AND NICKLES' NEGOTIABLE INSTRUMENTS AND CHECK COLLECTION IN A NUTSHELL, Fourth Edition, 544 pages, 1993. Softcover. (Text)

STOCKTON AND MILLER'S SALES AND LEASES OF GOODS IN A NUTSHELL, Third Edition, 441 pages, 1992. Softcover. (Text)

STONE'S UNIFORM COMMERCIAL CODE IN A NUTSHELL, Third Edition, 580 pages, 1989. Softcover. (Text)

WHITE AND SUMMERS' HORNBOOK ON THE UNIFORM COMMERCIAL CODE, Third Edition, Student Edition, 1386 pages, 1988 with 1993 pocket part (covering Rev. Arts. 3, 4, new 2A, 4A). (Text)

Community Property

MENNELL AND BOYKOFF'S COMMUNITY PROPERTY IN A NUTSHELL, Second Edition, 432 pages, 1988. Softcover. (Text)

Comparative Law

GLENDON, GORDON AND OSAKWE'S COMPARATIVE LEGAL TRADITIONS IN A NUTSHELL. 402 pages, 1982. Softcover. (Text)

Conflict of Laws

HAY'S BLACK LETTER ON CONFLICT OF LAWS, 330 pages, 1989.

Softcover. (Review)

SCOLES AND HAY'S HORNBOOK ON CONFLICT OF LAWS, Student Edition, 1160 pages, 1992. (Text)

SIEGEL'S CONFLICTS IN A NUTSHELL, 470 pages, 1982. Softcover. (Text)

Constitutional Law—Civil Rights

BARRON AND DIENES' BLACK LETTER ON CONSTITUTIONAL LAW, Third Edition, 440 pages, 1991. Softcover. (Review)

BARRON AND DIENES' CONSTITUTIONAL LAW IN A NUTSHELL, Second Edition, 483 pages, 1991. Softcover. (Text)

ENGDAHL'S CONSTITUTIONAL FEDERALISM IN A NUTSHELL, Second Edition, 411 pages, 1987. Softcover. (Text)

MARKS AND COOPER'S STATE CONSTITUTIONAL LAW IN A NUTSHELL, 329 pages, 1988. Softcover. (Text)

NOWAK AND ROTUNDA'S HORNBOOK ON CONSTITUTIONAL LAW, Fourth Edition, 1357 pages, 1991. (Text)

VIEIRA'S CONSTITUTIONAL CIVIL RIGHTS IN A NUTSHELL, Second Edition, 322 pages, 1990. Softcover. (Text)

WILLIAMS' CONSTITUTIONAL ANALYSIS IN A NUTSHELL, 388 pages, 1979. Softcover. (Text)

Consumer Law—see also Commercial Law

EPSTEIN AND NICKLES' CONSUMER LAW IN A NUTSHELL, Second Edition, 418 pages, 1981. Softcover. (Text)

Contracts

CALAMARI AND PERILLO'S BLACK LETTER ON CONTRACTS, Second Edition, 462 pages, 1990. Softcover. (Review)

CALAMARI AND PERILLO'S HORNBOOK ON CONTRACTS, Third Edition, 1049 pages, 1987. (Text)

CORBIN'S TEXT ON CONTRACTS, One Volume Student Edition, 1224 pages, 1952. (Text)

FRIEDMAN'S CONTRACT REMEDIES IN A NUTSHELL, 323 pages, 1981. Softcover. (Text)

KEYES' GOVERNMENT CONTRACTS IN A NUTSHELL, Second Edition, 557 pages, 1990. Softcover. (Text)

SCHABER AND ROHWER'S CONTRACTS IN A NUTSHELL, Third Edition, 457 pages, 1990. Softcover. (Text)

Copyright—see Intellectual Property

Corporations

HAMILTON'S BLACK LETTER ON CORPORATIONS, Third Edition, 732 pages, 1992. Softcover. (Review)

HAMILTON'S THE LAW OF CORPO-RATIONS IN A NUTSHELL, Third Edition, 518 pages, 1991. Softcover. (Text)

HENN AND ALEXANDER'S HORNBOOK ON LAWS OF CORPORATIONS, Third Edition, Student Edition, 1371 pages, 1983, with 1986 pocket part. (Text)

Corrections

KRANTZ' THE LAW OF CORRECTIONS AND PRISONERS' RIGHTS IN A NUTSHELL, Third Edition, 407 pages, 1988. Softcover. (Text)

Creditors' Rights

EPSTEIN'S DEBTOR–CREDITOR LAW IN A NUTSHELL, Fourth Edition, 401 pages, 1991. Softcover. (Text)

EPSTEIN, NICKLES AND WHITE'S HORNBOOK ON BANKRUPTCY, 1077 pages, 1992. (Text)

NICKLES AND EPSTEIN'S BLACK LETTER ON CREDITORS' RIGHTS AND BANKRUPTCY, 576 pages, 1989. (Review)

Criminal Law and Criminal Procedure—see also Corrections, Juvenile Justice

ISRAEL AND LAFAVE'S CRIMINAL PROCEDURE—CONSTITUTIONAL LIMITATIONS IN A NUTSHELL, Fifth Edition, 475 pages, 1993. Softcover. (Text)

LAFAVE AND ISRAEL'S HORNBOOK ON CRIMINAL PROCEDURE, Second Edition, 1309 pages, 1992 with 1992 pocket part. (Text)

Environmental Law—Continued Softcover. (Text)

RODGERS' HORNBOOK ON ENVIRONMENTAL LAW, 956 pages, 1977, with 1984 pocket part. (Text)

Equity—see Remedies

Estate Planning—see also Trusts and Estates; Taxation—Estate and Gift

LYNN'S INTRODUCTION TO ESTATE PLANNING IN A NUTSHELL, Fourth Edition, 352 pages, 1992. Softcover. (Text)

Evidence

BROUN AND BLAKEY'S BLACK LETTER ON EVIDENCE, 269 pages, 1984. Softcover. (Review)

GRAHAM'S FEDERAL RULES OF EVIDENCE IN A NUTSHELL, Third Edition, 486 pages, 1992. Softcover. (Text)

LILLY'S AN INTRODUCTION TO THE LAW OF EVIDENCE, Second Edition, 585 pages, 1987. (Text)

MCCORMICK'S HORNBOOK ON EVIDENCE, Fourth Edition, Student Edition, 672 pages, 1992. (Text)

ROTHSTEIN'S EVIDENCE IN A NUTSHELL: STATE AND FEDERAL RULES, Second Edition, 514 pages, 1981. Softcover. (Text)

Federal Jurisdiction and Procedure

CURRIE'S FEDERAL JURISDICTION

IN A NUTSHELL, Third Edition, 242 pages, 1990. Softcover. (Text)

REDISH'S BLACK LETTER ON FEDERAL JURISDICTION, Second Edition, 234 pages, 1991. Softcover. (Review)

WRIGHT'S HORNBOOK ON FEDERAL COURTS, Fourth Edition, Student Edition, 870 pages, 1983. (Text)

First Amendment

BARRON AND DIENES' FIRST AMENDMENT LAW IN A NUTSHELL, Approximately 450 pages, September, 1993 pub. Softcover. (Text)

GARVEY AND SCHAUER'S THE FIRST AMENDMENT: A READER, 527 pages, 1992. Softcover. (Reader)

Future Interests—see Trusts and Estates

Gender Discrimination—see also Employment Discrimination

THOMAS' SEX DISCRIMINATION IN A NUTSHELL, Second Edition, 395 pages, 1991. Softcover. (Text)

Health Law—see Medicine, Law and

Human Rights—see International Law

Immigration Law

WEISSBRODT'S IMMIGRATION LAW AND PROCEDURE IN A NUTSHELL,

Labor and Employment Law— Continued

LESLIE'S LABOR LAW IN A NUT-SHELL, Third Edition, 388 pages, 1992. Softcover. (Text)

NOLAN'S LABOR ARBITRATION LAW AND PRACTICE IN A NUT-SHELL, 358 pages, 1979. Softcover. (Text)

Land Finance—Property Security—see Real Estate Transactions

Land Use

HAGMAN AND JUERGENSMEYER'S HORNBOOK ON URBAN PLANNING AND LAND DEVELOPMENT CONTROL LAW, Second Edition, Student Edition, 680 pages, 1986. (Text)

WRIGHT AND WRIGHT'S LAND USE IN A NUTSHELL, Second Edition, 356 pages, 1985. Softcover. (Text)

Legal History—see also Legal Method and Legal System

Legal Method and Legal System—see also Legal Research, Legal Writing

KEMPIN'S HISTORICAL INTRODUCTION TO ANGLO-AMERICAN LAW IN A NUTSHELL, Third Edition, 323 pages, 1990. Softcover. (Text)

REYNOLDS' JUDICIAL PROCESS IN A NUTSHELL, Second Edition, 308 pages, 1991. Softcover. (Text)

Legal Research

COHEN AND OLSON'S LEGAL RESEARCH IN A NUTSHELL, Fifth Edition, 370 pages, 1992. Softcover. (Text)

COHEN, BERRING AND OLSON'S HORNBOOK ON HOW TO FIND THE LAW, Ninth Edition, 716 pages, 1989. (Text)

HAZELTON'S COMPUTER–ASSISTED LEGAL RESEARCH: THE BASICS, Approximately 70 pages, 1993. Softcover. (Coursebook)

Legal Writing and Drafting

MELLINKOFF'S DICTIONARY OF AMERICAN LEGAL USAGE, 703 pages, 1992. Softcover. (Text)

SQUIRES AND ROMBAUER'S LEGAL WRITING IN A NUTSHELL, 294 pages, 1982. Softcover. (Text)

Legislation—see also Legal Writing and Drafting

DAVIES' LEGISLATIVE LAW AND PROCESS IN A NUTSHELL, Second Edition, 346 pages, 1986. Softcover. (Text)

Local Government

MCCARTHY'S LOCAL GOVERNMENT LAW IN A NUTSHELL, Third Edition, 435 pages, 1990. Softcover. (Text)

REYNOLDS' HORNBOOK ON LOCAL GOVERNMENT LAW, 860 pages, 1982 with 1993 pocket part. (Text)

Mass Communication Law

ZUCKMAN, GAYNES, CARTER AND DEE'S MASS COMMUNICATIONS LAW IN A NUTSHELL, Third Edition, 538 pages, 1988. Softcover. (Text)

Medicine, Law and

HALL AND ELLMAN'S HEALTH CARE LAW AND ETHICS IN A NUTSHELL, 401 pages, 1990. Softcover (Text)

JARVIS, CLOSEN, HERMANN AND LEONARD'S AIDS LAW IN A NUTSHELL, 349 pages, 1991. Softcover. (Text)

KING'S THE LAW OF MEDICAL MALPRACTICE IN A NUTSHELL, Second Edition, 342 pages, 1986. Softcover. (Text)

Mining Law—see Energy and Natural Resources Law

Mortgages—see Real Estate Transactions

Natural Resources Law—see Energy and Natural Resources Law, Environmental Law

TEPLY'S LEGAL NEGOTIATION IN A NUTSHELL, 282 pages, 1992. Softcover. (Text)

Office Practice—see also Computers and Law, Interviewing and Counseling, Negotiation

Oil and Gas—see also Energy and Natural Resources Law

HEMINGWAY'S HORNBOOK ON THE LAW OF OIL AND GAS, Third Edition, Student Edition, 711 pages, 1992. (Text)

LOWE'S OIL AND GAS LAW IN A NUTSHELL, Second Edition, 465 pages, 1988. Softcover. (Text)

Patents—see Intellectual Property

Partnership—see Agency—Partnership

Products Liability

PHILLIPS' PRODUCTS LIABILITY IN A NUTSHELL, Fourth Edition, approximately 325 pages, 1993. Softcover. (Text)

Professional Responsibility

ARONSON AND WECKSTEIN'S PROFESSIONAL RESPONSIBILITY IN A NUTSHELL, Second Edition, 514 pages, 1991. Softcover. (Text)

LESNICK'S BEING A LAWYER: INDIVIDUAL CHOICE AND RESPONSIBILITY IN THE PRACTICE OF LAW, 422 pages, 1992. Softcover. Teacher's Manual available. (Coursebook)

ROTUNDA'S BLACK LETTER ON PROFESSIONAL RESPONSIBILITY, Third Edition, 492 pages, 1992. Softcover. (Review)

WOLFRAM'S HORNBOOK ON MODERN LEGAL ETHICS, Student Edition, 1120 pages, 1986. (Text)

WYDICK AND PERSCHBACHER'S CALIFORNIA LEGAL ETHICS, 439 pages, 1992. Softcover.

Professional Responsibility—
Continued
(Coursebook)

Property—see also Real Estate
Transactions, Land Use,
Trusts and Estates

BERNHARDT'S BLACK LETTER ON
PROPERTY, Second Edition, 388
pages, 1991. Softcover. (Review)

BERNHARDT'S REAL PROPERTY IN
A NUTSHELL, Third Edition, 475
pages, 1993. Softcover. (Text)

BOYER, HOVENKAMP AND KURTZ'
THE LAW OF PROPERTY, AN IN-
TRODUCTORY SURVEY, Fourth
Edition, 696 pages, 1991.
(Text)

BURKE'S PERSONAL PROPERTY IN
A NUTSHELL, Second Edition,
399 pages, 1993. Softcover.
(Text)

CUNNINGHAM, STOEBUCK AND
WHITMAN'S HORNBOOK ON THE
LAW OF PROPERTY, Second Edition, approximately 900 pages,
1993. (Text)

HILL'S LANDLORD AND TENANT
LAW IN A NUTSHELL, Second Edition, 311 pages, 1986. Softcover. (Text)

Real Estate Transactions

BRUCE'S REAL ESTATE FINANCE
IN A NUTSHELL, Third Edition,
287 pages, 1991. Softcover.
(Text)

NELSON AND WHITMAN'S BLACK
LETTER ON LAND TRANSACTIONS
AND FINANCE, Second Edition,
466 pages, 1988. Softcover.
(Review)

NELSON AND WHITMAN'S HORN-
BOOK ON REAL ESTATE FINANCE
LAW, Second Edition, 941 pages,
1985 with 1989 pocket part.
(Text)

Regulated Industries—see also
Mass Communication Law,
Banking Law

GELLHORN AND PIERCE'S REGU-
LATED INDUSTRIES IN A NUT-
SHELL, Second Edition, 389
pages, 1987. Softcover. (Text)

Remedies

DOBBS' HORNBOOK ON REMEDIES,
Second Edition, approximately
900 pages, 1993. (Text)

DOBBYN'S INJUNCTIONS IN A NUT-
SHELL, 264 pages, 1974. Softcover. (Text)

FRIEDMAN'S CONTRACT REMEDIES
IN A NUTSHELL, 323 pages, 1981.
Softcover. (Text)

O'CONNELL'S REMEDIES IN A NUT-
SHELL, Second Edition, 320
pages, 1985. Softcover. (Text)

Sea, Law of

SOHN AND GUSTAFSON'S THE LAW
OF THE SEA IN A NUTSHELL, 264
pages, 1984. Softcover. (Text)

Securities Regulation

HAZEN'S HORNBOOK ON THE LAW

Taxation—International—Continued

PARTNERSHIP TAXATION: A GUIDE TO THE LEADING CASES, STATUTES, AND REGULATIONS, 545 pages, 1990. Softcover. (Text)

BURKE'S FEDERAL INCOME TAXATION OF PARTNERSHIPS IN A NUTSHELL, 356 pages, 1992. Softcover. (Text)

SCHWARZ AND LATHROPE'S BLACK LETTER ON CORPORATE AND PARTNERSHIP TAXATION, 537 pages, 1991. Softcover. (Review)

Taxation—State & Local

GELFAND AND SALSICH'S STATE AND LOCAL TAXATION AND FINANCE IN A NUTSHELL, 309 pages, 1986. Softcover. (Text)

Torts—see also Products Liability

KIONKA'S BLACK LETTER ON TORTS, Second Edition, approximately 350 pages, 1993. Softcover. (Review)

KIONKA'S TORTS IN A NUTSHELL, Second Edition, 449 pages, 1992. Softcover. (Text)

PROSSER AND KEETON'S HORNBOOK ON TORTS, Fifth Edition, Student Edition, 1286 pages, 1984 with 1988 pocket part. (Text)

Trade Regulation—see also Antitrust, Regulated Industries

MCMANIS' UNFAIR TRADE PRACTICES IN A NUTSHELL, Third Edition, 471 pages, 1993. Softcover. (Text)

SCHECHTER'S BLACK LETTER ON UNFAIR TRADE PRACTICES AND INTELLECTUAL PROPERTY, Second Edition, approximately 300 pages, 1993. Softcover. (Review)

Trial and Appellate Advocacy—see also Civil Procedure

BERGMAN'S TRIAL ADVOCACY IN A NUTSHELL, Second Edition, 354 pages, 1989. Softcover. (Text)

CLARY'S PRIMER ON THE ANALYSIS AND PRESENTATION OF LEGAL ARGUMENT, 106 pages, 1992. Softcover. (Text)

DESSEM'S PRETRIAL LITIGATION IN A NUTSHELL, 382 pages, 1992. Softcover. (Text)

GOLDBERG'S THE FIRST TRIAL (WHERE DO I SIT? WHAT DO I SAY?) IN A NUTSHELL, 396 pages, 1982. Softcover. (Text)

HEGLAND'S TRIAL AND PRACTICE SKILLS IN A NUTSHELL, 346 pages, 1978. Softcover. (Text)

HORNSTEIN'S APPELLATE ADVOCACY IN A NUTSHELL, 325 pages, 1984. Softcover. (Text)

JEANS' TRIAL ADVOCACY, Second Edition, approximately 575

Advisory Board

[XIV]

CRIMINAL PROCEDURE

CONSTITUTIONAL LIMITATIONS

IN A NUTSHELL

Fifth Edition

By

JEROLD H. ISRAEL

Alene and Allan F. Smith Professor of Law,
University of Michigan
Ed Rood Eminent Scholar in Trial Advocacy and
Procedure, University of Florida, College of Law

WAYNE R. LaFAVE

Professor Emeritus in the College of Law and in the
Center for Advanced Study, University of Illinois

ST. PAUL, MINN.
WEST PUBLISHING CO.
1993

COPYRIGHT © 1971, 1975, 1980, 1988 WEST PUBLISHING CO.
COPYRIGHT © 1993 By WEST PUBLISHING CO.

610 Opperman Drive
P.O. Box 64526
St. Paul, MN 55164–0526
1–800–328–9352

Library of Congress Cataloging-in-Publication Data

Israel, Jerold H., 1934–
    Criminal procedure, constitutional limitations in a nutshell / by Jerold H. Israel, Wayne R. LaFave. — 5th ed.
        p.   cm. — (Nutshell series)
    Rev. ed. of: Criminal procedure in a nutshell.
    ISBN 0–314–02590–1
    1. Criminal procedure—United States.   I. LaFave, Wayne R.
II. Israel, Jerold H., 1934–   Criminal procedure in a nutshell.
III. Title.   IV. Series.
KF9619.3.I8   1993
345.73'05—dc20
[347.3055]   93–25581
                                                    CIP

ISBN 0–314–02590–1

PREFACE

This brief text is intended primarily for use by law students during their study of the ever-expanding field of criminal procedure. In preparing these materials, we have attempted to set forth as succinctly and clearly as possible an analysis of the consitutional standards of major current significance. In doing so, however, we have not wavered from our firm conviction—which we believe is manifested in our casebook on *Modern Criminal Procedure* (with Professor Yale Kamisar)—that there is no substitute for in-depth study of the basic sources: the leading cases in the field, and the critical and extended analysis of the cases to be found in the legal literature. Rather, we have undertaken this work on the assumption that the diligent student might also profit from a less cluttered look at some of the principal problems in the field. On the basis of our own experience with students and that reported to us by other teachers of criminal procedure, we believe this assumption is valid—that at some point it is useful for the student to examine only the forest and not the trees.

This is not a text on criminal procedure, but rather about *constitutional* criminal procedure. As anyone who has followed the work of the Supreme Court in recent years well knows, we have about reached the point—to borrow Judge Henry Friendly's phrase—where we may view "the Bill of Rights as a code of criminal procedure." Whatever one may think of this significant development, it is apparent that most of the difficult problem areas in the field of criminal procedure are now constitutional in dimension. In concentrating upon the "constitutionalized" parts of the criminal justice process, we have avoided the task—almost impossible for a book of this size— of describing the various non-constitutional standards applied to the criminal justice process in the 50 states and our federal system. Those standards are treated in much larger works, such as *Modern Criminal Procedure* and our treatise, *Criminal Procedure*.

For the sake of brevity and ease in reading this text, we have departed from the traditional citation style for cases. Where it would not be ambiguous, we have used abbreviations for the name of the governmental unit in the case name (eg., U.S., N.Y.), and have placed all citations in the table of cases itself. There, we have cited only the official reporter for Supreme Court decisions, unless that citation was not available. A previous discussion of the same case (or, occasionally a subsequent discussion) is noted by a section and subsection reference within a parentheses. Reference to subsections within the same section refer to the subsection letter—e.g. ((d) infra). Traditional introductory signals ("see," "see e.g.," and "accord") have been omitted where the case supports the text either through direct ruling, dicta, or the decision's general treatment of a particular case.

To make our sentence structure as short and direct as possible, we generally have not used the phrases "he or she" or "his and her." Consistent with traditional rules of construction in statutes and legal texts, masculine pronouns (which is what we usually use) should be read to refer to both male and female actors unless the context clearly indicates otherwise.

Space limitations have also caused us to cite only leading Supreme Court cases. This, we again emphasize, should not be taken to mean that secondary sources—books, law review articles, commission reports, and the like—cannot be of considerable use to the student. Those secondary materials which we have found most challenging and helpful are cited in *Modern Criminal Procedure*.

This text includes cases decided by the United States Supreme Court through July, 1993, the conclusion of the October 1992 Term.

J.H.I.
W.R.L.

September, 1993

OUTLINE

TABLE OF CASES

References are to Pages

TABLE OF CASES

*

CRIMINAL PROCEDURE

CONSTITUTIONAL LIMITATIONS

IN A NUTSHELL

Fifth Edition

*

CHAPTER 1

THE CONSTITUTIONALIZATION OF CRIMINAL PROCEDURE

---

§ 1.1 INTRODUCTION

(a) The "criminal justice revolution"

Over the past three decades, the law governing criminal procedure has undergone change so extensive and dramatic that commentators have spoken of a "criminal justice revolution." Perhaps the foremost component of that "revolution" has been the establishment through Supreme Court rulings of a substantial body of constitutional standards governing the structure and administration of both state and federal criminal justice systems. Our objective is to provide an overview and analysis of the most significant of those standards. Because of their special significance, we have concentrated upon the constitutional standards governing the investigative aspects of the criminal justice process and the standards defining the right to counsel. In the last chapter, however, we have sought as well to survey very briefly the constitutional standards applicable to the remaining stages of the process, starting with the decision to prosecute and ending with appellate review of convictions.

It would take far more space than we have available to restate even in the briefest fashion all of the Supreme Court rulings that have shaped the constitutional standards currently applicable to the criminal justice process. Thirty-five years ago, space limitations would not have been a problem. Indeed, those constitutional rulings applicable to the state criminal justice systems state proceedings—which produce the vast bulk of criminal investigations and criminal prosecutions in this country—could readily have been surveyed in less than a quarter of these pages. Since that time, however, no area of constitutional adjudication has consistently occupied a more substantial portion of the Supreme Court's efforts. Almost every Supreme Court term has been marked by several decisions producing significant new developments in constitutional criminal procedure, and by a larger group of rulings that finetuned previously announced standards. As a result, every major stage of the criminal justice process is today subject to significant constitutional standards developed in decisions of the past thirty-five years. Moreover, some basic elements of the process (e.g., police searches) are now subject to constitutional regulations, developed in a lengthy series of Supreme Court rulings, so extensive that they rival the most complex statutory codes in their comprehensiveness and intricacy.

(b) The Constitution and criminal procedure

To understand how constitutional limitations came to play such a significant role in the legal regulation of the criminal justice process, one must start with the Constitution itself. As originally proposed, the Constitution had only a few provisions relating to the administration of criminal law. But with the addition of the Bill of Rights, designed to ensure that the federal government did not encroach upon the rights of individuals, the criminal justice process took on a special significance in the Constitution.

Of the 23 separate rights noted in the first eight Amendments, 12 concern criminal procedure. The Fourth Amendment guarantees the right of the people to be secure against unreasonable searches and seizures and prohibits the issuance of warrants unless certain conditions are met. The Fifth Amendment requires prosecution by grand jury indictment for all infamous crimes (excepting certain military prosecutions) and prohibits placing a person "twice in jeopardy" or compelling him to be a "witness against himself." The Sixth Amendment lists several rights that apply "in all criminal prosecutions"—the rights to a speedy trial, to a public trial, to an impartial jury of the state and district in which the crime was committed, to notice of the "nature and cause of the accusation," to confrontation of opposing witnesses, to compulsory process for obtaining favorable witnesses, and to the assistance of counsel. The Eighth Amendment adds a prohibition against requiring excessive bail.

Finally, aside from these guarantees directed specifically at criminal procedure, there is the due
process clause of Fifth Amendment. That clause
encompasses the criminal justice process, along
with other legal processes, in its general prohibition against the "deprivat[ion] of life, liberty or
property without due process of law."

Taken together, the various Bill of Rights provisions offer an obvious potential for extensive constitutional regulation of the criminal justice process. Constitutional provisions, however, are not
self-defining. Their ultimate impact is dependent,
in large part, upon how they are interpreted by the
judiciary in the course of adjudicating individual
cases. Thus, it was not until the Supreme Court
came to adopt certain critical interpretations of the
Constitution's criminal procedure guarantees that
the potential for substantial constitutionalization
of the criminal justice process was realized.

(c) Constitutionalization and judicial interpre-
tation

Two important doctrinal developments were prerequisites to establishing, through Supreme Court
rulings, extensive constitutional regulation of the
nation's criminal justice procedures. First, the
relevant guarantees in the Bill of Rights had to be
made applicable in large part to state proceedings.
Although federal criminal jurisdiction has been
expanding over the years, almost 99% of all prosecutions still are brought in the state systems. For
the Constitution to have a major impact upon

criminal justice administration, its criminal procedure provisions had to be held applicable to state
as well as federal proceedings. That result eventually was reached through various Supreme Court
rulings interpreting the Fourteenth Amendment's
due process clause. Those rulings did not come,
however, until the Warren Court (i.e., the Court of
Chief Justice Earl Warren's tenure) adopted the
"selective incorporation" interpretation of the
Fourteenth Amendment in the 1960s, almost 100
years after the adoption of the Fourteenth Amendment. Section 1.2 of this chapter reviews this
development.

The second major doctrinal prerequisite for the
extensive constitutionalization of criminal procedure was adoption of expansive interpretations of
individual guarantees. Even though applied to the
states, the Bill of Rights guarantees, if interpreted
narrowly, would have only a limited impact upon
the criminal justice process. A narrow construction of each of the guarantees would produce a
constitutional regulatory scheme that governs only
a small portion of the total process and imposes
there limitations fairly restricted in scope and unlikely to have a significant impact upon traditional
state and federal criminal justice practices. Consider, for example, the Fifth Amendment clause
stating that "no person * * * shall be compelled in
any criminal case to be a witness against himself."
Read narrowly, that provision might be said simply
to prohibit the state from compelling the defendant
to testify in his criminal trial as to any incrimina-

ting aspects of his involvement in the offense charged. Such an interpretation would make constitutional an important structural element of an accusatorial process, but its significance would be limited to the trial, and even then, it would only restate a prohibition well accepted in all of the states and the federal system. The Supreme Court has, in fact, adopted a much broader view of the self-incrimination privilege, a view that gives rise to a wide-range of constitutional limitations. Reading the privilege to be "as broad as the mischief against which it seeks to guard," *Counselman v. Hitchcock* (1892), the Court has construed the self-incrimination clause to: guarantee to the accused an absolute right not to give any testimony at his trial (§ 8.8(e)); bar procedural restrictions that require an early decision as to the exercise of that right not to testify (§ 8.8(e)); prohibit comment by the prosecutor upon the defendant's failure to testify (§ 8.8(e)); prohibit the use of compulsory process in other proceedings besides the criminal trial (e.g., grand jury proceedings) to compel a witness to give testimony that could conceivably be used against that witness in a later criminal prosecution (§ 4.10); prohibit admission at trial of statements of the accused obtained by the state through the use of means deemed coercive, such as the threat of removal from public office, *Garrity v. N.J.* (1967); prohibit admission at trial of statements of the accused given in response to custodial interrogation by police unless the accused had been advised of certain rights (including the right to re-

main silent) and voluntarily waived those rights
(§ 4.4); and prohibit the compulsory production of
personal documents under some circumstances
(§ 4.10(c)).

As evidenced by the Court's Fifth Amendment
rulings, an expansive interpretation of a constitutional guarantee can result in the establishment of
restrictions that have a bearing upon numerous
aspects of the process. Such an interpretation can
also produce, as did the Court's Fifth Amendment
rulings on custodial interrogation, the prescription
of a series of procedures designed to safeguard the
constitutional right. So too, when expansive interpretations of various different constitutional guarantees are combined, the end product can be a
series of interrelated constitutional limitations
that extend throughout the process.

The adoption of expansive interpretations of the
Constitution's criminal procedure guarantees is not
a new phenomenon. *Counselman,* supra, held in
1892 that the prohibition against compulsory self-
incrimination was not limited to barring prosecution compulsion of defendant's testimony at trial
but extended to "any proceeding" in which a witness would otherwise be compelled to give testimony that might incriminate him in a subsequent
criminal case. Indeed, it is debatable whether any
Supreme Court ruling has adopted a broader view
of the Fourth Amendment than did *Boyd v. U.S.
(1886)* (§ 6.3(b)), also decided before the turn of the
century. Over the first century and a half of

constitutional interpretation, however, Supreme Court opinions adopting strikingly expansive interpretations of criminal procedure guarantees were fairly infrequent. It was not until the 1960s—the same period that saw the application of the various Bill of Rights guarantees to the states—that expansive rulings became relatively commonplace. Application of the criminal procedure guarantees to state proceedings gave the Court many more opportunities to rule on the scope of those guarantees, and in numerous instances, the Court responded with an expansive, far reaching interpretation of the particular guarantee.

Of course, the pattern of expansiveness has varied. The Warren Court period of the 1960s clearly marked the heyday of expansionist interpretation—although, even then, not every ruling adopted a broad reading of every guarantee. Over the 1970s, the 1980s, and so far, the 1990s, fewer and fewer dramatically expansionist rulings have been issued. Shifts in the makeup of the Court produced rulings that, in some instances, partially withdrew from the Warren Court's earlier expansionist rulings, but most often, dealt with issues at the margin or edges of the earlier rulings, and refused to extend those rulings. Indeed, the expansionism of the Court in the post-Warren Court era has consisted in large part of its acceptance of the core concepts of the Warren Court's expansionist rulings. However, over this period, the Court also has branched out on occasion to produce new, expansive interpretations in areas barely touched

upon by Warren Court rulings. So too, in other
instances, it has substantially extended the reach
of expansive Warren Court rulings.

The above characterization obviously can be disputed, particularly as to the Rehnquist Court,
which many commentators have described as de-
cidedly non-expansionist in approach. This is not
surprising, since any characterization of a Supreme Court ruling as "expansive" or "narrow"
rests, in considerable part, upon the eyes of the
beholder. A decision that one observer character-
izes as broadly expansive because it goes far beyond previous rulings will be seen by another as
simply taking a minor step beyond a very restricted starting point because it falls short of rejecting
the conceptual grounding of those earlier rulings
and leaves the law with a less than totally sweeping view of the particular guarantee. A decision
that some would characterize as a major retreat
from past expansive rulings others would characterize as largely consistent with those rulings but
simply refusing to extend them at the edges. Still,
notwithstanding the obvious influence of the individual's value judgments, most observers largely
agree as to what might be described as the "big
picture" or "general trend" presented by the
Court's rulings over a substantial period. On that
score, as compared to the overall character of judicial rulings prior to the midpoint of this century,
the Court's rulings since then generally have fa-
vored more expansive interpretations. The Court
has proceeded from the premise that a reading of

the Constitution's criminal procedure guarantees should be liberal rather than constricted, although it has vacillated, usually in response to shifts in personnel, in deciding how far it will carry this premise. Section 1.3 of this chapter explores some of the concerns that have been at the heart of both the Court's adoption and vacillating application of this general presumption, and § 1.4 treats a doctrine that arguably also has had an influence on the expansiveness of the Court's rulings.

§ 1.2 APPLICATION OF BILL OF RIGHTS GUARANTEES TO THE STATES

(a) Introduction

The first 10 Amendments were enacted as limitations solely upon the federal government. *Barron v. Baltimore* (1833). The adoption of the Fourteenth Amendment in 1868, however, significantly extended federal constitutional controls over the actions of state governments. That Amendment provides, inter alia, that "no State" may "deprive any person of life, liberty, and property, without due process of law." From the outset, the Supreme Court found troublesome the determination of the exact relationship of the Fourteenth Amendment's limitation upon the states to the Bill of Rights' limitations upon the federal government. Over the years, at least four separate views of that relationship were advanced by different members of the Court. The different viewpoints were debated in opinions spread over a period of almost a hundred years, with the sharpest exchanges often between concurring and dissenting opinions.

(b) The fundamental rights interpretation

The relationship between the Fourteenth Amendment and the Bill of Rights was first considered by the Supreme Court in the criminal procedure context in *Hurtado v. Cal.* (1884). The Court there adopted the "fundamental rights interpretation" of the Fourteenth Amendment's due process clause, an interpretation that prevailed until the early 1960s and that still influences some members of the Court. The fundamental rights interpretation finds no necessary relationship between the content of the Fourteenth Amendment and the guarantees of the Bill of Rights. The due process clause is viewed as simply incorporating all principles "implicit in the concept of ordered liberty." *Palko v. Conn.* (1937). As applied to criminal procedure, those principles require that the state afford the defendant "that fundamental fairness essential to the very concept of justice." *Lisenba v. Cal.* (1941). While a state's violation of a procedural right noted in the Bill of Rights is viewed as a likely indicator that fundamental fairness has been denied, it is not necessarily conclusive. Similarly, the absence of a specific Bill of Rights guarantee prohibiting a particular practice does not necessarily mean that the practice complies with fundamental fairness. The due process clause of the Fourteenth Amendment, like the due process clause of the Fifth Amendment, can reach beyond the specific guarantees.

In support of the fundamental rights interpretation, it frequently was argued that not all Bill of Rights guarantees necessarily reflect in all their aspects that process needed to achieve basic fairness. Some Bill of Rights guarantees were seen as reflecting only the "restricted views of Eighteenth Century England regarding the best method for the ascertainment of facts." *Adamson v. Cal.* (1947) (Frankfurter, J., con.). Others were viewed as encompassing fundamental rights in general, but not in every aspect of the guarantee. For example, the Fifth Amendment's double jeopardy clause had been held to prohibit the federal government from retrying a previously acquitted defendant both where the government's only justification for seeking a retrial was its interest in gaining a second chance to prove guilt and where it alleged that the original verdict of acquittal had been tainted by a trial error that worked to the prosecution's disadvantage. Several authorities had suggested, however, that a retrial violated basic fairness only in the former situation, since only there has the government had a fair opportunity to present its case. Proceeding from the independent perspective of the Fourteenth Amendment, the fundamental rights interpretation permitted a court to find that a retrial prohibition ordinarily is fundamental (and therefore applicable to the states) only where there was no error in the first trial. Indeed, the court could even shape its ruling to the facts of the particular case before it. Thus, while state retrials of acquitted defendants might ordinarily be acceptable where justified by trial errors, exercise of such retrial authority in a particular case, taking into consideration the "totality of the circumstances" (e.g., whether the prosecution "invited" the trial error), could still constitute a denial of due process.

Although the fundamental rights interpretation prevailed from *Hurtado* until the early 1960s, its application can be divided roughly into two periods. Prior to the early 1930s, the Supreme Court reviewed comparatively few criminal cases arising from state courts and generally ruled against Fourteenth Amendment protection of interests encompassed within the specific guarantees of the Bill of Rights. Although these decisions usually dealt with a single aspect of a particular right, the opinions often seemed to characterize all aspects of the right as "not fundamental." Thus, a decision dealing with prosecutorial comment upon defendant's refusal to take the stand was commonly characterized as holding that due process did not guarantee any element of the privilege against self-incrimination. The early 1930s, however, marked a change in direction. The Supreme Court began to display increasing interest in state criminal procedure, and state criminal cases occupied a more significant portion of its docket. During this period, the Court held that elements of several rights guaranteed by the first eight Amendments were also fundamental rights protected by the Fourteenth Amendment. In *Powell v. Ala.* (1932), for example, the Court recognized that the indigent's right to appointed counsel, an element of the Sixth Amendment guarantee of assistance of counsel, was a fundamental right as applied to certain types of state cases. At the same time, the Court rejected claims that elements of several other guarantees were fundamental. Most of these decisions, however, were carefully limited to the particular problem before the Court. Thus, in *Palko v. Conn.* (1937), the Court held that due process did not bar a state appeal from an acquittal where the trial court had committed errors favoring the defendant, but its opinion also indicated that other forms of double jeopardy (e.g., appeal from an acquittal in an error-free trial) might well violate the Fourteenth Amendment.

(c) The total incorporation interpretations

While it won majority support for many years, the fundamental rights interpretation was criticized over those years by several dissenting justices. They contended that the fundamental rights interpretation promoted a largely ad hoc, personal application of the Fourteenth Amendment. They argued that its general standards (e.g., "fundamental fairness") granted a largely "unconfined power" to the judiciary that was contrary to the basic premise of a written constitution. *Duncan v. La.* (1968) (Black, J., con.). In response to these contentions, the justices in the majority frequently stated that a fundamental rights analysis was not basically subjective, but rested upon the pervasive consensus of society, which could be determined independently of a justice's personal views. They also stressed that, in any event, the fundamental rights interpretation was consistent with the traditional view of "due process" as that concept had been developed prior to the adoption of the Fourteenth Amendment, most notably in the application of the Fifth Amendment due process clause.

The dissenting justices who criticized the fundamental rights interpretation generally argued for a much broader reading of the Fourteenth Amendment as "incorporating" the entire Bill of Rights and making all of its guarantees applicable to the states. Justice Black, the primary proponent of this view, found support for this incorporationist position in his reading of Fourteenth Amendment as a whole, taking into consideration the Amendment's prohibition against abridgement of the "privileges and immunities of citizens of the United States" as well as its due process clause. Justice Black saw the Fourteenth Amendment as reaching no farther than to incorporate each of the Bill of Rights guarantees. See *In re Winship* (1970) (Black, J., dis.). Other dissenting justices, however, argued for total incorporation plus inclusion of any unenumerated rights that were essential to "fairness" and "individual liberty." See *Adamson v. Cal.* (1947) (Murphy, J., dis.); *Poe v. Ullman* (1961) (Douglas, J., dis.).

Responding to the dissenting justices, concurring opinions supporting the then prevailing fundamental rights interpretation argued that neither the "total incorporation" nor "total incorporation plus" positions had support in the legislative history or the language of the Fourteenth Amendment. They argued that the drafters of the Amendment would have clearly stated that the Bill of Rights was applicable to the states if that had been their intent. They also rejected the contention that Justice Black's "total incorporation" position would avoid much of the subjectivity inherent in the fundamental rights approach. The focus of judicial inquiry, they argued, would simply be shifted from the flexible concept of "fundamental rights" to the equally flexible terms of the specific Amendments, such as "probable cause," "unreasonable search," and "speedy and public trial." The concurring opinions also warned that full application of the Bill of Rights would impose an undue burden on the states and "deprive [them] of opportunity for reforms in legal process designed for extending the area of freedom." *Adamson v. Cal.,* supra (Frankfurter, J., con.). Although neither total incorporation position gained majority support, the debate over total incorporation versus fundamental rights did have a substantial influence on the development of the selective incorporation doctrine, which became the prevailing view in the 1960s.

(d) The shift to selective incorporation

The fundamental rights approach lost majority support during the early 1960s, although the leading fundamental rights ruling in *Palko* (§ 1.2(b)) was not overruled until 1969. In 1961, Mr. Justice Brennan, in a dissenting opinion, advanced what is commonly described as the "selective incorporation" view of the Fourteenth Amendment. *Cohen v. Hurley* (1961) (Brennan, J., dis.). This view combines aspects of both the "fundamental rights" and "total incorporation" interpretations of the Fourteenth Amendment. Selective incorporation accepts the basic premise of the fundamental rights interpretation that the Fourteenth Amendment encompasses rights, substantive or procedural, that are "of the very essence of the scheme of ordered liberty." It recognizes too that not all rights enumerated in the Bill of Rights are necessarily fundamental, and that other rights may be fundamental even though not within the specific guarantees of the Bill of Rights. It rejects the fundamental rights interpretation, however, insofar as that view stresses the "totality of circumstances" in the particular case. Evaluating the fundamental nature of an enumerated right in terms of the "factual circumstances surrounding each individual case" is viewed as "extremely subjective and excessively discretionary." Limiting a decision to only one aspect of the particular right also is rejected as presenting the same difficulty. Accordingly, in determining whether an enumerated right is fundamental, the selective incorporation doctrine requires that the Court look at the total right guaranteed by the particular Bill of Rights provision, not merely at a single aspect of that right nor the application of that aspect in the particular case. If it is decided that a particular guarantee is fundamental, that right will be incorporated into the Fourteenth Amendment "whole and intact." The enumerated right will then be enforced against the states in every case according to the same standards applied to the federal government. With respect to those guarantees within the Bill of Rights held to be fundamental, there is, as Justice Douglas put it, "coextensive coverage" under the Fourteenth Amendment and the Bill of Rights. *Johnson v. La.* (1972). See also *Pointer v. Tex.* (1965) (Goldberg, J., con.).

The selective incorporation doctrine gained majority support during the early 1960s. Because that support included two justices who remained supporters of total incorporation, the opinions for the Court majority generally did not label their approach as one of "selective incorporation" (thereby rejecting total incorporation). However, the reasoning of those opinions clearly indicated that this was the standard being applied. See e.g., *Benton v. Md.* (1969) ("Once it is decided that a Bill of Rights guarantee is fundamental * * * the same constitutional standards apply against both the State and Federal governments"). Dissenting opinions clearly recognized and challenged this shift from traditional fundamental fairness analysis to what was a new approach, even though clothed in the overall standard of "fundamental fairness." They argued that what the majority had adopted was no more than an artificial compromise between the traditional fundamental fairness and the total incorporation doctrines. *Duncan v. La.* (1968) (Harlan, J., dis.).

The adoption of the selective incorporation position during the early 1960s was accompanied by a movement towards a broader view of the nature of a "fundamental procedural right." Consistent with selective incorporation, the Court's assessment was directed at the significance of the right when viewed as a whole, rather than concentrating solely on the particular aspect presented in the case at hand. In addition, the right was viewed with reference to its operation within the "common law system of [criminal procedure] * * * that has been developing * * * in this country, rather than its theoretical justification as a necessary element of a 'fair and equitable procedure.'" *Duncan v. La.* (1968). Finally, greater emphasis was placed upon the very presence of a right within the Bill of Rights as strong evidence of its fundamental nature.

Applying this approach, the Supreme Court during the 1960s held fundamental (and therefore applicable to the states under the same standards applied to federal government) the following Bill of Rights guarantees: the freedom from unreasonable searches and seizures and the right to have excluded from criminal trials any evidence obtained in violation thereof, *Mapp v. Ohio* (1961), and *Ker v. Cal.* (1963); the privilege against self-incrimination, *Malloy v. Hogan* (1964); the guarantee against double jeopardy, *Benton v. Md.* (1969); the right to the assistance of counsel, *Gideon v. Wainwright* (1963); the right to a speedy trial, *Klopfer v. N.C.* (1967); the right to jury trial, *Duncan v. La.* (1968); the right to confront opposing witnesses, *Pointer v. Tex.* (1965); the right to compulsory process for obtaining witnesses, *Washington v. Tex.* (1967); and the prohibition against cruel and unusual punishment, *Robinson v. Cal.* (1962). Moreover, in light of these rulings, two earlier cases were characterized as incorporating within the Fourteenth Amendment the Sixth Amendment rights to a public trial and to notice of the nature and cause of the accusation. See *In re Oliver* (1948); *Cole v. Ark.* (1948). See also *Gannett Co., Inc. v. DePasquale* (1979) (all Sixth Amendment rights applicable to the states through the Fourteenth Amendment). The only remaining guarantees addressed specifically to criminal procedure are the Eighth Amendment prohibition against excessive bail and the Fifth Amendment requirement of prosecution of infamous crimes by grand jury indictment. The Supreme Court has not ruled directly on the bail clause, but the Court's characterization of that clause in *Schilb v. Kuebel* (1971) suggests that it would be incorporated within the Fourteenth Amendment if the issue were squarely presented. Prosecution by grand jury indictment, on the other hand, was found not to be fundamental, and therefore not required of the states, in *Hurtado v. Cal.* (1884); that decision continues to be followed as valid precedent and appears unlikely to be overruled. See *Gerstein v. Pugh* (1975).

(e) Subsequent developments

As new justices come to the Court in the years since the adoption of selective incorporation, they have accepted and applied the selective incorporation principle even though they might not have supported it as a matter of first impression. One reason for this acceptance has been the Court's ability, in dealing with new issues, to find in the incorporated guarantees room to accommodate those special administrative needs of the states that are not concerns of the federal criminal justice system. See e.g., *Shadwick v. Tampa* (1972) ("stiff and unrelenting" caseloads borne by municipal government considered in allowing ordinance arrest warrants to be issued by non-lawyer clerks of municipal courts). The greatest obstacle to imposing the same constitutional standards under the incorporated guarantees to both state and federal governments has been the extension to the states of pre-selective-incorporation precedents developed in what the Court has described as the "limited environment" of the federal judicial system. *Duncan v. La.* (1968). Here, the Court has noted its willingness to reexamine the earlier precedents in light of the necessity of now making them applicable to the states as well as the federal system. The leading illustrations of such reassessments have occurred in the interpretation of the Sixth Amendment right to jury trial.

In holding that the Fourteenth Amendment fully absorbed the Sixth Amendment's jury trial right, the majority in *Duncan,* supra, noted the state's contention that incorporation could disrupt long established state practices by requiring adherence to past interpretations of the Sixth Amendment that were developed solely in terms of federal court practice. The majority responded, in part, that those past interpretations were "always subject to reconsideration" in light of new developments. Subsequently, in *Williams v. Fla.* (1970), the Court reconsidered the scope of the Sixth Amendment, ruled that it did not require a twelve-person jury as utilized in the federal courts, and consequently upheld the state's use of a six person jury in a non-capital felony case.

A similar approach was taken in *Apodaca v. Or.* (1972), although there a division over incorporationist theory did influence the result. Eight justices agreed that the constitutionality of non-unanimous jury verdicts should be resolved in the same way for both state and federal prosecutions, with any shift away from a unanimity requirement coming through a reexamination of the implications of earlier Sixth Amendment decisions. The eight divided equally, however, as to whether a 10–2 verdict should be acceptable in light of that reexamination. The deciding vote was therefore cast by Justice Powell, the only justice who challenged the premise that the same constitutional standards should apply to federal and state cases. Applying a fundamental rights analysis, he concluded that unanimity should not be required of the states, but should be required of the federal government under the prior Sixth Amendment rulings.

It should be noted that the reexamination route followed in *Williams* and *Apodaca* does not necessarily require alteration of federal court practice even though the Court rejects the constitutional foundation of a procedural standard previously applied to federal courts. Although the Constitution no longer requires adherence to that standard, the Supreme Court can continue to apply the standard to the federal courts pursuant to its special authority over those courts. Thus, the Federal Rules of Criminal Procedure (proposed by the Court and accepted by Congress) continue to require twelve person juries and unanimous verdicts. See Fed. R.Crim.P. 23, 31. So too, in several cases, the Court, after rejecting the contention that certain standards were constitutionally mandated, has imposed those standards upon the federal system pursuant to its "supervisory power over the administration of justice in the federal courts." *McNabb v. U.S.* (1943). See e.g., *Rosales-Lopez v. U.S.* (1981) (requiring voir dire questioning beyond what is constitutionally mandated). The Court has noted, however, that federal appellate courts may not use this supervisory authority simply because they view the current interpretation of constitutional requirements as not sufficiently broad to meet desirable procedural goals. See *U.S. v. Payner* (1980) (lower court could not rely on its supervisory power to effectively bypass standing requirement (§ 6.8) for raising Fourth Amendment objections); *U.S. v. Hasting* (1983) (lower court could not rely on supervisory power to reverse a conviction based on a constitutional violation without regard to the harmless error doctrine (§ 8.10) ordinarily applied to such violations).

Another characteristic of the post-selective-incorporation rulings is their frequent return to the fundamental fairness standard to impose constitutional requirements under the due process clause standing apart from the incorporated guarantees. The selective incorporation doctrine does not reject the view, recognized in the early fundamental fairness cases (§ 1.2(b)), that due process may bar state action that is not prohibited under a specific guarantee if that action results in a denial of fundamental fairness. This use of due process often allows for a more flexible, case-by-case analysis than reliance upon a specific guarantee, and the Court in post-incorporationist rulings has often looked to it even in regulating procedures that arguably may have been reached under specific guarantees. Thus, preindictment delay has been held to be governed by the due process standard rather than the Sixth Amendment's speedy trial guarantee, *U.S. v. Lovasco* (1977), and rulings relating to the seating of prospective jurors who are aware of prejudicial pretrial publicity have been based on the due process clause rather than the Sixth Amendment's right to an impartial jury, *Murphy v. Fla.* (1975), as have also rulings governing inflammatory closing arguments by the prosecution before the jury, *Darden v. Wainwright* (1986). So too, due process has been the grounding of various constitutional rights that bear upon the interests protected in specific guarantees, such as the right of the defendant to be present during every stage of the trial, *U.S. v. Gagnon* (1985), the right of the defendant to testify at his trial, *Rock v. Ark.* (1987), and the right to an impartial judge, *Mayberry v. Pa.* (1971). Of course, due process may also provide the grounding for rulings that are far removed from the specific guarantees, as the Court has continued to recognize that due process may have a completely independent content in prohibiting practices that violate fundamental fairness. See e.g., *Blackledge v. Perry,* (1974) (prohibiting the vindictive prosecutorial raising of a charge because defendant exercised a procedural right provided under state law).

§ 1.3 EXPANSIVE INTERPRETATIONS OF INDIVIDUAL GUARANTEES

As noted in § 1.1, the current state of constitutional regulation of criminal procedure has been the product of both the extension of various Bill of Rights guarantees to the states and the adoption of expansive interpretations of those guarantees. In this section, we will consider several general concerns that have influenced the Court with respect to the adoption of expansive interpretations of individual guarantees. Some of these concerns have made the Court more receptive to interpreting liberally the Constitution's criminal procedure guarantees, but others have suggested caution in extending constitutional regulation of the criminal justice process. Whether one or another set of concerns prevails in the particular case has depended upon a variety of factors, not the least of which has been the composition of the Court. Significant shifts by the Court in the weighing of these concerns provide further evidence that criminal procedure is one of those areas of constitutional adjudication most susceptible to swings of the pendulum with changes in personnel.

(a) Judicial protection of civil liberties

At least since the end of World War I, the Supreme Court has viewed as a primary function of constitutional judicial review the safeguarding of the civil liberties of individuals. This focus has produced a willingness to extend the reach of guarantees protecting these basic liberties, responding particularly to the growth of modern-day governmental authority. Thus, provisions such as the First Amendment guarantee of free speech have received far more expansive interpretations than provisions dealing with property rights, such as the prohibition against state impairment of the obligation of contracts. For at least the past several decades, the Court has viewed the criminal procedural guarantees of the Constitution as among those provisions that safeguard basic civil liberties. Thus, in one of the Warren Court's most significant expansionist rulings, the Court noted that "the quality of a nation's civilization can be largely measured by the methods it uses in the enforcement of the criminal law." *Miranda v. Ariz.* (1966) (§ 4.4). A fair criminal justice process is viewed, in somewhat the same fashion as the right of free speech, as a "bulwark" against "governmental oppression."

Closely connected to the protection of civil liberties has been a recognition of the need for especially close judicial scrutiny where the burdens of governmental regulation fall upon "discrete and insular minorities" who cannot count on the protection of the political process. *U.S. v. Carolene Products Co.* (1938). Safeguarding the rights of the accused has been viewed, at least by some justices, as a critical aspect of protecting the rights of minorities. Justice Frankfurter, for example, described accused persons as themselves constituting a highly unpopular minority (noting that "those accused of crime * * * have few friends"), and argued that the judiciary therefore had a special obligation to provide "alert and strenuous resistance" to infringements of criminal procedural safeguards. *Harris v. U.S.* (1947) (dis.). Commentators have suggested that the fact that accused persons so frequently are members of disadvantaged groups also has contributed to the Court's heightened concern that the criminal justice process be fairly administered. It is certainly true that the Court has taken significant steps to eliminate the traditional disadvantages that precluded the indigent defendant from fully exercising his procedural rights (see § 7.1). So too, the Court has noted on several occasions that, to preserve the integrity of the criminal justice process, constitutional standards must preclude any suggestion of racial discrimination in its administration. See *Rose v. Mitchell* (§ 8.2(b)); *Batson v. Ky.* (§ 8.6(b)).

Another factor arguably contributing to the Court's view of the criminal process as an especially appropriate subject for extensive judicial review is the relatively firm constitutional grounding for the exercise of such review. The Court has noted that it is "most vulnerable and comes nearest to illegitimacy when it deals with judge made constitutional law having little or no cognizable roots in the language or design of the Constitution." *Bowers v. Hardwick* (1986) (upholding a state's criminal prohibition of homosexual sodomy). That difficulty is far less likely to arise in the criminal justice area than in many other areas of constitutional adjudication. The specificity of many of the guarantees found in the Fourth, Fifth, and Sixth Amendments arguably permits criminal procedure rulings to be more firmly rooted in the text and underlying purpose of the constitutional provision being applied. Even where the Court's ruling is based upon the more open-ended due process clause, it has the benefit of the clear recognition that that clause was designed to provide procedural safeguards, as compared to its more debatable function of establishing substantive rights.

Criminal procedure rulings may also be seen as resting on a less controversial exercise of judicial review because they so infrequently produce the kind of direct conflict with representative institutions that give rise to criticism of the Court's rulings as anti-majoritarian. Unlike constitutional rulings treating other aspects of individual liberty, criminal procedure rulings ordinarily do not require the Court to review the constitutionality of legislation. Most challenges are to practices that have been instituted by the police without specific legislative approval or procedures adopted by the state judiciary on its own initiative. Indeed, the failure of the legislatures to prescribe standards designed to protect the rights of the accused has often been cited by commentators as a justification for the Court's assumption of a special responsibility for maintaining the decency of the criminal justice process through judicial review.

(b) The priority of reliability guarantees

Over the years, various justices have maintained that a higher priority should be given to those procedural guarantees that serve primarily to ensure that the truth is established at trial. Such justices tend to be much more willing to give a broad reading, particularly in the construction of remedies, to those guarantees that seek to achieve factfinding accuracy, as opposed to guarantees that serve other interests (e.g., the protection of privacy under the Fourth Amendment or the recognition of individual dignity in the Fifth Amendment's self-

incrimination clause). Of course, certain constitutional guarantees serve both to promote accuracy
and to protect other interests as well. In such
cases, justices arguing that factfinding reliability
should receive higher priority may be willing to
extend the scope of the guarantee only insofar as it
achieves the reliability objective. Thus, they
would refuse to apply the self-incrimination privilege to bar most police interrogation, but would
extend the policies of the privilege to exclude from
evidence potentially unreliable confessions obtained through interrogation so abusive as to encourage false admissions of guilt. Similarly, the
double jeopardy protection against reprosecution
following an acquittal would be given a more expansive interpretation than the double jeopardy
protection against multiple punishment for the
commission of a single offense.

Other justices have flatly rejected the contention
that priority should be given to those guarantees
that seek to ensure factfinding integrity. They
argue that all constitutional guarantees should be
treated alike and extensive relief should be available for any constitutional violation. They acknowledge that some remedies afforded for violations of guarantees protecting other interests (such
as the exclusion of evidence obtained through a
Fourth Amendment violation) often operate to protect the "guilty," but they note that those remedies
also serve the interests of society as a whole. They
also contend that attempts to separate the different interests protected by a single guarantee pro-

duce uneven interpretations of the guarantee that only serve to undermine the Court's authority. Expansive protection of all guarantees is essential, in their view, to ensure respect for the place of the Constitution in regulating the criminal justice process.

The significance of the concept of giving priority to truthfinding guarantees has varied with the composition of the Court and the nature of the issue being considered. That concept may well have had considerable influence in the development of the "fundamental fairness" standard of due process prior to the 1930s. In the post-incorporationist era, its greatest influence has been in determining the appropriate scope of remedial measures, with the broader remedies available for guarantees central to factfinding accuracy. That influence is seen in the standards developed for determining when new rulings will be given full retroactive application. Truthfinding guarantees were given special weight initially in the first prong of the *Linkletter-Stovall* standards (see § 1.4(a)), and then when those standards were overturned, in the second exception recognized in *Teague v. Lane* to the law-at-the-time standard applied in habeas review (see § 1.4(a)). Similarly, in restricting the reach of the exclusionary rule, which bars use of evidence obtained in violation of the Fourth Amendment, the Court frequently has stressed that this remedy impairs truthfinding by excluding reliable evidence. See § 6.5(c)–(g); § 6.7(a). The preference does not appear to have played a major role, however, in determining whether the Court would give an expansive reading to the basic content of particular guarantees, as opposed to the scope of remedies. While the Court occasionally has noted that a particular guarantee impairs truthfinding in the course of adopting an arguably narrow view of its coverage, see e.g., *Schneckloth v. Bustamonte* (§ 2.12), those rulings were also tied to other characteristics of the guarantee in question.

(c) Historical acceptance

Another issue bearing on the adoption of expansive interpretations relates to the appropriate treatment of the historical acceptance of a procedural practice. In particular, what weight should be given to the fact that a particular practice was well accepted and thought to create no constitutional difficulties at the time of the adoption of the Bill of Rights, or at the time of the adoption of the Fourteenth Amendment? In some instances, historical acceptance has been advanced in challenging the constitutionality of a state's modification of a traditional practice in a way that arguably lessens the procedural protection afforded the accused. See e.g., *Williams v. Fla.* (1970) (argument advanced that the Sixth Amendment jury trial guarantee incorporated the common law requirement of a 12 person jury). More often, however, where historical acceptance has been cited as bearing upon the constitutionality of a particular practice, it has been advanced in support of the thesis that a practice accepted at the time of a guarantee's adoption (or its extension to the states under the Fourteenth Amendment) cannot appropriately now be held to violate that guarantee. Thus, treating historical acceptance as strong evidence of constitutional content commonly is seen as working against adoption of expansive interpretations of constitutional guarantees.

Historical acceptance has been emphasized by the Court in many opinions rejecting challenges to practices accepted at early common law. Indeed, it has been cited as critical even where the challenged practice is seemingly inconsistent with the function commonly attributed to the guarantee in question. See e.g., *U.S. v. Watson* (1976) (upholding police authority to make arrests in public without warrants, notwithstanding ample opportunity to obtain a warrant prior to the arrest). The Court has reasoned in such cases that the historical acceptance of a practice seemingly inconsistent with the function of a guarantee indicates that the purpose of the guarantee was more limited than what a logical extension of that function might suggest. The assumed "logic" of the guarantee "must defer to history and experience," *U.S. v. Watson* (1976) (Powell, J., con.), as the Court must recognize that, in determining the intended purpose of many guarantees, "a page of history is worth a volume of logic." *Ullmann v. U.S.* (1956) (Frankfurter, J., con.).

In contrast to the above cases, various other Supreme Court rulings have held unconstitutional

practices that were well accepted at the time of the
adoption of the Bill of Rights and that continued to
be accepted through the adoption of the Fourteenth Amendment. See e.g., *Tenn. v. Garner*
(1985) (holding unconstitutional a statute permitting police to use deadly force to prevent the escape of apparently unarmed, nondangerous suspected felons). So too, the Court has held that the
Constitution recognizes rights of the accused that
were flatly rejected at early common law. See e.g.,
Rock v. Ark. (1987) (right of the accused to testify is
constitutionally guaranteed, although the "historic
common-law view" was that the defendant was
disqualified from testifying). The opinions in such
cases have discounted on various grounds the significance of historical acceptance. Some have reasoned that, in light of "sweeping change in the
legal and technological context, reliance on the
common-law rule * * * would be a mistaken liter-
alism that ignores the purposes of a historical
inquiry." *Tenn. v. Garner* (1985) (constitutionality
of police use of deadly force against fleeing felons
must be assessed in light of the greatly expanded
classification of crimes as felonies, the greatly restricted authorization of the death penalty, and the
use of handguns by modern-day police). Also cited
has been "open-ended" constitutional language
(e.g., the "reasonableness" requirement of the
Fourth Amendment) that argues against treating a
guarantee as having "frozen into constitutional
law those * * * practices that existed at the time
of the [guarantee's] adoption." *Payton v. N.Y.*

(1980). Some opinions have suggested that the historical acceptance of a particular practice did not reflect a basic value judgment bearing upon the meaning of relevant constitutional guarantee, but was based on unrelated factual assumptions now commonly rejected. See e.g., *Rock v. Ark.* (1987) (common law disqualification of defendant as witness was based upon a now discredited assumption that the testimony of any party to a litigation was so untrustworthy as to require exclusion).

As several commentators have noted, the reasons offered by the Court for relying upon or discounting historical acceptance do not always provide a fully satisfactory explanation of the differing treatment of such history from one case to another. Many of the factors cited by the Court are quite flexible, as evidenced by frequent divisions among the justices in applying those factors. Consider, for example, the reliance upon changed circumstances that place an historically accepted practice in a quite different setting than existed at the time of its original acceptance. Because of various fundamental changes that have occurred in the criminal justice process since the adoption of the Bill of Rights (e.g., the creation of the modern police department), a justice who is looking for such a reason often will have little difficulty finding it. In the end, the critical element in determining the weight given to historical acceptance often will be the personal philosophy of the individual justice with respect to such matters as the proper role of "original intent" in constitutional interpretation and the appropriateness of infusing new meaning into constitutional guarantees so as to reflect current societal aspirations for a more fair and just society.

(d) The desirability of a per se analysis

Still another issue on which the judicial philosophy of the individual justice will have considerable bearing is the appropriateness of adopting what is sometimes described as a "per se" analysis. Such an analysis substitutes a per se or flat constitutional prohibition for a case-by-case determination of whether the particular circumstances presented resulted in a violation of the rights of the accused. Of course, the underlying purpose of a constitutional guarantee will often require by its logic a flat prohibition. The self-incrimination clause, for example, necessarily prohibits under all circumstances the compulsion of a defendant to testify against himself in his criminal trial. Adoption of a flat prohibition becomes controversial, however, where the Court acknowledges that under a case-by-case analysis the circumstances of the particular case could establish that a particular practice did not there operate contrary to the constitutional guarantee, but nonetheless that practice will be treated as a per se constitutional violation because of difficulties that would be presented in evaluating its operation in the special setting of each case. *Miranda v. Ariz.* (§ 4.4) has been described by the Court as relying upon such a per se analysis.

Miranda held that custodial interrogation not accompanied by certain warnings constituted proscribed "compulsion" under the Fifth Amendment no matter how short the interrogation, how sophisticated and knowledgeable the suspect, or how unpressured the setting in which the interrogation took place. *Miranda*, the Court later noted, created an "irrebuttable presumption" of compulsion where warnings were not given in preference to attempting to ascertain whether compulsion existed under all of the circumstances of the particular custodial interrogation. *Ore. v. Elstad* (1985).

Depending upon a justice's interpretation of the basic thrust of a guarantee, a "flat" or "bright line" rule may be seen as either a direct mandate of the constitutional guarantee or a product of a per se analysis. Consider, for example, the *Gideon v. Wainwright* (§ 7.1(b)) requirement that an indigent felony defendant be provided with court appointed counsel. Justice Harlan, concurring in *Gideon*, concluded that the Constitution required the appointment of counsel only where the special circumstances of the particular case made counsel's assistance necessary to ensure a fair trial, but he nonetheless accepted the *Gideon* ruling under a per se analysis—because of the great difficulties experienced by the lower courts in determining after-the-fact whether the absence of counsel had deprived the indigent of a fair trial, it was appropriate to mandate the appointment of counsel in all felony cases. Justice Black's opinion for the Court in *Gideon*, on the other hand, apparently read the Sixth Amendment as prescribing the assistance of counsel as an invariable prerequisite for a constitutionally acceptable felony trial, and reasoned that the state therefore was mandated to provide counsel for the indigent in all such trials, just as it provided other procedural rights (e.g., notice of charges).

What factors justify adoption of a per se analysis where the justices agree that a flat prohibition can only be grounded upon such an analysis? Most frequently the Court has cited various difficulties that would flow from adopting the alternative of a constitutional standard that focused upon the circumstances of the particular case. These difficulties include the failure to provide a clear direction to officials bound by the standard (a deficiency viewed as especially pernicious in regulating police activities), the possibility of inviting abuse by those officials in the form of fabricated testimony as to relevant circumstances, the significant adjudicatory burdens that would be placed upon lower courts, and the special problems presented in assessing certain types of circumstances (e.g., the motive of the official involved). In some instances, the Court has pointed to actual experience with a "totality of the circumstances" approach as evidence that the failings of such an approach require the Court to move to a flat rule based on a per se analysis. In others, a per se analysis has been adopted in a matter of first impression, in anticipation of the problems that presumably would arise under a more flexible standard.

In the latter situation, in particular, judicial philosophy may be the critical factor in determining whether a justice is willing to adopt a per se analysis. Some justices believe the Court should always be willing to cast a protective cloak around a guarantee where that will be helpful in ensuring its fullest implementation. Others, however, believe the Court should be more cautious in taking such action where its cost is to make the state's criminal justice process less efficient by taking from the state authority that could be exercised consistent with that guarantee under various circumstances. They would restrict the adoption of a per se rule to situations where "the factual premises for [the] rule are so generally prevalent that little would be lost and much would be gained by abandoning case-by-case analysis." *Rakas v. Ill.* (1978). This difference in philosophy is reflected in the division among the justices in various cases that speak to the adoption of a per se analysis. See e.g., *Maine v. Moulton* (§ 4.3(e)) (division as to the propriety of barring under the Sixth Amendment government use of information police obtained from an unrepresented, charged defendant relating to the offense charged where the police investigation could conceivably be justified as directed at other activities for which charges had not yet been brought).

While the Court's willingness to adopt a per se approach is commonly seen as favoring the adoption of expansive interpretations of individual guarantees, that approach can also be "turned

around" to produce constitutional protection narrower than that which would be available under an
examination of all of the circumstances of a particular case. Some justices have argued, for example,
that there is special need in interpreting the
Fourth Amendment to provide police with clear
guidelines, permitting the adoption of standardized
procedures. Accordingly, they have been willing
to carve out generalized areas of acceptable police
authority even though in some instances the exercise of that authority may not be justified by the
exigency that supports its constitutionality. Thus,
police authority to conduct a warrantless search
incident to an arrest, justified by the need to prevent the arrestee from destroying evidence or seizing hidden weapons, has been held under a "bright
line rule" to permit the search of the entire passenger compartment of an automobile, even though it
might have been physically impossible for the arrestee to have reached into that area under the
circumstances of the case (e.g., because he was
handcuffed and removed from the car). *N.Y. v.
Belton* (§ 2.8(a)).

(e) The desirability of prophylactic require-
ments

Closely related to, although arguably distinguishable from, the adoption of a per se analysis is the
mandating of prophylactic safeguards. Whereas a
per se analysis carves out a bright line prohibition
to avoid the difficulties that would be presented by
looking to the particular circumstances of the indi-

vidual case, a prophylactic rule arguably moves a step beyond that analysis by requiring the state to take certain affirmative steps to ensure against the possible violation of an individual's rights. The most prominent prophylactic safeguard was that imposed in *Miranda v. Ariz.* (§ 4.4), where the Court required that the police give various warnings to an interrogated suspect in order to ensure that he was not compelled by the interrogation to incriminate himself. Other rulings described by the Court as imposing prophylactic safeguards are *N.C. v. Pearce* (§ 8.9(b)) (requiring a judge imposing a higher sentence on retrial to set forth the reasons for a higher sentence and to rely on justifications that will ensure that the higher sentence is not vindictive) and *Anders v. Cal.* (§ 7.3(h)) (prescribing procedures that must be followed by appointed appellate counsel in withdrawing from a case in order to ensure that such withdrawals are limited to "wholly frivolous" appeals).

Some justices see the prophylactic safeguard as simply a form of per se rulemaking, to be governed by the considerations commonly applied in determining the appropriateness of adopting a flat prohibition based on a conclusive presumption. Others, however, see the adoption of prophylactic safeguards as going beyond the Court's authority to generalize where there is a need either to avoid adjudicatory burdens or to preclude evasion of constitutional guarantees through the limitations of situational factfinding. Here, they argue, by prescribing additional procedures solely as a prophy-

laxis, the Court engages in "pure legislation."
N.C. v. Pearce, supra (Black, J., dis.). The questionable constitutional grounding for such rulings is
said to be evidenced by the Court's acknowledgment in *Miranda* that the affirmative safeguards
required there could be replaced by equally protective alternative procedures prescribed by the legislature. See §§ 4.4(a). See also *U.S. v. Wade*
(§ 5.2(c)).

(f) Administrative burdens

The more expansive a constitutional ruling, the
more likely that it will impose a substantial burden upon the administration of the criminal justice
process. That burden can take various forms, including increased expenses for an already under-
funded system, additional hearings for already con-
gested court dockets, and perhaps even insur-
mountable obstacles to the solution of some crimes.
The extent to which such "practical costs" should
be considered by the Court has been a matter of
continuing debate among the justices. The clash
of viewpoints on this score is most often found in
the fashioning of standards (particularly per se
standards) under the more flexible, open-ended
procedural guarantees (e.g., the due process
clause), and in the application of the more concrete
guarantees to new settings. Thus, the Court has
noted that where the text or history of a particular
provision produces a "constitutional command that
* * * is unequivocal," the practical costs incurred
in applying that command become irrelevant.

Payton v. N.Y. (1980). The command itself strikes a balance between the rights of the accused and society's need for effective enforcement of the criminal law, and the Court is bound to accept that balance.

Where the application of a guarantee is acknowledged to be less than clear, the justices generally tend to be spread along a continuum with respect to the weighing of practical costs. At one end of the continuum are justices who believe that administrative burdens should never be considered in reaching a result, or should be considered only where there is considerable doubt that the proposed standard would be more effective in protecting constitutional rights than a less burdensome standard. At the other end are justices who believe that, where the burden imposed would be great, the Court should extend the guarantee only if the particular extension is absolutely essential to fulfilling the function of the guarantee. In between are justices who give practical costs varying weight depending upon a variety of circumstances. They will look to such factors as whether the burden will be substantial and clear (asking, for example, whether other jurisdictions have accommodated such a burden under state law standards similar to the proposed constitutional standard), whether the burden relates to an important state interest (thus, perhaps giving less weight to a mere increase in the state's financial costs than to an increase in the inconvenience to witnesses), and whether the burden can be offset by other measures (e.g., police use of more advanced technology).

Very often differences in perspective are reflected not only as to the weighing of the administrative burden but also in the justices' evaluation of the likely scope of the burden. Thus, in *Miranda*, though looking at the same data, the majority concluded that its decision would "not in any way preclude police from carrying out their traditional investigatory role" and thus "should not constitute an undue interference with a proper system of law enforcement," while one dissenter (Harlan, J.) found that the Court was taking "a real risk with society's welfare" and another (White, J.) concluded that the Court's ruling would "measurably weaken" the enforcement of the criminal law and result in an inability to prosecute successfully a "good many criminal defendants."

§ 1.4 THE DOCTRINE OF LIMITED RETROACTIVE APPLICATION

(a) The *Linkletter* approach

In 1965, in *Linkletter v. Walker*, the Supreme Court for the first time held that a constitutional ruling imposing a new limitation upon government need not be given full retroactive application. Prior to *Linkletter*, a newly announced constitutional limitation was applied to: (1) all prosecutions initiated thereafter; (2) previously initiated prosecutions that had not yet been tried or that had resulted in a trial conviction that was still subject to appellate review within the ordinary framework for appeals; and (3) previous convictions that had became "final" (i.e., direct appellate review had been exhausted), but were subject to challenge through the collateral remedy of federal habeas corpus. The application of new rulings to federal habeas petitions was especially significant because the federal writ remained available to challenge a state or federal conviction on constitutional grounds so long as the convicted person remained "in custody" (which included persons on probation or parole as well as those actually imprisoned). Thus, a person receiving a long sentence could overturn his conviction many years after his trial on the basis of a new ruling that rendered unconstitutional a procedure that was well accepted as constitutional at the time of that trial. While that newly established constitutional error typically would not bar a reprosecution, the time lapse between the offense and the habeas overturning of the conviction often would make a retrial impracticable.

Linkletter, a habeas case, rejected the concept that all new constitutional rulings required automatic retroactivity. That concept rested on a Blackstonian view of the judicial process that treated new rulings as merely setting forth the law as it always existed. Modern day jurisprudence recognized that courts do not simply "discover" the law, but actually "make (law) interstitially." Accordingly, the principles governing retroactivity must recognize that earlier precedent was an "existing fact until overruled," and that where the new ruling went beyond that earlier precedent, retroactive application often imposed a hardship upon a criminal justice administration that had relied upon the earlier precedent. *Linkletter* therefore concluded that retroactivity should be evaluated ruling by ruling, taking into consideration that hardship factor as well as the values served by the new ruling.

Since the *Linkletter* analysis was keyed to the possible hardship resulting from the government having relied upon the law as it previously stood, the possibility of limiting retroactive application was tied to the new decision having actually broken new ground. Less than fully retroactive application was not appropriate, as no true hardship was imposed, when the new decision "merely * * * applied settled precedents to a new and different fact situation." *U.S. v. Johnson* (1982). Yet, as the Court itself later acknowledged, the precise degree of "newness" that was needed to bring the *Linkletter* analysis into play was sometimes "unclear". *Solem v. Stumes* (1984). That newness clearly was present when a Supreme Court decision overruled prior precedent, but it could also be present in a Supreme Court ruling of first impression, at least where that ruling went against the weight of the lower court precedent. *U.S. v. Peltier* (1975).

Once it was found that a particular decision had indeed established a "new" rule, *Linkletter* directed that three factors be considered in determining whether that rule should be given less than full retroactive application. Those factors were commonly described as the "*Stovall*" criteria, based upon their reformulation in *Stovall v. Denno* (1967). The "criteria guiding the resolution of the question" of retroactivity, *Stovall* noted, "implicate (a) the purpose to be served by the new standards, (b) the extent of the reliance by law enforcement authorities on the old standards, and (c) the effect on the administration of justice of a retroactive application of the new standards."

The first of the *Stovall* criteria—the purpose to be served by the newly announced constitutional standard—was in itself controlling in two situations. First, where the new ruling established a state's lack of authority to convict, without regard to the procedures employed, the ruling automatically would be given full retroactive application. What such a ruling established was the state's lack of jurisdiction and inherent in such a finding was the premise that an earlier obtained conviction could not stand, even if based on prior rulings that had accepted the state's authority. Second, where the new rule's "major purpose" was to "overcome an aspect of the criminal trial that substantially impairs its truthfinding function", and thereby "raise[d] serious questions about the accuracy of guilty verdicts", here again, "complete retroactive effect" was required. *Williams v. U.S.* (1971). The importance of achieving accuracy (see § 1.3(b)), as it related to the protection of the possibly innocent, overrode any possible hardship to the state in applying the rule retroactively.

On the other side, the purpose of some new rules, such as those designed only to serve a deterrent function in future cases, pointed against retroactive application. If the rule had such a purpose, or any other that did not fall in the two categories of automatic retroactivity, the two other *Stovall* criteria would be examined. The reliance factor was evaluated in light of the unexpectedness of the new ruling. A decision could announce a "new rule" because it departed from the previous law, yet pose a weak reliance factor, as where it was "distinctly foreshadowed" by earlier rulings. On the other hand, a very strong reliance factor was presented where the new rule constituted a "clear break" from previous precedent, as in the overruling of a firmly established past decision. In weighing the third *Stovall* factor, the impact of retroactivity on the administration of justice, the primary consideration was the administrative and enforcement costs of retroactive application. The costs were increased, for example, when the new rule held unconstitutional a practice widely followed throughout the United States, or when the retroactive application would require extensive hearings that would rest on factual issues difficult to determine long after the critical events had transpired.

Linkletter opened the door to nonretroactivity during the midst of the Warren Court's adoption of both selective incorporation and expansive interpretations of various individual guarantees. As the Court itself later acknowledged, the capacity to announce a new ruling while ensuring that it could not be used to "open * * * wide the prison doors" for those previously convicted, provided an "impetus" for the "implementation of long overdue reforms, which otherwise could not be practicably effected". *Jenkins v. Del.* (1969). Relying upon the *Linkletter* analysis, the Court denied retroactive application to several of the most dramatic expansive rulings of the 1960s. Although not always consistent in defining the excluded retroactive application, the Court's usual policy was to tie subsequent application of the new rule to the date of the operative event governed by the rule. Thus, if the new rule dealt with a police practice in acquiring evidence, it would apply only to cases in which the police employed that practice after the date of the Supreme Court decision announcing that new rule. *Stovall,* for example, held the *Wade* rule on counsel at lineups (see § 5.2(a)) to be applicable only to lineups conducted after the date of the *Wade* ruling. Similarly, where the new rule related to a trial or other judicial hearing, the nonretroactivity doctrine would result in its application only to trials or hearings held after the date of the new ruling. Of course, there was one exception: the defendant in the case in which the new rule was adopted received the benefit of that rule even though the operative event as to him obviously occurred beforehand. This exception was justified as "an unavoidable consequence of the necessi-

ty that constitutional adjudication not stand as
mere dictum." *Jenkins,* supra.

(b) Restricting *Linkletter:* Full retroactivity prior to conviction finality

Starting with *U.S. v. Johnson* (1982), a series of
cases overturned *Linkletter* as to proceedings that
had not yet reached the point where a conviction
became final. *Johnson* held that full retroactivity
was required prior to the point of conviction finality as to new Fourth Amendment rulings. *Shea v.
La* (1985) held that this requirement was not limited to Fourth Amendment rulings, and *Griffith v.
Ky.* (1987) held that it applied even where the new
ruling constituted a "clear break" from past precedent. For the purpose of this line of cases, a
conviction did not become final until "the availability of appeal [was] exhausted and the time for a
petition for certiorari [to the Supreme Court]
elapsed or a petition was denied." Thus, a new
ruling was now given retroactive effect (1) to all
cases that came to trial after the date of the new
ruling even if the operative event had occurred
beforehand, and (2) to prior adjudications that had
resulted in a conviction where the opportunity for
direct appellate review (through to petition for
certiorari) was still available.

The *Johnson* line of cases offered several reasons
for rejecting the *Linkletter* analysis insofar as it
applied to cases not yet final. To fail to apply a
newly adopted rule to a prosecution that had not
yet come to trial or was still pending upon direct

appellate review would be contrary to "basic norms of constitutional adjudication." It undermines the integrity of judicial review to "simply fish * * * one case from the stream of appellate review, using it as a vehicle for pronouncing new constitutional standards, and then permitting a stream of similar cases subsequently to flow by unaffected by the new rule." So too, such selective application of the new rule was said to violate "the principle of treating similarly situated defendants the same." As earlier critics had noted, giving the benefit of the new rule to the defendant whose case constituted the vehicle for announcing the rule and denying it to others whose cases were at the same stage could result in "different standards for the protection of constitutional rights * * * [being] applied to two defendants simultaneously tried in the same courthouse for similar offenses." Dissenters maintained that the line the majority was drawing, between final and non-final cases, was equally based on the fortuity of timing and produced an inequality in the treatment of like cases as great as that which arose under the *Linkletter* approach. The Court majority, however, found a greater sense of consistency provided where the distinction was tied to an appellate court's responsibility "to resolve all cases before us on direct review in light of our best understanding of governing constitutional principle." Also, direct review was more likely than collateral review to be dealing with events of a relatively recent vintage. Thus, the distinction drawn between direct and collateral review had a rough correspondence to the degree of difficulty posed by the time lapse when the retroactive application of a new rule forced the state to retry a defendant.

(c) Rejecting *Linkletter:* The *Teague* standards for finalized convictions

The *Johnson* line of cases left the *Linkletter* approach governing only the application of new rules to convictions that had become final with the exhaustion of direct appellate review and now were subject to challenge only collaterally through habeas corpus. *Teague v. Lane* (1989) rejected the *Linkletter* approach for habeas review as well. Unlike *Johnson,* which rejected *Linkletter* because of its failure to provide complete retroactivity as to nonfinal convictions, *Teague* rejected *Linkletter* because it provided too much retroactivity on habeas review.

Although there was no opinion for the Court in *Teague,* the reasoning and standards set forth in Justice O'Connor's plurality opinion subsequently were adopted by the Court majority. See e.g., *Sawyer v. Smith* (1990). Justice O'Connor's opinion started from the premise that the *Linkletter* analysis was flawed in its focus solely upon the function and impact of the new rule. The proper frame of reference, where the issue of retroactivity is presented in a habeas context, should be the function of federal habeas review. That review was designed in large part to provide "a necessary incentive for trial and appellate judges throughout the land to conduct their proceedings in a manner consistent with established constitutional principles." Federal habeas review thus served basically a "deterrent function." State courts knew that, because of habeas review, they could not fail conscientiously to apply previously announced constitutional principles and escape federal court reversal because of the docket limitations of the Supreme Court on direct review through certiorari; any such state rulings would be subject to review by lower federal courts through the habeas writ so long as the convicted defendant was in custody. This deterrent function, the *Teague* opinion reasoned, was adequately fulfilled when the state conviction was tested against the law that prevailed at the time of the final direct appellate review. The state courts could not be expected, in their duty to conscientiously apply constitutional principles, to do more than apply conscientiously the law as it stood at the time of their decisions.

Teague thus replaced the *Linkletter–Stovall* analysis with the general requirement that a habeas court review a conviction by reference to "the law prevailing at the time [the] conviction became final" (i.e. when the opportunity for direct review, including petition for certiorari, was exhausted). The Federal habeas court, with two exceptions, was not to apply later precedent that created a new rule or itself adopt a constitutional interpretation that created a new rule. Moreover, since the objective of this prohibition, consistent with the deterrent function of habeas review, was to "validate reasonable good faith interpretations of existing precedents made by state courts", *Butler v. McKellar* (1990), a broad reading would be given to the concept of a "new rule" that could not be applied by the habeas court.

Teague, in describing the "new rule" concept, stated that a "a case announces a new rule if the result was not *dictated* by precedent existing at the time the defendant's conviction became final." Later cases added that a result was not so dictated simply because it followed from the general rationale of that precedent. Thus, where two interpretations of existing precedent were "susceptible to debate among reasonable minds," the habeas court could not override the state court's adoption of the narrower of the two by applying retroactively the broader interpretation. Where "it would not have been an illogical or even a grudging application of [existing] Supreme Court precedent" to sustain a conviction, the habeas court applies a new rule where it reads that precedent to overturn that conviction, even if its reading might be more in keeping with the flavor, spirit, or logic of that precedent. *Butler,* supra.

Teague did recognize, however, two situations in which the habeas court could overturn a final conviction based on a new rule. The first was a new ruling that "place[s] certain kinds of primary, private individual conduct beyond the power of the criminal-law making authority". This exception was similar to one of those instances were *Linkletter–Stovall* imposed automatic retroactivity. If the new rule established that the criminal offense itself was unconstitutional, that rule could be applied even though the state court's earlier conclusion to the contrary may have been consistent with the precedent at the time. Such jurisdictional defects had long been recognized on habeas review, and respect for a state court's good faith application of existing precedent did not carry so far as to allow continued custody for conduct that could not constitutionally be punished.

The second exception similarly was designed "to assure that no man has been incarcerated under a procedure which creates an impermissibly large risk that the innocent will be convicted." It allowed for application of a new rule that implicates fundamental fairness by mandating a procedure "central to an accurate determination of innocence or guilt." The *Teague* plurality noted that it "seemed unlikely that many such components of basic due process have yet to emerge," but should that occur, they would be applied even though not established by precedent at the time the conviction became final. Later cases emphasized that this exception applied only to a truly "watershed ruling" that altered "bedrock procedural elements essential to a fair trial" and not simply refinements of earlier established limitations designed to ensure factfinding accuracy. *Sawyer v. Smith* (1990). Thus, this exception appears to be substantially narrower than the class of rulings that would have been given automatic retroactivity under *Linkletter–Stovall* because of their contribution to avoiding conviction of the innocent.

CHAPTER 2

ARREST, SEARCH AND SEIZURE

§ 2.1 INTRODUCTION

(a) The Fourth Amendment

The Fourth Amendment to the U.S. Constitution reads: "The right of the people to be secure in their persons, houses, papers, and effects, against unreasonable searches and seizures, shall not be violated, and no Warrants shall issue, but upon probable cause, supported by Oath or affirmation, and particularly describing the place to be searched, and the persons or things to be seized." The Amendment is applicable to the states through the due process clause of the Fourteenth Amendment (see § 6.3(a)), but on both the federal and state levels governs only conduct by agents of the government (police, other government employees, and private persons acting at the direction or request of government officials). *Burdeau v. McDowell* (1921). A plurality of the Court concluded in *U.S. v. Verdugo–Urquidez* (1990) that the word "people" in the Amendment covers only members of our "national community" and not nonresident aliens, so that the Amendment is inapplicable to the search of such a person's Mexican residence. (Perhaps the three dissenters, together with the two concurring Justices who instead stressed the inapplicability of the Amendment's warrant clause to foreign searches, would have produced a different result had the objection been not lack of a warrant but absence of probable cause.) Evidence obtained in violation of the Amendment is subject to exclusion in the state courts, *Mapp v. Ohio* (1961), as well as the federal courts, *Weeks v. U.S.* (1914), subject to the *Leon* exception (see § 6.4). The same standards of reasonableness and probable cause govern both federal and state activities. *Ker v. Cal.* (1963); *Aguilar v. Tex.* (1964).

(b) Seizure of the person

Because of the exclusionary sanction, the Fourth Amendment is more commonly thought of as a limitation on the power of police to search for and seize evidence, instrumentalities, and fruits of crime. However, an illegal arrest or other unreasonable seizure of the person is itself a violation of the Fourth and Fourteenth Amendments, *Terry v. Ohio* (1968); *Henry v. U.S.* (1959), although it is no defense to a state or federal criminal prosecution that the defendant was illegally arrested or forcibly brought within the jurisdiction of the court, *Frisbie v. Collins* (1952), except perhaps when the circumstances are particularly shocking. (Even abduction of the defendant in lieu of resort to an extradition treaty is no bar to prosecution when the treaty does not provide otherwise. *U.S. v. Alvarez-Machain* (1992).)

Whether an arrest or other seizure of the person conforms to the requirements of the Constitution is nonetheless frequently a matter of practical importance. The police are authorized to conduct a limited search without warrant incident to a lawful arrest (see §§ 2.6(b), 2.7(c), 2.8(a)), and thus the admissibility of physical evidence acquired in this way depends upon the validity of the arrest. The same is true of certain other evidentiary "fruits" obtained subsequent to and as a consequence of the arrest (see § 6.6(e)).

(c) The major issues

Several Fourth Amendment issues of current significance are surveyed in this Chapter. Consideration is first given to the areas and interests protected by the Amendment (see § 2.2), for they determine what constitutes a "search" and thus what activities are subject to the requirements of the Amendment. The most pervasive requirement of the Amendment is that of "probable cause," needed for lawful arrests and searches both with and without warrant, and special attention is therefore given to the meaning and significance of this quantum-of-evidence standard (see § 2.3). Other constitutional requirements for obtaining physical evidence by search warrant (see §§ 2.4, 2.5), without a warrant (see §§ 2.6, 2.7, 2.8), and with consent (see § 2.12) are separately considered. Finally, to illustrate the flexibility of the Fourth

Amendment limitations, this Chapter also covers some unique practices for which separate rules have been developed because of the limited intrusion or special need attending their use: brief detentions for purposes of investigation (see § 2.9); grand jury subpoenas (see § 2.10); and inspections and regulatory searches (see § 2.11).

§ 2.2 PROTECTED AREAS AND INTERESTS

(a) Property interests vs. privacy interests

What is a search under the Fourth Amendment? The traditional approach was to speak of intrusion into certain "constitutionally protected areas," in that the Fourth Amendment protects the "right of the people to be secure in their persons, houses, papers, and effects, against unreasonable searches and seizures." This property approach was rejected in *Katz v. U.S.* (1967), in favor of a privacy approach. In concluding that a nontrespassory eavesdropping into a public telephone booth constituted a search, the Court declined to characterize the booth as a "constitutionally protected area": "For the Fourth Amendment protects people, not places. What a person knowingly exposes to the public, even in his own home or office, is not a subject of Fourth Amendment protection * * *. But what he seeks to preserve as private, even in an area accessible to the public, may be constitutionally protected."

The majority opinion in *Katz* does not elaborate upon the privacy approach, except for the helpful observation that defendant's activities were protected because the government intrusion "violated the privacy upon which he justifiably relied." Justice Harlan's oft-quoted concurrence suggested a "two-fold requirement: first, that a person have exhibited an actual (subjective) expectation of privacy; and, second, that the expectation be one that society is prepared to recognize as 'reasonable.'" (But later, dissenting in *U.S. v. White* (1971), he cautioned against undue emphasis upon actual expectations, which "are in large part reflections" of what the law permits.) He also noted, quite correctly, that in asking what protection the Fourth Amendment affords people (i.e., where an expectation of privacy is reasonable), it is generally necessary to answer with reference to a place, so that many of the earlier property-based decisions are not disturbed by *Katz*.

The Fourth Amendment proscription on unreasonable "searches and seizures" extends not only to cases involving both a search and a related seizure, but also to those in which either a search *or* a seizure has occurred alone. *Soldal v. Cook County* (1992). While the "searches" part of the Amendment has to do mainly with the privacy interest, as in *Katz,* the "seizures" part concerns the interests in possession of property and liberty of person. See *U.S. v. Place* (1983) (detention of traveler's luggage 90 minutes an unreasonable deprivation of defendant's "possessory interest in his luggage" and his "liberty interest in proceeding with his itinerary").

(b) Plain view, smell and hearing

It is not a search under *Katz* for an officer, lawfully present at a certain location, to detect something by one of his natural senses (e.g., to hear "by the naked ear" conversation in adjoining motel room). But, while "plain touch" has been analogized to plain view for some purposes, ordinarily the touching will itself constitute search activity for which a justification must be shown. *Minn. v. Dickerson* (1993).

The result is ordinarily the same when common means of enhancing the senses, such as a flashlight or binoculars, are used. *U.S. v. Dunn* (1987); *U.S. v. Lee* (1927). But the use of such devices in particular circumstances may be so highly intrusive as to justify the conclusion that a search has occurred, as where a highpowered telescope is used to determine from a distance of a quarter mile the contents of papers being read in a high-rise apartment. In holding aerial photography of the outdoor areas of an industrial complex was no search, the Court in *Dow Chem. Co. v. U.S.* (1986) intimated the result would be different if (1) the place of surveillance had been "an area immediately adjacent to a private home, where privacy expectations are most heightened," (2) "any identifiable human faces or secret documents [were] captured in such a fashion," or (3) the surveillance involved "highly sophisticated surveillance not generally available to the public."

Also, it is a search to utilize other sophisticated means, such as an x-ray machine or magnetometer. But use of a drug dog to detect narcotics in a suitcase is no search because, unlike any other investigative procedure, it "discloses only the presence or absence of * * * a contraband item" and "does not expose noncontraband items that otherwise would remain hidden from public view." *U.S. v. Place* (1983). By similar reasoning, it was held in *U.S. v. Jacobsen* (1984) that field testing of a white powder uncovered by a private search was no search, as it would only reveal whether the powder was an illegal substance.

Sometimes even police action in opening a package will be treated like a plain view situation on the ground that the opening did not intrude upon any reasonable expectation of privacy. This is so as to containers whose "contents can be inferred from their outward appearance," *Ark. v. Sanders* (1979), and as to reopening of a package after controlled delivery following an earlier lawful government inspection of the package's contents, *Ill. v. Andreas* (1983), or after the private person who summoned police had opened the package to the same extent but then closed it, *U.S. v. Jacobsen* (1984).

While the characterization of an observation as a nonsearch plain view situation settles the lawfulness of the observation itself, it does not inevitably follow that a warrantless seizure of the observed object would be lawful. As explained in *Ill. v. Andreas* (1983), the plain view doctrine "authorizes seizure of illegal or evidentiary items visible to a police officer" only if the officer's "access to the object" itself has a "Fourth Amendment justification."

(c) Residential premises

Even entry and examination of residential premises is not a search if those premises have been abandoned. *Abel v. U.S.* (1960). Consistent with *Katz*, the proper test for abandonment in this context is not whether all formal property rights have been relinquished, but whether the complaining party retains a reasonable expectation of privacy in the place allegedly abandoned. As for premises not abandoned, it is a search for an officer to make an uninvited entry into even the hallway of a single-family dwelling, but the result is otherwise if the entry is into the common hallway of an apartment building. In the latter instance, some courts reach a contrary result if the building is sufficiently secured so that even common areas are not accessible to the general public.

Looking in or listening at a residence or other structure within the curtilage is no search if the officer uses his natural senses and is positioned on nearby public property, on the adjacent property of a neighbor, or on part of the curtilage of the premises being observed which is the normal means of access to and egress from the house. As for entry of the curtilage (an area to be ascertained on a case-by-case basis "with particular reference to four factors: the proximity of the area claimed to be curtilage to the home, whether the area is included within an enclosure surrounding the home, the nature of the uses to which the area is put, and other steps taken by the resident to protect the area from observation by people passing by," *U.S. v. Dunn* (1987)), the question is whether the conduct intrudes upon a justified expectation of privacy. Relevant to that determination are the place of entry (was it along a normal route of access?) and the degree of scrutiny. Mere looking into these lands from adjacent property will seldom constitute a search, though some courts deem this a search under *Katz* if the viewing can be accomplished only by most extraordinary efforts unlikely to be utilized by any curious passerby. In *Cal. v. Ciraolo* (1986), the Court held viewing from a plane in public navigable airspace was no search because "any member of the public flying in this airspace who glanced down would have seen everything that these officers observed." *Ciraolo* was followed in *Fla. v. Riley* (1989), involving a helicopter hovering at 400 ft., but the Court cautioned flights could be so rare at some lower level, albeit within navigable air space, as to constitute a search.

(d) Other premises and places

Before *Katz,* the protections of the Fourth Amendment were "not extended to the open fields," *Hester v. U.S.* (1924), typically viewed as all lands not falling within the curtilage. *Hester* was reaffirmed in *Oliver v. U.S.* (1984), where the Court reasoned that such places were not covered by the Fourth Amendment's "persons, houses, papers, and effects" language, and that a case-by-case assessment of the privacy expectation in such areas (e.g., that in *Oliver* the land was fenced, locked and posted with "No Trespassing" signs) would make it too "difficult for the policeman to discern the scope of his authority." In *U.S. v. Dunn* (1987) the Court assumed that a justified expectation of privacy could exist as to a barn outside the curtilage, so that entry of it would be a search, but held it was no search merely to look into the barn from an open field vantage point.

Though the Fourth Amendment mentions only "houses," offices, stores and other commercial premises are also protected. *See v. City of Seattle* (1967). Whether a particular investigative practice directed at such a place is a search often involves considerations similar to those discussed above as to residences, though it is no search for an officer to enter where and when there is an implied invitation for customers to come in. *Md. v. Macon* (1985). Even if certain business premises are generally open to the public, surveillance into private areas therein, such as fitting rooms and rest rooms, constitutes a search. The outdoor area of business premises, such as the fenced grounds of an industrial plant, can "be seen as falling somewhere between 'open fields' and curtilage," so that it is no search to use sophisticated aerial photography at such a place, even though physical entry probably would be deemed a search. *Dow Chem. Co. v. U.S.* (1986).

(e) Vehicles

It is no search for the police, from a lawful vantage point, to examine the exterior of a vehicle, *Cardwell v. Lewis* (1974), or to see the contents by looking through the windows, *N.Y. v. Class* (1986). Entry of the car is a search under *Katz, N.Y. v. Class* (1986), unless of course the vehicle had been abandoned in such a way that the user no longer had a reasonable expectation that the automobile would be free from governmental intrusion.

(f) Effects

It has long been accepted that the protections of the Fourth Amendment do not extend to effects which have been abandoned. *Hester v. U.S.* (1924) (containers thrown into field); *Abel v. U.S.* (1960) (items left in waste basket upon hotel checkout). After *Katz*, the question is not whether the object has been abandoned in the property sense, but rather whether the defendant has, in discarding the property, relinquished his reasonable expectation of privacy as to it. (See e.g., *Smith v. Ohio* (1990), holding there was no abandonment of a grocery bag defendant placed on the hood of a car at police order and then attempted to protect from police inspection.) One has no expectation of privacy as to "trash left for collection in an area accessible to the public" (e.g., in plastic bags placed at the curb), as garbage so placed is "readily accessible" to the public; moreover, the garbage was so placed "for the express purpose of conveying it to a third party, the trash collector," who could search it or allow others to do so. *Cal. v. Greenwood* (1988). Because only the latter reason would apply, it is unclear what result should obtain where the collector at police request takes the garbage from well within the curtilage and then turns it over to the police.

In *Warden v. Hayden* (1967), the Court discarded the so-called "mere evidence" rule, whereunder objects of evidential value only could not be seized pursuant to a warrant, *Gouled v. U.S.* (1921), or incident to arrest, *U.S. v. Lefkowitz* (1932). This rejection of the distinction between "mere evidence" and instrumentalities, fruits of crime, and contraband was based upon the conclusions that (1) nothing in the language of the Fourth Amendment supports the distinction; (2) privacy is disturbed no more by a search for evidentiary material than other property; (3) the Fourth Amendment protects privacy rather than property, so that the defendant's or the government's property interest in the items seized is not relevant; and (4) the distinction had spawned numerous exceptions and great confusion.

The Court in *Hayden* was careful to emphasize that "the items of clothing involved in this case are not 'testimonial' or 'communicative' in nature, and their introduction therefore did not compel respondent to become a witness against himself in violation of the Fifth Amendment." This led some courts to conclude that the result would be otherwise if private papers were seized, but that position was rejected in *Andresen v. Md.* (1976). The Court there held that though the Fifth Amendment privilege against self-incrimination protects a person from having to produce testimonial documents in response to a subpoena, the privilege against self-incrimination affords no protection against a search warrant, as when a warrant is utilized the person in possession has not been compelled to make the record or to authenticate it by production.

The fact that "mere evidence" is being sought, or that it is being sought from a "third party," does not limit the manner of seizure. In *Zurcher v. Stanford Daily* (1978), the respondent, a college newspaper, argued that, because it had not been a participant in the crime being investigated, the prosecutor had violated the Fourth and First Amendments by seeking evidence allegedly in its possession (photographs) through a warrant-authorized search of its offices rather than through a subpoena duces tecum. Rejecting this claim, the Court noted that nothing in the Fourth Amendment suggests third parties are entitled to greater protection against searches than suspects; indeed, a contrary rule would be unworkable in that search warrants are often obtained when the identity of all those involved in the crime under investigation is not known. The First Amendment also did not require use of a subpoena duces tecum instead of a warrant, but only that the Fourth Amendment requirements be applied with "particular exactitude."

(g) Surveillance of relationships and movements

The courts have upheld a number of surveillance practices on the questionable ground that no justified expectation of privacy was infringed because what was discovered had been revealed in a limited way to a limited group for a limited purpose. In *Smith v. Md.* (1979), for example, police use of a pen register to record the numbers called on a phone was held to be no search, as the defendant had conveyed such information to the telephone company equipment when dialing. By an equally narrow view of the *Katz* expectation of privacy test, it has been held that use of a mail cover, recording information on the outside of incoming mail, is no search. The Court similarly has said that a bank depositor "takes the risk, in revealing his affairs to [his bank]," that the information will be conveyed by the bank to police, and thus has no Fourth Amendment protection against such transfer. *U.S. v. Miller* (1976).

As for use of an electronic tracking device or "beeper" to keep track of an object's movements, the mere installation of a "beeper" in an object and its transfer to a suspect is no search because it "conveyed no information," and is no seizure because no one's possessory interest "was interfered with in a meaningful way." *U.S. v. Karo* (1984). Monitoring a beeper to keep track of one's public movements, even if visual surveillance would not have been practicable, is no search, as one "travelling in an automobile on public thoroughfares has no reasonable expectation of privacy in his movements from one place to another." *U.S. v. Knotts* (1983). But "monitoring of a beeper falls within the ambit of the Fourth Amendment when it reveals information that could not have been obtained through visual surveillance," such as that a certain object remains inside private premises. *U.S. v. Karo* (1984).

§ 2.3 "PROBABLE CAUSE" AND RELATED PROBLEMS

(a) When and why "probable cause" in issue

The Fourth Amendment provides that "no Warrants shall issue, but upon probable cause," and thus it is apparent that a valid arrest warrant or search warrant may only be issued upon an affidavit or complaint which sets forth facts establishing probable cause. Those arrests and searches which may be made without a warrant must not be "unreasonable" under the Fourth Amendment, and because the requirements in such cases "surely cannot be less stringent" than when a warrant is obtained, *Wong Sun v. U.S.* (1963), probable cause is also required in such circumstances. *Draper v. U.S.* (1959).

When the police act without a warrant, they initially make the probable cause decision themselves, although it will be subject to after-the-fact review by a judicial officer upon a motion to suppress evidence found because of the arrest or search. When the police act with a warrant, the probable cause decision is made by a magistrate in the first instance, but his decision may likewise be challenged in an adversary setting upon a motion to suppress. However, because of the *Leon* "good faith" rule (see § 6.4), a finding of no probable cause in a with-warrant case will not often result in suppression. But *Leon* is inapplicable when the affidavit was "so lacking in indicia of probable cause as to render official belief in its existence entirely unreasonable." *Leon* indicates that as far as the executing officer is concerned, the question is "whether a reasonably well-trained officer would have known that the search was illegal despite the magistrate's authorization." But *Leon* also requires good faith on the part of the officer applying for the warrant, and as to him the fact the magistrate acted favorably on the warrant request is irrelevant. *Malley v. Briggs* (1986).

Although there are many circumstances in which arrests and searches may be made without a warrant (see §§ 2.6, 2.7, 2.8), the Supreme Court has expressed a strong preference for arrest warrants, *Beck v. Ohio* (1964), and search warrants, *U.S. v. Ventresca* (1965), on the ground that interposing an orderly procedure whereby a neutral and detached magistrate makes the decision is better

than allowing those engaged in the competitive
enterprise of ferreting out crime to make hurried
decisions which would be reviewable by a magistrate only after the fact and by hindsight judgment. This preference has even resulted in a
subtle difference between the probable cause required when there is no warrant and that required
when there is; "in a doubtful or marginal case a
search under a warrant may be sustainable where
without one it would fall." *U.S. v. Ventresca*
(1965).

Although there is reason to question whether
before-the-fact review when warrants are sought is
always as cautious as presumed by the Supreme
Court, the warrant process at least has the advantage of providing a before-the-fact record of the
facts upon which probable cause is based. If the
police have acted without a warrant, the probable
cause determination must be made primarily upon
the basis of the officer's testimony on the motion to
suppress, and thus there is some risk that the facts
brought out at that time may not be limited to
those upon which the officer acted. But when the
police have acted with a warrant, the factual justification is under the prevailing practice set out in a
complaint or affidavit, and at the motion to suppress hearing the issue is whether those pre-record-
ed facts show probable cause. Thus, a defective
complaint or affidavit may not be saved by police
testimony that they actually had additional facts,
Whiteley v. Warden (1971), although where not
barred by statute it is possible to receive testimony

that additional facts were orally presented to the magistrate under oath at the time of the warrant application.

Even an affidavit sufficient on its face may be challenged upon a later motion to suppress. If the defendant makes a substantial preliminary showing that a false statement was included therein by an affiant who either knew the statement was false or acted with reckless disregard for the truth, and it appears that the allegedly false statement was material (i.e., necessary to the earlier probable cause finding), the Fourth Amendment requires that a hearing be held at defendant's request. If the defendant then proves the allegation of perjury or reckless disregard by a preponderance of the evidence, the affidavit must then be judged with the false material excised. *Franks v. Del.* (1978). This is an express exception to the "good faith" rule of *U.S. v. Leon* (1984). The Court in *Franks* did not require invalidation because of a material false statement negligently made, as a few courts had previously done, or because of an immaterial but deliberately false statement, as many courts had previously done.

Probable cause for arrest does not necessarily constitute probable cause for a search warrant, nor does probable cause for a search warrant necessarily provide grounds for arrest; each requires the same quantum of evidence, but as to somewhat different facts and circumstances. For a search warrant, two conclusions must be supported by substantial evidence: (1) that the items sought are connected with criminal activity; and (2) that the items will be found in the place to be searched. By comparison, for arrest there must be probable cause (1) that an offense has been committed; and (2) that the person to be arrested committed it. Thus, a showing of the probable guilt of the person whose premises are to be searched is no substitute for a showing that items connected with the crime are likely to be found there, and an affidavit for a search warrant need not identify any particular person as the offender.

(b) Degree of probability

The Court in *Brinegar v. U.S.* (1949) declared that "in dealing with probable cause * * * we deal with probabilities," but did not identify the degree of probability needed other than to say that "more than bare suspicion" and "less than evidence which would justify * * * conviction" was required. Some of the Supreme Court's decisions may be read as adopting a more-probable-than-not test, so that, for example, there would not be grounds to arrest unless the information at hand provided a basis for singling out but one person. E.g., *Mallory v. U.S.* (1957). But the lower court cases generally do not go this far, and instead merely require that the facts permit a fairly narrow focus, so that descriptions fitting large numbers of people or a large segment of the community will not suffice. This permits an arrest to be made on the somewhat general descriptions often given by crime victims or witnesses, though courts are not inclined to be as lenient when the uncertainty goes to whether any crime has occurred, as when the police observe suspicious activity. As to this latter situation, it is commonly said that arrest and search based on events as consistent with innocent as with criminal activity are unlawful.

Brinegar also characterized the probable cause requirement as "the best compromise that has been found for accommodating" the often opposing interests of privacy and effective law enforcement. This raises the question of whether this "compromise" must always be struck in precisely the same way, or whether instead probable cause may require a greater or a lesser quantum of evidence, depending upon the facts and circumstances of the individual case. As discussed later herein (see §§ 2.9, 2.11), certain unique investigative techniques which involve significantly lesser intrusions into freedom and privacy are governed by a less demanding probable cause standard. Also, some investigative activities are so intrusive that more than the usual probable cause showing is needed. *Winston v. Lee* (1985) (obtaining evidence by surgery requires, inter alia, strong need for that evidence). Compare *N.Y. v. P.J. Video, Inc.* (1986) (fact First Amendment interests involved does not require higher probable cause standard). The Court has wisely declined to adopt a sliding-scale probable cause formulation which would require a weighing and balancing of the competing interests in each and every case. *Dunaway v. N.Y.* (1979).

(c) Information which may be considered

Probative evidence may be considered in determining whether there is probable cause, without regard to whether such evidence would be admissible at trial. Thus, it is proper to consider hearsay, *Draper v. U.S.* (1959), and a prior police record, *Brinegar v. U.S.* (1949). As the Court explained in *Brinegar,* those rules of evidence at trial which exclude probative evidence because of "possible misunderstanding or misuse by the jury" have no place at the probable cause determination, where "we deal with probabilities. These are not technical; they are the factual and practical considerations of everyday life on which reasonable and prudent men, not legal technicians, act." Probable cause may not be established by showing the arresting or searching officer subjectively believed he had grounds for his action. *Beck v. Ohio* (1964).

(d) Information from informants

Those probable cause cases which have reached the Supreme Court have dealt almost exclusively with the troublesome question of when probable cause may be established solely upon the basis of information from an informant or upon such information plus some corroborating facts. Under the traditional view, if probable cause is to be based solely upon the informant's information, then the warrant application or the testimony at the suppression hearing if there was no warrant must reveal (1) underlying circumstances showing reason to believe that the informant is a credible person, and (2) underlying circumstances showing the basis of the conclusions reached by the informant. *Aguilar v. Tex.* (1964). This "two-pronged test" of *Aguilar* was abandoned in *Ill. v. Gates* (1983), discussed below, but *Gates* declares that "veracity" and "basis of knowledge" remain "highly relevant," so it is still useful to think about those two factors.

For example, a search warrant affidavit which merely states that a credible informant reported that narcotics are concealed in certain premises (as in *Aguilar*) is defective in two respects. First, there no disclosure of why the informant is believed to be a credible person, such as that he provided information on past occasions which investigation proved to be correct, *McCray v. Ill.* (1967), or that his statement constituted an admission against his own penal interest, *U.S. v. Harris* (1971). But this alone should not be enough, for even a credible person may reach unjustified conclusions on the basis of circumstantial evidence or information from unreliable sources. That is, even if it were established that the informant was a credible person, it would still be unclear whether he asserted that there were narcotics in the house because (a) he saw them there, (b) he assumed they were there because of defendant's suspicious conduct, or (c) he was told by someone that they were there. Probable cause cannot be reliably determined without deciding which is the case, for while an informant's direct observation of criminal conduct would suffice, *McCray v. Ill.* (1967), it cannot be decided whether the suspicious conduct is adequate unless the precise nature of that conduct is revealed to the judge, *U.S. v. Ventresca* (1965), while hearsay-upon-hearsay can hardly be adequate unless it is determined that the ultimate source of the information was also credible and in a position to know of what he speaks.

If the underlying circumstances concerning the informant's credibility are shown, but the source of his information is not disclosed, it must then be considered whether the informant's tip is "in sufficient detail that the magistrate may know that he is relying on something more substantial than a casual rumor circulating in the underworld or an accusation based merely on an individual's general reputation." *Spinelli v. U.S.* (1969). The Court in *Spinelli* said that the detail provided in *Draper v. U.S.* (1959), "provides a suitable benchmark." There, when an informant who had given reliable information in the past indicated that one Draper was peddling narcotics and that he would return from Chicago by train on one of two days with narcotics, and also described Draper and his clothing and said he would be carrying a tan zipper bag and that he habitually walked fast, there was at that moment probable cause for arrest. The officers knew from their past experience that the informant was credible, but they did not know the exact source of his information; yet there was probable cause, for, as the Court later explained in *Spinelli,* the agents had been given so many details that they could "reasonably infer that the informant had gained his information in a reliable way." That is, the informant had given enough details to justify the conclusion that his source was reliable—either direct observation, admissions by the defendant, fair conclusions drawn from circumstantial evidence, or information given by another who was reliable and in a position to know.

This self-verifying detail analysis must be distinguished from the question whether it is significant that there has been partial corroboration of the informant's tale. The Supreme Court has relied upon corroboration when neither the informant's basis of knowledge nor his veracity was otherwise clearly established. Thus in *Ill. v. Gates* (1983), where an anonymous letter said a named couple made their living selling drugs and predicted the husband would soon fly to Florida and drive back with another supply, and later police surveillance established he did fly to Florida and then drive northward on an interstate highway, this was deemed sufficient corroboration to show probable cause. The Court stressed that "future actions of third parties ordinarily are not easily predicted," and that the observed conduct, though on its face innocent activity, was "as suggestive of a pre-arranged drug run, as it is of an ordinary vacation trip." (Some cases are much easier than *Gates* because the informer's story will prompt a surveillance by which police see actions so highly suggestive of criminal conduct that the observation itself will amount to probable cause, in which case neither the credibility of the informant nor the basis of his knowledge is important. *Adams v. Williams* (1972).)

But the greater significance of *Gates* lies in the Court's abandonment of the *Aguilar* "two-pronged test" in favor of a "totality of the circumstances analysis." Two unconvincing reasons were given for such a shift: (1) that such a "flexible" standard would be easier for laymen police and magistrates to understand and apply; and (2) that veracity and basis of knowledge should not have "independent status" because "a deficiency in one may be compensated for * * * by a strong showing as to the other." Logically, that is not so. A described basis of knowledge coming from an informant of unknown veracity does not establish veracity (as compared to detailed prevarication). Also, known veracity does not show a basis of knowledge, as is reflected by the Court's repeated holdings "that the unsupported assertion or belief of [a presumptively reliable] officer does not satisfy the probable cause requirement." *Ill. v. Gates* (1983) (White, J., conc.). Just how much *Gates* has "watered down" the probable cause standard is uncertain, but it is clear that a "bare bones" affidavit of the *Aguilar* variety is still far off the mark. *Gates* cautions: "Sufficient information must be presented to the magistrate to allow that official to determine probable cause; his action cannot be a mere ratification of the bare conclusions of others."

When probable cause is based in whole or in part upon information from an informant, his identity need not always be disclosed at the suppression hearing. Disclosure is not required when the officer has testified in full and has been cross-examined as to what the informant told him and as to why the information was believed trustworthy. *McCray v. Ill.* (1967). Although disclosure may be compelled if there is good reason to doubt the officer's credibility, many courts protect more broadly against perjury and at the same time honor the informer privilege by requiring disclosure only in camera when the defendant has fairly put into issue the existence of the informant or the correctness of the officer's report of the informer's tale or prior performance.

(e) Information from other sources

The reliability of informants used to uncover narcotics and gambling offenses has been a matter of special concern because they are often engaged in criminal conduct themselves. Thus, when the facts are provided by a police officer, *U.S. v. Ventresca* (1965), a crime victim, an eyewitness, a cooperative citizen, *Jaben v. U.S.* (1965), or an informant not from the criminal milieu, there is no comparable need for establishing credibility. It is still necessary to show why the person giving the information has a basis for his knowledge, although the number of details which need be disclosed varies depending upon the circumstances. See *Jaben v. U.S.* (1965), pointing out that tax evasion is not a crime which one might directly observe and that therefore there need not be disclosure of the details of the investigation into defendant's income. A warrantless arrest based upon the conclusory statements or directive of another policeman (i.e., that a certain person should be arrested) is not per se illegal, but will be upheld only upon a subsequent showing that the instigating official possessed facts constituting probable cause. *Whiteley v. Warden* (1971).

(f) Unconstitutional statute

What if the officer has information providing probable cause to believe that the suspect has violated a criminal statute, but the statute itself is later held unconstitutional? In *Mich. v. DeFillippo* (1979), the defendant was arrested pursuant to a local ordinance, later held unconstitutional, making it a violation for a person lawfully stopped to refuse to produce evidence of his identity. Upholding the admission of drugs seized in a search incident to that arrest, the Court noted that a "prudent officer" could not be required "to anticipate that a court would later hold the ordinance unconstitutional."

§ 2.4   SEARCH WARRANTS: ISSUANCE

(a) Who may issue

Where a state attorney general, as authorized by state law, issued a search warrant in the context of an investigation of which he had taken personal charge, this procedure violated the Fourth Amendment, as he "was not the neutral and detached magistrate required by the Constitution." *Coolidge v. N.H.* (1971). But it is not necessary "that all warrant authority must reside exclusively in a lawyer or judge"; an issuing magistrate need only be "neutral and detached" and "capable of determining whether probable cause exists," and thus a clerk of court could be authorized to issue arrest warrants for municipal ordinance violations. *Shadwick v. City of Tampa* (1972). It does not necessarily follow that a clerk could be permitted to issue search warrants, as to which the probable cause issues are often much more complex.

Even a judicial officer may not issue a warrant if he has such a personal interest in the matter that his impartiality is in doubt, as where a magistrate receives a fee only when he responds affirmatively to warrant requests. *Connally v. Ga.* (1977). A magistrate's conduct may show he is not "neutral and detached," as in *Lo-Ji Sales, Inc. v. N.Y.* (1979), where the judge allowed himself to become "the leader of the search party which was essentially a police operation." If a magistrate conducts himself in such a fashion in a particular case that he is not "neutral and detached," it appears that under the *Leon* "good faith" doctrine (see § 6.4(b)) suppression is required only if the police actually knew that the magistrate had "wholly abandoned his judicial role."

(b) Passage of time since facts gathered

If information showing probable cause that a crime was committed is gathered, and assuming no other evidence to the contrary is later uncovered, this probable cause will still be present weeks, months, or years later. The same is not true, however, as to information showing probable cause to believe that certain items are to be found at a particular place. As time passes, the chances increase that the goods have since been removed from that location. For this reason, an affidavit in support of a search warrant must contain a statement as to the time when the facts relied upon occurred. This statement of time must be reasonably definite, but declarations that the observations were made "recently" or "within" or "during" a named period have been approved. *Rugendorf v. U.S.* (1964).

Just how long a time period may elapse without probable cause vanishing "must be determined by the circumstances of each case." *Sgro v. U.S.* (1932). Generally, a longer time will be allowed as to an ongoing criminal enterprise as compared to a one-shot criminal episode. Thus 49 days is not too long re a search for forged tax stamps being used in an elaborate and extensive counterfeiting scheme, but 4 days might be deemed too long as to a one-time illegal sale of liquor. It is also generally true that more time will be tolerated when the search is for items which have continuing utility and are not strongly incriminating. Thus, the passage of 3 months from a bank robbery is not too long as to search for clothing worn by the robber, but is too long as to search for the bank's money bag. Likewise relevant is the extent to which the criminal would have had access to the place to be searched during the time which has elapsed.

(c) Particular description of place or person to be searched

The Fourth Amendment provides that no warrants shall issue except those "particularly describing the place to be searched." This means the description must be such that the executing officer can "with reasonable effort ascertain and identify the place intended." *Steele v. U.S.* (1925). (However, under the *Leon* "good faith" exception to the exclusionary rule, see § 6.4(b), suppression is required only if the warrant is "so facially deficient—i.e., in failing to particularize the place to be searched or the things to be seized—that the executing officers cannot reasonably presume it to be valid.")

In describing premises to be searched, more care is generally required in urban areas than in rural areas. Farm property, for example, might merely be described in a general way and identified by section, township and range number. In a city, however, a building must be identified by street and number or by an equally specific description. *Steele v. U.S.* (1925). Minor errors in description, such as an incorrect street number, will not invalidate a warrant if it is still apparent what building or what part of a building is to be searched. In multiple-occupancy structures, the particular unit to be searched must be identified by occupant, room number, or apartment number, unless the multi-unit character of the property was reasonably not known to the officers applying for or executing the warrant and was not externally apparent. Similarly, full execution of a warrant authorizing search of an apartment covering the entire third floor is lawful where the police failure to perceive at execution that there were two apartments on that floor "was objectively understandable and reasonable." *Md. v. Garrison* (1987).

If a search warrant is obtained for search of an automobile, the description must direct the executing officer to one specific vehicle, either by license number or by the make of the car and the name of the operator. As to misdescription, the question again is whether the officer could select the proper vehicle, and thus a license number is sufficient notwithstanding a mistake as to the color and model year of the car.

A valid warrant for the search of a certain person must indicate the person's name, if known. If his name is not known, an otherwise complete description, listing such facts as the individual's aliases, approximate age, height and weight, race, and clothing, is adequate.

(d) Particular description of things to be seized

The Fourth Amendment also provides that no search warrants shall issue except those "particularly describing the * * * things to be seized." "The requirement that warrants shall particularly describe the things to be seized makes general searches under them impossible * * *. As to what is to be taken, nothing is left to the discretion of the officer executing the warrant." *Marron v. U.S.* (1927). (Here again, it must be noted that under the *Leon* rule, see § 6.4(b), suppression is necessary only if the warrant is "so facially deficient—i.e., in failing to particularize the place to be searched or the things to be seized—that the executing officers cannot reasonably presume to be valid." A somewhat different application of this "good faith" exception was involved in *Mass. v. Sheppard* (1984), holding the evidence need not be suppressed when the search warrant misdescribed the items to be seized but the police officer relied on the magistrate's representation he had corrected the description to match that officer's correct description in his affidavit.)

The degree of particularity required varies somewhat depending upon the nature of the materials to be seized. Greater leeway is permitted in describing contraband (property the possession of which is a crime), and thus during Prohibition a description merely of "cases of whiskey" would suffice. *Steele v. U.S.* (1925). By comparison, innocuous property must be described more specifically so that executing officers will not be confused between the items sought and other property of a similar nature which might well be found on the premises. The particularity requirement requires even closer scrutiny of warrants for documents because of the potential they carry for very serious intrusions into privacy. *Andresen v. Md.* (1976).

Because of First Amendment considerations, this constitutional requirement "is to be accorded the most scrupulous exactitude when the 'things' are books, and the basis for their seizure is the ideas they contain," *Stanford v. Tex.* (1965), or when they are the papers of a newsgathering organization. *Zurcher v. Stanford Daily* (1978). Also, in obscenity cases a search warrant may not authorize the seizure of great quantities of the same publication before the owner has had an opportunity to litigate the question of obscenity, for this would be an unconstitutional prior restraint. *A Quantity of Copies of Books v. Kan.* (1964). For the same reason, seizure of even a single copy of a film may not continue if it would prevent further showing of that picture by the exhibitor. *Heller v. N.Y.* (1973).

§ 2.5 SEARCH WARRANTS: EXECUTION

(a) Time of execution

Even where statutes or court rules purport to authorize execution within a fixed period of time, e.g., 10 days, the better view is that execution even within that time is permissible only if the probable cause recited in the affidavit continues until the time of execution, giving consideration to the intervening knowledge of the officers and the passage of time. Three members of the Court have suggested that a search warrant may be executed at night only upon a special showing of a need to do so, as provided by law in several jurisdictions, because of the "Fourth Amendment doctrine that increasingly severe standards of probable cause are necessary to justify increasingly intrusive searches." *Gooding v. U.S.* (1974). A search warrant may be executed in the absence of the occupant.

(b) Entry without notice

18 U.S.C.A. § 3109 provides that an officer may break into premises to execute a search warrant only "if, after notice of his authority and purpose, he is refused admittance," and many states have comparable statutes. The breaking referred to in such statutes includes any unannounced intrusion, even by opening a closed but unlocked door, *Sabbath v. U.S.* (1968), but apparently not entry by subterfuge. By analogy to the cases dealing with entry for purposes of arrest (see § 2.7(b)), it may be concluded that these statutes state the requirements of the Fourth Amendment, subject to exceptions when exigent circumstances are present. *Ker v. Cal.* (1963); *Sabbath v. U.S.* (1968).

The exigent circumstances most likely to be present when a search warrant is to be executed is the risk that notice would result in destruction of the evidence sought. Some courts hold entry without notice can be justified merely by the type of crime or evidence involved. But most instead require a specific showing of facts and circumstances involved in that particular case indicating there was a risk that the evidence would be destroyed. Under the "useless gesture" exception, notice is not required when it is evident from the circumstances that the authority and purpose of the police was already known to those within.

(c) Detention and search of persons on the premises to be searched

An individual who merely happens to be present in premises where a search warrant is being executed may not, by virtue of that fact alone, be subjected to a search of his person. This is because such a search "must be supported by probable cause particularized with respect to that person," a requirement which "cannot be undercut or avoided by simply pointing to the fact that coincidentally there exists probable cause * * * to search the premises where the person may happen to be." *Ybarra v. Ill.* (1979).

Of course, if probable cause to search that person did exist and was established when the warrant to search the premises was obtained, that warrant could also authorize search of the person. During execution of a warrant lacking such authorization, a person might be discovered within as to whom there are grounds for arrest, in which case a search of the person could be undertaken incident to arrest and without reliance upon the search warrant. *Marron v. U.S.* (1927). Or, if there are not grounds to arrest but yet probable cause that the person has in his possession the items named in the search warrant, this would appear to be an additional basis for the search, for there would not be time to seek an additional warrant. But an

actual search of such a person may not be undertaken merely because of suspicion that person may
have the objects named in the search warrant.
Ybarra v. Ill. (1979). If there is some basis for
thinking that the person may be armed, and if only
a frisk is undertaken, this would seem proper. Cf.
Terry v. Ohio (1968) (discussed in § 2.9).

In *Mich. v. Summers* (1981), the Court held that
a resident of premises where a search warrant for
contraband is to be executed may be detained there
during warrant execution. The Court explained
that such detention would serve three important
government interests: (1) preventing flight in the
event incriminating evidence was found; (2) mini-
mizing the risk of harm to the police; and (3)
facilitating the orderly completion of the search.

(d) Seizure of items not named in the warrant

Even if, as required, the police look within the
described place only where the described items
might be located, *Harris v. U.S.* (1947), and terminate the search once those items are discovered,
they may discover supposed incriminating evidence
other than that named in the warrant. As to this
situation, the Court stated in *Coolidge v. N.H.*
(1971): "Where, once an otherwise lawful search is
in progress, the police inadvertently come upon a
piece of evidence [in plain view], it would often be a
needless inconvenience, and sometimes dangerous—to the evidence or to the police themselves—
to require them to ignore it until they have obtained a warrant particularly describing it." The

requirement that the discovery be "inadvertent" was abandoned in *Horton v. Cal.* (1990), where the Court explained it disapproved of Fourth Amendment "standards that depend upon the subjective state of mind of the officer" and believed the Amendment's particularity-of-description requirement would serve "the interest in limiting the area and duration of the search that the inadvertence requirement inadequately protects." But the observed item may be seized only if there is probable cause it constitutes the fruits, instrumentalities or evidence of crime. Reasonable suspicion that the article is of such character is an insufficient basis for a closer examination of the item (e.g., picking it up to reveal a serial number) not otherwise permissible in executing the warrant. *Ariz. v. Hicks* (1987).

§ 2.6 WARRANTLESS SEARCHES AND SEIZURES OF PERSONS

(a) Arrest

The prevailing view, as a matter of state law, is that an arrest warrant is not required in serious cases notwithstanding the practicability of obtaining one before arrest. Arrest without warrant was lawful at common law when the officer had "reasonable grounds to believe" that a felony had been committed and that the person to be arrested had committed it, and this is the prevailing rule today either as a matter of statute or court decision. This "reasonable grounds" test and the "probable cause" requirement of the Fourth Amendment "are substantial equivalents." *Draper v. U.S.* (1959). On the other hand, warrants are sometimes required for minor offenses notwithstanding the need for immediate action. The traditional view is that an officer may arrest without warrant for all misdemeanors committed in his presence, but that he must obtain a warrant even when he has overwhelming evidence of a misdemeanor which occurred out of his presence. This requirement, even when interpreted to mean that the officer must only have reasonable grounds to believe that a misdemeanor occurred in his presence, is sometimes too restrictive, in that there may be a need for immediate arrest even though the officer did not witness the misdemeanor. Several jurisdictions have thus provided by statute for arrest without warrant on "reasonable grounds" for all offenses.

With the exception of the case in which private premises must be entered to make the arrest (see § 2.7(a)), there is no constitutional requirement that an arrest warrant be obtained when it is practicable to do so. While the Court has expressed a "preference for the use of arrest warrants when feasible," see *Gerstein v. Pugh* (1975), it also has declined "to transform this judicial preference into a constitutional rule," *U.S. v. Watson* (1976). Such a rule, it noted in *Watson,* would "encumber criminal prosecutions with endless litigation with respect to the existence of exigent circumstances." On the other hand, *Gerstein v.*

Pugh (1975) held that once a warrantless arrest is made, the Fourth Amendment "requires a [prompt] judicial determination of probable cause as a prerequisite to extended restraint on liberty following [the warrantless] arrest." That determination, upon a standard which "is the same as that for arrest," may be made in an ex parte proceeding (i.e., without defense participation) in the same manner as the issuance of a warrant. A probable cause determination within 48 hours of arrest is presumptively reasonable, though a particular defendant may show such a delay was unreasonable because "for the purpose of gathering additional evidence to justify the arrest, a delay motivated by ill will against the arrested individual, or delay for delay's sake." On the other hand, a later probable cause determination is presumptively unreasonable, meaning "the burden shifts to the government to demonstrate the existence of a bona fide emergency or other extraordinary circumstance." *County of Riverside v. McLaughlin* (1991).

Rejecting the contention that *Watson* means the Fourth Amendment has nothing to say about *how* a seizure is made, the Court in *Tenn. v. Garner* (1985) held that the use of deadly force to arrest a fleeing felon is unreasonable unless "the suspect threatens the officer with a weapon or there is probable cause to believe that he has committed a crime involving the infliction or threatened infliction of serious physical harm." The Fourth Amendment reasonableness standard (1) applies to "*all* claims that law enforcement officers have used

excessive force—deadly or not—in the course of"
any seizure; (2) "requires careful attention to the
facts and circumstances of each particular case,
including the severity of the crime at issue, whether the suspect poses an immediate threat to the
safety of the officers or others, and whether he is
actively resisting arrest or attempting to evade
arrest by flight"; (3) "must embody allowance for
the fact that police officers are often forced to
make split-second judgments *** about the amount
of force that is necessary in a particular situation";
and (4) asks "whether the officers' actions are
'objectively reasonable' in light of the facts and
circumstances confronting them, without regard to
their underlying intent or motivation." *Graham v.
Connor* (1989).

(b)   Search incident to arrest

"When an arrest is made, it is reasonable for the
arresting officer to search the person arrested in
order to remove any weapons that the latter might
seek to use in order to resist arrest or effect his
escape [and to] seize any evidence on the arrestee's
person in order to prevent its concealment or destruction." *Chimel v. Cal.* (1969). Given this justification, doubt existed for some time as to whether
a search could be undertaken incident to an arrest
for a lesser offense, such as a minor traffic violation, where there would be no evidence to search
for and a relatively lesser risk that the arrestee
would be armed. But in *U.S. v. Robinson* (1973),
the Court held that a full search of the person

incident to a "full custody arrest" (i.e., one made for the purpose of taking the person to the station) may be undertaken without regard to "what a court may later decide was the probability in a particular arrest situation that weapons or evidence would in fact be found upon the person of the suspect," apparently on the ground that it would be unwise to have courts second-guessing such a "quick *ad hoc* judgment" by arresting officers. The limited frisk alternative of *Terry* (see § 2.9(d)) was deemed insufficient in the case of arrest, as "the danger to an officer is far greater in the case of the extended exposure which follows the taking of a suspect into custody and transporting him to the police station."

What then of the situation in which the arrest is not of the "full custody" type referred to in *Robinson,* as where a traffic violator is arrested in the expectation that he will be released at the scene after signing a promise to appear? At least when the offense is not one for which evidence could be found on the person, it appears that only a frisk may be undertaken and that even this step is impermissible unless the *Terry* grounds for frisk are present. Even absent such grounds, the officer may direct a motorist lawfully seized for a violation to alight from his car during the encounter. *Pa. v. Mimms* (1977).

The Supreme Court's ruling in *Robinson* makes more significant the longstanding issue of what items are subject to seizure once discovered. Clearly seizure is not limited to the items sought;

"when an article subject to lawful seizure properly comes into an officer's possession in the course of a lawful search it would be entirely without reason to say that he must return it because it was not one of the things it was his business to look for." *Abel v. U.S.* (1960). But in *Abel* there was probable cause to seize the item in question, and on this ground *Abel* was distinguished in a case where the officer seized an unlabeled bottle of pills from the pocket of a defendant arrested for public intoxication. The court, noting the absence of cases in point, concluded that the seizure was improper because the officer acted only upon suspicion that the pills might be narcotics and not upon reasonable grounds to believe that the article he has discovered is contraband. Compare the situation as to seizure of items not named in a search warrant, § 2.5(d), which likewise raises the question of how much discretion should be left to the searching officer; and consider *Warden v. Hayden* (1967), where the court, in rejecting the contention that abolition of the "mere evidence" rule would result in indiscriminate seizures, emphasized that there "must, of course, be a nexus * * * between the item to be seized and criminal behavior," and that "probable cause must be examined in terms of cause to believe that the evidence sought will aid in a particular apprehension or conviction."

(c) Time of search; inventory

It is clear that a search cannot be justified as being "incident" to arrest if the search is conducted without arrest and at a time when a lawful arrest could not be made because sufficient grounds are lacking or because of physical inability to make an arrest at that time. But a search of the person qualifies as a search incident to arrest if "the formal arrest followed quickly on the heels" of that search and was sufficiently grounded upon facts other than those uncovered by the search. *Rawlings v. Ky.* (1980). This is a sound position, as a search before arrest when there are grounds to arrest involves no greater invasion of the person's security and privacy, and has the advantage that if the search is not productive the individual may not be arrested at all. If there was no present intent to arrest and arrest does not promptly follow the search, then the search is not properly characterized as "incident" to arrest, but it is still lawful if made upon probable cause and limited to the extent "necessary to preserve highly evanescent evidence [e.g., fingernail scrapings]." *Cupp v. Murphy* (1973).

Courts have generally upheld delayed searches of the person arrested (such as those made on the way to or at the station), either on the theory that police control of the person by arrest is so substantial that it of necessity carries with it a continuing right of search, or on the ground that the police are entitled to inventory the property found on a person before placing him in a cell. A contrary result has sometimes been reached because of a prior failure of the police to permit the defendant to exercise his right of stationhouse release. Police need not resort to less intrusive means than the inventory of all effects found on or in possession of a person arrested, provided such searches are pursuant to "standardized inventory procedures." *Ill. v. Lafayette* (1983). In *U.S. v. Edwards* (1974), the Court held that "once the defendant is lawfully arrested and is in custody, the effects in his possession at the place of detention that were subject to search at the time and place of his arrest may lawfully be searched and seized without a warrant even though a substantial period of time has elapsed between the arrest and subsequent administrative processing on the one hand and the taking of the property for use as evidence on the other," at least where such searches are not unreasonable "either because of their number or their manner of perpetration." This qualification suggests that neither *Robinson* nor *Edwards* disturb the holding in *Schmerber v. Cal.* (1966) that, except where delay would threaten loss of the evidence, a search warrant is required to intrude into an arrestee's body.

(d) "Subterfuge" arrests

Robinson has been criticized on the ground that it opens the door to "subterfuge" arrests for minor offenses made to support searches of persons for evidence of more serious offenses as to which probable cause is lacking, particularly in light of the fact that *Robinson* was applied in the companion case of *Gustafson v. Fla.* (1973) to a situation in which the officer had complete discretion as to whether to arrest or give a citation and whether to search if an arrest was made. Evidence has sometimes been suppressed upon a showing that the desire to seek such evidence was the motivation behind arrest for such minor crimes as vagrancy or a traffic violation, but some courts have overlooked strong evidence of such a "subterfuge." Because the Supreme Court stated in *Scott v. U.S.* (1978) that a Fourth Amendment claim should be evaluated by "an objective assessment of an officer's actions in light of the facts and circumstances then known to him" and "without regard to the underlying intent or motivation of the officers involved," lower courts are increasingly reluctant to inquire into the pretext issue.

(e) The significance of booking

"Booking" is an administrative step taken after the arrested person is brought to the police station, which involves entry of the person's name, the crime for which the arrest was made, and other relevant facts on the police "blotter," and which may also include photographing, fingerprinting, and the like. Because booking results in a record of some of the circumstances of arrest, the question has arisen whether the entries made are relevant in determining the lawfulness of the arrest. A few courts have taken the position that an entry that the defendant was arrested "on suspicion of" or "for investigation of" a certain offense shows that the arrest was without probable cause, but in practice such entries are often made solely for the purpose of identifying those cases being referred to the detective division. It has been held that if a person was booked for one offense, his arrest may thereafter be upheld on the ground that the police had sufficient evidence of a quite different offense. A contrary conclusion, it is argued, would prevent arrest "on a trumped-up charge," *Wainwright v. New Orleans* (1968) (dissent of Chief Justice to dismissal of writ of certiorari), and on this basis some courts have declined to inquire into the existence of probable cause for an offense unrelated to that for which the defendant was booked.

§ 2.7 WARRANTLESS SEARCHES AND SEIZURES OF PREMISES

(a) Entry to arrest

In *Payton v. N.Y.* (1980), the Court held that the Fourth Amendment prohibits the police from making a warrantless nonconsensual entry into a suspect's home to make a routine arrest. The Court reasoned that the "basic principle of Fourth Amendment law" that searches and seizures inside a home without a warrant are presumptively unreasonable, long applied when the purpose was to search for an object, "has equal force when the seizure of a person is involved." This is because "any differences in the intrusiveness of entries to search and entries to arrest are merely ones of degree rather than kind," and they "share this fundamental characteristic: the breach of the entrance to an individual's home." As for the argument that a warrant requirement was impractical, the Court, after noting it had been provided with no "evidence that effective law enforcement has suffered in those States that already have such a requirement," declared that "such arguments of policy must give way to a constitutional command that we consider to be unequivocal."

Prior to *Payton*, the Court had held that police may enter premises without a warrant in immediate pursuit of a person to be arrested who sought refuge therein on seeing the police approach, *U.S. v. Santana* (1976). Such an entry may also be made in hot pursuit of an offender, as in *Warden v. Hayden* (1967), where the police were informed that an armed robbery had taken place and that the suspect had entered a certain house five minutes before they reached it, as delay under these circumstances would endanger the lives of the police and others. Once inside, the Court concluded in *Hayden*, the police were justified in looking everywhere in the house where the suspect might be hiding and also (before his capture) where weapons might be hidden.

Payton casts no doubt on those decisions, for the Court emphasized it was dealing with in-premises arrests for which no exigent circumstances claim had been made. Thus, the Court in *Payton* had no occasion to elaborate upon what would amount to exigent circumstances. The Court did, however, place considerable reliance upon a case in which exigent circumstances were found to be present based upon these factors: (1) a crime of violence was involved; (2) the suspect was reasonably believed to be armed; (3) there was a very clear showing of probable cause; (4) there was a strong reason to believe the suspect was within the premises; (5) there was a likelihood the suspect would escape if not swiftly apprehended; and (6) the entry was made peaceably. Emphasizing the absence of the first of these factors, the Court in *Welsh v. Wis.* (1984) held illegal a warrantless entry to arrest for driving under the influence, made to ensure that defendant's blood-alcohol level was determined before it dissipated. Noting the crime was a civil offense not punishable by imprisonment, the Court found it "difficult to conceive of a warrantless home arrest that would not be unreasonable under the Fourth Amendment when the underlying offense is extremely minor."

In response to the "suggestion that only a search warrant based on probable cause to believe the suspect is at home at a given time can adequately protect the privacy interests at stake," the Court in *Payton* concluded that an arrest warrant, though affording less protection than a search warrant, would suffice: "If there is sufficient evidence of a citizen's participation in a felony to persuade a judicial officer that his arrest is justified, it is constitutionally reasonable to require him to open his doors to the officers of the law. Thus, for Fourth Amendment purposes, an arrest warrant founded on probable cause implicitly carries with it the limited authority to enter a dwelling in which the suspect lives when there is reason to believe the suspect is within." But a search warrant, issued on probable cause the person to be arrested is now present within, is needed to enter premises of a third party. *Steagald v. U.S.* (1981).

(b) Entry without notice

Many jurisdictions have statutes which expressly provide that an officer may not break into private premises for purposes of arrest unless he has been denied admittance after giving "notice of his office and purpose." However, these statutes have generally been interpreted as codifying the common law rule with its exceptions for "exigent circumstances." These laws apply to actual breaking of doors and windows as well as merely opening an unlocked door, but not to entry by subterfuge. Courts have excused notice and demand when it reasonably appeared that: (1) the occupants were already aware of the presence of the police and their objective; (2) prompt action was required for the protection of a person within; (3) unannounced entry was required for protection of the officer; (4) unannounced entry was required to prevent the destruction of evidence; (5) by unannounced entry actual commission of the offense could be observed; or (6) by unannounced entry escape of the person to be arrested could be prevented. Such belief must be based upon the facts of the particular case, and cannot be justified by a general assumption that certain classes of persons are more likely than others to resist arrest, attempt escape, or destroy evidence.

The Supreme Court has yet to speak clearly to the issue. In *Ker v. Cal.* (1963), four members of the Court concluded that entry without notice and demand was proper because the evidence (narcotics) could easily be disposed of and it appeared from the defendant's earlier furtive conduct that he was expecting the police. Another justice concurred on the ground that state searches and seizures should be judged by "concepts of fundamental fairness," while the remaining members of the Court argued that under the Fourth Amendment the only exceptions to the demand-notice requirements were "(1) where the persons within already know of the officers' authority and purpose or (2) where the officers are justified in the belief that persons within are in imminent peril of bodily harm, or (3) where those within, made aware of the presence of someone outside (because, for example, there has been a knock at the door) are then engaged in activity which justifies the officers in the belief that an escape or the destruction of evidence is being attempted."

(c) Search incident to and after arrest

For many years, it could be said that the right to make a warrantless search incident to arrest was one exception which came close to swallowing up the search warrant requirement. Per *Harris v. U.S.* (1947), and *U.S. v. Rabinowitz* (1950), such searches were permitted of the premises where the

arrest occurred, without regard to the practicality
of obtaining a search warrant. Under the *Harris-Rabinowitz* rule, the scope of the search extended
to the entire premises in which the defendant had
a possessory interest, and such searches were usually upheld without any showing of probable cause
that the objects sought would be found there. In
Chimel v. Cal. (1969), the Court, noting that in
more recent decisions such searches had been justified solely upon the need to prevent the arrested
person from obtaining a weapon or destroying evidence, overruled *Harris* and *Rabinowitz* and limited the scope of warrantless searches incident to
arrest consistent with that purpose:

"When an arrest is made, it is reasonable for the
arresting officer to search the person arrested in
order to remove any weapons that the latter might
seek to use in order to resist arrest or effect his
escape. * * * In addition, it is entirely reasonable
for the arresting officer to search for and seize any
evidence on the arrestee's person in order to prevent its concealment or destruction. And the area
into which an arrestee might reach in order to
grab a weapon or evidentiary items must, of
course, be governed by a like rule. A gun on a
table or in a drawer in front of one who is arrested
can be as dangerous to the arresting officer as one
concealed in the clothing of the person arrested.
There is ample justification, therefore, for a search
of the arrestee's person and the area 'within his
immediate control'—construing that phrase to
mean the area from within which he might gain

possession of a weapon or destructible evidence." A broader search of the place of arrest "may be made only under the authority of a search warrant." *Chimel* involved a search of an entire house, but the Court made it clear that the new rule would also bar more limited searches, such as the one-room search in *Rabinowitz* and the four-room search in *Harris*.

Chimel is not inconsistent with the notion that if it is necessary for the arrestee to put on clothing or do other things before he is taken to the station, then the police may examine closets and other places to which the arrestee is permitted to move. Such accompanying of the arrestee about the premises is always reasonable, without regard to the degree of risk in the particular case, even if the arrest took place off the premises. *Wash. v. Chrisman* (1982). Subsequent to an in-premises arrest, police may conduct a protective sweep of the area for their own protection, extending (i) to "closets and other spaces immediately adjoining the place of arrest from which an attack could be immediately launched," even without reasonable suspicion such a risk is present; and (ii) to other parts of the premises, on a reasonable belief "that the area to be swept harbors an individual posing a danger to those on the arrest scene." *Md. v. Buie* (1990). If a "potential accomplice" is found, he may be frisked for weapons, and the area within his immediate control may also be searched for weapons and evidence.

(d) Plain view

As noted in *Coolidge v. N.H.* (1971), "an object which comes into view during a search incident to arrest that is appropriately limited in scope under existing law may be seized without a warrant." Thus, if an object is discovered by the officer from a place where he is lawfully present, that discovery is not illegal, and this is so even if an arrest has been made but the object itself is not within the control of the arrestee under *Chimel.* While in *Coolidge* it was indicated that the item may be seized only if its discovery was "inadvertent," that limitation was later abandoned as unnecessary in *Horton v. Cal.* (1990) (see § 2.5(d)).

Assuming no problems in the manner in which the plain view is acquired, it does not necessarily follow that the observed object may be seized. As stated in *Coolidge,* it must be "an incriminating object," meaning that there must be probable cause that the object is the fruit, instrumentality, or evidence of crime. That determination must be made by the police without exceeding their authority, and even the lesser intrusion of picking up an object and looking at it is impermissible on reasonable suspicion short of probable cause. *Ariz. v. Hicks* (1987).

(e) Search to prevent loss of evidence

In *Agnello v. U.S.* (1925), the Court held that "belief, however well founded, that an article sought is concealed in a dwelling house furnishes no justification for a search of that place without a warrant." But in *Johnson v. U.S.* (1948), and *Chapman v. U.S.* (1961), reference was made to the possibility of a warrantless dwelling search being upheld upon a showing of a need for immediate action. This issue also took on increased importance because of the *Chimel* decision, and was not directly confronted in *Chimel* because no emergency was present there; the police had sufficient opportunity to obtain a search warrant before they tipped their hand by making an arrest.

But in *Vale v. La.* (1970), the circumstances were different; the police had come to arrest the defendant on another matter, observed what reasonably appeared to be a sale of narcotics by the defendant to a person who drove up to his house, arrested the defendant in front of his house, made a cursory inspection of the house to determine if any one else was there, and then (after the defendant's mother and brother entered the house during the inspection) made a warrantless search of the house for the additional narcotics they believed were hidden there. Yet the Court concluded that the state had not met its burden "to show the existence of such an exceptional situation" as to justify a warrantless search, as the goods seized were not actually in the process of destruction or removal from the jurisdiction. The Court also asserted that because the officers had arrest warrants for Vale, "there is thus no reason * * * to suppose that it was impracticable for them to obtain a search warrant as well," but this is a questionable conclusion in view of the fact that here (unlike *Chimel*) the probable cause for search did not exist until the officers on the scene observed the illegal transaction. *Vale,* therefore, cannot easily be squared with the search-of-vehicles cases (see § 2.8(b)), but does show that the Court is much more protective of dwellings then vehicles. Although some courts have resisted a broader formulation on the ground that the police can too easily conjure up reasons why evidence within premises might be subject to future destruction or disposal, the lower courts have generally not accepted the *Vale* formulation as controlling. They have been inclined to state the exception in broader terms, covering instances in which the police reasonably conclude that the evidence would be destroyed or removed if they delayed the search while a warrant was obtained. But the mere fact that a homicide has occurred in certain premises does not of itself establish exigent circumstances justifying a warrantless search. *Mincey v. Ariz.* (1978).

Some lower courts have held that the police may respond to this emergency by impounding the premises and keeping the occupants thereof under surveillance while a search warrant is being obtained. In *Segura v. U.S.* (1984), dealing with a somewhat easier case in which the 19–hour impoundment was of unoccupied premises belonging to persons then under lawful arrest, the Court held "that where officers, having probable cause, enter premises, and with probable cause, arrest the occupants who have legitimate possessory interests in its contents and take them into custody and, for no more than the period here involved, secure the premises from within to preserve the status quo while others, in good faith, are in the process of obtaining a warrant, they do not violate the Fourth Amendment's proscription against unreasonable seizures." The Court went on to hold that in any event any illegality in the initial entry would not require suppression of the evidence first discovered in the later execution of the search warrant.

§ 2.8 WARRANTLESS SEARCHES AND SEIZURES OF AUTOMOBILES

(a) Search incident to arrest

Although *Chimel* involved search of premises, the more limited rule of that case was also applied for a time to a search of an automobile incident to arrest. But the need for such case-by-case assessment was largely obviated by *N.Y. v. Belton* (1981), where the Court reasoned: (1) Fourth Amendment protections "can only be realized if the police are acting under a set of rules which, in most instances, make it possible to reach a correct determination beforehand as to whether an invasion of privacy is justified in the interest of law enforcement"; (2) "no straightforward rule has emerged from the litigated cases respecting the question involved here"; (3) this has caused the courts "difficulty" and has put the appellate cases into "disarray"; (4) the cases suggest "the generalization that articles inside the relatively narrow compass of the passenger compartment of an automobile are in fact generally, even if not inevitably, within 'the area into which an arrestee might reach in order to grab a weapon or evidentiary item' "; and thus (5) "the workable rule this category of cases requires" is best achieved by holding "that when a policeman has made a lawful custodial arrest of the occupant of an automobile, he may, as a contemporaneous incident of that arrest, search the passenger compartment of that automobile," inclusive of "the contents of any containers found within the passenger compartment."

(b) Search on probable cause

In *Carroll v. U.S.* (1925), the Court upheld a warrantless search of a vehicle being operated on the highway upon probable cause that it contained contraband, because the driver was not subject to lawful arrest and thus the car could be quickly moved out of the locality. Some courts concluded *Carroll* could not be relied upon to justify a warrantless search of the car after arrest of the driver because "exigencies do not exist when the vehicle and the suspect are both in police custody." But in *Chambers v. Maroney* (1970), the Supreme Court reached a contrary conclusion. In response to the contention that *Carroll* was not applicable on these facts because the car in which the defendant was arrested could simply be held until a search warrant was obtained, the Court in *Chambers* responded: "For constitutional purposes, we see no difference between on the one hand seizing and holding a car before presenting the probable cause issue to a magistrate and on the other hand carrying out an immediate search without a warrant." Neither *Chambers* nor later decisions of the Court (e.g., *Cardwell v. Lewis* (1974), allowing warrantless seizure and search of a car parked in a public parking lot after arrest of the driver elsewhere; *Tex. v. White* (1975), allowing search of the vehicle at the station after the driver's arrest though, unlike *Chambers,* there was no indication an immediate at-the-scene search would have been impractical) could be explained in terms of the oft-stated principle that a search warrant is required except in exigent circumstances.   Finally, the Court acknowledged in *U.S. v. Chadwick* (1977) that warrantless vehicle searches are being permitted "in cases in which the possibilities of the vehicle's being removed or evidence in it destroyed were remote, if not non-existent."   Why?   Because, the Court explained: "One has a lower expectation of privacy in a motor vehicle because its function is transportation and it seldom serves as one's residence or as the repository of personal effects. * * *.   It travels public thoroughfares where both its occupants and its contents are in plain view."

In *Cal. v. Carney* (1985), this reformulated vehicle exception was even applied to a motor home which "is being used on the highways, or if it is readily capable of such use and is found stationary in a place not regularly used for residential purposes."   The majority emphasized both justifications for the vehicle exception, noting that a motor home in such circumstances is "readily mobile"

and has "a reduced expectation of privacy stem-
ming from its use as a licensed motor vehicle
subject to a range of police regulation inapplicable
to a fixed dwelling." One consequence of the
Court's alternative reliance upon the "reduced expectation" theory is that warrantless car searches
are not likely to be jeopardized by more substantial
delay between seizure of the vehicle and search of
it than existed in *Chambers.* Cf. *U.S. v. Johns*
(1985).

(c) Search of containers and persons therein

Despite the "lesser expectation of privacy in a
motor vehicle" of which the Court spoke in *Chadwick,* there is no comparable lesser expectation as
to containers such as luggage, and thus they can be
searched without a warrant only upon a genuine
showing of exigent circumstances, *U.S. v. Chadwick* (1977). (This is so even if the police have
lawful possession of the object, as "an officer's
authority to possess a package is distinct from his
authority to examine it." *Walter v. U.S.* (1980).)
But what if the container is in an automobile? In
an effort to reconcile the *Chadwick* and *Chambers-
Carney* lines of authority, the Court has held that if
there exists probable cause to search the entire
car, then the authority to make a warrantless
search of the vehicle (as with the authority to
execute a search warrant for a vehicle) extends to
containers within the vehicle in which the objects
sought might be concealed, *U.S. v. Ross* (1982),
even if the police earlier removed the container

from the vehicle but still had lawful possession of it, *U.S. v. Johns* (1985). By contrast, it was once the rule that absent true exigent circumstances a search warrant was required to search a container within a car if there was probable cause only as to the container (e.g., a suitcase placed in a taxi by a passenger), *Ark. v. Sanders* (1979), but *Sanders* was later overruled because of a perceived need for "one clear-cut rule to govern automobile searches": that containers in cars may be searched without a warrant whether the probable cause is specific or general. *Cal. v. Acevedo* (1991).

Assuming a lawful warrantless search of a vehicle, may it automatically extend to the person of an occupant? No, the Supreme Court held in *U.S. v. Di Re* (1948), for the need to do so is no greater than the necessity "for searching guests of a house for which a search warrant had issued," which the government conceded would not be lawful. Some argue the *Di Re* analogy is unsound because it is too easy, while police are trying to stop a moving vehicle, for incriminating evidence to be transferred to an occupant.

(d) Inventory

If the police have lawfully impounded a vehicle (e.g., because it was found illegally parked in such a way as to constitute a traffic hazard), they may, pursuant to an established standard procedure, secure and inventory the vehicle's contents in order to (i) protect the owner's property while it remains in police custody, (ii) protect the police from claims or disputes over lost or stolen property, and (iii) protect the police from potential danger. *So. Dak. v. Opperman* (1976). If the driver was stopped on the street while operating the vehicle and then arrested, some lower courts have held that the police must honor the driver's request that the car instead be lawfully parked there or turned over to a friend; some cases indicate the police must even take the initiative and inquire of the driver what disposition he prefers; and some others declare that if the car is impounded, the driver must be allowed to decide between inventory and waiver of any claims against the police. But in *Colo. v. Bertine* (1987) the Court held vehicle inventory procedures are reasonable under the Fourth Amendment without regard to the existence of such "alternative 'less intrusive' means."

An inventory is unlawful if it was not undertaken pursuant to standard policy or practice in the department, but *Bertine* holds that it is not objectionable that "departmental regulations gave the police officers discretion to choose between impounding * * * and parking, * * * so long as that discretion is exercised according to standard criteria." An inventory is illegal if it appears to have been undertaken solely for some other motive (as shown, for example, by the failure to use inventory forms or to complete the inventory once contraband was discovered), In terms of scope, the inventory must be limited to areas of the car in which valuables might be found, and may not extend to examination of "materials such as letters or checkbooks, that 'touch upon intimate areas of an individual's personal affairs,' " *So. Dak. v. Opperman,* supra (Powell, J., conc.). The inventory may extend to containers (such as suitcases) found in the car. *Colo. v. Bertine,* supra. Though that case declared it "permissible for police officers to open closed containers in an inventory search only if they are following standard police procedures that mandate the opening of such containers in every impounded vehicle," more recent and seemingly conflicting dictum says police "may be allowed sufficient latitude to determine whether a particular container should or should not be opened in light of the nature of the search and characteristics of the container itself." *Fla. v. Wells* (1990).

§ 2.9 STOP–AND–FRISK AND OTHER BRIEF DETENTION

(a) Background

Police have long followed the practice of stopping suspicious persons on the street or other public places for purposes of questioning them or conducting some other form of investigation, and, incident to many stoppings, of searching the person for dangerous weapons. Because this investigative technique, commonly referred to as stop-and-frisk, is ordinarily employed when there are not grounds to arrest the suspect and to search him incident to arrest, it was often questioned whether the practice could be squared with the Fourth Amendment.

The Supreme Court provided some answers in *Terry v. Ohio* (1968).

In *Terry,* where an officer observed three men who appeared to be "casing" a store for a robbery and then approached them for questioning and frisked them, finding weapons on two of them, the Court held "that where a police officer observes unusual conduct which leads him reasonably to conclude in light of his experience that criminal activity may be afoot and that the persons with whom he is dealing may be armed and presently dangerous; where in the course of investigating this behavior he identifies himself as a policeman and makes reasonable inquiries; and where nothing in the initial stages of the encounter serves to dispel his reasonable fear for his own or others' safety, he is entitled for the protection of himself and others in the area to conduct a carefully limited search of the outer clothing of such persons in an attempt to discover weapons which might be used to assault him."

The result in *Terry* rests upon three fundamental conclusions the Court reached concerning Fourth Amendment theory. First of all, the Court concluded that restraining a person on the street is a "seizure" and that exploring the outer surfaces of his clothing is a "search," and thus rejected "the notions that the Fourth Amendment does not come into play at all as a limitation upon police conduct if the officers stop short of something called a 'technical arrest' or a 'fullblown search.'" Secondly, after noting that the police conduct here was without a warrant and thus subject to the reasonableness rather than the probable cause part of the Fourth Amendment, the Court utilized the balancing test of the *Camara* case (see § 2.11(a)) to conclude that a frisk could be undertaken upon facts which would not support an arrest and full search. (Justice Douglas objected in dissent that the Court had in effect said that the police have more power without a warrant than with a warrant, which could have been answered—but was not—by observing that the balancing test applies in determining both the reasonableness of warrantless searches and seizures and, as in *Camara,* the probable cause for those with warrant.) Finally, in response to the defendant's observation that some stops and frisks are employed for harassment and other improper purposes, the Court noted that the exclusionary rule is ineffective when the police have no interest in prosecution and that consequently a flat prohibition of all stops and frisks would not deter those undertaken for improper objectives.

(b) Temporary seizure for investigation

As for what Fourth Amendment evidentiary test is to be applied to temporary seizures, in *U.S. v. Cortez* (1981), the Court stated that the essence of the standard is that "the detaining officers must have a particularized and objective basis for suspecting the particular person stopped of criminal activity." The Court's emphasis in *Terry* was upon the situation "where a police officer observes unusual conduct which leads him reasonably to conclude in light of his experience that criminal activity may be afoot." If this language is compared with that usually employed to describe the evidentiary test for arrest, it appears that some difference exists in the degree of probability required. As to the probability required for arrest, it may generally be stated that it must be more probable than not that the person has committed an offense; that is, there must be a more than 50% probability that a crime has been committed, and at least sometimes a more than 50% probability that the person arrested committed it, *Wong Sun v. U.S.* (1963) (see § 2.3(b)). But for a *Terry* stop a reasonable suspicion, even less than a preponderance of the evidence, that a crime has been or is about to be committed and that the suspect is the person who committed or is planning the offense will suffice. *U.S. v. Sokolow* (1989). Thus, the stopping of a suspect near the scene of a recent robbery because he fitted the general description given by the victim is proper even if arrest would not be proper because the description would also fit several others in the area. (This is so without regard to whether a less intrusive investigative technique is available. *Sokolow*, supra.) The reasonable suspicion for a stop may differ from probable cause to arrest in a quite different way, namely, in the extent to which the information must be shown to be reliable. *Ala. v. White* (1990).

In *Adams v. Williams* (1972), the Court, 6–3, upheld a stop based upon information the suspect possessed a gun and narcotics, given by a known informant who had provided information in the past. Because the informer could have been prosecuted for making a false complaint if his tip proved false, the tip (though insufficient for arrest) was deemed to have sufficient "indicia of reliability" to justify a stop. As for an anonymous tip from an informant regarding criminal activity, such a tip (i) is insufficient standing alone when the tip gives no indication of the informant's reliability or basis of knowledge; and (ii) is also insufficient despite corroboration of part of the informant's story re innocent existing circumstances (e.g., that a certain car is presently parked at a certain location), as virtually anyone could predict such a continuing circumstance; but (iii) is sufficient when corroboration of the informant's prediction of future events (e.g., that a certain person will travel to a certain place) demonstrates "a special familiarity with" the suspect's affairs. *White*, supra.

In *U.S. v. Hensley* (1985), the Court applied the *Whiteley* approach (see § 2.3(e)) in this context, and thus held that a stopping on the basis of a conclusory police bulletin was lawful provided the bulletin had been "issued on the basis of articulable facts supporting a reasonable suspicion." But in *Brown v. Tex.* (1979), where in the afternoon officers saw defendant and another man walk away from each other in an alley in an area with a high incidence of drug traffic, but there was no indication it was unusual for people to be in the alley and the police did not point to any facts supporting their conclusion the situation "looked suspicious," the Court held there were not grounds for a stop. Similarly, merely consorting with narcotic addicts does not constitute grounds for a stop. *Sibron v. N.Y.* (1968).

Although the results in *Brown* and *Sibron* may have been influenced to some degree by doubts about whether *Terry* should apply to suspicion of minor possessory offenses, the Court has recognized an offense category limitation only in the somewhat different situation presented by *U.S. v. Hensley* (1985). The Court there held a *Terry* stop was also permissible to investigate *past* criminal activity, but only as to "felonies or crimes involving a threat to public safety," where "it is in the public interest that the crime be solved and the suspect detained as promptly as possible."

A detention for investigation of a somewhat different kind was involved in *U.S. v. Van Leeuwen* (1970), where the Court, citing *Terry,* upheld the holding of mailed packages for approximately one day while the police promptly investigated the suspicious circumstances of the mailing and obtained a search warrant for the packages. Similarly, in *U.S. v. Place* (1983), the Court held a traveler's luggage could be seized on reasonable suspicion for purposes of investigation, but wisely added that because such a seizure affects the suspect's travel plans the luggage may be held no longer than if the traveler himself were detained.

(c) No seizure and arrest distinguished

If it turns out that grounds for a *Terry* stop were lacking, the police-citizen encounter is still lawful if no seizure occurred. While stopping a vehicle is a seizure, *U.S. v. Hensley* (1985), many police contacts with pedestrians are not. A person "has been 'seized' within the meaning of the Fourth Amendment only if, in view of all the circumstances surrounding the incident, a reasonable person would have believed that he was not free to leave," which means that the "subjective intention" of the police officer "is irrelevant except insofar as that may have been conveyed to the" suspect. *U.S. v. Mendenhall* (1980), followed in *Fla. v. Royer* (1983), and elaborated in *Fla. v. Bostick* (1991) as presupposing "an *innocent* person". Lower court decisions reflect the view that there is no Fourth Amendment seizure when the policeman, although perhaps making inquiries which a private citizen would not be expected to make, has otherwise conducted himself in a manner consistent with what would be viewed as a nonoffensive contact if it occurred between two ordinary citizens. *I.N.S. v. Delgado* (1984) held a "factory survey" involved no seizure where it was apparent INS agents were only questioning workers and those questioned were obligated to remain on the premises anyway by virtue of their obligation to their employer. Similarly, in *Fla. v. Bostick*, supra, the Court recognized that literal application of the "free to leave" test is inappropriate in some circumstances (e.g., where defendant was questioned on a bus he did not want to leave), and concluded that in such cases the proper question "is whether a reasonable person would feel free to decline the officers' requests or otherwise terminate the encounter." In *Cal. v. Hodari D.* (1991), the word "seizure" in the Fourth Amendment was construed to cover "application of physical force to restrain movement, even when it is ultimately unsuccessful," as well as "*submission* to the assertion of authority," but not a "show of authority" to which "the subject does not yield." This means a suspect's act of discarding contraband is not the fruit of an illegal seizure when, at the time of that act, an officer lacking reasonable suspicion was vigorously chasing but had not yet caught the suspect.

If the dimensions of a permissible stop are exceeded when only a reasonable suspicion exists, the result is an illegal arrest. This can occur because of excessive force or threats of force, but it is not excessive for the police to draw weapons when they have reason to suspect the person is armed and dangerous. *U.S. v. Hensley* (1985). There is no per se rule that the passage of a certain time, such as 20 minutes, escalates the stop into an arrest. In determining whether the time was excessive, it is useful to ask whether the police were diligently pursuing a means of investigation likely to resolve the matter one way or another very soon. *U.S. v. Sharpe* (1985). Movement of the suspect to a nearby location to facilitate the investigation does not inevitably escalate the detention into an arrest. But, as *Fla. v. Royer* (1983) illustrates, such escalation can occur from a wrong choice of investigative techniques by the police. There, the Court held taking the suspected drug courier a mere 40 feet to an airport police office for questioning was an arrest, as resort to "the least intrusive means reasonably available" would have resulted in the summoning of a drug detection dog to the corridor. More recently, however, the Court has cautioned against "unrealistic second-guessing," and has declared that the "question is not simply whether some other alternative was available, but whether the police acted unreasonably in failing to recognize or to pursue it." *U.S. v. Sharpe* (1985).

(d) Protective search

Terry makes it clear that whether it is proper to make a protective search incident to a stopping for investigation is a question separate from the issue of whether it is permissible to stop the suspect. For a protective search, it must reasonably appear that the suspect "may be armed and presently dangerous," which would again appear to require only a substantial possibility, rather than the more than 50% probability which would justify an arrest and full search for carrying a concealed weapon. Although *Terry* also emphasizes that the officer frisked only after he had made some initial inquiries and the responses did not "dispel his reasonable fear," the frisk upheld in *Adams* was not preceded by inquiries.

Terry indicates that a two-step process must ordinarily be followed: the officer must pat down first and then intrude beneath the surface of the suspect's clothing only if he comes upon something which feels like a weapon. In *Adams,* the Court approved the officer's conduct in reaching directly into the suspect's pocket, apparently because the informant had indicated the precise location of the weapon. But in any event, the search is limited by its recognized purpose, that is, "to an intrusion reasonably designed to discover guns, knives, clubs, or other hidden instruments for the assault of the police officer." This means that the search must be limited to those places to which the suspect has immediate access, and may not otherwise go beyond what is necessary to determine if the suspect is armed. *Minn. v. Dickerson* (1993) (prohibiting further squeezing of suspect's pocket to determine if lump was cocaine).

As for a protective search beyond the person, the Court in *Mich. v. Long* (1983) held "that the search of the passenger compartment of an automobile, limited to those areas in which a weapon may be placed or hidden, is permissible if the police officer possesses a reasonable belief based on 'specific and articulable facts which, taken together with the rational inferences from those facts, reasonably warrant' the officers in believing that the suspect is dangerous and the suspect may gain immediate control of weapons." But the Court then reached the questionable conclusion that such a risk can be present, even as to a suspect outside the car, because of the possibility he would "break away" from the police during the investigation or merely would reenter the car at its conclusion.

(e) Brief detention at the station

It remains unclear whether the *Terry* balancing test may be utilized to support a brief detention for investigation at the station on grounds slightly short of that required for arrest. In *Davis v. Miss.* (1969), holding fingerprints inadmissible because obtained after an illegal arrest, the Court noted it was arguable "that because of the unique nature of the fingerprinting process, such detention might, under narrowly defined circumstances, be found to comply with the Fourth Amendment even though there is no probable cause in the traditional sense," in that it "may constitute a much less serious intrusion upon personal security than other types of police searches and detentions." The Court added that a warrant would be required for such a detention, a matter which concurring Justice Harlan preferred to leave open.

Davis suggests that the intended investigative technique is a relevant consideration; the Court emphasized that detention for fingerprinting "involves none of the probing into an individual's private life and thoughts which marks an interrogation or search," cannot "be employed repeatedly to harass any individual," and "is an inherently more reliable and effective crime-solving tool than eyewitness identifications or confessions and is not subject to such abuses as the improper line-up and the 'third degree.' " Consistent with this, it was held in *Dunaway v. N.Y.* (1979) that custodial questioning at the station on less than probable cause for a full-fledged arrest was unlawful. But there is case authority that a properly conducted lineup would be reliable and that therefore detention to facilitate it would be permissible on less than the grounds needed for arrest.

Statutes authorizing stationhouse detention for other investigative purposes, such as fingerprinting or taking voice or handwriting exemplars, have been upheld. The status of these provisions is not entirely clear, as *Dunaway* can be read broadly as barring all at-the-station detention on less than full probable cause, or narrowly as dealing only with interrogation and allowing detention for other types of investigation, at least if there is judicial authorization and the suspect is ordinarily given a chance to respond to a summons. But it is noteworthy that in more recently reasserting the *Davis* dictum, the Court made seemingly favorable reference to those statutes. *Hayes v. Fla.* (1985).

§ 2.10 GRAND JURY SUBPOENAS

Unlike the detentions for the purpose of collecting evidence considered in *Davis* and *Dunaway,* supra, the grand jury subpoena operates largely free of Fourth Amendment restrictions. Insofar as the Constitution is concerned, a subpoena directing a person to testify or produce specific physical evidence before a grand jury need not be supported by a showing of probable cause, reasonable suspicion, or any other factual foundation. *U.S. v. Dionisio* (1973) (subpoena requiring production of voice exemplars); *U.S. v. Mara* (1973) (subpoena requiring handwriting exemplars). As the Court noted in *Dionisio,* "a subpoena to appear before the grand jury is not a 'seizure' in the Fourth Amendment sense." Unlike an arrest or an "investigative stop," it does not produce an "abrupt" detention, "effected with force or the threat of it," or result "in a record [like an arrest record] involving social stigma." A subpoena, the Court has noted "is served in the same manner as other legal process [and] involves no stigma whatever." *U.S. v. Dionisio,* supra. The Court has acknowledged that the compulsion to appear or produce evidence does require some "personal sacrifice," but that obligation is characterized as simply a "part of the necessary contribution of the individual to the welfare of the public." *Blair v. U.S.* (1919). The Court also has stressed, in this connection, that a person subpoenaed retains his privilege against self-incrimination (see § 4.10) and, where applicable, judicial protection against abuse of the grand jury process. A subpoena issued on the basis of "tips [or] rumors" is not abusive, however, since a grand jury has an obligation to "run down" every "available clue" in conducting its investigation. *U.S. v. Dionisio,* supra.

While the Fourth Amendment does not require a showing of some factual foundation for a subpoena, it does prohibit a subpoena duces tecum too sweeping in its terms "to be regarded as reasonable." *Hale v. Henkel* (1906). This prohibition, arguably resting more appropriately on the due process clause, has application primarily to subpoenas requesting production of numerous documents. In barring overly broad subpoenas duces tecum, courts have sought to ensure that a subpoena (1) commands production only of documents relevant to the investigation being pursued, (2) specifies the documents to be produced with reasonable particularity, and (3) includes records covering only a reasonable period of time.

§ 2.11 INSPECTIONS; REGULATORY SEARCHES

The Fourth Amendment has been held to apply to a variety of searches and inspections conducted as part of regulatory schemes. In each case, however, the standards applied have been somewhat different than those applied to searches conducted in the course of criminal investigations.

(a) Inspection of premises

Administrative inspections of residential and commercial premises for fire, health and safety violations may not be undertaken without a search warrant unless the occupant consents to the inspection or the inspection is made in an emergency. The occupant is thus usually free to challenge the inspector's decision to search without the risk of suffering criminal penalties for his refusal. However, a search warrant for such an inspection does not require a showing of probable cause that a particular dwelling contains violations of the code being enforced, but only that reasonable legislative or administrative standards for conducting an area inspection are satisfied with respect to a particular building. This special probable cause test was arrived at "by balancing the need to search against the invasion which the search entails," considering (1) the long history of acceptance of such inspection programs; (2) the public interest in abating all dangerous conditions, even those which are not observable from outside the building; and (3) the fact that the inspections are neither personal in nature nor aimed at discovery of evidence of crime, and thus involve a relatively limited invasion of privacy. *Camara v. Mun. Ct.* (1967); *See v. City of Seattle* (1967).

The *Camara-See* warrant requirement has been held inapplicable to certain business inspection schemes. The latest case of that genre, *N.Y. v. Burger* (1987), involving warrantless inspection of an auto junkyard, stressed these factors: (1) the business was "closely regulated," considering the long tradition of regulation and its extensive nature; (2) "a 'substantial' government interest," combatting auto theft, supports the regulatory scheme; (3) warrantless inspections are "necessary to further [the] regulatory scheme," as frequent and unannounced inspections are necessary to detect stolen cars and parts; (4) the statutory scheme "provides a 'constitutionally adequate substitute for a warrant'" by informing the businessman inspections will occur regularly, of their permissible scope, and who may conduct them; and (5) the permitted inspection is "carefully limited in time, place, and scope" (business hours only, auto dismantling businesses only, of records, cars and parts only).

Entry of premises to fight a fire and thereafter find the cause may be made without a warrant, but subsequent entries on probable cause of arson require a regular criminal warrant on full probable cause. *Mich. v. Tyler* (1978). A post-fire entry merely to ascertain the cause of the fire may be made without even an administrative warrant if notice is given. *Mich. v. Clifford* (1984).

(b) Border searches

As noted in *Carroll v. U.S.* (1925), quoted with approval in *Almeida-Sanchez v. U.S.* (1973): "Travellers may be stopped in crossing an international boundary because of national self protection reasonably requiring one entering the country to identify himself as entitled to come in, and his belongings as effects which may be lawfully brought in." Border searches are considered unique, and a person crossing the border may be required to submit to a warrantless search of his person, baggage, and vehicle without the slightest suspicion, just as is true of incoming international mail (at least if correspondence is not read). *U.S. v. Ramsey* (1977). However, some evidence short of probable cause must exist to justify more intrusive and embarrassing searches; "a real suspicion" is said to be required for a strip search, and a "clear indication" for examination of body cavities. On a reasonable suspicion of alimentary canal drug smuggling, a person may be detained at the border until the suspicion is verified or dispelled (by submission to x-ray or a bowel movement). *U.S. v. Montoya de Hernandez* (1985).

The special rules on border searches also apply to persons who have already travelled some distance into the country, if the circumstances indicate that any contraband which might be found was in the place searched at the time of entry. But, a border search must occur at the border or "its functional equivalent," and thus a car found near the border but not known to have crossed the border may not be subjected to a warrantless search for illegal aliens, either by a roving patrol or at a fixed checkpoint, in the absence of consent or probable cause. *Almeida-Sanchez v. U.S.* (1973); *U.S. v. Ortiz* (1975). Such a vehicle may be stopped briefly to enable questioning of the occupants about their citizenship and immigration status if (a) the stopping occurs at a reasonably located fixed checkpoint, *U.S. v. Martinez-Fuerte* (1976), or (b) the officer is aware of specific articulable facts which, together with rational inferences from those facts, reasonably warrant suspicion that the car contains aliens who may be illegally in the country. *U.S. v. Brignoni-Ponce* (1975).

(c) Driver's license, vehicle registration and DWI checks

When the police observe a traffic violation, they may stop the vehicle and demand to see the driver's license and the vehicle's registration and vehicle identification number. *N.Y. v. Class* (1986). A stopping for a license-registration check is also permissible when there is articulable and reasonable suspicion that a motorist is unlicensed or that a vehicle is not registered, or that either the vehicle or occupant is otherwise subject to seizure for violation of law, but the random stopping of an auto and detaining the driver in order to check the license and registration is unreasonable. This does not preclude use of methods for spot checks that involve less intrusion or less discretion, such as stopping all traffic at a roadblock. *Del. v. Prouse* (1979). Checkpoints may also be utilized to seek out intoxicated drivers, *Mich. Dep't of State Police v. Sitz* (1990), and many lower courts have upheld such checkpoints which were carefully planned by police supervisory personnel, were operated with a minimum of discretion by on-the-scene officers, and resulted in only very brief detentions.

(d) Airport inspections

When airport hijacker detection searches were conducted selectively by use of the government's hijacker "profile," they were upheld by reliance on

Terry v. Ohio, § 2.9(a). Now that all passengers
and carry-on luggage are checked, the program can
be upheld as a form of administrative search under
Camara, at least so long as prospective passengers
retain the right to leave rather than submit to
inspection.

(e) Supervision of prisoners, probationers and parolees

A prisoner's cell and effects are not protected by
the Fourth Amendment; "the prisoner's expectation of privacy [must] always yield to what must be
considered the paramount interest in institutional
security." *Hudson v. Palmer* (1984). *Hudson* may
not apply to searches of a prisoner's person or to
searches in pretrial detention facilities, in which
case such searches must be undertaken on reasonable suspicion or pursuant to an established routine or plan.

Probationers and parolees may be subjected to
searches without arrest or a search warrant and
upon evidence which falls short of the usual probable cause requirement. In *Griffin v. Wis.* (1987),
involving a warrantless search of a probationer's
home, the Court explained this was because of the
"special needs" of the probation system, where
restrictions on freedom and privacy are necessary
"to assure that the probation serves as a period of
genuine rehabilitation and that the community is
not harmed by the probationer's being at large."
The warrant requirement was deemed inappropriate for probation officers, who "have in mind the

welfare of the probationer" and must "respond quickly to evidence of misconduct." The usual probable cause standard was deemed inapplicable because it "would reduce the deterrent effect of the supervisory arrangement" and because "the probation agency must be able to act based upon a lesser degree of certainty * * * in order to intervene before a probationer does damage to himself or society."

(f) Supervision of students

In *N.J. v. T.L.O.* (1985), the Court held that "the Fourth Amendment applies to searches conducted by school authorities," but that under the *Camara* balancing test neither a warrant nor full probable cause is needed. Rather, the search is reasonable if limited in scope, taking into account the age and sex of the student and the nature of the infraction, and if there are "reasonable grounds for suspecting" the search will uncover evidence of a violation of law or school regulation. *T.L.O.* left unanswered whether individualized suspicion is always necessary, whether students have an expectation of privacy in school desks and lockers, and whether a higher standard applies if there is some police involvement.

(g) Supervision of employees

Government employees have a justified expectation of privacy in certain work areas, such as individual offices and the desk and filing cabinets therein. If a search of such an area is conducted by a public employer, no warrant is needed for intrusions "for legitimate work-related reasons wholly unrelated to illegal conduct," and intrusions "for noninvestigatory, work-related purposes, as well as for investigation of work-related misconduct, should be judged by the standard of reasonableness under all the circumstances" rather than the traditional quantum of probable cause. *O'Connor v. Ortega* (1987). Public employees may be required to submit to drug testing upon individualized reasonable suspicion or, absent such suspicion, where testing is triggered by a specific event and in additional a special need for testing exists. *Skinner v. Railway Labor Executives' Ass'n* (1989) (testing of crew after train accident or violation of safety rules); *National Treasury Employees Union v. Von Raab* (1989) (testing of customs agents upon transfer or promotion to position involving drug interdiction or carrying firearms).

§ 2.12 CONSENT SEARCHES

(a) Background

Where effective consent is given, a search may be conducted without a warrant and without probable cause. At one time, the consent doctrine was assumed to be grounded on the concept of waiver, *Stoner v. Cal.* (1964). But in *Schneckloth v. Bustamonte* (1973), the Court concluded that "a [traditional] 'waiver' approach to consent searches would be thoroughly inconsistent with our decisions," and thus held that the issue is whether the person's consent was "voluntary." Although this voluntariness test would appear to focus primarily upon the state of mind of the person allegedly consenting, the Court in *Schneckloth* did not have occasion to consider the validity of the position taken by some courts: that because it is the Fourth Amendment prohibition against unreasonable searches which is at issue, the question is whether the officers could reasonably conclude that defendant's consent was given.

(b) Warning of rights

Schneckloth v. Bustamonte (1973) holds that, while a person's knowledge of his right to refuse is a factor to be taken into account in determining (based on the totality of the circumstances) whether his consent was voluntary, the prosecution is not required to prove that he was so warned or otherwise had such knowledge where the consent was obtained while the person was not in custody. The *Johnson v. Zerbst* (see § 7.4(a)) test of waiver, "an intentional relinquishment or abandonment of a known right or privilege," was distinguished as applicable only to those constitutional rights which, unlike the Fourth Amendment, are intended to protect a fair trial and the reliability of the truth-determining process; the *Miranda* requirement of Fifth Amendment warnings (see § 4.4(b)) was distinguished because it only governs interrogation of those in custody. While this latter distinction suggests that the *Miranda* analogy might be persuasive as to a consent to search given by one in custody, it was held in *U.S. v. Watson* (1976), that failure to give Fourth Amendment warnings is not controlling where, as there, the defendant "had been arrested and was in custody, but his consent was given while on a public street, not in the confines of the police station." Most courts view the *Schneckloth* totality of circumstances test as equally applicable to consent obtained from one in custody at the station.

Some courts have taken the position that a consent to search given during custodial interrogation must be preceded by *Miranda* warnings because the request to search is a request that the defendant be a witness against himself which he is privileged to refuse under the Fifth Amendment. The prevailing view, however, is to the contrary, on the ground that a consent to search is neither testimonial nor communicative in the Fifth Amendment sense. But if the police first obtain statements in violation of *Miranda,* the subsequently obtained consent may be found to be a fruit of the earlier *Miranda* violation.

(c) Consent subsequent to a claim of authority

A search may not be justified on the basis of consent when that "consent" was given only after the official conducting the search asserted that he possessed a search warrant, but in fact there was no warrant or an invalid warrant. Such a claim of authority is, in effect, an announcement that the occupant has no right to resist the search, and thus acquiescence under these circumstances cannot be construed as consent. *Bumper v. N.C.* (1968). By comparison, the consent is valid if given in response to an officer's declaration that he will *seek* a warrant, as no false or overstated claim of authority has occurred. But if the officer said he would *obtain* a warrant, this invalidates the consent if there were not grounds on which such a warrant could issue. Even when there is no assertion of a warrant or threat to obtain one, submission to such declarations as "I am here to search your house" or "I have come to search your house" are almost certain to be viewed as coercive. *Amos v. U.S.* (1921).

(d) Other relevant factors

The voluntariness of a consent to search is "to be determined from the totality of all the circumstances," *Schneckloth v. Bustamonte* (1973). Among the other factors to be considered in determining the effectiveness of an alleged consent to search are whether the defendant (1) had minimal schooling or was of low intelligence; (2) was mentally ill or intoxicated; (3) was under arrest at the time the consent was given; (4) was overpowered by arresting officers, handcuffed, or similarly subject to physical restrictions; (5) had seized from him by police the keys to the premises thereafter searched; (6) employed evasive conduct or attempted to mislead the police; (7) denied guilt or the presence of any incriminatory objects in his premises; (8) earlier gave a valid confession or otherwise cooperated, as by initiating the search, or at least the investigation leading to the search; (9) was hesitant in agreeing to the search; or (10) was refused his request to consult with counsel. The presence of some of these factors is not controlling, however, as each case must stand or fall on its own special facts.

(e) Scope of consent

Assuming a valid consent, the police may not exceed the physical bounds of the area as to which consent was granted, such as by looking through private papers after a consent to allow search for narcotics. The standard for determining the scope of the consent "is that of 'objective' reasonableness—what would the typical reasonable person have understood by the exchange between the officer and the suspect." *Fla. v. Jimeno* (1991). Assuming consent to search a certain place, the police may look inside unlocked (but not locked) containers large enough to contain the object the police stated they were looking for. *Jimeno,* supra. There is disagreement as to whether a voluntary consent may be used to justify a second search of the same place after a fruitless first search; at least where there has been a significant passage of time, the second search involves re-entry of defendant's home, and defendant's status has changed from suspect to accused, the second search cannot be justified on the assumption that defendant's consent is continuing. In any event, a consent may be withdrawn or limited at any time prior to the completion of the search, though such a revocation does not operate retroactively so as to make invalid a search conducted prior to revocation.

(f) Consent by deception

A somewhat related problem concerning the scope of the consent arises when the consent was obtained by deception, as where the suspect gives the policeman a gun on the representation that the officer will aid him in selling it, but the officer then has a ballistics test run on the weapon, or where the suspect gives a blood sample to the police on the representation that it will be tested for alcohol content but it is in fact matched with blood found at the scene of a rape. The "misplaced trust" cases, upholding the admissibility of voluntary disclosures of criminal conduct to an undercover officer or police agent, *Lewis v. U.S.* (1966), *Hoffa v. U.S.* (1966), are probably distinguishable. The above situations are more like *Gouled v. U.S.* (1921) (where an old acquaintance acting for the police obtained defendant's consent to enter his office, but then conducted an extensive search when defendant left the room), in that the officer exceeded the reasonably anticipated scope of the consensual intrusion. That is, in *Lewis* and *Hoffa* the defendant voluntarily revealed his criminal activity to another, but this was not so in *Gouled* or the above illustrations.

§ 2.13 THIRD PARTY CONSENT

(a) Background

In the area of consent searches, courts have long recognized that certain third parties may give consent which will permit use of the seized evidence against the defendant.   Various theories have been utilized to explain this result.   An agency theory was relied upon in *Stoner v. Cal.* (1964), where the Court held that Fourth Amendment rights can only be waived by the defendant "either directly or through an agent."   But in *Bumper v. N.C.* (1968), the Court seemed to rely upon a property theory in intimating that the grandmother's consent to search of her house for a rifle, had it been voluntary, would have been effective against the grandson who lived there because she "owned both the house and the rifle."   In *Frazier v. Cupp* (1969), consent by defendant's cousin Rawls to search of a duffel bag jointly used by them was held to be effective against the defendant because he "must be taken to have assumed the risk that Rawls would allow someone else to look inside."   Similarly, in *U.S. v. Matlock* (1974), the Court indicated that where two or more persons have joint access to or control of premises "it is reasonable to recognize that any of the coinhabitants has the right to permit the inspection in his own right and that the others have assumed the risk that one of their number might permit the common area to be searched."   This assumption-of-risk theory is consistent with the justified-expectation-of-privacy approach to the Fourth Amendment in *Katz v. U.S.* (1967) (see § 2.2(a)).

This shift in theoretical basis may affect the result. Under the agency theory it has been held that a wife's consent is ineffective against her husband if she called the police because she was angry at him, but the contrary result is correct under the assumption-of-risk theory. By like reasoning, under the latter theory A's consent may be upheld as against B even though B instructed A not to consent, even though the police passed up the opportunity to seek B's consent, *U.S. v. Matlock* (1974) or even though B's consent was earlier sought and refused. The most difficult issue is whether A's consent is effective against co-occupant B who is then present and objecting. One view is that it is because this risk has been assumed by joint occupancy, a position which finds support in the assertion in *Matlock* that each occupant is free "to act in his own or the public interest." The contrary view rests upon the notions that ordinarily a co-occupant would not consent in this situation and that to allow police to proceed on A's consent in such a case would likely produce an untoward confrontation.

(b) Relationship of third party to defendant and place searched

Most of the third party consent cases have involved the husband-wife relationship, and the prevailing view is that when a husband and wife jointly own or occupy the premises in question, either may consent to a search of those premises for items which may incriminate the other. *Coolidge v. N.H.* (1971). Recent decisions have also upheld consents given by paramours who actually shared the premises on a continuing basis. *U.S. v. Matlock* (1974).

If a child is living at the home of his parents, a parent may consent to a search of the child's living quarters. On the other hand, a child may not give effective consent to a full search of the parents' home, although where it is not unusual or unauthorized for the child to admit visitors into the home, the mere entry of police on the premises with the consent of the child is not improper.

A landlord may not consent to the search of rented premises occupied by a tenant, and this is so even though the landlord may have some limited right of entry for purposes of inspecting or cleaning the premises. *Chapman v. U.S.* (1961). A person who rents a hotel room is treated as any other tenant, *Stoner v. Cal.,* supra, although once the time of occupancy has expired and the guest has checked out, a hotel representative may then consent to a search for anything the guest has left behind. *Abel v. U.S.* (1960). However, the landlord or his agents (such as a building custodian or superintendent) may consent to a search of hallways, basements, and other area to which all tenants have common access. A tenant may not consent to search of the part of the premises retained by the landlord, *Weeks v. U.S.* (1914), but may consent to search of the premises rented to him for items the landlord may have hidden there. A person sharing a house or apartment with another may consent to a search of areas of common usage, and a person in lawful possession of premises may give consent to search of the premises which will be effective against a nonpaying guest or casual visitor.

An employer may consent to a search of an employee's work and storage areas on the employer's premises, but he may not consent to a search of areas in which the employee is permitted to keep personal items not connected with the employment. Whether an employee can give a valid consent to a search of his employer's premises depends upon the scope of his authority. Generally, the courts have been of the view that a lesser employee, such as a secretary, may not give consent. However, if the employee is a manager or other person of considerable authority who is left in complete charge for a substantial period of time, then the prevailing view is that such a person can waive his employer's rights.

Whether a bailee, who does not own the property but has lawful possession of it, can consent to a police search of the property which will be effective against the bailor depends upon whether the nature of the bailment is such that the bailor has assumed the risk. *Frazier v. Cupp* (1969). The risk is assumed when, as in that case, a duffel bag is turned over on the understanding that the bailee may use part of it to store his effects, but not when a locked container is involved and the bailee has no key. The extent to which the bailor has surrendered control and the length of the bailment are important; perhaps an attendant in a public garage may consent to the opening of the car door to see items on the floor of the car, but for the bailee to consent to search of the trunk it must appear that the bailee was authorized to open the trunk.

(c) Apparent authority

In *Stoner v. Cal.* (1964), in response to the state's contention that a police search of defendant's hotel room was proper because they reasonably believed that the clerk had authority to consent, the Court emphasized "that the rights protected by the Fourth Amendment are not to be eroded by strained applications of the law of agency or by unrealistic doctrines of 'apparent authority.'" This means only that an officer's mistake as to someone's *legal* authority cannot, in effect, expand the limits of third party consent. But, because the Fourth Amendment only proscribes "unreasonable" searches, a consent search is lawful despite an officer's reasonable mistake of *fact* (e.g., that the person giving consent actually has the property interest in the premises searched which he claims to have or otherwise appears to have but in fact does not have). *Ill. v. Rodriguez* (1990). In ambiguous circumstances the police may not accept even an explicit claim of authority without further inquiry. *Rodriguez,* supra.

(d) Exclusive control

In third party consent situations, it is necessary to consider the various relationships discussed above as they relate to the particular area or object searched. In *U.S. v. Matlock* (1974), the Court said the effectiveness of the consent depended upon whether there was "common authority" over the premises, which was said to rest on "mutual use of the property" by one "having joint access or control for most purposes." Consistent with this language is the notion that even if *A* and *B* generally share premises together, they each may still have areas therein of mutually exclusive use. Such is least likely to be true in husband-wife situations, where ordinarily the personal effects of each spouse are not thought to be "off limits" to the other, but the result may well be different in the case of friends sharing an apartment.

CHAPTER 3

WIRETAPPING, ELECTRONIC EAVESDROPPING, AND THE USE OF SECRET AGENTS

---

§ 3.1 HISTORICAL BACKGROUND; APPLICATION OF FOURTH AMENDMENT

(a) The *Olmstead* case

In *Olmstead v. U.S.* (1928), the first wiretap case to reach the Supreme Court, the police intercepted communications by placing a tap on defendant's telephone line. In a 5–4 decision, the majority read the Fourth Amendment literally in concluding that the police conduct did not constitute a search and seizure. Two reasons were given: (1) at no time did the police trespass upon defendant's premises, so that no "place" was searched; and (2) only conversations were obtained, so that no "things" were seized.

As indicated herein, both of these grounds have since been rejected, and thus it is not surprising that in recent years the forceful dissents in *Olmstead* have more often been quoted. Justice Brandeis argued that the Amendment did cover wiretapping, and also that the government, as "the omnipresent teacher," should not be upheld in its admitted violation of a state wiretapping law. Justice Holmes, dissenting on the latter ground only, characterized wiretapping in violation of state law as "dirty business" and contended that "it is a less evil that some criminals should escape than that the government should play an ignoble part."

(b) Section 605

Congress later enacted the Federal Communications Act of 1934, which provided in § 605: "[N]o person not being authorized by the sender shall intercept any communication and divulge or publish the existence, contents, substance, purport, effect, or meaning of such intercepted communication to any person." On the basis of this language, it was held that a person with standing, i.e., a party to the conversation, *Goldstein v. U.S.* (1942), could suppress in a federal prosecution evidence obtained by state or federal officers, *Nardone v. U.S.* (1937); *Benanti v. U.S.* (1957), by wiretapping interstate or intrastate communications, *Weiss v. U.S.* (1939), unless done with the consent of one of the parties to the conversation. *Rathbun v. U.S.* (1957). The ruling that wiretap evidence gathered by state officials was admissible in state prosecutions, *Schwartz v. Tex.* (1952), was finally overruled in *Lee v. Fla.* (1968), where the Court emphasized the constitutional extension of the exclusionary rule in *Mapp v. Ohio* (1961) and the lack of other effective sanctions for violation of § 605. *Lee* was

decided just two days before the Crime Control Act
(see § 3.2) superceded the wiretapping prohibition
of § 605.

(c) Non-telephonic electronic eavesdropping

Goldman v. U.S. (1942), was the "bugging" counterpart of *Olmstead:* because federal officers had
merely placed a detectaphone against the outer
wall of a private office, the Court held there had
been no trespass and thus no Fourth Amendment
violation. Similarly, in *On Lee v. U.S.* (1952),
where incriminating statements were picked up
via a "wired for sound" acquaintance of defendant,
a 5–4 majority rejected the contention that a trespass by fraud had occurred and thus found no
constitutional violation.

In *Silverman v. U.S.* (1961), a unanimous Court
held that listening to incriminating conversations
within a house by inserting a "spike mike" into a
party wall and making contact with a heating duct
serving that house amounted to an illegal search
and seizure. The opinion did not clearly indicate
whether the "intrusion" by the spike into defendants' premises was a critical fact, but any remaining doubts were dispelled by *Katz v. U.S.* (1967).
The issue in *Katz* was whether recordings of defendant's end of telephone conversations, obtained by
attaching an electronic listening and recording device to the outside of a public telephone booth, had
been obtained in violation of the Fourth Amendment. In a 7–1 decision, the Court expressly rejected the "trespass" doctrine of *Olmstead* and

Goldman, and held that the government action constituted a search and seizure within the meaning of the Fourth Amendment because it "violated the privacy upon which [the defendant] justifiably relied while using the telephone booth." *Katz* thus made it clear that, with the possible exception of the case in which a conversation is overheard or recorded with the consent of a party to the conversation (see § 3.3), wiretapping and electronic eavesdropping are subject to the limitations of the Fourth Amendment.

§ 3.2 CONSTITUTIONALITY OF TITLE III OF THE CRIME CONTROL ACT

(a) Background

Under what circumstances, then, may wiretapping and electronic eavesdropping without the prior consent of a party to the conversations be conducted consistent with the Fourth Amendment? Because such surveillance is authorized in limited circumstances by Title III of the Omnibus Crime Control and Safe Streets Act of 1968, 18 U.S.C.A. §§ 2510–2520, the appropriate inquiry is into the constitutionality of that legislation. Though the Supreme Court has never passed upon the Act, guidance on the issues involved may be found in certain decisions of the Court: *Osborn v. U.S.* (1966), upholding a judicially authorized use of an undercover agent with a concealed tape recorder; *Berger v. N.Y.* (1967), holding the New York eavesdropping law unconstitutional; and *Katz v. U.S.*

(1967), indicating that the limited eavesdropping undertaken there would have been constitutional if a warrant had first been obtained.

(b) Summary of Title III

Under the Act, the Attorney General or various other officials down to a specially designated Deputy Assistant Attorney General in the Criminal Division may authorize application to a federal judge for an order permitting interception of wire or oral communications (i.e., wiretapping or electronic eavesdropping) by a federal agency having responsibility for investigation of the offense as to which application is made, when such interception may provide evidence of certain enumerated federal crimes. (Use of a "pen register" to keep a record of telephone numbers dialed is not an interception under the Act, *U.S. v. N.Y. Telephone Co.* (1977), and is not a search, *Smith v. Md.* (1979).) A comparable provision permits, when authorized by state law, application by a state or county prosecutor to a state judge when the interception may provide evidence of "murder, kidnapping, gambling, robbery, bribery, extortion, or dealing in narcotic drugs, marijuana or other dangerous drugs, or other crime dangerous to life, limb, or property, and punishable by imprisonment for more than one year." The judge may only grant an interception order as provided in § 2518 of the Act, and evidence obtained in the lawful execution of such order is admissible in court. Other willful interception or disclosure of any wire or oral communication without the prior consent of a party thereto is made criminal, and evidence so obtained is inadmissible in any state or federal proceedings, but suppression is not required merely because of noncompliance with those requirements in the Act which do not play a "substantive role" in the regulatory system. *U.S. v. Donovan* (1977).

The Act originally provided that it did not limit the constitutional power of the President to take such measures as he deems necessary to, inter alia, "obtain foreign intelligence information deemed essential to the security of the United States." Those powers do not extend to warrantless tapping in *domestic* security cases, as Fourth Amendment protections are "the more necessary" for "those suspected of unorthodoxy in their political beliefs." *U.S. v. U.S. District Court* (1972). (The matter is now dealt with in the Foreign Intelligence Surveillance Act of 1978, 50 U.S.C.A. §§ 1801–1811, which establishes a warrant procedure and also provides that the President "may authorize electronic surveillance without a court order under this title to acquire foreign intelligence information for periods of up to one year" if, inter alia, the Attorney General certifies in writing under oath that the surveillance is "solely directed at" the acquisition of the contents of communications "transmitted by means of communications used exclusively between or among foreign powers" and that "there is no substantial likelihood that the surveillance will acquire the contents of any communication to which a United States person is a party.")

Under § 2518, an interception order may be issued only if the judge determines on the basis of facts submitted that there is probable cause for belief that an individual is committing, has committed, or is about to commit one of the enumerated offenses; probable cause for belief that particular communications concerning that offense will be obtained through such interception; that normal investigative procedures have been tried and have failed to reasonably appear to be unlikely to succeed if tried or to be too dangerous; and probable cause for belief that the facilities from which, or the place where, the communications are to be intercepted are being used, or are about to be used, in connection with the commission of such offense, or are leased to, listed in the name of, or commonly used by such person. Each interception order must specify the identity of the person, if known, whose communications are to be intercepted; the nature and location of the communications facilities as to which, or the place where, authority to intercept is granted (except that a so-called "roving tap" may be authorized upon a particularized showing of need); a particular description of the type of communication sought to be intercepted, and a statement of the particular offense to which it relates; the identity of the agency authorized to intercept the communications and of the person authorizing the application; and the period of time during which such interception is authorized, including a statement as to whether or not the interception shall automatically terminate when the described communication has been first obtained. No order may permit interception "for any period longer than is necessary to achieve the objective of the authorization, nor in any event longer than thirty days." Extensions of an order may be granted for like periods, but only by resort to the procedures required in obtaining the initial order.

Interception without prior judicial authorization is permitted upon a specifically designated enforcement officer's reasonable determination that "(a) an emergency situation exists that involves (i) immediate danger of death or serious physical injury to any person, (ii) conspiratorial activities threatening the national security interest, or (iii) conspiratorial activities characteristic of organized crime, that requires a wire or oral communication to be intercepted before an order authorizing such interception can with due diligence be obtained, and (b) there are grounds upon which an order could be entered." In such a case, application for an order must be made within 48 hours after the interception commences, and, in the absence of an order, the interception must terminate when the communication sought is obtained or when the application for the order is denied, whichever is earlier.

Within a reasonable time but not later than 90 days after the filing of an application which is denied or the termination of an authorized period of interception, the judge must cause to be served on the persons named in the order or application and other parties to the intercepted communications, an inventory which shall include notice of (1) the fact of the entry of the order or application; (2) the date of the entry and the period of authorized interception, or the denial of the application; and (3) the fact that during the period communications were or were not intercepted. A similar inventory is required as to interceptions terminated without an order having been issued.

(c) Continued surveillance

The most obvious difference between a search for tangible items and the search for wire or oral communications allowed under Title III is the time dimension of the latter kind of search. A search warrant for some physical object permits a single entry and prompt search of the described premises, while Title III permits continuing surveillance up to 30 days, with extensions possible. During the authorized time, all conversations over the tapped line or within the bugged room may be overheard and recorded without regard to their relevance.

As reflected in *Berger*, this striking difference accounts for the major constitutional obstacle to legalized electronic surveillance. In holding a New York law unconstitutional, the Court emphasized that it (1) permitted installation and operation of surveillance equipment for 60 days, "the equivalent of a series of intrusions, searches, and seizures pursuant to a single showing of probable cause"; (2) permitted renewal of the order "without a showing of present probable cause for the continuance of the eavesdrop"; and (3) placed "no termination date on the eavesdrop once the conversation sought is seized." While Title III permits extensions only upon a new showing of probable cause and requires that interception cease once "the objective of the authorization" is achieved, it does permit continued surveillance for up to 30 days upon a single showing of probable cause, and thus goes well beyond the kind of with-warrant electronic surveillance the Supreme Court has approved or indicated would be permitted.

As emphasized in *Berger,* the bugging of a secret agent upheld in *Osborn* was pursuant to an order which "authorized one limited intrusion rather than a series or a continuous surveillance. And, we note that a new order was issued when the officer sought to resume the search and probable cause was shown for the succeeding one. Moreover, the order was executed by the officer with dispatch, not over a prolonged and extended period." And in *Katz* the Court noted that the "surveillance was so narrowly circumscribed that a duly authorized magistrate * * * clearly apprised of the precise intrusion * * * could constitutionally have authorized * * * the very limited search and seizure that the Government asserts in fact took place." The surveillance was limited in that the agents had probable cause to believe defendant was using certain public telephones for gambling purposes about the same time almost every day and thus activated the surveillance equipment attached to the outside of the phone booth only when defendant entered the booth.

Decisions holding that continued surveillance may also be squared with the Fourth Amendment rely upon the analysis of Justices Harlan and White, dissenting in *Berger*. First, they contend that an electronic surveillance which is continued over a span of time is no more a general search than the typical execution of a search warrant over a described area. As Justice White argued: "Petitioner suggests that the search is inherently overbroad because the eavesdropper will overhear conversations which do not relate to criminal activity. But the same is true of almost all searches of private property which the Fourth Amendment permits. In searching for seizable matters, the police must necessarily see or hear, and comprehend, items which do not relate to the purpose of the search. That this occurs, however, does not render the search invalid, so long as it is authorized by a suitable search warrant and so long as the police, in executing that warrant, limit themselves to searching for items which may constitutionally be seized."

This analogy holds only if it may be concluded that the overhearing or recording of a series of conversations is merely a search, from which certain particularly described conversations will thereafter be seized, as Justice Harlan contended: "Just as some exercise of dominion, beyond mere perception, is necessary for the seizure of tangibles, so some use of the conversation beyond the initial listening process is required for the seizures of the spoken word." A majority of the Court has yet to speak clearly on this point, although in *Katz* there is language characterizing the "electronically listening to and recording" of defendant's words as a "search and seizure." This has not deterred lower courts from consistently holding Title III is not unconstitutional merely because it authorizes wiretaps which may last several days and encompass multiple conversations.

(d) Lack of notice

The Court in *Berger* also found the New York law "offensive" because it "has no requirement for notice, as do conventional warrants, nor does it overcome this defect by requiring some showing of special facts. On the contrary, it permits uncontested entry without any showing of exigent circumstances. Such a showing of exigency, in order to avoid notice would appear more important in eavesdropping, with its inherent dangers, than that required when conventional procedures of search and seizure are utilized." This criticism goes to the heart of all eavesdropping practices, as the Court noted, in that success depends upon secrecy.

The *Berger* Court did not explore this matter in greater detail, and thus it is not entirely clear whether Title III might be challenged on this basis. In decisions upholding the statute, the following arguments have been made: (1) One reason for advance notice, as emphasized by four members of the Court in *Ker v. Cal.* (1963), is to guard the entering officer from attack on the mistaken belief he is making a criminal entry, and this danger is not present in most eavesdropping cases—including all which do not require a trespass. (2) Another reason for notice is so that the individual will be aware that a search was conducted, but in the more typical search case this notice may come only after the event by discovery of the warrant and a receipt at the place searched, which is comparable to the Title III requirement of service of an inventory within 90 days. (3) Prior notice is not required when there is reason to believe it would result in destruction of the evidence sought (see 2.5(b)), and while the Court in *Berger* may have been unwilling to uphold all eavesdropping without notice on this ground, this "exigency" is sufficiently established upon a showing that "normal investigative procedures have been tried and have failed or reasonably appear to be unlikely to succeed if tried or to be too dangerous," as required by Title III. An extensive footnote (n. 16) on the subject in *Katz* suggests that the Court finds these arguments compelling.

(e) Other considerations

An exhaustive analysis of Title III would reveal a number of other problems, primarily going to how the Act must be construed in light of the Fourth Amendment. Four of these problems deserve brief mention here. First of all, what meaning is to be given to the "probable cause" requirement in this context? If, as discussed earlier, the Fourth Amendment has some flexibility, so that somewhat less evidence is needed to justify such lesser intrusions as a building inspection, stop-and-frisk, or brief seizure for fingerprinting (see §§ 2.9, 2.11), then it may be equally true that more evidence than usual will be required to establish probable cause for the unusual degree of intrusion which results from electronic surveillance. Justice Stewart, concurring in *Berger,* took this approach and thus found the affidavits in that case adequate for a "conventional search or arrest" but insufficient for a 60–day eavesdrop. However, defendants who have made this type of argument in the lower courts have not prevailed.

Title III requires a particular description of the "type of communication sought to be intercepted, and a statement of the particular offense to which it relates," but it is unclear how this language is to be interpreted. The statute in *Berger* merely required the naming of "the person or persons whose communications * * * are to be overheard or recorded"; the Court held this did not meet the Fourth Amendment requirement that the things to be seized be particularly described and declared that the "need for particularity * * * is especially great in the case of eavesdropping [because it] involves an intrusion on privacy that is broad in scope." Yet, as Justice Harlan noted in dissent, the cases on search for tangible items make it clear that the particularity requirement of the Amendment is a flexible one, depending upon the nature of the described things and whether the description readily permits identification by the executing officer (see § 2.4(d)). From this it might be concluded, as the lower courts have rather consistently held, that specification of conversations as relating to a certain kind of criminal activity should suffice.

Next, there is the question whether an interception order may be executed by covert entry in the absence of specific judicial authorization for such execution based upon a showing of necessity therefor. In *Dalia v. U.S.* (1979), the Court held that neither Title III nor the Fourth Amendment required such specific authorization. The latter holding was based upon the conclusion that nothing in the Amendment suggests "search warrants also must include a specification of the precise manner in which they are to be executed."

Finally, there is the provision in Title III which permits interception without prior judicial approval when there are grounds for an interception order but an emergency exists with respect to "(i) immediate danger of death or serious physical injury to any person, (ii) conspiratorial activities threatening the national security interest, or (iii) conspiratorial activities characteristic of organized crime" that require interception before an order could with due diligence be obtained. If strictly construed to ensure that warrantless interceptions are not being upheld after the fact on the basis of what was discovered, this provision is consistent with Fourth Amendment decisions on search for physical evidence without warrant to prevent loss of the evidence (see § 2.7(e)). *Katz* condemned the warrantless eavesdropping challenged in that case, but the facts make it clear that there was ample time to secure a warrant.

§ 3.3 THE USE OF SECRET AGENTS TO OBTAIN INCRIMINATING STATEMENTS

(a) "Wired" agents: *On Lee* and *Lopez*

In *On Lee v. U.S.* (1952), a wired-for-sound informant entered the laundry of the defendant, an old acquaintance, and engaged him in conversation, resulting in defendant's incriminating statements being transmitted to a narcotics agent outside. At trial, the agent testified as to these statements, but the informer was not called as a witness. A 5–4 majority rejected the claim that the informant committed a trespass by fraud, dismissed as "verging on the frivolous" the contention that the narcotics agent was trespassing by use of the transmitter and receiver, and concluded that in the absence of a trespass there was no Fourth Amendment violation.

Lopez v. U.S. (1963) concerned an internal revenue agent who, after receiving a bribe offer from the defendant, engaged defendant in subsequent incriminating conversations in the agent's office while equipped with a pocket recorder. The recordings were admitted at trial in support of the agent's testimony. In a 6–3 decision, the Court held no eavesdropping had occurred, in that there had been no invasion of the defendant's premises and the recording revealed only what the defendant willingly disclosed to the agent and what the agent in turn was entitled to disclose to others. The Chief Justice, concurring specially, asserted that *On Lee* was "wrongly decided" and was distinguishable from *Lopez* because in *On Lee* the eavesdropping deprived the defendant of an opportunity to cross-examine the informer. The three dissenters saw no difference between the two cases, and asserted that the Fourth Amendment should protect a person against the risk that third parties may give independent evidence of conversations engaged in with another.

(b) Without "bugging": *Lewis* and *Hoffa*

In *Lewis v. U.S.* (1966), a federal narcotics agent misrepresented his identity and expressed a willingness to purchase narcotics, which resulted in his being invited into defendant's home, where an unlawful narcotics sale occurred. Because the agent did not "see, hear, or take anything that was not contemplated and in fact intended by petitioner as a necessary part of his illegal business," but merely entered a home "converted into a commercial center to which outsiders are invited for purposes of transacting unlawful business," the Court found no Fourth Amendment violation. *Gouled v. U.S.* (1921), was distinguished in that there a business acquaintance, acting on police order, gained entry to defendant's office as a social visitor and then searched for and seized papers in the defendant's absence.

In *Hoffa v. U.S.* (1966), the defendant unsuccessfully challenged on Fourth, Fifth, and Sixth Amendment grounds the admission of evidence obtained by a Teamsters official who at government instigation visited Hoffa during the latter's earlier trial and overheard conversations between Hoffa and his associates concerning an attempt to bribe jurors. As to the contention that the failure of the informer to disclose his role vitiated the consent to his entry of a constitutionally protected area, Hoffa's hotel suite, the Court noted that Hoffa "was not relying on the security of the hotel room [but rather] upon his misplaced confidence that [the informer] would not reveal his wrongdoing," which is not protected by the Fourth Amendment. The Fifth Amendment claim was summarily dismissed with the observation that "a necessary element of compulsory self-incrimination is some kind of compulsion," absent here because Hoffa's conversations with and in the presence of the informer were "wholly voluntary." As to the Sixth Amendment claim that the informer had intruded upon the confidential attorney-client relationship, the Court concluded that, at least on these facts, such a violation of Sixth Amendment rights in one trial does not render evidence obtained thereby inadmissible in a different trial on other charges. (It was later held in *Weatherford v. Bursey* (1977), that if an informer was present at pretrial attorney-client meetings, but he never communicated what he learned thereby, no Sixth Amendment violation has occurred.) Another Sixth Amendment argument, that from the time when there was evidence for arrest Hoffa was entitled to the same protection afforded an arrested person under *Massiah* and *Escobedo* (see § 4.3), was quickly disposed of on the ground that "there is no constitutional right to be arrested," for otherwise the police would be in the perilous position of having to guess at the precise moment they had probable cause.

(c) The impact of *Katz*

The thrust of these four cases is that such uses of secret agents, with or without listening or recording devices, are not covered by the Fourth Amendment. It is apparently on this basis that the electronic eavesdropping provisions of Title III expressly exclude from the warrant requirement the interception of communications with the consent of a party to the conversation. However, doubts about the continued vitality of *On Lee, Lopez, Lewis,* and *Hoffa* emerged when the Court in *Katz v. U.S.* (see § 2.2(a)), rejected the old trespass-into-constitutionally-protected-areas analysis in favor of an expectation-of-privacy approach to Fourth Amendment issues.

The question reached the Court in *U.S. v. White* (1971), where an informer, carrying a concealed transmitter, engaged the defendant in conversations in a restaurant, defendant's home and the informer's car. The informer did not testify at the trial, but the narcotics agents who electronically overheard the conversations did, resulting in defen-

dant's conviction. In a 4–man plurality opinion by
White, J., it was concluded (1) that one may not
have a "justifiable" expectation that his trusted
associates neither are nor will become police
agents, and (2) that a different result is not called
for when the agent has recorded or transmitted the
conversations: "Given the possibility or probability
that one of his colleagues is cooperating with the
police, it is only speculation to assert that the
defendant's utterances would be substantially different or his sense of security any less if he also
thought it possible that the suspected colleague is
wired for sound." Black, J., concurred on the basis
of his *Katz* dissent, which contended the Fourth
Amendment did not apply to intangibles.

Brennan, J., concurred in the result in *White* on
the ground that *Katz* should not be applied retroactively, but contended that *On Lee* and *Lopez* both
should be viewed as overruled by *Katz,* the position
apparently taken in each of the three dissenting
opinions. None of the dissenters specifically questioned the status of *Lewis* and *Hoffa,* and Harlan,
J., in particular, emphasized the difference between the practices involved in those cases and the
instant case: "The interest *On Lee* fails to protect
is the expectation of the ordinary citizen, who has
never engaged in illegal conduct in his life, that he
may carry on his private discourse freely, openly,
and spontaneously without measuring his every
word against the connotations it might carry when
instantaneously heard by others unknown to him
and unfamiliar with his situation or analyzed in a

cold, formal record played days, months, or years after the conversation."

§ 3.4 DISCLOSURE OF ELECTRONIC SURVEILLANCE RECORDS

(a) The "fruits" of surveillance

If conversations have been overheard or recorded by electronic surveillance in violation of the Fourth Amendment, testimony concerning or recordings of these conversations may be suppressed by a defendant with standing. Under the "fruit of the poisonous tree" doctrine (see § 6.6(a)), other evidence which was the product of illegal surveillance is also subject to suppression. This has given rise to the issue of what procedures are required to facilitate a determination whether other evidence is in fact the fruit of such a surveillance.

(b) The *Alderman* disclosure requirement

This issue was decided in *Alderman v. U.S.* (1969) involving convictions for conspiring to transmit murderous threats in interstate commerce and two other cases of convictions for transmitting national defense information to the Soviet Union. The defendants sought disclosure of all surveillance records so that they might show that some of the evidence admitted against them grew out of illegally overheard conversations. The government urged that in order to protect innocent third parties participating or referred to in irrelevant conversations overheard by the government, surveillance records should first be subjected to in camera inspection by the trial judge. He would then turn over to defendants and their counsel only those materials "arguably relevant" to defendants' convictions, in the sense that the overheard conversations arguably underlay some item of evidence offered at trial.

The Court, in a 5–3 decision, held that a defendant should receive all surveillance records as to which he has standing. The government's proposal was rejected on the ground that the trial judge often would not be in a position to determine what conversations were relevant: "An apparently innocent phrase, a chance remark, a reference to what appears to be a neutral person or event, the identity of a caller or the individual on the other end of a telephone, or even the manner of speaking or using words may have special significance to one who knows the more intimate facts of an accused's life. And yet that information may be wholly colorless and devoid of meaning to one less well acquainted with all relevant circumstances. Unavoidably, this is a matter of judgment, but in our view the task is too complex, and the margin for error too great, to rely wholly on the in camera judgment of the trial court to identify those records which might have contributed to the Government's case." To protect innocent third parties, the Court added, the trial court could place defendants and counsel under enforceable orders against unwarranted disclosure of the materials they would be entitled to inspect.

In *Giordano v. U.S.* (1969), the Court emphasized
that the disclosure required in *Alderman* was expressly limited to situations where the surveillance
had been determined to be in violation of the
Fourth Amendment. Justice Stewart, concurring,
suggested that this preliminary determination
might sometimes be made in ex parte, in camera
proceedings. And in *Taglianetti v. U.S.* (1969), the
Court rejected defendant's contention that he was
entitled to examine additional surveillance records
to establish that he might be a party to some other
conversations. Distinguishing *Alderman,* the
Court concluded that the trial judge could be expected to identify defendant's voice without the
defendant's assistance.

(c) The statutory limitation

By Title VII of the Organized Crime Control Act
of 1970, 18 U.S.C.A. § 3504, Congress has attempted to limit the impact of *Alderman* in the federal
courts. For one thing, records of an unlawful
surveillance which occurred prior to June 19, 1968,
(the date that the Omnibus Crime Control and Safe
Streets Act of 1968 became law) need not be disclosed "unless such information may be relevant to
a pending claim of * * * inadmissibility," which
presumably is to be determined by the judge in
camera. For another, on the legislative finding
that "there is virtually no likelihood" that evidence offered to prove an event would have been
obtained by exploitation of an unlawful surveillance occurring more than five years prior to that

event, no such claim is to be considered. The constitutionality of these provisions is open to some doubt, considering the fact that the *Alderman* decision was cast in terms of "the scrutiny which the Fourth Amendment exclusionary rule demands."

§ 3.5   THE USE OF SECRET AGENTS TO "ENCOURAGE" CRIMINAL CONDUCT

(a) Entrapment

Secret agents—sometimes undercover police officers but very often private citizens acting as informants—are frequently utilized to "encourage" others to engage in criminal conduct. Such tactics are for the most part confined to the crimes of prostitution, homosexuality, liquor and narcotic sales, and gambling; normal detection methods are virtually impossible as to these offenses, as they are committed privately with a willing victim who will not complain. The encouragement very frequently involves little more than a feigned offer by the agent to purchase criminal services from the suspect, but on occasion the agent may use considerably more pressure to gain the suspect's agreement to commit an offense.

The Supreme Court has held that techniques of encouragement may not reach the point where they constitute "entrapment"; if they do, the presence of entrapment constitutes a defense to the defendant's otherwise criminal act. The exact definition of entrapment is a matter of dispute, but it clearly includes the situation in which "the criminal design originates with the [police agents] and they implant in the mind of an innocent person the disposition to commit the offense and induce its commission in order that they may prosecute." *Sorrells v. U.S.* (1932). The prosecution, which has the burden of proof, can defeat the defense by showing defendant's predisposition to such criminality was independent of any government contacts with him. *Jacobson v. U.S.* (1992). So far, the Court has based the defense upon other than constitutional grounds; some of the Justices have relied upon general principles of substantive criminal law and others upon the supervisory power of the Court over the administration of justice in federal courts. *U.S. v. Russell* (1973); *Sherman v. U.S.* (1958).

(b) Possible constitutional bases

While the entrapment defense is also recognized in the state courts, which for the most part purport to use the *Sorrells-Sherman* test, state convictions are sometimes affirmed notwithstanding evidence of what would constitute entrapment under those decisions. This has given rise to the question of whether freedom from entrapment is a federal constitutional right for which relief may be granted upon federal habeas corpus, to which the courts have so far responded in the negative.

In support of the contention that freedom from entrapment is a right protected under the due process clause, commentators have suggested that: (1) by analogy to the Fourth Amendment protection against unreasonable searches or by application of the penumbral "right of privacy," *Griswold v. Conn.* (1965), secret agents may encourage only those individuals as to whom there exists "probable cause" (under the balancing approach, see §§ 2.9, 2.11, a lesser quantum of evidence than would be required for arrest); (2) by analogy to the constitutional prohibition on illegally obtained confessions, under which ruses and appeals to sympathy are relevant considerations, *Spano v. N.Y.* (1959), secret agents may not overbear a person's will to get him to perpetrate a crime; (3) by analogy to the doctrine that it is cruel and unusual punishment to convict for mere status and without the proof of any act, *Robinson v. Cal.* (1962), the acts which serve as the basis for conviction must be attributable to the defendant rather than to the police or their agents; (4) by analogy to the constitutional limitation on abolition of *mens rea, Lambert v. Cal.* (1957), the necessary mental element for the crime may not be implanted by entrapment; and (5) by analogy to the constitutional defense of estoppel, which bars conviction for actions undertaken upon official advice that such conduct would not violate the law, *Cox v. La.* (1965), secret agents may not induce actions in which the defendant was not predisposed to engage.

In *U.S. v. Russell* (1973), the Supreme Court, while noting that the entrapment defense "is not of a constitutional dimension," acknowledged that there might be "a situation in which the conduct of law enforcement agents is so outrageous that due process principles would absolutely bar the government from invoking judicial processes to obtain a conviction." Due process does not bar conviction of a defendant for sale of narcotics supplied to him by a government agent. *Hampton v. U.S.* (1976). Lower courts have but seldom found government "overinvolvement" to violate due process, and have indicated that for such a violation it must appear that (a) the plan did not originate with the defendant, (b) the defendant was not reasonably suspected of criminal conduct or design, and (c) a government agent supplied indispensible and not otherwise readily available goods or services to the illegal enterprise.

CHAPTER 4

POLICE INTERROGATION AND CONFESSIONS

---

§ 4.1 INTRODUCTION

(a) The confession dilemma

No area of constitutional criminal procedure has provoked more debate over the years than that dealing with police interrogation. In large measure, the debate has centered upon the extent of police abuse in seeking confessions and the importance of confessions in obtaining convictions—two matters on which conclusive evidence is lacking.

Because the questioning of suspects has traditionally been undertaken behind station-house doors (for some, a sufficient indication in itself of abuse), there is not sufficient empirical evidence to assert with confidence what always, usually, or often occurs in the course of police interrogation. Attention thus has often turned to celebrated cases of confessions later proved false or to judicial opinions (including many Supreme Court cases, see § 4.2) revealing outrageous police tactics. Those who assert that police abuses have been widespread contend that these cases are fairly representative, while those of a contrary persuasion claim that these are unusual cases having no relation to day-to-day police work. There is similar disagreement as to what may be logically presumed from the nature of the police and their task: whether it is proper to presume that policemen usually abide by their sworn duty to comply with the law in enforcing the law; or whether the correct assumption is that the police are so caught up in the difficult task of fighting crime that they believe anything goes.

Hard facts about the need for confessions are also lacking. It may be true, as Justice Frankfurter declared in *Culombe v. Conn.* (1961), that "despite modern advances in the technology of crime detection, offenses frequently occur about which things cannot be made to speak," but just how frequently they occur is uncertain. Statistics have been offered to establish that confessions are seldom utilized in serious criminal cases and also to show the contrary. The former are challengeable on the ground that they fail to take account of the overwhelming majority of cases disposed of by pleas of guilty, while the latter are contested because they may only demonstrate that the police often fail to use other investigative techniques.

Assuming other techniques are available, there is still disagreement as to whether interrogation is nonetheless desirable. Some hold to the view, as expressed by Justice Goldberg in *Escobedo v. Ill.* (1964), that "a system of criminal law enforcement which comes to depend on the 'confession' will, in the long run, be less reliable and more subject to abuses than a system which depends on extrinsic evidence independently secured through skillful investigation." Others question this assumption and suggest that greater use of certain "extrinsic evidence," such as eyewitness identifications (see ch. 5), would result in even less reliability.

(b) The Supreme Court's response

From 1936 to nearly 30 years later, the Court dealt with confessions admitted in state criminal proceedings in terms of the fundamental fairness required by the Fourteenth Amendment due process clause (see § 1.2(b)). A so-called "voluntariness" test, which depended upon the "totality of the circumstances," was used to determine whether the Constitution required exclusion of a confession (see § 4.2). Over the years, it became increasingly apparent that this test was most difficult to administer because it required a finding and appraisal of all relevant facts surrounding each challenged confession.

Essentially the same approach was used by the Court during this period on the infrequent occasions when confessions admitted in federal prosecutions were reviewed. In such instances, it might logically be thought that the Court was then relying upon the due process clause of the Fifth Amendment, although the tendency was to refer to earlier holdings in which the basis of exclusion was the Fifth Amendment privilege against self-incrimination or a common law rule of evidence. *U.S. v. Carignan* (1951). Beginning in 1943, a confession obtained by federal officers and offered in a federal prosecution could also be excluded on the ground that it was received during a period of "unnecessary delay" in taking the arrested person before a judicial officer. *McNabb v. U.S.* (1943); *Mallory v. U.S.* (1957). Although these decisions were grounded upon the Court's supervisory power over the federal courts, most commentators viewed them as attempts by the Court to avoid the tremendous problems inherent in the due process voluntariness test, and thus there was some expectation that the *McNabb-Mallory* rule (finally abolished by Title II of the Omnibus Crime Control and Safe Streets Act of 1968) would ultimately be rested upon a constitutional foundation and applied to the states.

This did not come to pass, perhaps because subsequent decisions holding that there was a constitutional right to counsel at certain pretrial "critical stages" provided a better stepping stone. The anticipated move away from sole reliance upon the voluntariness test occurred in *Escobedo v. Ill.* (1964), suppressing the defendant's confession because it was obtained in violation of his right to counsel at the time of interrogation. *Escobedo* was a cautious step, for the holding was carefully limited to the unique facts of the case (see § 4.3(b), (c)), but it was generally assumed that this newly established right to counsel in the police station would thereafter be expanded on a case-by-case basis.

Instead, the Court just two years later decided *Miranda v. Ariz.* (1966), which was grounded upon the Fifth Amendment privilege against self-incrimination and prescribed a specific set of warnings as prerequisites to all future custodial interrogations (see § 4.4).

It is *Miranda* which is of major current significance, and thus the emphasis in this chapter is upon the basis and meaning of that decision. But the voluntariness approach also deserves further attention, as does the right to counsel approach, which the Court has more recently utilized in certain cases not amenable to easy resolution under *Miranda,* e.g., *Brewer v. Williams* (1977).

§ 4.2   THE "VOLUNTARINESS"— "TOTALITY OF CIRCUM- STANCES" TEST

(a) Objectives of the test

Although the Supreme Court earlier had occasion to review the admissibility of confessions in the federal courts, first under the common law rule of evidence barring confessions obtained by threats or promises, *Hopt v. Utah* (1884), and later—at least in one case—under a voluntariness test apparently derived from the Fifth Amendment privilege against self-incrimination, *Bram v. U.S.* (1897), it was not until *Brown v. Miss.* (1936), that the Court barred the use of a confession in the state courts. It could not, of course, dispose of the state confession on the same grounds as were resorted to in the earlier cases; under our federal system, the Supreme Court could not proscribe mere rules of evidence for the states, and the Fifth Amendment privilege was then not applicable to the states, *Twining v. N.J.* (1908), overruled by *Malloy v. Hogan* (1964). Thus the confessions in *Brown,* obtained by brutally beating the suspects, were struck down on the notion that interrogation is part of the process by which a state procures a conviction and thus subject to the requirements of the Fourteenth Amendment due process clause.

The interests to be protected under the due process test, and thus the true dimensions of that constitutional protection, remained somewhat obscure in the earlier cases. In *Brown,* the confessions clearly were of doubtful reliability, and thus that case might be read as announcing a due process test for excluding confessions obtained under circumstances presenting a fair risk that the statements are false. Concern with this risk was emphasized in subsequent cases, such as *Chambers v. Fla.* (1940); *Ward v. Tex.* (1942); and *Lyons v. Okla.* (1944), and this led many state courts to the conclusion that unfairness in violation of due process exists when a confession is obtained by means of pressure exerted upon the accused under such circumstances that it affects the testimonial trustworthiness of the confession.

While it is fair to say that ensuring the reliability of confessions is a goal under the due process voluntariness standard, it is incorrect to define the standard in terms of that one objective. In *Rogers v. Richmond* (1961), defendant's confession was obtained after the police pretended to order his ailing wife arrested for questioning, and the state court had ruled that the statement need not be excluded "if the artifice or deception was not calculated to procure an untrue statement." The Supreme Court disagreed, emphasizing that convictions based upon coerced confessions must be overturned "not because such confessions are unlikely to be true but because the methods used to extract them offend an underlying principle in the enforcement of our criminal law: that ours is an accusatorial and not an inquisitorial system." *Rogers* thus made certain what was strongly intimated in several earlier cases, e.g., *Ashcraft v. Tenn.* (1944); *Haley v. Ohio* (1948), namely, that the exclusionary rule for confessions (in much the same way as the Fourth Amendment exclusionary rule, see § 6.3(d)) is also intended to deter improper police conduct. See § 6.2(c).

In *Townsend v. Sain* (1963), the ailing defendant had been given a drug with the properties of a truth serum, after which he gave a confession in response to questioning by police who were unaware of the drug's effect. Although the confession was not obtained by conscious police wrongdoing and apparently was reliable, the Court nonetheless held its use impermissible: "Any questioning by police officers which *in fact* produces a confession which is not the product of free intellect renders that confession inadmissible." *Townsend* thus highlights another theme which runs through many of the earlier cases, e.g., *Lisenba v. Cal.* (1941); *Watts v. Ind.* (1949): the confession must be a product of the defendant's "free and rational choice." This phrase, however, was not used in an absolute sense, but rather in conjunction with a recognized need to exert some pressure to obtain confessions. As the Court seems to have acknowledged in *Miranda,* the question of whether a confession was "voluntary" had theretofore been determined by a lesser standard than, say, the question of whether a testator's will was his voluntary act.

Viewing the voluntariness test in terms of its objectives, then, it could until recently be said that the test was designed to bar admission of those confessions which: (a) were of doubtful reliability because of the practices used to obtain them; (b) were obtained by offensive police practices even if reliability was not in question (e.g., where there is strong corroborating evidence); or (c) were obtained under circumstances in which the defendant's free choice was significantly impaired, even if the police did not resort to offensive practices. But in *Colo. v. Connelly* (1986) the Court refuted the existence of the last category in holding the state court had erred in excluding a confession volunteered to police by a defendant who suffered from a psychosis that interfered with his ability to make free and rational choices. The "crucial element of police overreaching" was absent, the Court reasoned, and thus "there is simply no basis for concluding that any state actor has deprived a criminal defendant of due process." *Townsend* was distinguished as a case involving "police wrongdoing" in questioning a person who had been given a truth serum, though in fact the Court in that earlier case had proceeded on the assumption that neither the police doctor who administered the painkiller nor the police who interrogated were aware of the drug's truth serum character.

(b) The relevant circumstances

Under the voluntariness test, the Supreme Court undertook a continuing re-evaluation on the facts of each case of how much pressure on the suspect was permissible. The rule required examination of the "totality of circumstances" surrounding each confession. *Haynes v. Wash.* (1963). The factors deemed most important were: (1) physical abuse, *Lee v. Miss.* (1948); (2) threats, *Payne v. Ark.* (1958); (3) extensive questioning, *Turner v. Pa.* (1949); (4) incommunicado detention, *Davis v. N.C.* (1966); (5) denial of the right to consult with counsel, *Fay v. Noia* (1963); and (6) the characteristics and status of the suspect, such as his lack of education, *Culombe v. Conn.* (1961), emotional instability, *Spano v. N.Y.* (1959), youth, *Gallegos v. Colo.* (1962), or sickness, *Jackson v. Denno* (1964). However, the voluntariness test is by its nature imprecise, and thus it could rarely be said that the presence of any one of these factors or any fixed combination of them clearly required exclusion of a confession. But *Connelly,* discussed above, makes

(I. & L.) Crim.Proc. 5th Ed. NS—9

it clear that item (6), in isolation, cannot "ever dispose of the inquiry into constitutional 'involuntariness.' "

(c) Administration of the test

Although the *Miranda* dissenters saw the voluntariness test as "a workable and effective means of dealing with confessions in a judicial manner," many critics of the totality-of-circumstances approach had long been of the contrary view. The amorphous character of the test, together with the seeming reluctance of some courts to overturn the conviction of an apparently guilty defendant, led to divergent results in the lower courts. Not infrequently, confessions were upheld although they quite clearly appeared to have been obtained under circumstances previously condemned by the Supreme Court. For example, in *Davis v. N.C.* (1966) it was uncontested that no one other than the police had spoken to the defendant during the 16 days of detention and interrogation which preceded his confessions. The Court reversed, noting it had "never sustained the use of a confession obtained after such a lengthy period of detention and interrogation," but two state courts and two federal courts had previously upheld the confession notwithstanding these objective facts.

Davis was unique in that the relevant circumstances were revealed by police records; usually, an attempt at the trial level to ascertain the "totality of circumstances" has resulted in what has been commonly referred to as a "swearing contest" between the defendant and the police. The ultimate determination of whether the confession should be excluded, therefore, typically had to be made upon the basis of several hotly disputed questions of fact.

§ 4.3 THE RIGHT TO COUNSEL

(a) Pre-*Escobedo* developments

Several developments in the late 1950's and early 1960's enhanced the prospect that the Supreme Court might ultimately resolve the confession issue in terms of the right to counsel. In *Crooker v. Cal.* (1958), where defendant's confession was obtained following denial of his request to call an attorney, the Court held the confession voluntary and also rejected defendant's separate contention that he had a right to counsel at the police station. But the four dissenters asserted that under due process "the accused who wants a counsel should have one at any time after the moment of arrest." *Crooker* was followed in *Cicenia v. La Gay* (1958), where defendant's requests to see his attorney were refused and his counsel turned away at the station, but again there was a strong dissent. The confession in *Spano v. N.Y.* (1959), was found involuntary on traditional grounds, but four concurring justices accepted defendant's contention that his absolute right to counsel in a capital case attached at the time he was indicted (which was prior to his confession).

In *White v. Md.* (1963), the absolute right to counsel in a capital case was held applicable to a pretrial "critical stage," a preliminary arraignment at which a guilty plea later introduced into evidence was obtained. Some commentators suggested that if, as in *White,* an uncounseled guilty plea could not be admitted as evidence of guilt at trial, then it followed that the same should be true of an uncounseled confession. *White* took on greater significance when the *Betts* rule (§ 7.1(b), relied upon in *Crooker*) was overruled in *Gideon v. Wainwright* (1963), holding that the absolute right to counsel for indigent state defendants existed as to all serious cases and not merely capital cases.

The argument that the right to counsel attaches when the defendant is indicted and his status thereby changes from "suspect" to "accused," not reached by the majority in *Spano,* was accepted in a somewhat different context in *Massiah v. U.S.* (1964). After defendant's indictment, he was engaged in an incriminating conversation by a bugged codefendant-turned-informer, about which the overhearing agent testified at trial. The Court held, 6–3, that the Sixth Amendment prohibits extraction of incriminating statements from an indicted person without presence of counsel. The majority indicated this would be equally true had the incriminating statements been obtained by police interrogation. *Massiah* was not limited to federal prosecutions or to cases in which the defendant had already retained counsel, *McLeod v. Ohio* (1965), but most lower courts refused to extend

Massiah back to the point of earlier tentative charges.

(b) The *Escobedo* case

The confession in *Escobedo v. Ill.* (1964), was obtained after defendant's repeated requests to consult with retained counsel were refused and after his attorney had actually been turned away at the station. The Court, 5–4, concluded that this pre-indictment interrogation was just as much a "critical stage" as the preliminary hearing in *White,* in that what happened then could "affect the whole trial," and that *Massiah* was apposite because "no meaningful distinction can be drawn between interrogation of an accused before and after formal indictment." Yet the Court did not announce a broad right-to-counsel-at-the-station rule, but instead cautiously limited the holding to the facts of the case:

"We hold * * * that where, as here, [1] the investigation is no longer a general inquiry into an unsolved crime but has begun to focus on a particular suspect, [2] the suspect has been taken into police custody, [3] the police carry out a process of interrogations that lends itself to eliciting incriminating statements, [4] the suspect has requested and been denied an opportunity to consult with his lawyer, and [5] the police have not effectively warned him of his absolute constitutional right to remain silent, the accused has been denied 'the Assistance of Counsel' in violation of the Sixth Amendment to the Constitution as 'made obligato-

ry upon the States by the Fourteenth Amendment,'
* * * and that no statement elicited by the police
during the interrogation may be used against him
at a criminal trial."

(c) The meaning of *Escobedo*

Because the much broader *Miranda* decision is
not retroactive (see § 1.4(c)), the precise meaning of
Escobedo became a matter of significance only as to
confessions admitted at trials occurring between
the two decisions. This matter of interpretation
largely fell upon the lower courts, which usually
attributed significance to each of the five "elements" in the *Escobedo* holding.

Thus: (1) While the Court said in *Miranda* that
the focus requirement of *Escobedo* was really intended to mean deprivation of freedom in a significant way, this requirement has been utilized to
find *Escobedo* inapplicable where the suspect was
in custody on another charge and the interrogation
was undertaken while the case was in the investigatory rather than accusatory stage. (2) *Escobedo*
does not apply when the suspect is not in police
custody, although custody may be present without
a formal arrest. (3) *Escobedo* does not govern
volunteered statements or even interrogation undertaken primarily for another purpose, such as to
locate a kidnap victim. (4) *Escobedo* does not require a warning of the right to counsel, but applies
only if the suspect makes a clear and unambiguous
request for counsel. *Frazier v. Cupp* (1969). (5)

Escobedo is inapplicable if the police have warned the suspect of his right to remain silent.

Consider also *Kirby v. Ill.* (discussed in § 5.2(e)), where the Court concluded that the Sixth Amendment right to counsel attaches "only at or after the time that adversary judicial proceedings have been initiated." Because *Escobedo* was the "only seeming deviation" from a long line of cases accepting this starting point, the Court "in retrospect concluded that the " 'prime purpose' of *Escobedo* was not to vindicate the constitutional right to counsel as such, but, like *Miranda* to guarantee full effectuation of the privilege against self-incrimination." Moreover, *Kirby* noted, *Escobedo* is now limited in its "holding * * * to its own facts."

(d) The *Williams* case

More then ten years following the *Miranda* decision, the Court "resurrected" the *Massiah* rule in *Brewer v. Williams* (1977). Williams was arraigned in Davenport, Iowa, on an outstanding arrest warrant prior to his transportation to Des Moines on a murder charge. Though the police had assured Williams' lawyer that he would not be interrogated during the trip, a detective made a "Christian burial speech," to the effect that because of the worsening weather it would be necessary to find the body now to ensure the victim a Christian burial, after which Williams directed the police to the body. The Supreme Court, noting (i) that the right to counsel attaches when "judicial proceedings have been initiated" against the defendant,

clearly the case here in light of the warrant issuance, arraignment on the warrant, and commitment to jail by the court, and (ii) that the detective
"set out to elicit information from Williams" by a
means "tantamount to interrogation," concluded
the case fell within "the clear rule of *Massiah*
* * * that once adversary proceedings have com-
menced against an individual, he has a right to
legal representation when the government interro-
gates him." Though declining to hold that the
right to counsel could be waived only upon notice
to counsel, the Court rejected the state court's
conclusion that waiver had occurred here merely
because during the trip Williams did not assert
that right or a desire not to talk in the absence of
counsel.

(e) When the right attaches

In *Williams,* supra, the Court declared that "the
right to counsel granted by the Sixth and Fourteenth Amendments means at least that a person
is entitled to the help of a lawyer at or after the
time that judicial proceedings have been initiated
against him—'whether by way of formal charge,
preliminary hearing, indictment, information, or
arraignment.'" Later, in *Mich. v. Jackson* (1986),
the Court elaborated that arraignment (in the
sense of the initial appearance, not the pleading
stage) "signals the initiation of adversary judicial
proceedings" without regard to whether it has the
particular characteristics which would make "the
arraignment itself * * * a critical stage requiring

the presence of counsel." The right to counsel does not attach merely because the defendant has been arrested without a warrant, nor is it sufficient that the investigation has "focused" on him. *Hoffa v. U.S.* (1966). There is a split of authority as to whether the filing of a complaint or such filing plus the issuance of an arrest warrant suffices. Considering the teaching of *Kirby v. Ill.* (1972) that the right attaches once the government has "committed itself to prosecute, and * * * the adverse positions of government and defendant have solidified," it may make a difference whether the complaint-warrant process manifests a charging decision or serves some other purpose (e.g., to justify an in-premises arrest; see § 2.7(a)).

If the necessary stage in the proceedings has been reached, then the right to counsel attaches even if, unlike the *Williams* case, defendant is not yet represented by an attorney. *U.S. v. Henry* (1980). If that stage has not been reached, then the right does not attach even if defendant has already retained counsel, for "it makes little sense to say that the Sixth Amendment right to counsel attaches at different times depending on the fortuity of whether the suspect or his family happens to have retained counsel." *Moran v. Burbine* (1986). What then if the requisite stage in the proceedings has been reached as to one offense, but the police are thereafter engaged in an investigation of some new or different offense involving the same person? In *Me. v. Moulton* (1985), the Court concluded that "to exclude evidence pertaining to charges as to which the Sixth Amendment right to counsel had not attached at the time the evidence was obtained, simply because other charges were pending at that time, would unnecessarily frustrate the public's interest in the investigation of criminal activities." The dissenters argued it followed from this that evidence obtained in that investigation bearing on the charged offense should be admissible in the prosecution of that offense, but the *Moulton* majority rejected that approach because it "invites abuse by law enforcement personnel in the form of fabricated investigations."

(f) Waiver of counsel

The Court in *Williams,* supra, acknowledged that the right to counsel could be waived and that, because it is the right of the client rather than the attorney, waiver by the client-defendant is possible without the lawyer's participation. Seemingly inconsistent with that conclusion is the statement in *Escobedo,* supra, that the conduct of the police in turning away the lawyer was by itself "a violation of the Sixth Amendment." But in *Escobedo* the defendant was aware of that police conduct, which certainly should cast a heavy cloud over any subsequent "waiver" by the defendant. When the defendant is not aware, however, it appears the police conduct has no bearing upon the validity of the waiver. Such a conclusion, already reached by the Court in a *Miranda* context, *Moran v. Burbine* (1986), is also appropriate here unless a much more demanding waiver standard applies in a *Williams*

Sixth Amendment context. That is not the case; "because the role of counsel at questioning is relatively simple and limited," the waiver standard here is the same as under *Miranda* (see § 4.9), in contrast to the relatively high at-trial standard (see § 7.4(a)). *Patterson v. Ill.* (1988). In any event, it is apparent that "the concept of a knowing and voluntary waiver of Sixth Amendment rights does not apply in the context of communications with an undisclosed undercover informant acting for the government." *U.S. v. Henry* (1980).

The special waiver-after-assertion-of-rights rules which govern in the *Miranda* area as to a defendant who has invoked his right to counsel, see § 4.9(c), also apply to the Sixth Amendment right. Thus, when that right has attached, "if police initiate interrogation after a defendant's assertion, at an arraignment or similar proceeding, of his right to counsel, any waiver of the defendant's right to counsel for that police-initiated interrogation is invalid." *Mich. v. Jackson* (1986). The Court added this is so even though the request for counsel at arraignment was not specifically tied to the matter of police questioning and even if the police were unaware of that invocation of the right. But because this Sixth Amendment right is "offense-specific" and "cannot be invoked once for all future prosecutions," the *Jackson* rule is likewise offense-specific, so that if a defendant exercises his Sixth Amendment right to counsel when brought into court on a robbery charge, that is no bar to police-initiated questioning about an unrelated murder. *McNeil v. Wis.* (1991).

(g) Infringement of the right

In *Massiah,* supra, the violation of the right to counsel occurred when the police, using a cooperating and wired-for-sound codefendant, "deliberately elicited" incriminating statements from the defendant. Similarly, in *Williams* the Christian burial speech infringed upon the right because the detective "deliberately and designedly set out to elicit information from Williams." But these cases, which indicate that they extend to police conduct other than interrogation in the narrow sense of that word, do not require that the police have initiated the contact. Though the Sixth Amendment is not violated when the state obtains incriminating statements by mere "luck or happenstance", "knowing exploitation by the State of an opportunity" to confront the accused without counsel being present is as much a breach of the State's obligation not to circumvent the right to assistance of counsel as is the intentional creation of such an opportunity." *Me. v. Moulton* (1985).

Though *Massiah* and *Williams* seem to require "action undertaken with the specific intent to evoke an inculpatory disclosure," *U.S. v. Henry* (1980) (Blackmun, J., diss.), whether that is still so after the "jail plant" *Henry* case is unclear. The conduct of the police in asking the cellmate to report back defendant's incriminating comments, the Court held, met the "deliberately elicited" test

by virtue of the government "intentionally creating a situation likely to induce Henry to make
incriminating statements." Though that language,
if read literally, would seem to cover even negligent triggering of events resulting in an incriminating response by the defendant, the *Henry* majority
appears to have viewed the case as a true "deliberately elicited" type of case. That is, they deem the
government's instructions to the informant not to
question Henry about the robbery, in light of all
the circumstances, as not manifesting a lack of
intent to obtain incriminating statements or to
have the informant take some affirmative steps to
achieve that result. It is apparently still true,
therefore, that there is no *Massiah-Williams* violation if the person acting with the intention of
eliciting an incriminating statement is not a government agent, or if the government agent who
elicits an incriminating response does so exclusively for some other legitimate purpose.

Because the majority in *Henry* did not think it
was dealing with a truly "passive" situation in
terms of the actions of the government's informant, the Court did not have occasion to decide
whether the *Massiah-Williams* doctrine applies to
both active and passive efforts to obtain incriminating statements. But in *Kuhlmann v. Wilson*
(1986), on the ground that "the primary concern of
the *Massiah* line of decisions is secret interrogation
by investigatory techniques that are the equivalent
of direct police interrogation," the Court ruled that
it was not a violation of defendant's right to coun-

sel for police merely to arrange for an informant to report back to police any overheard incriminating comments of the defendant. But *Kuhlmann* illustrates the difficulty of drawing the line between active and passive efforts; defendant's incriminating comments followed the informant's assertion that his original nonincriminating version "didn't sound too good," but the majority felt this was not enough under all the circumstances to bring the case within the "deliberately elicited" test. That problem is not present when the police " 'listening post' is an inanimate electronic device"; its use clearly does not infringe upon the right to counsel, as it "has no capability of leading the conversation into any particular subject or prompting any particular replies." *U.S. v. Henry* (1980).

§ 4.4 THE PRIVILEGE AGAINST SELF–INCRIMINATION

(a) The privilege in the police station

The Fifth Amendment provides that no person "shall be compelled in any criminal case to be a witness against himself." Although a literal reading of this language suggests that the privilege against self-incrimination has no application to unsworn statements obtained by station-house interrogation, in *Bram v. U.S.* (1897) the Court asserted that "in criminal trials, in the courts of the United States, wherever a question arises whether a confession is incompetent because not voluntary, the issue is controlled by that portion of the Fifth

Amendment." The Court's conclusion that there was a historical connection between the privilege and the confession doctrine appears incorrect, and was subsequently challenged by many commentators. The privilege was not expressly relied upon in later cases concerning the admissibility of confessions in federal courts, while the Court dealt with confessions used in state courts solely in terms of the due process voluntariness test (see § 4.2). But in *Malloy v. Hogan* (1964), which did not involve a confession, the Court held the privilege applicable to the states, and in support of this result noted that the admissibility of a confession in a state trial had long been tested by the same standard as applied to federal prosecutions by *Bram*. Promptly thereafter, the Court decided the *Escobedo* case (see § 4.3(b)), which, while grounded upon the Sixth Amendment right to counsel, spoke of "the right of the accused to be advised by his lawyer of his privilege against self-incrimination."

Any remaining doubts were dispelled by *Miranda v. Ariz.* (1966), holding that the privilege against self-incrimination "is fully applicable during a period of custodial interrogation." Although the apparent assumption of the *Miranda* majority that this proposition was "settled" in the precedents is subject to question, this of course does not compel the conclusion that the *Miranda* holding was in error. Even the dissenters in *Miranda* conceded that the Fifth Amendment privilege "embodies basic principles always capable of expansion," although they forcefully argued that those principles would not be served by extending the privilege to the police station.

(b) The *Miranda* rules

Apart from this reliance upon the Fifth Amendment rather than the Sixth, *Miranda* is striking in its contrast to *Escobedo*. The latter holding was carefully limited to the facts of the case before the Court, while *Miranda* sets forth what the dissenters called a "constitutional code of rules for confessions":

(1) These rules are required to safeguard the privilege against self-incrimination, and thus must be followed in the absence of "other procedures which are at least as effective in apprising accused persons of their right of silence and in assuring a continuous opportunity to exercise it."

(2) These rules apply "when the individual is first subjected to police interrogation while in custody at the station or otherwise deprived of his freedom of action in any significant way," and not to "general on-the-scene questioning as to facts surrounding a crime or other general questioning of citizens in the fact-finding process" or to "volunteered statements of any kind."

(3) Without regard to his prior awareness of his rights, if a person in custody is to be subjected to questioning, "he must first be informed in clear and unequivocal terms that he has the right to remain silent," so that the ignorant may learn of this right and so that the pressures of the interro-

gation atmosphere will be overcome for those previously aware of the right.

(4) The above warning "must be accompanied by
the explanation that anything said can and will be
used against the individual in court," so as to
ensure that the suspect fully understands the consequences of foregoing the privilege.

(5) Because this is indispensible to protection of
the privilege, the individual also "must be clearly
informed that he has the right to consult with a
lawyer and to have the lawyer with him during
interrogation," without regard to whether it appears that he is already aware of this right.

(6) The individual must also be warned "that if
he is indigent a lawyer will be appointed to represent him," for otherwise the above warning would
be understood as meaning only that an individual
may consult a lawyer if he has the funds to obtain
one.

(7) The individual is always free to exercise the
privilege, and thus if he "indicates in any manner,
at any time prior to or during questioning, that he
wishes to remain silent, the interrogation must
cease"; and likewise, if he "states that he wants an
attorney, the interrogation must cease until an
attorney is present."

(8) If a statement is obtained without the presence of an attorney, "a heavy burden rests on the
Government to demonstrate that the defendant
knowingly and intelligently waived his privilege
against self-incrimination and his right to retained

or appointed counsel," and such waiver may not be presumed from the individual's silence after the warnings or from the fact that a confession was eventually obtained.

(9) Any statement obtained in violation of these rules may not be admitted into evidence, without regard to whether it is a confession or only an admission of part of an offense or whether it is inculpatory or allegedly exculpatory.

(10) Likewise, exercise of the privilege may not be penalized, and thus the prosecution may not "use at trial the fact that [the defendant] stood mute or claimed his privilege in the face of accusation."

The Supreme Court has more recently asserted that *Miranda* "recognized that these procedural safeguards were not themselves rights protected by the Constitution but were instead measures to insure that the right against compulsory self-incrimination was protected. * * * The suggested safeguards were not intended to 'create a constitutional straightjacket,' but rather to provide practical reinforcement for the right against compulsory self-incrimination." *Mich. v. Tucker* (1974). This approach is reflected generally in the cases interpreting *Miranda* (see §§ 4.5–4.9).

(c) Criticism of *Miranda*

Not unexpectedly, the *Miranda* decision was greeted with criticism from many quarters. It was contended that police abuse was not so widespread as to call for such a far-reaching decision, and that confessions were essential to law enforcement but would be unobtainable under the new rules (see § 4.1(a)). Recent empirical studies, however, have concluded that the impact of *Miranda* has been quite different than predicted by the Court's critics. In most instances the *Miranda* warnings have not appreciably reduced the amount of talking by a suspect, and the police are now obtaining about as many confessions as before *Miranda*.

These conclusions lend some support to the views of another group of critics, those who find a fundamental inconsistency in the majority's reasoning. They claim that the heavy emphasis on the inability of an uncounseled defendant to decide whether to incriminate himself when subject to the inherent pressures of custody is inconsistent with the conclusion that the decision whether to dispense with counsel can be voluntary in the same circumstances. As stated in one of the *Miranda* dissents: "But if the defendant may not answer without a warning a question such as 'Where were you last night?' without having his answer be a compelled one, how can the court ever accept his negative answer to the question of whether he wants to consult his retained counsel or counsel whom the court will appoint?"

(d) The Crime Control Act

Title II of the Omnibus Crime Control and Safe Streets Act of 1968 amends existing legislation by adding 18 U.S.C.A. § 3501, which purports to "repeal" *Miranda* in federal prosecutions. The Act states that a confession is admissible in the federal courts if voluntarily given, and that whether the defendant was advised of his right to remain silent or his right to counsel and whether he was without counsel when he confessed are merely to be taken into consideration as circumstances bearing on the issue of voluntariness.

If viewed as a total "repeal" of *Miranda,* this statute is quite clearly unconstitutional, for rights derived from the Constitution cannot be repealed by legislation. However, in support of this legislation it has been noted that the *Miranda* Court indicated Congress might devise equally effective safeguards for protecting the privilege, and the argument is made that Title II does this by a less rigid formula than *Miranda,* permitting a confession to be used where a less than perfect warning was given or a less than conclusive waiver was obtained. In response, the contention can be made that compliance with Title II would result in courts returning to the old practice of considering all of the circumstances of the individual case, a procedure which the *Miranda* Court concluded had proven ineffective in protecting a suspect's constitutional rights.

§ 4.5 *MIRANDA:* WHAT OFFENSES ARE COVERED?

(a) Traffic and other minor offenses

Although a number of lower courts held *Miranda* inapplicable to traffic and other minor crimes, a unanimous Court held otherwise in *Berkemer v. McCarty* (1984). The Court concluded that such an exception would undermine *Miranda*'s clarity (especially when a misdemeanor investigation escalated into or was a pretext for a felony investigation), and that the purposes of *Miranda* are served even as to minor traffic offenses.

(b) Tax investigations

In *Mathis v. U.S.* (1968), statements were obtained by an internal revenue agent from a defendant incarcerated in jail on another matter. The government contended that the *Miranda* warnings were not required because the questions were asked as "part of a routine tax investigation where no criminal proceedings might even be brought," but the Court ruled otherwise because there is always the possibility that criminal prosecution will result.

(c) Proceeding at which confession offered

Because *Miranda* is grounded in the privilege against self-incrimination, it protects only against compulsion "in any criminal case." Thus the *Miranda* exclusionary rule applies in criminal cases at stages of the proceedings having to do with guilt or punishment. *Estelle v. Smith* (1981). It does not apply, however, *Estelle* concluded, at a hearing to ascertain defendant's competence to stand trial. Nor does it apply in such noncriminal contexts as prison discipline hearings, *Baxter v. Palmigiano* (1976), or in a civil sexually dangerous persons proceeding which was not "punitive either in purpose or effect," *Allen v. Ill.* (1986).

§ 4.6 *MIRANDA:* WHEN IS INTERROGATION "CUSTODIAL"?

(a) "Custody" vs. "focus"

In defining that interrogation which is "custodial," the *Miranda* Court dropped a footnote stating that was "what we meant in *Escobedo* when we spoke of an investigation which had focused on an accused." Though this might be taken to mean that custody and focus are alternative grounds for requiring the warnings, a more likely explanation for this footnote is that the Court was attempting to maintain some continuity between *Escobedo* and the new approach of *Miranda,* while in fact making a fresh start in describing the point at which the constitutional protections begin. The Court has since rejected the claim that "focus" involves psychological restraints equivalent of custody, necessitating the *Miranda* warnings. *Beckwith v. U.S.* (1976).

(b) Purpose of the custody

Mathis v. U.S. (1968) posed the question whether *Miranda* applies when the purpose of the custody is unrelated to the purpose of the interrogation, as there the defendant was in jail serving a state sentence when questioned by a revenue agent about his tax returns. The Court, 5–3, answered in the affirmative, asserting that a contrary result would go "against the whole purpose of the *Miranda* decision." The dissenters were unwilling to accept this conclusion, for they read *Miranda* as resting "not on the mere fact of physical restriction but on a conclusion that coercion—pressure to answer questions—usually flows from a certain type of custody, police station interrogation of someone charged with or suspected of a crime."

(c) Subjective vs. objective approach

A most fundamental question concerning the "custody" element of *Miranda* is whether it is to be determined by (1) the subjective state of mind of the suspect, which would square with the "potentiality for compulsion" concern expressed in *Miranda* but would make it difficult for police to ascertain when warnings are required; (2) the subjective state of mind of the officer, the approach used in *Orozco v. Tex.* (1969), which would be easy for the police to apply but would not square with the "potentiality for compulsion" to the extent that it made the unstated intentions of the officer determinative; or (3) an objective approach. The first two have the added defect that the "custody" issue would be decided by swearing contests concerning intentions, and thus the Court wisely concluded in *Berkemer v. McCarty* (1984) that an objective standard should be used. The Court thus rejected the argument that "custody" existed because of the officer's uncommunicated intention to make an arrest, and reasoned that a "policeman's unarticulated plan has no bearing on the question whether a suspect was 'in custody' at a particular time; the only relevant inquiry is how a reasonable man in the suspect's position would have understood his situation."

This objective approach will often require a careful examination of all the circumstances of the particular case. Account must be taken of those facts intrinsic to the interrogation: when and where it occurred, how long it lasted, how many police were present, what the officers and the defendant said and did, the presence of physical restraint or the equivalent (e.g., drawn weapons, a guard at the door), and whether the defendant was being questioned as a suspect or as a witness. Events before the interrogation, such as how the defendant got to the place of questioning, are also relevant. The Supreme Court has also taken into account events after the questioning, e.g., in *Ore. v. Mathiason* (1977), that defendant was then permitted to depart, though such facts would seem to have nothing to do with how a reasonable person would have perceived the situation at the time of the questioning.

(d) Presence at station

Though *Miranda* expressly covers the case of a
person "in custody at the station," not all presence
at a police station is custodial. Thus in *Ore. v.
Mathiason* (1977), where the defendant came to the
station in response to the written request of a
police officer that he come by to "discuss something," the Court correctly concluded defendant
"came voluntarily to the police station." The
Court's other conclusion that the situation did not
later become custodial when the defendant, a parolee, was told his fingerprints had been found at a
burglary scene, is open to question. A supposed
"invitation" which involves the suspect going to
the station in the company of a police officer, at
least when the officer has not unequivocally advised the defendant he is free to leave at any time,
is much more likely to support a finding of "custody" for *Miranda* purposes. Cf. *Dunaway v. N.Y.*
(1979).

(e) Presence elsewhere

Courts are much less likely to find the circumstances custodial when the interrogation occurs in
familiar or at least neutral surroundings. See,
e.g., *Beckwith v. U.S.* (1976) (questioning in suspect's home noncustodial). But, the circumstances
of each case must be carefully examined. See, e.g.,
Orozco v. Tex. (1969) (questioning at suspect's home
custodial where four police entered defendant's
bedroom at 4 a.m.). In *Minn. v. Murphy* (1984),
concluding defendant's meeting with his probation

officer at her office and pursuant to her order was not custodial, the Court emphasized that such interviews were "arranged by appointment at a mutually convenient time" and that Murphy, by virtue of past interviews, was familiar with the officer and that environment.

Although the Court in *Miranda* excluded "general on-the-scene questioning" from the holding in that case, this does not mean crime scene interrogation is never custodial. As stated in *N.Y. v. Quarles* (1984), "the ultimate inquiry is simply whether there is a 'formal arrest or restraint on freedom of movement' of the degree associated with a formal arrest." Such was the case in *Quarles,* where the questioning occurred in a supermarket minutes after defendant had been arrested by four officers with guns drawn and then handcuffed. But such was not the case in *Berkemer v. McCarty* (1984), involving roadside questioning during a routine traffic stop. Thus a *Terry* type of stop, see § 2.9, though a seizure for Fourth Amendment purposes, is not an "in custody" situation for purposes of *Miranda.*

§ 4.7 *MIRANDA:* WHAT CONSTITUTES "INTERROGATION"?

(a) "Volunteered" statements

The *Miranda* Court emphasized that "there is no requirement that police stop a person who enters a police station and states that he wishes to confess to a crime, or a person who calls the police to offer a confession or any other statement he desires to make. Volunteered statements of any kind are not barred by the Fifth Amendment and their admissibility is not affected by our holding today." Thus, it is clear that a statement not preceded by the *Miranda* warnings will be admissible when, for example, the defendant walks into a station and confesses or blurts out an admission when approached by an officer near a crime scene. Also, because the *Miranda* Court found custody-plus-interrogation coercive, rather than mere custody, it likewise seems clear that a statement may qualify as "volunteered" even though made by one in custody.

(b) Follow-up questioning

Assuming a truly volunteered statement, may the police follow up that statement with some questions? *Miranda* is not entirely clear on this issue; at one point custodial interrogation is defined as "questioning initiated by law enforcement officers," suggesting that police questioning designed to clarify or amplify a volunteered statement is permissible, but elsewhere it is said that the suspect must be warned "prior to any questioning." So far, courts have been quite willing to admit the answers to follow-up questions on the ground that these answers are a continuation of the volunteered statement. It may well be, however, that a distinction should be drawn between questions designed to clarify an ambiguous statement (e.g., "did what"? in response to "I did it"), and those which seek to enhance the defendant's guilt or raise the offense to a higher degree (e.g., "why did you do it?").

(c) The "functional equivalent" of questioning

What if the police have done something (other than questioning the suspect) which appears to have prompted his statement, such as showing him incriminating physical evidence or confronting him with a confessing accomplice or the accusing victim?   Such actions will usually fall within the Court's holding in *R.I. v. Innis* (1980):

"We conclude that the *Miranda* safeguards come into play whenever a person in custody is subjected to either express questioning or its functional equivalent.   That is to say, the term 'interrogation' under *Miranda* refers not only to express questioning, but also to any words or actions on the part of the police (other than those normally attendant to arrest and custody) that the police should know are reasonably likely to elicit an incriminating response from the suspect.   The latter portion of this definition focuses primarily upon the perceptions of the suspect, rather than the intent of the police. This focus reflects the fact that the *Miranda* safeguards were designed to vest a suspect in custody with an added measure of protection against coercive police practices, without regard to objective proof of the underlying intent of the police.   A practice that the police should know is reasonably likely to evoke an incriminating response from a suspect thus amounts to interrogation.   But, since the police surely cannot be held accountable for the unforeseeable results of their words or actions, the definition of interrogation can extend only to words or actions on the part of police officers that they *should have known* were reasonably likely to elicit an incriminating response."

In *Innis,* the defendant, who had already asserted his *Miranda* rights, made incriminating statements after one officer said to another, as they took defendant to the station after his arrest, that the missing shotgun might fall into the hands of students at a nearby school for handicapped children. The majority concluded this was a dialog between the police rather than questioning, and that it was not the "functional equivalent" of questioning because there was nothing in the record to suggest the officers "should have known" the brief conversation would prompt defendant to make an incriminating response. (This is not to suggest that comments directed at the suspect are inevitably interrogation; under the *Innis* test, it is not interrogation for the police to ask the suspect to perform physical sobriety tests, *Pa. v. Muniz* (1990), or take a blood alcohol test, *So. Dak. v. Neville* (1983).) The Court in *Innis* then confused matters further by a footnote assertion that the intent of the police was not irrelevant on the question of what they "should have known." But neither the probability of an incriminating response nor the undisclosed intentions of the police is directly relevant to the concerns underlying *Miranda,* and thus a much more appealing interpretation of *Innis* is that the test is whether an objective observer of the officer's actions would conclude they were designed to elicit an incriminating response. This avoids the factfinding difficulties of a subjective test, but yet for the most part identifies those situations in which the suspect may have experienced the *Miranda* "potentiality for compulsion" by perceiving that the police were trying to get him to make an incriminating response.

Notwithstanding the language in *Innis, Ariz. v. Mauro* (1987) indicates that it is not inevitably interrogation for police to allow a scenario to occur which they know will likely prompt the defendant to incriminate himself. The Court there held, 5–4, that it was not interrogation for police to accede to the request of defendant's wife, also a suspect in the death of their son, to speak with defendant and then to have a police officer and tape recorder conspicuously present at the meeting. Stressing that "Mauro was not subjected to compelling influences, psychological ploys, or direct questioning," the majority concluded the police action did not implicate the purpose underlying *Miranda:* "preventing government officials from using the coercive nature of confinement to extract confessions that would not be given in an unrestrained environment."

It must be remembered that conduct which does not constitute "interrogation" under *Innis* may still amount to the eliciting of an incriminating statement in violation of defendant's right to counsel; see § 4.3(g). Such is the case as to questioning by an undercover "jail plant." Though such conduct in a post-charge setting violates defendant's Sixth Amendment rights, see § 4.3(g), it does not violate *Miranda,* for it is the impact on the suspect's mind of the interplay between police interrogation and police custody—each reinforcing the pressures and anxieties produced by the other—that the Court in *Miranda* correctly discerned makes "custodial police interrogation" so devastating. *Ill. v. Perkins* (1990).

(d) Purpose of the questioning

The Supreme Court has held that the privilege against self-incrimination offers no protection against requiring a suspect to appear in a lineup, to give a handwriting sample, or to speak for identification the words uttered by the offender at the scene of the crime (see § 5.1). Thus, *Miranda*-type warnings are not a prerequisite to these procedures. The claim that a psychiatric examination to determine a defendant's prior state of mind is like taking handwriting exemplars and thus is not covered by *Miranda* was rejected in *Estelle v. Smith* (1981), but the Court went on to indicate that a defendant who asserted an insanity defense and introduced supporting psychiatric testimony could be required to submit to examination by a government psychiatrist. Following *Smith,* the Court held in *Buchanan v. Ky.* (1987) that "if a defendant requests [a psychiatric] evaluation or

presents psychiatric evidence [here, to make out
the affirmative defense of extreme emotional dis-
turbance], then, at the very least, the prosecution
may rebut this presentation with evidence from
the reports of the examination that the defendant
requested."

Pa. v. Muniz (1990) illustrates the point that
Miranda requirements are inapplicable to questioning which produces an incriminating response
other than a "testimonial" one. The defendant,
under arrest for driving under the influence, was
asked a series of questions about his name, address,
birthday, age, etc. The absence of *Miranda* warnings did not require suppression of the videotape of
his slurred-speech responses, as requiring one to
reveal the physical manner in which he speaks is
not testimonial in character. But the content of
one of defendant's answers, that he did not know
the date of his sixth birthday, was incriminating,
as the inference his mental state was confused was
derived from a "testimonial act," that is, one in
which the defendant was required "to communicate an express or implied assertion of fact or
belief." *Muniz* supports those lower court decisions holding that routine inquiries during booking
are lawful even absent *Miranda* warnings. Indeed,
it may well be that questions asked for purposes of
identification (e.g., "what is your name?", "where
do you live?") on other occasions are likewise outside the privilege, and that therefore they may be
put to a suspect in custody without first giving him
the *Miranda* warnings. Cf. *Cal. v. Byers* (1971),

holding that a statute requiring a driver of a car involved in an accident to stop and give the driver of the other car his name and address does not violate the privilege. This conclusion is consistent with the *Innis* definition of "interrogation," supra.

Still another type of case is that in which the authorities claim that they were questioning for the purpose of protecting themselves or others from weapons by asking the defendant whether he had a gun or where a gun was located. In *N.Y. v. Quarles* (1984) the Court recognized "a 'public safety' exception to the requirement that *Miranda* warnings be given," reasoning that "the need for answers to questions in a situation posing a threat to the public safety outweighs the need for the prophylactic rule protecting the Fifth Amendment's privilege against self-incrimination." Somewhat similar is the so-called "rescue doctrine," under which it has been held that *Miranda* warnings are unnecessary before custodial questioning undertaken to save life (e.g., in an effort to locate a kidnap victim).

(e) Questioning by non-police

In *Miranda*, the Court defined interrogation as "questioning initiated by law enforcement officers." This language has been relied upon by courts in holding *Miranda* inapplicable to questioning by such persons as a private investigator, a high school principal, and the victim. It has also been held that *Miranda* is not applicable to interrogation by the defendant's parole or probation officer, although the Supreme Court has intimated the contrary because such an official "is a peace officer, and as such is allied, to a greater or lesser extent, with his fellow peace officers." *Minn. v. Murphy* (1984), quoting *Fare v. Michael C.* (1979). Also, the Court has on other occasions held *Miranda* applicable to questioning by persons not primarily responsible for criminal law enforcement. *Estelle v. Smith* (1981) ("a psychiatrist designated by the trial court"); *Mathis v. U.S.* (1968) (IRS "civil investigator," where a possibility "his work would end up in a criminal prosecution").

§ 4.8 *MIRANDA* : WHAT WARNINGS ARE REQUIRED?

(a) Adequacy of the warnings

Miranda does not require slavish adherence to the precise words used therein for the necessary warnings; the warnings given are adequate if they convey the substance of the *Miranda* requirements. *Cal. v. Prysock* (1981). Thus, it is sufficient that the police told the defendant that "he didn't have to make any statement" (instead of that he had a right to remain silent). Warnings that anything the suspect says "might," "may," "can," or "could" be used against him have been sustained, but a warning that the statement may be used "for or against" the suspect contains an improper inducement to speak.

Failure to advise the defendant of his right to have counsel appointed is fatally defective. A con-

trary result has sometimes been reached where the
defendant later had retained counsel at trial and
on appeal, which seems inconsistent with footnote
43 in *Miranda:* "While a warning that the indigent may have counsel appointed need not be given
to the person who is known to have an attorney or
is known to have ample funds to secure one, the
expedient of giving a warning is too simple and the
rights involved too important to engage in *ex post
facto* inquiries into financial ability when there is
any doubt at all on that score." Informing a
defendant of "his right to have a lawyer present
prior to and during interrogation" and of "his right
to have a lawyer appointed at no cost if he could
not afford one" is sufficient, as collectively it indicates the right to appointed counsel prior to and
during interrogation. *Cal. v. Prysock* (1981). Indeed, even a warning of a right to counsel before
and during questioning accompanied by a statement that appointment of counsel will only occur
"if and when you go to court" is sufficient, as
Miranda does not require "that attorneys be pro-
ducible on call," but only that police not interrogate if they cannot provide appointed counsel.
Duckworth v. Eagan (1989).

(b) "Cutting off" the warnings

What if the warning officer never completes his
task because the suspect cuts him off with the
assertion that the warnings are unnecessary because he is fully aware of all of his rights? The
view that this is no excuse for not completing the

warnings is consistent with the language in *Miranda* which emphasizes that the expedient of giving adequate warnings is so simple that "we will not pause to inquire in individual cases whether the defendant was aware of his rights without a warning being given."

(c) Multiple interrogation sessions

Once the warnings have been completely given and the defendant has given an effective waiver, must the warnings be repeated again at the outset of a subsequent interview? The courts have quite consistently answered in the negative, both when the later interview follows promptly after the first and when several days have intervened. It might be argued, however, that the *Miranda* concern with the suspect's continuing right to invoke the privilege means that a substantial interval or change in interrogators calls for repetition of the warnings, particularly so that the "warning will show the individual that his interrogators are prepared to recognize his privilege should he choose to exercise it."

(d) Additional admonitions

Because *Miranda* stresses that many suspects will assume that "silence in the face of accusation is itself damning and will bode ill when presented to a jury," it has been argued that suspects should be warned about another important part of the *Miranda* holding—that the "prosecution may not * * * use at trial the fact that he stood mute or

claimed his privilege in the face of accusation."
But the courts have not mandated the giving of
such a warning.

Likewise, there is no requirement that the suspect be advised of the nature of the crime about
which the police wish to interrogate, and this is so
even when the circumstances suggest the desired
questioning is about a matter quite different from
that later encompassed by the interrogation. *Colo.
v. Spring* (1987) (arrest by federal ATF agents for
firearms violations, questioning about an unreport-
ed homicide in another state). The Court reasoned
that since the defendant had been told he had a
right to remain silent and that *anything* he said
could be used against him, he had all the information necessary for a knowing and intelligent waiver
of his Fifth Amendment rights; "the additional
information could affect only the wisdom of a *Miranda* waiver, not its essentially voluntary and
knowing nature." As for the statement in *Miranda* that "any evidence that the accused was
threatened, tricked, or cajoled into a waiver will
* * * show that the defendant did not voluntarily
waive his privilege," the Court in *Spring* responded
that mere "official silence" about the desire to
question about the murder did not constitute trick-
ery, and cautiously left unresolved whether a waiver of *Miranda* rights would be valid had there been
"an affirmative misrepresentation by law enforcement officials as to the scope of the interrogation."

§ 4.9 *MIRANDA*: **WHAT CONSTITUTES WAIVER?**

(a) Express or implied

In *No. Car. v. Butler* (1979), it was held: "An express written or oral statement of waiver [of *Miranda* rights] is usually strong proof of the validity of that waiver, but is not inevitably either necessary or sufficient to establish waiver. The question is not one of form, but rather whether the defendant in fact knowingly and voluntarily waived [the *Miranda* rights]. The courts must presume that a defendant did not waive his rights; the prosecution's burden is great; but in at least some cases waiver can be clearly inferred from the actions and words of the person interrogated." But this does not mean waiver is established merely by the fact that the defendant thereafter answered questions, *Tague v. La.* (1980), as *Miranda* cautions that "a valid waiver will not be presumed simply from the silence of the accused after warnings are given or simply from the fact that a confession was in fact eventually obtained."

(b) Facts bearing on the waiver

Butler instructs that the waiver issue is to be decided on "the particular facts and circumstances surrounding that case, including the background, experience, and conduct of the accused." However, the voluntariness of a *Miranda* waiver depends upon the absence of police overreaching, not of "free choice" in the broad sense of that term, and thus a waiver is voluntary though produced by moral and psychological pressures emanating from sources other than official coercion. *Colo. v. Connelly* (1986). As for police overreaching, courts have held waivers involuntary when obtained by threats or promises or only after extended detention or persistent questioning. A waiver is not invalid merely because police withheld from the defendant information that an attorney had sought to consult him, as "events occurring outside the presence of the suspect and entirely unknown to him" have no bearing on whether the waiver was "knowing and intelligent." *Moran v. Burbine* (1986).

If the defendant requests an attorney, this is per se an invocation of his Fifth Amendment rights, requiring that all interrogation cease. This is because of the "pivotal role" of counsel in the criminal process, and thus a comparable per se approach is not applicable to a request for a probation officer, clergyman, or close friend. *Fare v. Michael C.* (1979). If the defendant's invocation of his right to counsel is limited in some way, it does not prohibit further police contact with the defendant consistent with that limitation. *Conn. v. Barrett* (1987) (counsel invoked only as to giving of written statement; police could still seek oral statement).

On the question of whether an effective waiver can be established in the face of defendant's refusal to sign a waiver-of-rights form, or to have his confession reduced to writing, the prevailing view is yes. That position is supported by the Supreme Court's approach in *No. Car. v. Butler*, discussed above. However, it does seem that under such circumstances no waiver should be found if other indications of the suspect's intentions to waive are at all ambiguous. In *Barrett*, supra, the Court stressed that the defendant had "made clear his intentions."

Another type of scope-of-waiver issue was presented in *Wyrick v. Fields* (1982), where Fields after consultation with counsel agreed to take a polygraph test, which was preceded by a *Miranda* waiver. After the test, Fields was asked to explain why his answers indicated deceit, and he made an incriminating response. The Court held the waiver extended to that questioning, as neither Fields nor his attorney could have reasonably assumed "that Fields would not be informed of the polygraph readings and asked to explain any unfavorable result."

(c) Waiver after assertion of rights

A suspect who has once refused to waive his *Miranda* rights may in some circumstances execute an effective waiver at a subsequent interrogation session. In *Mich. v. Mosley* (1975), the Court rejected the claim that assertion of *Miranda* rights creates "a per se proscription of indefinite duration upon any further questioning by any police officer on any subject," and concluded that instead the test is whether the defendant's right to cut off questioning was "scrupulously honored." In *Mos-*

ley, the defendant, after receiving the *Miranda* warnings, declined to discuss the robberies for which he was arrested, but two hours later waived his *Miranda* rights to a different officer with respect to an unrelated homicide. In holding his incriminating statements admissible, the Court stressed that this was not a case "where the police failed to honor a decision of a person in custody to cut off questioning, either by refusing to discontinue the interrogation upon request or by persisting in repeated efforts to wear down his resistance and make him change his mind." Rather, "the police here [i] immediately ceased the interrogation, [ii] resumed questioning only after the passage of a significant period of time and the provision of a fresh set of warnings, and [iii] restricted the second interrogation to a crime that had not been a subject of the earlier interrogation."

The *Mosley* "scrupulously honored" test applies when the defendant has invoked his right to silence, but is insufficient when the defendant has invoked his right to counsel; "an accused, * * * having expressed his desire to deal with the police only through counsel, is not subject to further interrogation by the authorities until counsel has been made available to him, unless the accused himself initiates further communication, exchanges or conversations with the police." *Edwards v. Ariz.* (1981). The "available to him" part of *Edwards* means "that when counsel is requested, interrogation must cease, and officials may not reinitiate interrogation without counsel present, whether or not the accused has consulted with his attorney" in the interim. *Minnick v. Miss.* (1990). When *Edwards* applies, a two-step analysis must be used: it must be determined (i) whether the defendant "initiated" the further conversation and, if so, (ii) whether he thereafter waived his right to silence and to counsel. *Ore v. Bradshaw* (1983). The Court in *Bradshaw* was divided as to just what "initiation" means (e.g., whether defendant's inquiry of "what is going to happen to me now?" should suffice).

Uncertainties about whether *Edwards* applies occur when the defendant's actions or statements preceding or contemporaneous with the purported request for counsel make that request ambiguous or equivocal. Courts have dealt with such situations in various ways: requiring that all questioning cease notwithstanding the equivocal or ambiguous nature of the request; requiring a specified degree of clarity to trigger the right to counsel; or permitting only that interrogation designed to clarify the earlier statement. The Court had no occasion to consider such circumstances in *Smith v. Ill.* (1984), but did hold that a defendant's "post-request responses to further interrogation may not be used to cast retrospective doubt on the clarity of the initial request itself."

Edwards presents no bar to a police-initiated waiver of the *Miranda* right to counsel occurring subsequent to that defendant's assertion of his *Sixth Amendment* right to counsel at a court proceeding. Such invocation of the Sixth Amendment right (which is offense-specific) does not also constitute invocation of *Miranda* as to other, uncharged offenses, for a defendant "might be quite willing to speak to the police without counsel present concerning many matters, but not the matter under prosecution." *McNeil v. Wis.* (1991). On the other hand, *Edwards* does apply when the defendant has invoked his *Miranda* right to counsel even when the later interrogation concerns a wholly unrelated crime. This conclusion maintains *Edwards* as "a bright-line rule" without qualification or exceptions, and is grounded in the notion that a defendant's claim he does not want to submit to custodial interrogation without counsel is no more limited to a particular offense than a waiver of *Miranda* rights. *Ariz. v. Roberson* (1988).

§ 4.10 SELF–INCRIMINATION AND THE GRAND JURY WITNESS

(a) Application of the privilege

Although this chapter is concerned primarily with police interrogation, it should be noted that prosecutors have even broader authority in interrogating witnesses before the grand jury. Acting as the legal advisor to the grand jury, the prosecutor may obtain a subpoena requiring that a person appear before the grand jury and testify under oath. While the police are subject to Fourth Amendment requirements in detaining a person for questioning (see § 2.9), those requirements do not apply to the decision to issue a grand jury subpoena (see § 2.10). Similarly, while the police have no authority to require a person to respond to interrogation, even apart from his self-incrimination privilege, the witness before the grand jury is required to respond to each question. Failure to do so may subject him to contempt, and if he lies under oath, he may be prosecuted for perjury. However, the witness may not be compelled to incriminate himself, and he may respond by claiming the privilege where it applies. *Counselman v. Hitchcock* (1892). The privilege is available not only where the witness' answer would acknowledge an element of a crime, but wherever it would furnish "a link in the chain of evidence" that might be used to institute a prosecution. *Hoffman v. U.S.* (1951). This standard applies to any potential state or federal prosecution, and thus the privilege may be claimed even though the potential incrimination applies to a jurisdiction other than that which compels the testimony. *Murphy v. Waterfront Comm.* (1964).

(b) Need for self-incrimination warnings

A subpoenaed grand jury witness may be an innocent third party or a potential defendant who is a "target" of the grand jury's investigation. A few courts have suggested that the "target witness" is in a position comparable to the arrestee subject to custodial interrogation and therefore must be given *Miranda* warnings. However, most of the courts that have confronted that issue have held otherwise. In *U.S. v. Mandujano* (1976), the full Court found it unnecessary to reach this issue. Although the witness there had not been given full *Miranda* warnings, he was being prosecuted for having given false testimony before the grand jury; even if the lack of full *Miranda* warnings had resulted in a denial of his Fifth Amendment privilege, it would provide "no protection for the commission of perjury." See also *U.S. v. Wong* (1977) (grand jury witness who misunderstood self-incrimination warnings cannot suppress her false testimony in subsequent perjury prosecution).

While the full Court did not reach the issue, a four-justice plurality opinion in *Mandujano* did consider and reject the need for full *Miranda* warnings. It stressed that: (1) grand jury questioning "takes place in a setting wholly different from custodial police interrogation"; (2) a grand jury witness has no absolute right to remain silent comparable to that of the person being interrogated by the police, but rather has an "absolute duty to answer all questions, subject only to a valid Fifth Amendment claim"; and (3) there was no Sixth Amendment basis for providing the witness with appointed counsel since "no criminal proceedings had [yet] been instituted" and the "Sixth Amendment right to counsel [therefore] had not come into play." Because the witness in *Mandujano* was told that he had a right not to answer incriminatory questions, the plurality noted it therefore was "unnecessary to consider whether any warning is required." Consistent with federal practice, the witness in *Mandujano* also had been told that he could consult with retained counsel (which he did not have) outside of the grand jury room. Two concurring justices argued that a witness could not be assumed to have knowingly waived his self-incrimination privilege without more complete warnings, including a notification that he was the target of the investigation. However, in a later case, *U.S. v. Washington* (1977), the Court specifically rejected the need for a target notification, noting that a witness' target status "neither enlarges nor diminishes the constitutional protection against compelled self-incrimination."

(c) Subpoenas for documents

The privilege also may apply to a subpoena duces tecum requiring the production of incriminating documents before the grand jury. Here, however, several limitations on the scope of the privilege sharply restrict its application. First, the privilege does not apply to the required production of records of corporations or similar collective entities (e.g., a labor union, or an ongoing business enterprise organized as a partnership). *Bellis v. U.S.* (1974); *U.S. v. White* (1944). As the Court noted in *Bellis* and *White,* the Fifth Amendment "respects a private inner sanctum of individual feeling and thought" which is not possessed by a corporation or other entity that "has a character so impersonal in the scope of its membership and activities that it cannot be said to embody or represent the purely private or personal interests of its constituents."

Since the individual officer of the entity who presents the records is acting in a custodial, representative capacity, he also cannot claim the privilege even though the records are highly incriminating to him personally. Moreover, even after the Court expressly recognized that sometimes the very act of production could be incriminatory (see the *Fisher* case, infra), an entity agent to whom a subpoena is directed cannot claim the privilege based upon his act of production, for that is not "a personal act" but rather that of the entity, from which it follows that the government "may make no evidentiary use of the 'individual act' against the individual." *Braswell v. U.S.* (1988).

Second, the privilege can only be raised by the person actually being compelled to produce the records. Thus, a taxpayer could not claim the privilege where his accountant was required to produce the taxpayer's records that were in the accountant's possession. *Couch v. U.S.* (1973). The accountant in that situation also could not claim the privilege since it is available only where the person compelled to produce the records will himself be incriminated, not where the only incrimination is to others. *Fisher v. U.S.* (1976). See also *Rogers v. U.S.* (1951) (where a witness testifying before a grand jury had waived the privilege by acknowledging her own possession of records, she could not claim the privilege as to questions that might prove incriminating to others). However, in the case of an attorney possessing the records of a client, the attorney-client privilege will bar production if the self-incrimination privilege would have barred production from the client if he had possessed the records. *Fisher v. U.S.* (1976).

Finally, even where the subpoenaed records are not those of a collective entity and are incriminating to the person subpoenaed, the privilege does not apply unless the records are the "private papers" of the subpoenaed person. *Fisher v. U.S.* (1976) suggests that incriminatory records will constitute private papers for this purpose only if the testimonial aspects of their production are themselves incriminatory. Those testimonial aspects consist of (1) the implicit acknowledgment through production that the records exist and are in the possession of the subpoenaed person, and (2) the implicit authentication that the records produced are those described in the subpoena. *Fisher* noted that these testimonial aspects of production would not be incriminatory (and therefore the privilege would not apply) where a taxpayer was required to produce workpapers prepared by his accountant. The taxpayer's production of the workpapers would not authenticate their content since the taxpayer "did not prepare the papers and could not vouch for their accuracy," and the existence and location of the workpapers had been independently established without regard to the taxpayer's act. (Consider also *Doe v. U.S.* (1988), holding that requiring an individual to sign a form directing a bank to release records did not compel testimony, as the form did not acknowledge the existence of any account in any particular bank, did not indicate whether the requested documents existed, and offered no assistance in authenticating any records produced.)

Fisher was distinguished in *U.S. v. Doe* (1984), involving a subpoena to a sole proprietor for his business records. Though acknowledging that the risk of incrimination must be "substantial and real" and not merely "trifling or imaginary," the Court concluded all three of the kinds of risks identified in *Fisher* were apparently present. Respondent had never conceded that the records existed or were in his possession, and his production of them would constitute authentication "even if the government could obtain the documents from another source." That is, the government had failed to show that possession, existence and authentication were a "foregone conclusion," as in *Fisher.* Failing in that, the Court added in *Doe,* any Fifth Amendment claim could be defeated by a grant of use/derivative-use immunity (see § 4.10(d)) limited to the act of production (that is, not covering the contents of the documents). But a court may not confer such immunity upon the government's disclaimer of an intent to use the subpoenaed party's act of production against him, as Congress has by statute delegated the immunity decision to appropriate Justice Department officials.

(d) Immunity

The state may preclude a witness' reliance on the privilege against self-incrimination, with respect to either testimony or the production of documents, by an appropriate grant of immunity. The object of the privilege is to protect the witness against criminal prosecution, not to protect him against being compelled to give information that might tend to "disgrace him or bring him into disrepute." *Brown v. Walker* (1896). Accordingly, if the state guarantees to the witness protection against prosecution equal to that which would exist if he claimed the privilege, it has effectively replaced the privilege and can compel him to testify. At one time, it was thought that equivalent protection required a grant of "transactional immunity"—i.e. immunity from prosecution for any offenses based on the transaction as to which the witness is compelled to testify. *Brown v. Walker,* supra. Under this type of immunity, which is still utilized in many states, a witness compelled to furnish information relating to a particular offense may not be prosecuted for that offense even if the state has obtained sufficient evidence to establish his guilt through sources other than his compelled testimony. In *Kastigar v. U.S.* (1972), the Court held that it was sufficient to grant a less extensive immunity known as "use and derivative use" immunity. Such immunity, the Court noted, was coextensive with the privilege because it barred prosecution use of the witness' compelled statement and any information derived from that statement. Cf. § 6.6(a) (discussing the "fruit of the poison tree" doctrine). However, since the privilege extends to possible incrimination under both federal or state law, the protection against use and derivative use must extend to both jurisdictions. *Murphy v. Waterfront Comm.* (1964). Although the states lack the power to preclude federal prosecutions, the Supreme Court has lent the necessary scope to state immunity grants by holding that state immunized testimony and its fruits cannot be used in federal prosecutions. Congress has provided that federal witness immunity bars use and derivative use in both federal and state prosecutions. 18 U.S.C.A. § 6002.

For a grant of immunity to provide protection "coextensive" with the Fifth Amendment, it need not treat the witness as if he had remained silent. Thus, if the witness granted immunity gives false testimony, he may be prosecuted for that criminal conduct, and at his criminal trial the allegedly false testimony and also other testimony relevant to prove that the false statements charged were knowingly made are admissible in evidence. *U.S. v. Apfelbaum* (1980).

CHAPTER 5

LINEUPS AND OTHER PRE-TRIAL IDENTIFICATION PROCEDURES

---

§ 5.1 THE PRIVILEGE AGAINST SELF-INCRIMINATION

(a) The *Schmerber* case

In *Schmerber v. Cal.* (1966), the Court upheld the taking of a blood sample by a physician at police direction from a defendant over his objection after his arrest for drunken driving. Among the grounds upon which the defendant challenged the admission of this sample in evidence against him was that it violated his Fifth Amendment privilege not to "be compelled in any criminal case to be a witness against himself." The Court, in a 5–4 decision, rejected this contention and held that "the privilege protects an accused only from being compelled to testify against himself, or otherwise provide the State with evidence of a testimonial or communicative nature." As the Court later put it, the privilege only protects one from being compelled to express the "contents of his mind" *Doe v. U.S.* (1988).

In defining the scope of the privilege, the *Schmerber* majority noted that many identification procedures were not protected by the Fifth Amendment. *Holt v. U.S.* (1910), holding that a defendant could be compelled to model a blouse, was cited as the "leading case," and it was observed that "both federal and state courts have usually held that it offers no protection against compulsion to submit to fingerprinting, photographing or measurements, to write or speak for identification, to appear in court, to stand, to assume a stance, to walk, or to make a particular gesture."

(b) Application to pretrial identification

It is thus not surprising that the Court has subsequently relied upon *Schmerber* in holding that several identification practices do not conflict with the privilege: requiring the defendant to appear in a lineup and to speak for identification, *U.S. v. Wade* (1967); or to provide handwriting exemplars, *Gilbert v. Cal.* (1967). In both cases the Court split 5–4 on this issue. The majority relied upon the *Schmerber* distinction between an accused's "communications" in whatever form, vocal or physical, and "compulsion which makes a suspect or accused the source of 'real or physical evidence.' " The dissenters argued that *Schmerber* was wrongly decided, in that the privilege is designed to bar the government from forcing a person to supply proof of his own crime, and that even assuming the correctness of *Schmerber* the instant cases were distinguishable because each defendant was required "actively to cooperate—to accuse himself by a volitional act." Other courts have followed the majority view and have thus held the privilege inapplicable to such other identification procedures as fingerprinting or examination by ultraviolet light.

(c) Consequences of failure to cooperate

Although not protected by the Fifth Amendment, some identification procedures (such as speaking or writing for identification) require the active participation of the suspect. But, what if the suspect will not cooperate? One possibility, feared the dissenters in *Wade,* is that "an accused may be jailed—indefinitely—until he is willing to" cooperate. Indeed, some courts have utilized civil contempt and criminal contempt as a means to coerce or punish the suspect who failed to comply with a court order to participate in some identification proceeding. Another possibility is that the prosecution may be permitted to comment at trial on the lack of cooperation. Cf. *So. Dak. v. Neville* (1983), holding refusal to give a blood sample is admissible at a criminal trial, as the refusal "is not an act coerced by the officer." But comment on the defendant's refusal to speak for identification is improper if it was the direct result of a prior police warning of the right to remain silent, for then the silence is insolubly ambiguous.

(d) Change in appearance

If a suspect drastically alters his appearance between the time of the crime and of identification procedures, this is admissible at trial as an indication of consciousness of guilt. Also, the identification procedure may be conducted in such a way as to simulate the defendant's prior appearance (e.g., by having him wear a false beard), but interference with the suspect's due process right to determine his personal appearance (e.g., by having him shave off a beard) requires a showing of substantial justification.

§ 5.2   THE RIGHT TO COUNSEL AND CONFRONTATION: LINEUPS

(a) Procedures required

At least after the accused has been indicted, ruled the Court in *U.S. v. Wade* (1967), and *Gilbert v. Cal.* (1967), he should not be exhibited to witnesses in a lineup conducted for identification purposes without notice to and in the absence of his counsel. Rather, both the accused and his counsel must be notified of the impending lineup, and the lineup must not be conducted until counsel is present (expressly left open was the possibility that the presence of substitute counsel might suffice where notification and presence of the suspect's own counsel would result in prejudicial delay). In the absence of "legislative or other regulations * * * which eliminate the risks of abuse and unintentional suggestion at lineup proceedings," the Court emphasized in *Wade,* the above procedures are required by virtue of the defendant's constitutional right to confrontation and his right to counsel at a critical stage of the proceedings. (Apparently no court has yet held any set of regulations to be adequate.

As explained by the Court, the right to counsel in this context is supportive of another right—here, the right to confrontation—in much the same way that the *Miranda* counsel requirement rests upon the privilege against self-incrimination. (But see *Kirby v. Ill.,* discussed in § 5.2(e).) Under past lineup practices, the defense was often unable "meaningfully to attack the credibility of the witness' courtroom identification" because of several factors which militate against developing fully the circumstances of a prior lineup identification by that witness: (a) other participants in the lineup are often police officers, or, if not, their names are rarely recorded or divulged at trial; (b) neither witnesses nor lineup participants are apt to be alert for or schooled in the detection of prejudicial conditions; (c) the suspect (often staring into bright lights) may not be in a position to observe prejudicial conditions, and, in any event, might not detect them because of his emotional tension; (d) even if the suspect observes abuse, he may nonetheless be reluctant to take the stand and open up the admission of prior convictions; and (e) even if he takes the stand, his version of what transpired at the lineup is unlikely to be accepted if it conflicts with police testimony. Moreover, the Court pointed out, the need to learn what occurred at the lineup is great; the risk of improper suggestion is substantial, and once the witness has picked out the accused in a lineup, he is unlikely to go back on his word in court.

The three dissenters to this aspect of *Wade* and *Gilbert* saw no need for the imposition of such a "broad prophylactic rule" in the absence of evidence that improper police practices at lineups were widespread. They also expressed concern that the delays required to comply with the procedures prescribed by the majority would make prompt and certain identification impossible.

Although there are cases to the contrary, the better view is that *Wade* and *Gilbert* apply at the moment of actual identification and not merely the moment of viewing, as it is important for counsel to be able to reconstruct the former at trial. The contrary position is bolstered to some extent by the *Ash* decision (see § 5.3(a)). *Wade* and *Gilbert* apply to a one-on-one identification procedure as well, even if conducted in the course of a judicial proceeding. *Moore v. Ill.* (1977).

(b) Waiver of counsel

The Court in *Wade* indicated that there might be an "intelligent waiver" of counsel, in which case notice to and presence of an attorney would not be required. Although this may seem consistent with the waiver permitted in *Miranda* (see § 4.4(b)), some have questioned whether the right to counsel at the lineup should be subject to waiver. The argument is that while waiver of counsel under *Miranda* serves the legitimate objective of permitting the suspect to bear witness to the truth, no comparable value is served by waiver under *Wade*.

The *Wade* opinion does not dwell upon the question of what is required to show an effective waiver, although it seems likely that the approach in *Miranda* is to be followed here. This means the defendant must be advised that he has a right to counsel for this particular purpose and that counsel will be provided for him if he is indigent, and "a heavy burden" rests upon the government to show an express waiver following the warnings. Moreover, waiver of counsel for another purpose will not suffice, and thus a waiver of counsel following the *Miranda* warnings does not carry over to the lineup.

(c) Consequences of violation

If the required lineup procedures are not followed, then testimony as to the fact of identification at the lineup is inadmissible at trial. "Only a *per se* exclusionary rule as to such testimony can be an effective sanction to assure that law enforcement authorities will respect the accused's constitutional right to the presence of his counsel at the critical lineup." If such testimony is admitted, the defendant is entitled to a new trial unless it is determined that the error was harmless beyond a reasonable doubt (see § 8.10). *Gilbert v. Cal.* (1967).

But, what of subsequent in-court identification by a witness who earlier identified the defendant at an improperly conducted lineup? This presents a "fruit of the poisonous tree" problem, and consistent with the general approach to that kind of issue (see § 6.6(a)), it must be determined "whether, granting establishment of the primary illegality, the evidence to which instant objection is made has been come at by exploitation of that illegality or instead by means sufficiently distinguishable to be purged of the primary taint." Thus, the government will be afforded the opportunity to establish by clear and convincing evidence that the in-court identifications were based upon observations of the suspect other than the lineup identification. Relevant factors are "the prior opportunity to observe the alleged criminal act, the existence of any discrepancy between any pre-lineup description and the defendant's actual description, any identification prior to lineup of another person, the identification by picture of the defendant prior to the lineup, failure to identify the defendant on a prior occasion, and the lapse of time between the alleged act and the lineup identification," in addition to "those facts which, despite the absence of counsel, are disclosed concerning the conduct of the lineup." *U.S. v. Wade* (1967).

Justice Black, dissenting in part in *Wade,* argued that this "tainted fruit" determination is "practically impossible," in that the witness will be unable "to draw a sharp line between a courtroom identification due exclusively to an earlier lineup and a courtroom identification due to memory not based on the lineup." The majority rejected his contention that therefore all in-court identifications should be admissible, noting that if this were the case then the state could easily circumvent the lineup requirements by resting upon the witnesses' courtroom identification and thus leave the defendant in the same predicament as before. However, some have taken note of the difficulty in making the "tainted fruit" determination in questioning whether the Court went far enough; they fear that trial judges, inevitably left with considerable discretion in making this decision, will readily find an "independent source" for in-court identifications and in that way free the police from the necessity of complying with the *Wade-Gilbert* formula. Several commentators, upon review of lower court decisions, suggest that experience has shown this to be the case.

18 U.S.C.A. § 3502, a part of the Omnibus Crime Control and Safe Streets Act of 1968, provides that the "testimony of a witness that he saw the accused commit * * * the crime" is admissible in a federal court. This appears to be a patently unconstitutional attempt to "repeal" *Wade.* Though the Court in *Wade* said the need for counsel could be removed by statutes "which eliminate the risks of abuse and unintentional suggestion at lineup proceedings and the impediments to meaningful confrontation at trial," this statute hardly does that.

(d) Role of counsel

What, exactly, is the role of defense counsel at the lineup? *Wade* stresses the need to protect the defendant's "right meaningfully to cross-examine the witnesses against him and to have effective assistance of counsel at the trial itself," which most clearly suggests that counsel should function as an observer at the lineup. On the basis of his observations, he would then be in a position at trial to decide whether it is tactically wise to bring out the lineup identification in order to cast doubt upon an in-court identification. And, if he decides to do so, he will better know what questions to ask the witness about the circumstances of the lineup. The observer-counsel may also have to become a witness at the trial, for the Court in *Wade* emphasized that the suspect, other participants in the lineup, and the witnesses at the lineup are unlikely to observe or recognize prejudicial circumstances. Rule 3.7 of the ABA Model Rules of Professional Conduct, however, provides that if a lawyer learns he will be required to be a witness for his client, except as to merely formal or uncontested matters, he should withdraw from the case unless doing so "would work substantial hardship on the client."

The majority in *Wade* implies that counsel might also take a more active role at the lineup; they say that "presence of counsel itself can often avert prejudice" and assist law enforcement "by preventing the infiltration of taint in the prosecution's identification evidence." The dissenters find in *Wade* "an implicit invitation to counsel to suggest rules for the lineup and to manage and produce it as best he can." Defense counsel obviously cannot compel the police to conduct the lineup in a certain way, although he might point out unfair features of the identification process and even suggest corrective measures. As a matter of tactics, however, counsel may prefer simply to allow the prejudicial practices so that he might bring them out in cross-examination. But if, as at least one court has suggested, such a tactic should be treated as a waiver of any suggestive procedure not objected to by counsel at the time of the lineup, counsel would be confronted with some very hard choices at a very early stage of the case. If that is to be the consequence, then the notion of defense counsel playing an active role at the identification proceeding is unsound. (The situation is different as to a later in-court identification, and thus in *Moore v. Ill.* (1977), the Court quite correctly said that if counsel had been present at the preliminary hearing he could have acted in such a way as to avoid "some or all of this suggestiveness.")

(e) Pre-indictment identifications

Because both *Wade* and *Gilbert* involved lineups held after indictment and appointment of counsel, lower courts were in disagreement as to whether counsel was required at any pre-indictment identifications. In *Kirby v. Ill.* (1972), the Court held that the *Wade-Gilbert* rule applies only to lineups occurring "at or after the initiation of adversary judicial criminal proceedings—whether by way of formal charge, preliminary hearing, indictment, information, or arraignment." The rationale was

that the constitutional right to counsel has traditionally been so limited, and with good reason, in
that only after such initiation is a defendant "faced
with the prosecutorial forces of organized society,
and immersed in the intricacies of substantive and
procedural criminal law." This conclusion, the
three dissenters cogently pointed out, is based upon
a misreading of *Wade* and *Gilbert* as purely right
to counsel cases, rather than cases concerned with
protecting the right to confrontation at trial, and
ignores the fact that the practices condemned in
those cases may just as easily occur during a pre-
indictment lineup.

Except for the language quoted above, *Kirby* does
not explore what it takes to "initiate" adversary
judicial criminal proceedings, but that language
was later relied upon in holding that a preliminary
hearing suffices. *Moore v. Ill.* (1977). It is generally agreed that a warrantless arrest is not sufficient, but the courts are not in agreement as to
whether proceedings are initiated by issuance of an
arrest warrant upon information and oath. At
least where the warrant is not connected with a
decision to charge and serves only purposes relating to arrest, it would seem that neither issuance
nor execution of the warrant should be sufficient.
Compare *Brewer v. Williams* (1977) (concluding
that adversary judicial proceedings clearly had
been initiated where a warrant had been issued
and defendant had been arraigned on the warrant
and committed to jail).

§ 5.3 THE RIGHT TO COUNSEL AND CONFRONTATION: OTHER IDENTIFICATION PROCEDURES

(a) The use of pictures

Does it follow from *Wade* and *Gilbert* that an accused in custody has a right to have his counsel present while witnesses view still or motion pictures of him for purposes of identification? No, the Court concluded in *U.S. v. Ash* (1973). Throughout the expansion of the constitutional right to counsel to certain pretrial proceedings, said the majority, "the function of the lawyer has remained essentially the same as his function at trial," namely, to give the accused "aid in coping with legal problems or assistance in meeting his adversary." This being so, there is no such right at photo-identification, as unlike a lineup, there is no "trial-like confrontation" involving the "presence of the accused." Moreover, even if a broader view were taken of the right to counsel, it need not extend "to a portion of the prosecutor's trial-preparation interviews with witnesses," given "the equal ability of defense counsel to seek and interview witnesses himself." Stewart, J., concurring, while objecting to the majority's distinction of *Wade* as a situation where the lawyer is giving advice or assistance to the defendant at the lineup, concluded that the lawyer's role "as an observer" need not be extended to photo identification, where "there are few possibilities for unfair suggestiveness."

The three dissenters in *Ash* objected that the risk of "impermissible suggestiveness" which led to *Wade* and *Gilbert* was equally present in the case of identification by pictures, and that because the defendant is not personally present for such identification there is less "likelihood that irregularities in the procedure will ever come to light" if counsel has not observed the identification. As for the majority's characterization of the right to counsel, the dissenters argued that historically the right to counsel attached at certain pretrial procedures not because of the assistance the attorney could immediately render at that time, but rather "to protect the fairness of the trial itself."

(b) Scientific methods

In *Wade*, the government argued that a lineup is no different from other identification procedures, such as taking and analyzing "the accused's fingerprints, blood sample, clothing, hair, and the like," apparently in an attempt to bring the instant case within the ruling of *Schmerber v. Cal.* (1966). The majority in *Schmerber* held that the taking of a blood sample was not covered by the Fifth Amendment, and thus found "no issue of counsel's ability to assist petitioner in respect of any rights he did possess." The Court in *Wade* distinguished the other procedures listed by the government on the ground that they do not present the risks attendant lineups: "Knowledge of the techniques of science and technology is sufficiently available, and the variables in techniques few enough, that the

accused has the opportunity for a meaningful confrontation of the Government's case at trial
through the ordinary processes of cross-examination of the Government's expert witnesses and the
presentation of the evidence of his own experts."
On this basis, the Court held in *Gilbert* that the
taking of handwriting exemplars is not a critical
stage entitling the suspect to the assistance of
counsel. Thus, while the suspect might benefit
from counsel's advice as to whether to give the
exemplars or refuse and suffer the consequences
(see § 5.1(c)), this does not involve a constitutional
right to which the right to counsel might be linked.

§ 5.4 DUE PROCESS: "THE TOTALITY OF THE CIRCUMSTANCES"

(a) Generally

An identification made prior to the *Wade* and
Gilbert decisions (which are not retroactive, see
§ 1.4(b)), made thereafter but under circumstances
in which counsel is not required, or perhaps even
made in the presence of counsel, might be challenged on yet another ground. A "recognized
ground of attack upon a conviction independent of
any right to counsel claim" is that the defendant's
identification was "so unnecessarily suggestive and
conducive to irreparable mistaken identification
that he was denied due process of law." *Stovall v.
Denno* (1967). (The later congressional declaration
that testimony of an identification witness "shall
be admissible in evidence in a criminal prosecu-

tion," 18 U.S.C.A. § 3502, cannot "repeal" a defendant's right under *Stovall* not to be convicted on the basis of an identification so unreliable as to violate due process.)

If an identification was "suggestive" (e.g., a one-on-one confrontation) and also "unnecessarily" so (i.e., there was no good reason for foregoing more reliable procedures), that alone does not require the exclusion of evidence. The Court declined to hold otherwise as to an identification which predated the *Stovall* decision. *Neil v. Biggers* (1972). If there has been suggestiveness, a subsequent in-court identification is inadmissible only if there is "a very substantial likelihood of irreparable misidentification," and "with the deletion of 'irreparable', [that test] * * * serves equally well as a standard for the admissibility of testimony concerning the out-of-court identification itself." *Neil v. Biggers,* supra. The Court later refused to apply a per se rule to post-*Stovall* identifications, and instead adhered to the "totality of the circumstances" test. *Manson v. Brathwaite* (1977). Under *Manson,* the factors to be considered in evaluating the likelihood of misidentification "include the opportunity of the witness to view the criminal at the time of the crime, the witness' degree of attention, the accuracy of his prior description of the criminal, the level of certainty demonstrated at the confrontation, and the time between the crime and the confrontation."

In the *Wade-Gilbert* context, these same factors bear on the question of whether an in-court identi-

fication is a "fruit of the poisonous tree," as to
which the government has the burden of proof (see
§ 5.2(c)). But in the context of the *Stovall* rule,
these factors bear directly upon the question of
whether there has been a violation of due process,
which suggests the burden is on the defendant.
But courts have been inclined to place the burden
on the government here as well; the asserted justification is that the government gave rise to the
issue by using unfair procedures.

(b) Lineups

An apt illustration of a due process violation in a
lineup identification is provided by *Foster v. Cal.*
(1969). The Court concluded it was "all but inevitable" that the victim of a robbery would identify
defendant "whether or not he was in fact" the
robber, as: (1) defendant was placed in a lineup
with two other men who were half a foot shorter;
(2) only he wore a jacket similar to that worn by
the robber; (3) when this did not lead to positive
identification, the police permitted a one-to-one
confrontation; and (4) because the witness' identification was still tentative, some days later another
lineup was arranged, but defendant was the only
person in this lineup who had also appeared in the
first lineup.

(c) The use of pictures

In *Simmons v. U.S.* (1968), FBI agents identified
a bank robbery suspect on the basis of his use of a
car which was similar to that used in the robbery.

From a relative of the suspect they obtained six snapshots, mostly group pictures, in which the suspect appeared, from which five bank employees separately identified the suspect the day after the robbery. Balancing the need against the risks, the Court concluded that this procedure was not "unnecessarily suggestive." The use of the photos was justified, in that a serious felony had occurred, the perpetrators were still at large, inconclusive clues led to the suspect, and it was important for the FBI swiftly to determine whether they were on the right track so that they could properly deploy their forces. Also, there was little risk of misidentification, as the employees had all gotten a good look at the robber, they examined the pictures while their memories were still fresh, each witness examined the pictures separately, and the FBI agents disclosed nothing about the progress of the investigation or suggesting which persons in the pictures were under suspicion.

(d) One-man showups

In contrast to a properly conducted lineup, the display of a single suspect to a witness carries with it a considerable risk of misidentification: the witness may well conclude that the individual displayed must be the offender, for otherwise he would not be in custody and singly displayed. In *Stovall v. Denno* (1967), the Court noted that "the practice of showing suspects singly to persons for the purpose of identification, and not as part of a lineup, has been widely condemned," but held that under the unique circumstances of the case the one-man showup was justified. The defendant was arrested because keys found at the scene of the murder were traced to him. The wife of the murder victim, who herself had been repeatedly stabbed while defending her husband, was hospitalized for major surgery to save her life. Two days after the crime, defendant was brought to her hospital room, where she identified him after he spoke a few words. Defendant was handcuffed to one of the five police officers who were present with two members of the prosecutor's staff, and he was the only black in the room. The Court concluded that "an immediate hospital confrontation was imperative," as no one knew how long the witness might live, she could not visit the jail, and she was the only person who could have exonerated the defendant.

While *Stovall* thus rests upon a rather unique showing of need for the one-man showup—the fact that the sole eye witness was near death—there may be other reasons why this less reliable procedure is sometimes "imperative." For example, if *Stovall* is considered with *Simmons,* where the recognized need was for the police "swiftly to determine whether they were on the right track," it might be said that an on-the-scene one-man showup of a suspect who has just been arrested or detained for investigation does not violate due process. This is the conclusion which has been reached by the lower courts, who have also stressed the increased reliability of identifications made promptly after the event. Similarly, some courts have upheld a one-man showup where it was the suspect who was seriously injured. But failure to use a lineup is not excused merely because it would be inconvenient or difficult to assemble a group of persons physically comparable to the suspect. *Neil v. Biggers* (1972).

(e) In-court identifications

A one-on-one confrontation in court would seem even more suggestive, for the witness is given even a stronger impression that the authorities are satisfied they have the right man. As stated in *Moore v. Ill.* (1977), it "is difficult to imagine a more suggestive manner in which to present a suspect to a witness for their critical first confrontation." The Court in *Moore* stated defense counsel might have avoided such suggestiveness by seeking to have the court proceeding postponed until a lineup was conducted or by asking that the defendant be allowed to be seated in the audience before the identifying witness was called. But the lower courts often say that whether to require such safeguards is a matter left to the trial judge's discretion. Defense counsel's resort to self-help, such as by placing a "decoy" at his side in lieu of the defendant, has been viewed as unethical.

CHAPTER 6

THE EXCLUSIONARY RULES AND THEIR APPLICATION

---

§ 6.1 INTRODUCTION

A violation of the constitutional restraints discussed in chapters 2–5 can lead to a tort suit, the issuance of an injunction, the imposition of administrative sanctions, or even a criminal prosecution against the violator. But violations of constitutional restraints have their most direct impact upon the criminal justice process in the exclusion of evidence. Within the process itself, the issue of whether a particular police practice constitutes a violation almost invariably is raised through a motion challenging the prosecution's attempt to introduce at trial evidence obtained through that police practice. The constitutionality of a search will be raised by a motion seeking suppression of evidence obtained in that search. The constitutionality of an arrest ordinarily will be presented by a motion seeking suppression of evidence obtained through a search of the person incident to that arrest. The legality of electronic surveillance (including, but not limited to, its constitutionality)

will be raised by a motion under § 2515 of Title III
of the Crime Control Act, which states that no
illegally intercepted communication and "no evidence derived therefrom may be received in evidence in any trial, hearing, or other proceeding."
The constitutionality of a police interrogation will
be challenged via a motion to exclude from evidence statements of the accused that were the
fruits of that interrogation. Claims that an identification procedure violated constitutional limits
will be presented via a motion to exclude identification evidence obtained through that procedure.

In the context of the Fourth Amendment, the
prohibition against admission at trial of unconstitutionally obtained evidence has come to be known
as the "exclusionary rule." The barring of evidence under the other constitutional limitations
discussed in chapters 2–5 is less often described as
resting on an "exclusionary rule," but references to
a Sixth Amendment, due process, or even a self-
incrimination "exclusionary rule" are not uncommon. There are certain common issues presented
in the exclusion of evidence under each of the
different constitutional guarantees, and that ex-
plains why we discuss the different exclusionary
requirements in the same chapter. It should be
kept in mind, however, that each guarantee provides a separate grounding for its exclusionary
requirement, which may give that requirement a
somewhat different scope than the exclusionary
requirements of the other guarantees. Thus, the
title of this chapter refers in the plural to the

"exclusionary rules" rather than to the more common singular phrasing of "exclusionary rule."

§ 6.2 FIFTH AMENDMENT, SIXTH AMENDMENT, AND DUE PROCESS EXCLUSION

(a) Fifth Amendment exclusion

As the Supreme Court has noted in several contexts, but most notably in its rulings sustaining immunity grants (§ 3.10(d)), the crux of a violation of the Fifth Amendment's self-incrimination clause lies in the prosecution's use in a criminal trial of a statement obtained from the defendant through governmental compulsion. Thus, as Justice Black noted in his separate opinion in *Coolidge v. N.H.* (1971), "the Fifth Amendment in and of itself directly and explicitly commands its own exclusionary rule." If the statement of the defendant was obtained through methods that constitute "compulsion" under the self-incrimination clause, the trial court must bar that statement to prevent a violation of the Fifth Amendment.

Miranda's requirement of exclusion of statements obtained through custodial interrogation that failed to follow the *Miranda* rules (see § 4.3(b)) initially was viewed as based upon the Fifth Amendment's command of absolute exclusion. Today, however, the Court reads *Miranda* somewhat differently. The "*Miranda* exclusionary rule" is said to "sweep more broadly than the Fifth Amendment itself," triggering exclusion of defendant's statements "even in the absence of a Fifth Amendment violation" on the basis of a "prophylactic," "irrebuttable presumption" of compulsion. *Ore. v. Elstad* (1985). As will be seen, this distinction has lead to differences in the applicable scope of *Miranda*'s exclusionary rule and the core Fifth Amendment exclusionary rule.

(b) Sixth Amendment exclusion

An accused is entitled to the assistance of counsel at all critical stages of criminal process. See § 7.1. If the state obtains evidence at such a critical stage without counsel being present, and without a waiver of counsel, that evidence will not be admitted at trial. Thus, where an accused is subjected to a lineup without the Sixth Amendment protection required under *Wade* (§ 5.2), evidence of his identification at that lineup is inadmissible. So too, where the police deliberately elicit a statement from an accused without his waiver of counsel, that statement must be excluded under *Massiah* and its progeny (§ 4.3). *White v. Md.* (1963) similarly barred prosecution evidence of the defendant having entered a non-binding guilty plea at his first appearance because he had not received (or waived) the assistance of counsel at that proceeding. The Court has not offered any extensive explanation of why the Sixth Amendment requires a remedy of excluding evidence in such cases, but its opinions have suggested two quite different rationales for the Sixth Amendment's exclusionary rule.

Initially, the Court has suggested that exclusion under the Sixth Amendment, like exclusion under the Fifth Amendment, is necessary because the crux of the Sixth Amendment violation lies in the admission at trial of the evidence obtained without affording the accused the assistance of counsel. The Court has noted in other contexts that a Sixth Amendment violation is not present unless the action alleged to have constituted the violation, whether it be state interference with the lawyer-client relationship or ineffective assistance by counsel, has resulted in prejudice to the defendant at trial. See §§ 7.6, 7.7. Thus, where the state's undercover agent participated in a conference between the defendant and his counsel, but did not convey anything he learned to his superiors, the Court held that there was no realistic possibility that the state had gained an advantage and therefore no Sixth Amendment violation occurred, notwithstanding the state invasion of the lawyer-client relationship. *Weatherford v. Bursey* (1977). Applying this analysis to cases where the state has obtained evidence by undercutting the lawyer-client relationship, the Sixth Amendment violation comes into play only with the state's use of that evidence. *Massiah,* for example, described the violation there as the introduction of the statement after it had been deliberately elicited. Under this view, the evidence must be excluded to prevent the critical element of the violation (i.e., the trial prejudice) from occurring. But consider *Me. v.*

Moulton (1985) (suggesting the *Massiah* violation occurs with elicitation of the statement in itself).

The Court's opinions at times also have suggested that exclusion under the Sixth Amendment is based on a deterrence rationale similar to that offered in support of the Fourth Amendment's exclusionary rule. Thus, *Gilbert v. Cal.* (1967) held that violation of the *Wade* requirements would result in automatic exclusion of the subsequent lineup identification because, though the lineup without counsel may have been fairly conducted and the resulting identification may be sufficiently open to counsel's challenge at trial, "only a per se exclusionary rule" could constitute "an effective sanction to assure that law enforcement authorities will respect the accused's constitutional right to the presence of his counsel at the critical lineup." Similarly, *Nix v. Williams* (1984), in dealing with the admissibility of secondary evidence discovered through a Sixth Amendment violation, justified applying an inevitable discovery exception (see § 6.6(c)) by reference to the traditional "deterrence rationale" of "the exclusionary rule." The defendant there contended that the "Sixth Amendment exclusionary rule" played a role different than the "Fourth Amendment exclusionary rule" and therefore did not permit the approach adopted in Fourth Amendment cases (see § 6.3(d)) of balancing the incremental deterrence provided by expanding exclusion against the cost of keeping from the factfinder reliable and relevant evidence. However, at least as to the secondary evidence issue considered in *Nix v. Williams*, the Court did not find that contention persuasive, and looked to both of those factors.

(c) Due process exclusion

Where the Court holds a particular police practice to violate due process because it presents a grave potential for producing untrustworthy evidence, exclusion of that evidence follows logically from the grounding of the violation. Thus, the Court has held that identification evidence must be excluded where it is the product of identification procedures so suggestive as to violate due process. See § 5.4. Indeed, in this situation, it is probably the use of the evidence rather than the identification procedure itself that violates due process. In the case of prohibited interrogation techniques which are likely to produce an untrustworthy confession (e.g., police brutality), the offensive police practice presumably violates due process in itself. However, exclusion of the confession would still be mandated, apart from any attempt to remedy the deprivation of personal dignity involved in the prohibited police practice, by the danger to a fair trial posed by prosecution use of the potentially unreliable confession.

While the condemnation of police interrogation practices under the "voluntariness" standard of due process often rests at least in part on the potential for producing untrustworthy confessions, not all practices held to violate that standard have that characteristic. Police interrogation practices have been held to be "so offensive to a civilized system that they must be condemned," *Miller v. Fenton* (1985), even though the evidence produced is likely to be most reliable. See § 4.2(a). Indeed, in *Rochin v. Cal.* (1952), this concept was applied outside the area of "involuntary" confessions to require exclusion of evidence extracted from the body of a suspect. Decided at a time when the Fourth Amendment exclusionary rule did not apply to the states (see § 6.3(a)), *Rochin* held that the use of stomach pumping to obtain two morphine tablets the suspect had swallowed so "shock[ed] the conscience" of a "civilized society" as to violate due process and bar the state's use of those tablets in evidence. In *Rochin*, as in certain of the Court's voluntariness rulings, the exclusionary remedy must be based on a justification other than the "reliability analysis" that underlies the typical due process exclusion. Insofar as such due process rulings rest on respect for the principle that "ours is an accusatorial and not an inquisitorial system," *Rogers v. Richmond* (§ 4.2(a)), the exclusionary remedy may be explained in much the same manner as exclusion under the self-incrimination privilege. However, due process violations in this area often have been characterized as offensive because of the nature of the police practice itself, rather than the prosecution's use of evidence forced from the accused. Here, the due process exclusionary rule apparently is designed largely to deter police from engaging in such offensive conduct, as the

Supreme Court recognized in *Colo. v. Connelly* (§ 4.2(a)).

§ 6.3 FOURTH AMENDMENT EXCLUSION

(a) From *Weeks* to *Mapp*

The Fourth Amendment exclusionary rule dates back to a period marked generally by relatively narrow readings of the Fourth Amendment, but it remains today, even after the adoption in large part of a far more expansive view of the Amendment, as perhaps the most controversial element of Fourth Amendment doctrine. The 1914 decision in *Weeks v. U.S.* established the exclusionary rule as the governing standard for federal courts. *Weeks* held that evidence obtained by federal officials in violation of the Fourth Amendment would be barred from a federal prosecution. To rule otherwise, the Court noted, would be "to affirm by judicial decision a manifest neglect if not an open defiance of the prohibitions of the Constitution." Six years later, in *Silverthorne Lumber Co. v. U.S.* (1920), Justice Holmes added that without the remedy of exclusion, the Fourth Amendment would be reduced to "a form of words." Despite this strong language, the *Weeks* rule reflected at the time a distinctly minority position in the interpretation of fundamental law governing searches and seizures. A substantial majority of state courts, interpreting state constitutional provisions identical to the Fourth Amendment, refused to adopt an exclusionary rule. The most widely cited criticism of the "federal position," that by Justice Cardoza (then a state court judge), characterized *Weeks* as permitting the "criminal * * * to go free because the constable has blundered."

Since the Fourth Amendment did not apply to the states, the state courts could reject the exclusionary rule so long as their admission of illegally seized evidence did not violate due process under the then prevailing "fundamental rights" interpretation of the Fourth Amendment. See § 1.2(b). Although the Court was moving at the time toward a broader reading of the fundamental rights concept, and although it acknowledged that Fourteenth Amendment due process encompassed the "security of one's privacy which is at the core of the Fourth Amendment," *Wolf v. Colo.* (1949) held that the Fourteenth Amendment did not require states to exclude evidence obtained through an unconstitutional search. The *Wolf* opinion noted that the *Weeks* exclusionary rule was "not derived from the explicit requirements of the Fourth Amendment," was not followed in "most of the English-speaking world," and had been expressly rejected in 30 states. In 1961, with the Court moving toward an adoption of a selective incorporation interpretation of the Fourteenth Amendment (see § 1.2(d)), *Wolf* was overruled in *Mapp v. Ohio* (1961). A case marked like *Wolf* itself with sharp dissents, *Mapp* held that "all evidence obtained by searches and seizures in violation of the

Constitution is, by that same authority, inadmissible in a state court."

Justice Clark's opinion for the Court in *Mapp* contained an extensive discussion of the justifications for requiring exclusion of unconstitutionally seized evidence even though that evidence was likely to be reliable and relevant to proof of guilt. Prior to *Mapp*, Supreme Court opinions had suggested as many as five different justifications for the *Weeks* rule, and each of these found at least oblique support somewhere in the *Mapp* opinion. The five justifications argued for exclusion on the basis of: (1) the implications of the Fifth Amendment; (2) the need to prevent a continued violation of the individual's privacy through the introduction of the evidence; (3) the natural implications of the law of remedies; (4) the imperative of judicial integrity; and (5) the need to deter future violations. Since *Mapp*, the first three of those justifications have been flatly rejected by the Court, and the fourth has been given a clearly subordinate status. The fifth, the deterrence rationale, has emerged as the crucial justification, the one that controls the scope of the exclusionary rule.

(b) Rejected theories

In *Boyd v. U.S.* (1886), a pre-*Weeks* ruling, the Court held that the forced disclosure of papers through a court order violated the Fourth Amendment and that those papers therefore could not be used by the government as incriminatory evidence. The Court reached this result through a linking of the Fourth and Fifth Amendments, noting that it had "been unable to perceive that the seizure of a man's private books and papers to be used in evidence against him is substantially different from compelling him to be a witness against himself." The extension of this rationale to all forms of searches was questionable from the outset; searches generally result in the seizure of physical evidence, rather than documents, and the Fifth Amendment traditionally has been limited to compelled production of evidence of a "testimonial or communicative nature." See § 5.1(a). While the *Mapp* opinion did discuss *Boyd* and did at one point draw an analogy between the exclusion of unconstitutionally seized evidence and the exclusion of coerced confessions, it focused on exclusion as a remedy required under the Fourth Amendment standing alone. Subsequently, in *Andresen v. Md.* (1976), the Court rejected the possible application of the Fifth Amendment even as to a search for documents. It reasoned that the self-incrimination clause protects only against compelling the individual to himself produce the documents, as occurs with a subpoena (see § 4.10(c)), but not with a governmental search and seizure. See § 2.2(f).

Language in *Weeks* and other early exclusionary rule cases could be read to suggest that the admission into evidence of unconstitutionally seized items in itself constituted a violation of the Fourth Amendment. The underlying theory, developed more by commentators than judicial opinions, was that the admission of such evidence constitutes a further invasion of privacy and thereby exacerbates the Fourth Amendment violation. Exclusion under this theory, as exclusion under the Fifth Amendment, is designed to prevent the basic violation that would occur with the act of introducing the evidence. The Supreme Court found no need to consider the validity of this theory, apart from the other justifications for the exclusionary rule, until the theory was presented in a rather unusual context in *U.S. v. Calandra* (1974). There, a grand jury witness argued that he could not be asked questions based on information obtained through an unconstitutional police search because this further invasion of his privacy constituted a "distinct violation of his Fourth Amendment rights." Rejecting this contention, the Court reasoned that "the wrong condemned" by the Fourth Amendment, the "unreasonable governmental intrusion into the privacy of one's person, house, papers, or effects," was "fully accomplished by the original search without probable cause." Therefore, the questions based on the illegally obtained evidence "work[ed] no new Fourth Amendment wrong." What was at stake here was simply "the derivative use of the product of a past unlawful search," presenting "a question, not of rights, but of remedies."

Several of the earlier Supreme Court opinions also lent support to the view that the exclusion of evidence is a remedy inherent in the Fourth Amendment. Justice Holmes, for example, noted that "the essence of a provision forbidding the acquisition of evidence in a certain way" is that "evidence so acquired shall not be used." *Silverthorne Lumber Co. v. U.S.* (1920). The theory here is that concomitant to any prohibition is the requirement that the judiciary respond to a violation of that prohibition by providing such relief as will cure the violation, by restoring the status quo, if that is possible. In the case of an unconstitutional search and seizure, the exclusionary rule was seen as providing such relief, placing both the defendant and the government in the positions that they would have occupied had there not been an unconstitutional search and seizure. *Wolf v. Colo.* (1949), however, clearly rejected this view of the exclusionary remedy, and while *Wolf* itself was later overruled, that part of its analysis continues to have majority support.

Wolf viewed the invasion of privacy as the crux of the Fourth Amendment violation, and the exclusion of the seized evidence, as it noted, does not restore that privacy. Indeed, exclusion is not even an available remedy for the victim of an unconstitutional search which produced no incriminating evidence. Moreover, even as to the unlawfully seized evidence, the exclusionary rule falls short of restoring the victim to the status quo in some instances (e.g., illegally seized contraband need not also be returned to the search victim) and gives even greater protection in others (e.g., where exclusion is required because the government lacked a warrant, the government cannot now obtain the warrant based on the probable cause it always had and simply reseize and use the evidence). Thus, *Wolf* viewed exclusion as a less than perfect remedy, no more the natural or inherent remedy of the Fourth Amendment than any of the other remedies commonly provided (e.g., the tort remedy). Although *Mapp* overruled *Wolf,* and extolled the virtues of the exclusionary rule remedy, it fell short of describing exclusion as a remedy that cured the constitutional violation. Later cases, noting the limitations of the exclusionary rule, have more clearly characterized it as something other than such a natural remedy. Thus, the Court has noted that the exclusionary rule is "neither intended nor able to cure the invasion of the defendant's rights which he has already suffered." *U.S. v. Leon* (1984).

(c) The "imperative of judicial integrity"

The primary justification for the exclusionary rule offered in *Weeks* was the need to avoid judicial affirmance of the unconstitutional actions of the police. This rationale was later characterized as resting upon the "imperative of judicial integrity," the need that courts not become "accomplices in the willful disobedience of a Constitution they are sworn to uphold." *Elkins v. U.S.* (1960). This concern relates not only to the responsibilities of the judiciary but also to maintaining public confidence in the willingness of government to abide by "the charter of its own existence." *Mapp v. Ohio* (1961).

The judicial integrity rationale was cited as one of the primary underpinnings of the exclusionary rule in *Mapp,* but subsequent majority opinions gave it considerably less weight. In *Stone v. Powell* (1976), the Court majority contended that various aspects of the law governing the exclusionary rule "demonstrate the limited role of this [judicial integrity] justification in the determination whether to apply the rule in a particular context." The Court noted that the judicial integrity rationale was inconsistent with the restriction of exclusion to cases in which a timely objection was made by a party having standing to object to the unconstitutional search (§ 6.8), with the inapplicability of the rule to grand jury proceedings (§ 6.5(b)), with the permissible use of illegally seized evidence for impeachment (§ 6.7), and with the rule of *Frisbie v. Collins* (1952) (holding that even the most egregiously unconstitutional arrest of the defendant does not bar retaining jurisdiction over the person so that he can be tried on a properly founded charge). Indeed, in some (but not all) of the rulings establishing these limits upon the availability and scope of the exclusionary remedy, dissenting justices had argued against their adoption by emphasizing their inconsistency with the judicial integrity rationale.

(d) The deterrence rationale

Ever since *Wolf,* the deterrence rationale for the exclusionary rule has been on the ascendancy. That rationale was set forth quite succinctly in

Elkins v. U.S. (1960): "[The exclusionary rule's] purpose is to deter—to compel respect for the constitutional guarantee in the only effectively available way—by removing the incentive to disregard it." The *Wolf* opinion looked primarily to the deterrence rationale in holding that the exclusionary rule was not applicable to the states under a fundamental rights interpretation of the Fourteenth Amendment. *Mapp* rejected *Wolf*'s factual premise that other remedies (e.g., tort actions) served as an effective deterrent, but *Mapp* also stressed other justifications for the exclusionary rule, particularly the "imperative of judicial integrity." Subsequent opinions, however, characterized the deterrence rationale as the critical grounding for requiring exclusion of evidence seized in violation of the Fourth Amendment. In *U.S. v. Janis* (1976), the Court stated that "the 'prime purpose' of the [exclusionary] rule, if not the sole one, 'is to deter unlawful police conduct.' " *U.S. v. Calandra* (1974) characterized the exclusionary rule as a "judicially-created remedy designed to safeguard Fourth Amendment rights generally through its deterrent effect, rather than a personal right of the party aggrieved." This characterization has been repeated by the Court majority in almost every subsequent major discussion of the exclusionary rule. See e.g., *U.S. v. Leon* (1984).

Reliance upon the deterrence rationale as the primary grounding for the exclusionary rule has had its greatest impact in the Court's determination of the scope of the rule. Since the exclusionary remedy under this rationale is "calculated to prevent, not to repair," *Elkins,* exclusion need not follow automatically from the establishment of a Fourth Amendment violation. "As with any remedial device, the application of the rule * * * [will be] restricted to those areas where its remedial objectives are thought most effaciously served." *Calandra.* Thus, where the particular setting of a limited class of illegal searches suggests that exclusion would have no deterrent impact, the Court has held the remedy not to apply. See § 6.4. So too, when extension of the remedy to new proceedings or different aspects of the criminal trial would have some deterrent impact, but that deterrence will only add marginally to the basic deterrence that stems from excluding evidence from the prosecution's case-in-chief, the Court will weigh the benefits of that additional deterrence against the costs of further exclusion. See e.g., § 6.5.

While willing to reassess the potential for deterrence in some settings, and to apply a cost/benefit analysis as to exclusion beyond the prosecution's case-in-chief, the Court has not been willing to reopen its basic assumption that exclusion from that case-in-chief is necessary to deter most unconstitutional searches. Empirical studies, the Court has noted, are too frequently flawed to furnish a conclusive answer as to whether the exclusionary remedy is in fact an effective deterrent. *U.S. v. Janis* (1976). Moreover, the critical question is not whether there exists "specific deterrence" as to a particular case or particular police department.

"Over the long term," the Court has noted, "this demonstration [through exclusion] that our society attaches serious consequences to violation of constitutional rights is thought to encourage those who formulate law enforcement policies, and the officers who implement them, to incorporate Fourth Amendment ideals into their value system." *Stone v. Powell* (1976).

§ 6.4 THE "GOOD FAITH" EXCEPTION

(a) A Fourth Amendment doctrine

Justice White, dissenting in *Stone v. Powell* (1976), expressed the view that the Fourth Amendment exclusionary rule "should be substantially modified so as to prevent its application in those many circumstances where the evidence at issue was seized by an officer acting in the good-faith belief that his conduct comported with existing law and having reasonable grounds for this belief." There was no justification for keeping relevant and reliable evidence from the factfinder under such circumstances, Justice White argued, for where there is good faith and reasonable reliance by the police, "the exclusion can have no deterrent effect."

Justice White's proposal, based as it was on a deterrence rationale, would seem to have no bearing on exclusionary rules having other groundings. Certainly, the presence of good faith and reasonable belief in legality could not justify allowing into evidence a statement obtained through what a court later deems to be "compulsion" under the Fifth Amendment. Nor would good faith and reasonable reliance justify admission of the fruits of a lineup so inherently suggestive as to violate due process.

There was a single attempt to develop a good faith exception as to a Sixth Amendment exclusionary rule, which arguably finds support in a deterrence rationale (§ 6.2(b)), but it drew little support. Chief Justice Burger, dissenting in *Brewer v. Williams* (§ 4.3(d)), argued for a form of good faith exception in that case (contending that the officer could not have anticipated the extension of *Massiah* to his "Christian burial speech"), but the majority did not even speak to that possibility. As for exclusion pursuant to the voluntariness test of due process (see § 6.3(b)), police practices rejected due to their offensiveness are by their very nature not good candidates for claiming police good faith along the lines suggested by Justice White. Thus, adoption of any sort of good faith exception apart from the Fourth Amendment context discussed by Justice White appears unlikely. As for the Fourth Amendment, the Court majority has so far adopted limited versions of Justice White's approach for two special situations.

(b) Police reliance upon a warrant

In *U.S. v. Leon* (1984), the Supreme Court, with Justice White writing for the majority, held that "the Fourth Amendment exclusionary rule should be modified so as not to bar the use in the prosecution's case-in-chief of evidence obtained by officers acting in reasonable reliance on a search warrant issued by a detached and neutral magistrate but ultimately found to be unsupported by probable cause." Because the search warrant affidavit in *Leon* "provided evidence sufficient to create disagreement among thoughtful and competent judges as to the existence of probable cause," the Court concluded that the "officers' reliance on the magistrate's determination of probable cause was objectively reasonable, and application of the extreme sanction of exclusion * * * [was therefore] inappropriate." The Court added in this regard that what was "objectively reasonable" would be determined in light of what a "reasonably well-trained officer would have known." Moreover, where a case falls within the good-faith exception, that should not preclude judicial "resolution of [the] particular Fourth Amendment question * * * [where needed] to guide future action by law enforcement officers and magistrates."

In evaluating the costs and benefits of requiring exclusion in the search-with-warrant case, the *Leon* majority noted initially that exclusion to deter magistrates is inappropriate, as (i) "the exclusionary rule is designed to deter police misconduct rather than to punish the errors of judges," (ii) "there exists no evidence suggesting that judges and magistrates are inclined to ignore or subvert the Fourth Amendment," and (iii) there is no basis "for believing that exclusion of evidence seized pursuant to a warrant will have a significant deterrent effect on the issuing judge or magistrate." As to the police, in a with-warrant case, exclusion ordinarily also is inappropriate, for usually, with the officer justifiably relying upon the prior judgment of the magistrate, "there is no police illegality and thus nothing to deter." Accordingly, "the marginal or nonexistent benefits produced by suppressing evidence obtained in objectively reasonable reliance on a subsequently invalidated search warrant" could not "justify the substantial costs of exclusion," which include "interference with the criminal justice system's truth-finding function" and thereby allowing "some guilty defendants * * * [to] go free or receive reduced sentences as a result of favorable plea bargains."

Leon, it should be noted, does not hold that the exclusionary rule is totally inapplicable whenever a warrant had been obtained. Fourth Amendment violations relating to execution of the warrant are untouched by *Leon,* as is reflected by the majority caution that its discussion "assumes, of course, that the officers properly executed the warrant and searched only those places for those objects that it was reasonable to believe were covered by the warrant." The *Leon* Court also emphasized it was not suggesting "that exclusion is always inappropriate in cases where an officer has obtained a warrant and abided by its terms," and that exclusion is still called for whenever the officer lacks "reasonable grounds for believing that the warrant was properly issued." This limitation encompasses at least four situations.

First, the Court expressly left untouched the *Franks* doctrine, whereunder a warrant facially sufficient is invalid if based upon knowingly or recklessly made falsehoods in the affidavit (§ 2.3(a)). Second, there is the situation in which the officer knows that the magistrate has "wholly abandoned his judicial role." As an illustration of such a case, the Court cited the situation in *Lo-Ji Sales* (§ 2.4(a)), where the magistrate "allowed himself to become a member, if not the leader of the search party." Third, the Court said "a warrant may be so facially deficient—i.e., in failing to particularize the place to be searched or the things to be seized—that the executing officers cannot reasonably presume it to be valid." See § 2.4. Lastly, the good faith exception is inapplicable when the affidavit is "so lacking in indicia of probable cause as to render official belief in its existence entirely unreasonable."

(c) Police reliance upon a statute

In *Ill. v. Krull* (1987), the Court held that a "good faith exception to the exclusionary rule also should be recognized when officers act in objectively reasonable reliance upon a statute authorizing [the search in question], but where the statute is ultimately found to violate the Fourth Amendment." Held admissible under this standard was evidence seized pursuant to a state statute, subsequently ruled to be unconstitutional, that authorized warrantless administrative searches of the premises of licensed automobile-parts dealers. The *Krull* majority concluded that "[t]he approach used in *Leon* is equally applicable to the present case" because (i) application of the exclusionary rule when the police reasonably relied on a statute would "have as little deterrent effect on the officers' actions" as in the *Leon* situation, and (ii) "legislators, like judicial officers, are not the focus of the [exclusionary] rule," as there "is nothing to indicate that applying the exclusionary rule to evidence seized pursuant to the statute prior to the declaration of its invalidity will act as a significant, additional deterrent" to the occasional enactment of statutes later held to confer unconstitutional search authority. The dissenters, though conceding the good faith of the police who relied on the statute, stressed that statutes "authorizing unreasonable searches were the core concern of the Framers of the Fourth Amendment." Responding to this criticism, the majority noted that "a statute cannot support objectively reasonable reliance if, in passing the statute, the legislature wholly abandoned its responsibility to enact constitutional laws" and an officer cannot "be said to have acted in good-faith reliance upon a statute if its provisions are such that a reasonable officer should have known the statute was unconstitutional."

§ 6.5 APPLICATION TO PROCEEDINGS OTHER THAN THE TRIAL

(a) Introduction

Decisions dealing with exclusion of unconstitutionally obtained evidence from proceedings other than the trial have dealt primarily with the Fourth Amendment exclusionary rule. In part, this is because evidence of the kind typically obtained through practices other than searches (e.g., identification procedures) is less likely to have much bearing in related civil or quasi-criminal proceedings. So too, the Fifth Amendment by its very terms eliminates certain scope-issues unresolved as to the Fourth Amendment's exclusionary rule; the self-incrimination clause bars the use of compelled testimony only in a "criminal case." See §§ 4.5(c), 4.10(d). As for the Fourth Amendment rule, the overall approach of the Court majority has remained consistent from one area of possible application to another. The Court has relied upon what it has described as a "pragmatic analysis of the exclusionary rule's usefulness in the particular context," weighing the additional deterrence that would stem from the rule's application against the costs that would be entailed. *Stone v. Powell* (1976).

(b) Grand jury proceedings

It is the settled federal practice, sustained against constitutional attack in *Costello v. U.S.*

(1956), that "an indictment returned by a legally constituted and unbiased grand jury, * * * if valid on its face, is enough to call for trial of the charge on the merits." This means that a defendant cannot challenge an indictment on the ground that the grand jury considered unconstitutionally obtained evidence. *Lawn v. U.S.* (1958). The defendant has a sufficient remedy in being able to challenge the introduction of such evidence if it should be used at trial. *U.S. v. Blue* (1966). Of course, a grand jury witness who will not later be indicted lacks that remedy, and that is almost certainly the situation where the witness has been given immunity, as was the case in *U.S. v. Calandra* (1974). Nonetheless, *Calandra* held that a grand jury witness could not refuse to answer questions even though those questions were based on evidence obtained from an unlawful search of his premises. The *Calandra* majority concluded that the "speculative and undoubtedly minimal advance in the deterrence of police misconduct" that might result from allowing the witness' objection was outweighed by the deleterious impact such a ruling would have upon the effective and expeditious discharge of the grand jury's duties.

(c) Related civil or quasi-criminal proceedings

In *One 1958 Plymouth Sedan v. Pa.* (1965), the Fourth Amendment exclusionary rule was held applicable to a proceeding for the forfeiture of an automobile as having had been used in the illegal transportation of alcohol. The Court emphasized that the proceeding was "quasi-criminal in character" because its object was to "penalize for the commission of an offense against the law." In *U.S. v. Janis* (1976), the Court refused to extend *Plymouth Sedan* to a civil tax proceeding. In that case, local police seized Janis' wagering records and cash in an unconstitutional search, and then notified federal authorities, who imposed an assessment against Janis for wagering excise taxes and levied upon the seized cash. The majority opinion suggested that it would take strong evidence of a substantial additional deterrent effect before it would consider extending the exclusionary rule to what was simply a civil suit for liability that existed without regard to the criminality of defendant's wagering activities. Here, such evidence was lacking: "Working, as we must, with the absence of convincing empirical data, common sense dictates that the deterrent effect of the exclusion of relevant evidence is highly attenuated when the 'punishment' imposed upon the offending criminal enforcement officer is the removal of that evidence from a civil suit by or against a different sovereign."

(d) Administrative proceedings

I.N.S. v. Lopez-Mendoza (1984) concluded that the exclusionary rule should not be applied in civil deportation hearings. The deterrent value of excluding evidence seized by INS officers in the course of arresting illegal aliens was deemed to be reduced in this setting even though, as the dissent pointed out, the evidence was not being used in a "collateral" proceeding, but in the very proceeding "for which the evidence was gathered." Deterrence here was less effective because (i) "deportation will still be possible when evidence not derived directly from the arrest is sufficient to support deportation," and (ii) INS agents know "that it is highly unlikely that any particular arrestee will end up challenging the lawfulness of his arrest." Deterrence also was less needed because (i) "the INS has its own comprehensive scheme for deterring Fourth Amendment violations" by training and discipline, and (ii) "alternative remedies" including the "possibility of declaratory relief" are available for institutional practices violating the Fourth Amendment. On the cost side, the Court found that (i) application of the exclusionary rule "in proceedings that are intended not to punish past transgressions but to prevent their continuance or renewal would require courts to close their eyes to ongoing violations of the law," (ii) invocation of the exclusionary rule at deportation hearings, where "neither the hearing officers nor the attorneys * * * are likely to be well versed in the intricacies of Fourth Amendment law," "might significantly change and complicate the character of these proceedings," and (iii) because many INS arrests "occur in crowded and confused circumstances," application of the exclusionary rule "might well result in the suppression of large amounts of information that had been obtained entirely lawfully."

(e) Habeas corpus

Although the issue posed in federal habeas corpus review of Fourth Amendment claims is not one of applying the exclusionary rule to a proceeding other than the trial, as the habeas petitioner's challenge is to the allegedly erroneous admission of seized evidence at trial, the Court has applied the same basic balancing approach in sharply limiting the cognizability of Fourth Amendment claims on habeas review. *Stone v. Powell* (1976) held that, "where the State has provided an opportunity for full and fair litigation of a Fourth Amendment claim, the Constitution does not require that a state prisoner be granted federal habeas corpus relief on the ground that the evidence obtained in an unconstitutional search and seizure was introduced at his trial." In reaching this result, the *Stone* Court proceeded from the premise that the deterrent function of the exclusionary rule was effectively served by exclusion at trial and the subsequent review of a failure to exclude on direct appeal. There was no reason to assume that "any specific disincentive already created by [these proceedings] * * * would be enhanced if there were the further risk that a conviction obtained in a state court and affirmed on direct review might be overturned in collateral proceedings often occurring years after the incarceration of the defendant." Moreover, on the other side of the cost/benefit ledger was the combination of both the basic "costs of applying the exclusionary rule even at trial" and the additional costs of habeas corpus review. Those additional costs included the consumption of scarce federal judicial resources in providing a second review of exclusionary rule claims, and the delayed finality of the criminal process through collateral proceedings that could be brought long after the original proceedings were completed.

Subsequent rulings have stressed the special character of the Fourth Amendment exclusionary rule and have refused to extend *Stone* to other exclusionary rules. Habeas review has been held fully applicable to claims resting on the admission of evidence at trial in violation of the due process prohibition of unduly suggestive identification procedures, *Manson v. Brathwaite* (1977), the self-incrimination prohibition against use of compelled statements, *Estelle v. Smith* (1981), the due process "voluntariness" test, *Miller v. Fenton* (1985), and admission of statements obtained in violation of *Miranda, Withrow v. Williams* (1993). *Withrow,* in distinguishing *Miranda* violations, noted that *Miranda,* " 'prophylactic' though it may be, in protecting a defendant's Fifth Amendment privilege, * * * safeguards a fundamental trial right." Moreover, unlike *Mapp*'s exclusionary rule, that right did not serve only "some value necessarily divorced from the correct ascertainment of guilt"; by "bracing against the possibility of unreliable statements in every instance of in-custody interrogation, *Miranda* serves to guard against the use of unreliable statements at trial." "Finally and most importantly, eliminating [habeas] review of *Mi-*

randa claims would not significantly benefit the federal courts in their exercise of habeas jurisdiction, or advance the cause of federalism in any substantial way, * * * as [it] would not prevent a state prisoner from simply converting his barred *Miranda* claim into a due process [voluntariness] claim" that would still be cognizable on habeas review.

§ 6.6 DERIVATIVE EVIDENCE

(a) Fruits of the poisonous tree

In *Silverthorne Lumber Co. v. U.S.* (1920), the Court held invalid a subpoena that had been issued on the basis of information acquired through an illegal search. Just as the prosecution could not use in court evidence obtained directly from the unconstitutional search, neither would it be allowed to use evidence obtained indirectly via a subpoena based upon that search. The exclusionary rule was applicable to all evidence "tainted" by the unconstitutional search, and that taint extended to evidence subsequently obtained through the use of information acquired during that search. This *Silverthorne* requirement of exclusion of "secondary" or "derivative" evidence later came to be described as the "fruit of the poisonous tree" doctrine.

Though the "fruits doctrine" was formulated initially in applying the Fourth Amendment's exclusionary rule, it was later applied to other exclusionary rules. Thus, in *Wade*, the Court held that violation of accused's Sixth Amendment right to counsel at a lineup required not only the exclusion of evidence of identification at that lineup but also exclusion of a subsequent in-court identification if it was the fruit of the lineup identification. See § 5.2(c). The Court noted further that the governing standard for determining whether the in-court identification was tainted was the same as that applied in Fourth Amendment cases. So too, in *Nix v. Williams (Williams II)* (1984), considering the admission of secondary evidence (the body of the murder victim) discovered through the Sixth Amendment (*Massiah*) violation presented in *Brewer v. Williams* (§ 4.3(d)), the Court again looked to the "fruits" doctrine (and its "exceptions") as developed in Fourth Amendment cases.

Kastigar v. U.S. (1972), in holding that immunity rendered the self-incrimination privilege inapplicable only if it provided protection against both use and "derivative use" of compelled testimony (§ 4.10(d)), established a form of Fifth Amendment "fruits" doctrine. Indeed, *Kastigar's* description of the scope of the prohibition against derivative use ("barring the use of compelled testimony as an 'investigatory lead' and also barring the use of any evidence obtained by focusing on a witness") may prescribe a more stringent exclusion than the Fourth Amendment doctrine. *Kastigar's* derivative evidence ban arguably would not accept either the inevitable discovery or attenuation limitations (discussed in (c) and (d) infra) that are part of the traditional fruits doctrine. *Kastigar* noted that secondary evidence derived from a coerced confession also must be excluded, but whether the scope of that ban is governed by a standard akin to the Fourth Amendment's fruits doctrine or the arguably more rigorous derivative use prohibition of *Kastigar* remains unclear. Cf. *Harrison v. U.S.* (1968) (applying traditional fruits analysis to evidence derived from a *McNabb-Mallory* violation).

On the other hand, there is one exclusionary rule held not to reach such derivative evidence as would be encompassed by the traditional fruits doctrine, and that is the exclusionary rule of *Miranda*. However, as discussed in subsection (i) infra, the Court arguably has not closed the door to extending the *Miranda* exclusionary rule to at least a limited class of derivative evidence under at least some circumstances.

(b) The "independent source" limitation

In applying the poisonous tree rule, *Silverthorne* stressed that "facts" obtained through a constitutional violation were not necessarily "inaccessible" for court use. The facts could still be proved, the Court noted, "if knowledge of [the facts] is [also] gained from an independent source." Subsequent Supreme Court opinions have cited the second lower court ruling in *Bynum v. U.S.* as presenting a classic application of this independent source rule. See *U.S. v. Crews* (1980). The first *Bynum* decision excluded fingerprints obtained from the defendant after he had been illegally arrested. Cf. *Davis v. Miss.* (§ 2.9(e)). At the time of that arrest, the police had reason to suspect the defendant had been involved in the robbery under investigation, although they lacked probable cause. When Bynum was subsequently reprosecuted, the government sought to use an older set of prints obtained from F.B.I. files, which also matched prints found at the scene of the crime. Since the police had reason to check for Bynum's prints without regard to the illegal arrest, and since the older set of prints had been taken in connection with an unrelated matter, those prints were admitted as independently acquired evidence, "in no way connected with the unlawful arrest." *Bynum v. U.S.* (1960).

The independent source doctrine unlike the purged taint doctrine (see d infra), proceeds from the premise that the source producing the evidence stands apart from the influence of the Fourth Amendment violation, with no links between the two. The Supreme Court twice has spoken to assessing the requisite degree of separateness, and in both instances was sharply divided. In *Murray v. U.S.* (1988), the lower court applied the independent source doctrine on the belief that the police in that case (i) initially had probable cause to obtain a search warrant for contraband, (ii) then unlawfully entered the premises without a warrant, where it learned that the contraband sought was indeed there, (iii) then left the premises and obtained a warrant based only on the previously obtained probable cause (i.e., without any reference to information gathered during the unlawful entry), and (iv) then returned with the warrant and seized the

contraband in the execution of the warrant. The
Supreme Court remanded the case for further findings of fact, but the majority agreed that the independent source doctrine would apply to the situation described by the lower court, provided one
additional finding was made. It must also be
shown that the police decision to seek the warrant
had not been "prompted" by what was learned
during the earlier unlawful entry (i.e., the police
"would have sought a warrant [even] if they had
not earlier entered the [premises]"). Dissenters
argued that this standard was not sufficiently
stringent, and would actually encourage police to
enter premises illegally so as to make certain that
the contraband was there before undertaking the
"inconvenient and time-consuming task" of obtaining the warrant. They advocated what the majority described as "prophylactic rule" that would
mandate "per se inadmissibility" absent a police
demonstration by some "historically verifiable
fact" (e.g., a prior initiation of the warrant process)
that the "subsequent search was totally unaffected
by the prior illegal search." The majority saw no
need for such a requirement, noting that "we see
the incentives differently." An officer with probable cause would be "foolish to enter the premises
first in an unlawful manner" as that would "add to
the normal burden of convincing the magistrate
that there is probable cause the much more oner-
ous burden of convincing a trial court that no
information gained from the illegal entry affected
either the enforcement officers' decision to seek a

warrant or the magistrate's decision to grant it."
Moreover, the present case "provided no basis" for
suggesting a "search first, warrant later [police]
mentality" as the agents apparently had entered
the premises first to "apprehend participants"
rather than "to see if there was anything worth
getting a warrant for."

In *Segura v. U.S.* (1984), the police entered the
premises without a warrant, arrested the occupants and then remained on the scene unlawfully
for many hours while a search warrant was obtained (see § 2.8(e)). That warrant, however, had
been based solely on information acquired prior to
the entry, and the only issue before the court was
the suppression of evidence "not observed during
the initial entry [but] first discovered" in the execution of the "admittedly valid" search warrant.
The dissenters contended that this was not sufficient to establish an independent source, for the
agents "access to the evidence" might have rested
on the illegal entry (the district court having noted
that the evidence "might well" have been destroyed if not for the illegal entry). The majority
found this contention unpersuasive and held the
independent source doctrine applicable. The possibility that the evidence otherwise would have been
removed or destroyed was based on "pure speculation," especially since the police, if they had not
entered the premises, presumably would have utilized alternative tactics that would have prevented
removal (e.g., a "perimeter stakeout") and avoided
alerting the occupants. "Even more important,"

the majority added, "we decline to extend the exclusionary rule, which already exacts an enormous price from society and our system of justice, to further 'protect' criminal activity, as the dissent would have us do."

(c) The "inevitable discovery" limitation

In *Nix v. Williams (Williams II)* (1984), the Court concluded that the fruits doctrine did not bar admission of evidence derived from a constitutional violation if such evidence would "inevitably" have been discovered from lawful investigatory activities without regard to that violation. The inevitable discovery rule differs from the independent source rule in that the question presented is not whether the police did in fact acquire the evidence by reliance upon an untainted source but instead whether evidence in fact obtained through a constitutional violation would otherwise inevitably have been discovered from an untainted source. Yet, as the Supreme Court explained in *Williams II,* the inevitable discovery rule is analytically similar to the independent source rule, in that both are intended to ensure that exclusion does not outrun the deterrence objective: the prosecution is neither "put in a better position than it would have been if no illegality had transpired" nor "put in a worse position simply because of some earlier police error or misconduct." Relying on this rationale, *Williams II* also rejected a lower court ruling that would have allowed the prosecution to justify admissibility on inevitable discovery grounds only if it first established an absence of "bad faith" on the part of the police in engaging in the constitutional violation that actually produced the evidence. Such a limitation, the Court noted, "would place courts in the position of withholding from juries relevant and undoubted truth that would have been available to police absent any unlawful police activity." Contrary to the lower court's assumption, a "bad faith" exception was not needed to ensure that the inevitable discovery rule did not encourage police to take unconstitutional short cuts, since "a police officer who is faced with the opportunity to obtain evidence illegally will rarely, if ever, be in a position to calculate whether the evidence sought would inevitably be discovered."

Williams II does not allow lower courts to apply the inevitable discovery rule upon the basis of nothing more than a hunch or speculation as to what otherwise *might* or *could* have occurred. The prosecution must "establish by a preponderance of the evidence that the information ultimately or inevitably *would* have been discovered by lawful means." The *Williams II* majority concluded that the preponderance standard would suffice here, as it does for most suppression issues (see § 6.9(b)), because "inevitable discovery involves no speculative elements but focuses on demonstrated historical facts capable of ready verification or impeachment." Circumstances justifying application of the inevitable discovery rule are unlikely to be present unless, at the time of the illegal police conduct, there was already in progress an investigation that eventually would have resulted in the discovery of the evidence through routine investigatory procedure. In *Williams II,* a statement illegally obtained from defendant revealed the whereabouts of the murder victim in a roadside ditch, but a group of 200 volunteers was already searching for the body pursuant to a carefully developed plan that eventually would have encompassed the place where the body was found.

(d) The "purged taint" limitation

Even where the secondary evidence would not have been discovered except for the constitutional violation (i.e., there was no independent source or inevitability of discovery), that evidence need not necessarily be banned as the fruit of the poisonous tree. The Court's decisions clearly indicate that the poisonous tree doctrine does not extend as far as a "but for" causation test might take it. If the means of acquiring the secondary evidence are substantially removed and distinguishable from the initial illegality, neither the "deterrence" rationale nor the "judicial integrity" rationale requires application of the exclusionary rule. *Harrison v. U.S.* (1968). Accordingly, as the Court noted in *Wong Sun v. U.S.* (1963), the controlling question is: "[W]hether, granting establishment of the primary illegality, the evidence to which instant objection is made has been come at by exploitation of that illegality or instead by means sufficiently distinguishable to be purged of the primary taint." See also *U.S. v. Wade* (§ 5.2(c)) (discussing the doctrine as applied to an in-court identification as the fruit of a lineup conducted in violation of the Sixth Amendment).

The application of this "purged taint" limitation in the Fourth Amendment context is well illustrated by the Court's rulings in *Wong Sun*. Narcotics agents there entered a dwelling without probable cause and chased down and arrested A, who almost immediately thereafter made a statement accusing B of having sold narcotics. Narcotics were subsequently seized from B, who in turn, implicated C, who was also arrested illegally. Several days later, after having been arraigned and released on his own recognizance, C voluntarily made an oral confession to a narcotics agent during interrogation. A argued that his statement and the narcotics later seized from B were fruits of the illegal entry into his dwelling and his illegal arrest. The Court agreed and both items were excluded. It rejected, however, C's claim that his statement was the fruit of his illegal arrest. Even though C might never have confessed if he had never been arrested illegally, his voluntary action after having been released and warned of his rights had made the "connection between the arrest and the statement * * * so attenuated as to [have] dissipate[d] the taint."

As *Wong Sun* indicates, the taint of initial illegality may be purged by an "intervening independent act" by the defendant or a third party which breaks the causal chain linking illegality and evidence in such a way that the evidence is not viewed as having been obtained by "exploitation of that illegality." Determining whether there has been such an intervening independent act has proved troublesome in several different settings. The most prominent of these settings are discussed in subsections (e)–(h) infra.

(e) The illegal arrest as the poisonous tree

When an unconstitutional arrest leads directly and immediately to a search, the exclusion of evidence seized in that search presents no difficulties. Indeed, a search incident to an unconstitutional arrest is itself unconstitutional, so the Court need not even look to the arrest as the poison tree. The question of exclusion does become complicated, however, where the arrest leads to the production of evidence through the intervening act of the defendant or a third person, as in the case of a confession by the arrestee or an identification of the arrestee by the victim.

Wong Sun, as noted in the previous subsection, excluded from evidence the incriminating statement of one defendant (A) on the ground that it was the fruit of that defendant's illegal arrest. At the same time, the Court also admitted the incriminating statement of another defendant (C) as the product of an "independent act of free will" that purged the taint of his unconstitutional arrest. The two statements considered in *Wong Sun* have been viewed as involving "opposite ends of the pole." However, *Brown v. Ill.* (1975) offered some guidance to the lower courts in dealing with the wide range of fact situations that fall between those extremes.

The police in *Brown* arrested defendant without probable cause in order to question him concerning a murder. Defendant was then taken to the police station, warned of his *Miranda* rights, and interrogated. He made an initial incriminating statement within two hours after his arrest, was interrogated again several hours later (after the *Miranda* warnings were repeated), and then made a second incriminating statement. The state supreme court upheld the admission of both statements on the ground that the *Miranda* warnings automatically purged the taint of defendant's illegal arrest. The Supreme Court unanimously rejected the state court's view of the impact of the *Miranda* warnings. A majority also found that, on the facts of the case, both statements were the fruit of the illegal arrest.

With respect to the *Miranda* warnings, the *Brown* opinion noted: "[T]he *Miranda* warnings, *alone* and *per se,* cannot always make the act [of confessing] sufficiently a product of free will to break, for Fourth Amendment purposes, the causal connection between the illegality and the confession. * * * The *Miranda* warnings are an important factor, to be sure, in determining whether the confession is obtained by exploitation of an illegal arrest. But they are not the only factor to be considered. The temporal proximity of the arrest and the confession, the presence of intervening circumstances, and, particularly, the purpose and flagrancy of the official misconduct are all relevant."

After examining the *Brown* fact situation in light of the factors noted above, the majority concluded that the prosecution had failed to meet its burden of establishing the dissipation of the initial taint. Defendant's first statement was made within two hours of his arrest and the later, second statement was the fruit of the first. No intervening acts of significance (such as presentment before a magistrate, consultation with counsel, or release from custody) had occurred between the arrest and the first statement. Moreover, the majority emphasized, the illegality had "a quality of purposefulness." The "impropriety of the arrest was obvious"; it had been undertaken as an "expedition for evidence" and had been executed in a manner which "gave the appearance of having been calculated to cause surprise, fright, and confession." Compare *Rawlings v. Ky.* (1980) (where defendant was illegally detained for a short period in the "congenial atmosphere" of a friend's house, *Miranda* warnings were given shortly before he made an incriminating statement, the statement appeared to be a spontaneous reaction to a search of another person, and the police conduct did not rise to the level of "conscious or flagrant misconduct," the state had carried its burden of showing that the statement was not the fruit of the illegal detention).

A multifactored analysis similar to that adopted in *Brown* also has been applied in determining whether an eyewitness identification following an illegal arrest should be excluded as the fruit of the poisonous tree. Here the temporal proximity is likely to be an insignificant factor as the time which passes between the illegal arrest and the identification has little bearing in itself on the factors that produced the identification, although it may shed light on the purpose of the arrest. The two leading Supreme Court cases on post-illegal-arrest identifications involved arrests that apparently were not motivated by a desire to present the defendant for possible identification, so the Court had no reason to discuss there the element of "purposefulness"; but that element would seem to have a significance in the identification context similar to that which it had in *Brown.* The critical factor in both of the Supreme Court rulings was presence of an "intervening circumstance" that was viewed as having broken the causal connection.

In *Johnson v. La.* (1972), after being subjected to what he alleged to be an unlawful arrest, and before being placed in a lineup, defendant received the assistance of counsel and was brought before a magistrate, who advised him of his rights and set bail. The Supreme Court concluded that "at the time of the lineup, the detention of the [defendant] was under the authority of [the magistrate's] commitment," and "consequently the lineup was conducted not by 'exploitation' of the challenged arrest, but by 'means sufficiently distinguishable to be purged of the primary taint.' " In *U.S. v. Crews* (1980), the Court, on similar grounds, held that an at-trial identification of defendant by a robbery victim was not a fruit of the defendant's earlier illegal arrest. The Court noted that none of the "three distinct elements" of the victim's in-court identification—the victim's presence at trial, her ability to reconstruct the prior criminal occurrence and identify the offender, and the defendant's physical presence in the courtroom—"had been come at by exploitation of the violation of the defendant's Fourth Amendment rights." With respect to the third element, the Court noted that *Frisbie v. Collins* (§ 6.3(c)) and similar cases had firmly established that a defendant "cannot claim immunity from prosecution simply because his appearance in court was precipitated by an unlawful arrest."

In each of the above cases, the illegality of the arrest went to the foundation of the arrest. In *N.Y. v. Harris* (1990), the police had probable cause to make an arrest, but the Fourth Amendment had been violated when the police entered the dwelling to make the arrest without an arrest warrant, contrary to *Payton v. N.Y.* (§ 2.7(a)). The Court here turned from a multifactored analysis to a per se rule: "where the police have probable cause to arrest a suspect, the exclusionary rule does not bar the State's use of a statement made by the defendant outside of his home, even though the statement is taken after an arrest made in the home in

violation of *Payton.*" Once the defendant was removed from his home, the majority reasoned, his
continued custody was lawful (as the police did
have probable cause) and the statement should not
be treated as the fruit of an arrest occurring in the
home as opposed to somewhere else.

(f) The tainted witness

Prior to *U.S. v. Ceccolini* (1978), lower courts had
taken a variety of positions in cases in which a
constitutional violation had led to the discovery of
a prosecution witness. Some had argued that the
witness' testimony was never an inadmissible fruit
since the witness' decision to testify was always an
intervening act that purged the taint. Others had
argued that the witness' decision should largely be
ignored and the testimony treated no differently
than physical evidence. *Ceccolini* rejected both of
these positions, adopting a position that looked, as
in *Brown,* to a multifactored analysis of the particular situation.

The potentially tainted witness in *Ceccolini* was
a sales clerk in a flower shop who had been present
when a visiting patrolman conducted an illegal
search by opening an envelope lying on the cash
register. The officer found that the envelope contained policy slips, but he did not tell the clerk of
his discovery. Several months later, an F.B.I.
agent, informed of the patrolman's discovery, questioned the clerk about her employer's activities.
She expressed a willingness to help and related the
incident involving the patrolman and the envelope.

The issue before the Court was whether the sales clerk's subsequent testimony against her employer at trial should be suppressed as the fruit of the officer's search. The Supreme Court held that the fruits doctrine did not bar admission of her testimony.

The *Ceccolini* opinion initially rejected the contention that the case before it should be treated no differently than one in which police discovered physical evidence. The function of the exclusionary rule, the Court noted, requires that special consideration be given to the element of "free will" that might be involved in the witness' decision to testify. The "greater the willingness of the witness to freely testify, the greater the likelihood that he or she will be discovered by legal means and, concomitantly, the smaller the incentive to conduct an illegal search to discover the witness." The exclusion of a tainted witness also involves different considerations because it can "perpetually disable a witness from testifying about relevant and material facts, regardless of how unrelated such testimony might be to the purpose of the originally illegal search."

While *Ceccolini* stressed that the exclusionary rule should be invoked "with much greater reluctance" as applied to "live testimony" than to an "inanimate object," it refused to accept the government's position that the testimony of a witness should always be admissible "no matter how close and proximate the connection between it and a violation of the Fourth Amendment." In determining whether the taint was purged, consideration must be given to the "time, place, and manner," of the initial questioning of the witness and its relationship to the initial illegality. In this case, several factors led to the conclusion that the taint of the illegal search had been dissipated: (i) "the testimony given by the witness was an act of her own free will in no way coerced or even induced by official authority"; (ii) the illegally discovered slips were not used in questioning the witness; (iii) substantial time passed between the search and the F.B.I. officer's contact with the witness and between that contact and her eventual testimony; (iv) the flower shop had been under F.B.I. surveillance even before the patrolman discovered the slips; and (v) there was "not the slightest evidence" that the patrolman made the search "with the intent of finding a willing and knowledgeable witness to testify against [the defendant]."

(g) Multiple confessions

In *U.S. v. Bayer* (1947) the Supreme Court noted that, "after an accused has once let the cat out of the bag by confessing, no matter what the inducement, he is never thereafter free of the psychological and practical disadvantages of having confessed. * * * In such a sense, a later confession always may be looked upon as a fruit of the first." The Court refused, however, to adopt a "per se rule" that "perpetually disables the confessor from making a usable [confession] after those conditions [which produced the first inadmissible confession] have been removed." Post-*Bayer* rulings dealing with successive confessions have fashioned separate standards for determining the admissibility of the second confession, dependent upon the nature of the illegality that required exclusion of the first confession. Where that first confession was a fruit of a Fourth Amendment violation, the Court asks whether the second confession is, in turn, the fruit of the first. See *Brown v. Ill.* (§ 6.6(e)). On the other hand, where the original confession is inadmissible under the "voluntariness" standard of due process, the Court asks whether the impact of the coercion that rendered the first confession involuntary has also rendered the second confession involuntary. *Darwin v. Conn.* (1968). This difference in the statement of the governing standard arguably follows from the position that "the exclusionary rule, * * * when utilized to effectuate the Fourth Amendment, serves interests and policies that are distinct from those it serves under the Fifth." *Brown.* In application, the two standards tend to produce the same result, as each looks to whether, "considering the totality of the circumstances," there was a "break in the stream of events * * * sufficient to insulate the final events [producing the second confession] from the effect of all that went before." *Darwin.* However, as discussed in subsection (i) infra, the Court in *Ore. v. Elstad* obviously assumed that application of a voluntariness test in determining the admissibility

of the second confession will produce a quite different result than the fruits doctrine where the first
confession is inadmissible only because of a *Miranda* violation.

(h) Guilty pleas as the fruit of the poisonous tree

In *Pa. ex rel. Herman v. Claudy* (1956), the Court
noted that a plea of guilty entered by an uncounseled defendant was "involuntary" (and consequently invalid, see § 8.5(a)) if the plea was "based
on a confession extorted [from defendant] by violence or mental coercion." This aspect of the law
governing guilty pleas is viewed as a special application of the fruits doctrine since the characterization of the plea as involuntary rests largely on the
finding that it is the fruit of the coerced confession.
Consistent with this analysis, the fact that the plea
might not have been entered "but for" the earlier
constitutional violation does not necessarily render
it invalid; the taint of the initial violation may
have been "purged" by intervening events. Thus,
in *McMann v. Richardson* (1970), the Court held
that a defendant who pleaded guilty with assistance of counsel does not establish the invalidity of
that plea by alleging "that he pleaded guilty because of a prior coerced confession." Though defendant pleaded guilty as a result of counsel's
mistaken belief that the confession would probably
be admissible and produce a conviction, that causal
connection alone does not render the plea involuntary. Assuming that counsel's advice was compe-

tent, the consultation with counsel and the subsequent determination to plead are viewed as independent intervening acts that "purged" the taint. As the Court later noted, in the absence of special circumstances, a "guilty plea represents a break in the chain of events which has preceded it in the criminal process." *Tollett v. Henderson* (1973).

The *McMann* analysis does recognize certain exceptional circumstances which permit a successful challenge to a guilty plea based upon a prior constitutional violation in the acquisition of evidence. Thus, the *McMann* Court noted that a plea would be open to challenge where the defendant acted without counsel and entered the plea based upon such evidence. See *Pa. ex rel. Herman v. Claudy.* Similarly, a plea may be challenged where the oppressive circumstances that produced a constitutional violation (e.g., a coerced confession) had an "abiding impact and also taint[ed] the plea." Cf. *Chambers v. Fla.* (1940).

(i) *Miranda* violations and the fruits doctrine

In *Ore. v. Elstad* (1985), defendant initially made a brief incriminating statement after having been taken into custody at his home and questioned briefly by the arresting officers without *Miranda* warnings. He was questioned again at the police station, after having been given his *Miranda* warnings, and responded with a much more incriminating and extensive second statement. Noting the impact of having let the "cat out of the bag," the lower court held that the second statement was inadmissible as the fruit of the *Miranda* violation which invalidated the first statement. The Supreme Court disagreed, holding that the fruits doctrine was inapplicable to a *Miranda* violation. The admissibility of the second confession depended on whether it was voluntary, and the initial failure to provide *Miranda* warnings was insufficient to produce a coerced second confession even though the "cat had been let out of the bag."

In explaining why the fruits doctrine was inapplicable, the *Elstad* majority stressed "fundamental differences between the role of the Fourth Amendment exclusionary rule and the function of *Miranda* in guarding against prosecutorial use of compelled statements as prohibited by the Fifth Amendment." The fruits doctrine had been developed in the context of the Fourth Amendment exclusionary rule, where the objective was to deter unreasonable searches no matter how probative their fruits. *Miranda,* on the other hand, sought to serve the Fifth Amendment prohibition against the use of compelled statements. Moreover, it did so by adopting an exclusionary rule that "sweeps more broadly" than the Fifth itself by establishing an irrebuttable presumption that unwarned statements obtained through custodial interrogation are compelled. This prophylactic element of *Miranda* would not be carried, however, beyond prohibiting the state's use of the unwarned statement in its case in chief. Just as *Miranda* had been held not to bar use of an unwarned but voluntary statement for impeachment use (§ 6.7(b)), so too it should not bar use of a subsequently obtained statement where there was compliance with *Miranda* in obtaining that second statement and the earlier unwarned statement was voluntary. The critical question here simply should be whether the second statement was "knowingly and voluntarily made."

Having concluded that the standard governing the admissibility of second confession should be the due process voluntariness test, the *Elstad* Court discussed at length the appropriate application of that test in a case where the first confession was inadmissible solely because of a *Miranda* violation. That situation, the Court stressed, was quite different from previous multiple confession cases in which the first confession was itself involuntary (see (g) supra). There, because of the coercion employed in obtaining the first confession, a presumption of continuing compulsion could require a showing of substantial intervening events that offset the impact of the initial coercion. Where the initial confession was voluntary but unwarned, "a careful and thorough administration of *Miranda* warnings serves to cure the condition that rendered the unwarned statement inadmissible." Consistent with *Bayer* ((g) supra), the psychological impact of the voluntary disclosure in the first statement cannot be treated as "state compulsion" that "compromises the voluntariness of a subsequently informed waiver." Neither was it appropriate to deem that waiver less than fully informed because defendant had not been told that his first statement could not be used against him due to the

Miranda violation. "This Court," *Elstad* noted, "has never embraced the theory that the defendant's ignorance of the full consequences of his decisions vitiates their voluntariness." The officers here had not attempted to "exploit the [earlier] unwarned admission to pressure [the suspect] into waiving his right to remain silent," and they should not be expected to give the suspect legal advice as to the inadmissibility of his earlier statement.

Although the *Elstad* Court had before it only the question of whether the fruits doctrine should apply to a second confession following an initial *Miranda* violation, the Court's language certainly suggested that the fruits doctrine was not applicable to any type of secondary evidence derived from a *Miranda* violation. The *Elstad* opinion noted, for example, that application of the fruits doctrine assumes a "constitutional violation," but that unwarned questioning in itself violated only prophylactic standards laid down to safeguard against such a violation. The Court relied heavily in this regard upon *Mich. v. Tucker* (1974). *Tucker* rejected the applicability of the fruits doctrine in refusing to suppress the testimony of a witness whose identity had been discovered through a statement obtained in violation of *Miranda*. The *Tucker* case involved various factors that arguably limited its implications (e.g., the police interrogation had occurred prior to the date of the *Miranda* ruling, and the deviation between the warnings given and the *Miranda* requirements was not substantial), but the *Tucker* opinion spoke in general terms of the difference between a *Miranda* violation and the denial of rights "themselves * * * protected by the Constitution." Relying on this language, *Elstad* noted that "[*Tucker*'s] reasoning applies with equal force when the alleged 'fruit' of a noncoercive *Miranda* violation is neither a witness nor an article of evidence but the accused's own voluntary testimony." The implication of this statement surely is that the rejection of the fruits doctrine in *Elstad* and *Tucker* will be applied across the board to all secondary evidence derived from a *Miranda* violation.

The *Elstad* opinion also contained language, however, that could lead to a less sweeping rejection of the fruits doctrine in the context of *Miranda* violations. The Court did stress the various influences that may lead an arrested person to issue a second confession and the insulating quality of *Miranda* warning given prior to the obtaining of the second confession—factors that result in a causal connection far less direct than when a statement obtained in violation of *Miranda* leads police directly to physical evidence. This additional emphasis led Justice Brennan, dissenting in *Elstad*, to suggest that the Court's opinion "surely ought not be read as also foreclosing application of the traditional derivative-evidence presumption [of exclusion] to physical evidence obtained as a proximate result of a *Miranda* violation."

§ 6.7 IMPEACHMENT

(a) Fourth Amendment violations

In *Walder v. U.S.* (1954), the defendant, charged with purchasing and possessing heroin, asserted on direct examination that he had never purchased, sold or handled narcotics at any time "in my life." Responding to that claim, the prosecution sought to impeach defendant by reference to a heroin capsule that had been seized illegally from his home in his presence approximately two years earlier. Defense objected on the ground that the capsule had been suppressed as illegally seized in an earlier prosecution, but the trial court allowed the prosecution's line of questioning (and introduction of direct evidence when defendant denied the previous seizure), advising the jury that it could be considered "solely for the purpose of impeaching the defendant's credibility." The Supreme Court affirmed, noting that "it is one thing to say that the Government cannot make any affirmative use of evidence unlawfully obtained, [but] * * * quite another to say that the defendant can turn the illegal method by which evidence in the Government's possession was obtained to his own advantage, and provide him with a shield against contradiction of his untruths." The Court reasoned that the defendant "must be free to deny all the elements of the case against him without thereby giving lease to the Government to introduce by way of rebuttal evidence illegally secured to it * * *. Beyond that, however, there is hardly justification for letting the defendant affirmatively resort to perjurious testimony in reliance on the Government's disability to challenge his credibility."

In *Harris v. N.Y.* (1971), a divided Court relied upon *Walder* to uphold the use of defendant's prior statement to a police officer, obtained in violation of *Miranda,* to impeach his trial testimony. Unlike *Walder,* the illegally obtained evidence in *Harris* had been acquired in the investigation of the offense currently charged against defendant. Also, defendant was impeached "as to testimony bearing more directly on the crimes charged" than the "collateral" matter introduced in Walder's testimony. The majority concluded, however, that neither distinction suggested any "difference in principle that warrants a result different from * * * *Walder.*" The *Harris* opinion clearly indicated, as was substantiated in *U.S. v. Havens,* infra, that the same result would have been reached if the impeachment evidence had been obtained by a Fourth Amendment violation.

In *U.S. v. Havens* (1980), the Supreme Court partially accepted and partially rejected another possible limitation upon the impeachment exception to the exclusionary rule. The defendant in *Havens,* on direct examination, denied that he had been "engage[d]" in the smuggling activities of his traveling companion. On cross-examination, defendant was asked whether he had anything to do with his companion's makeshift underwear pockets

in which the smuggled cocaine was carried. When
defendant gave a negative response, the prosecutor
sought to impeach that denial by reference to an
illegal search of defendant's suitcase in which police found the material from which the pockets had
been cut. Defendant argued that the illegally
seized material should not be available for impeachment because that evidence did not "squarely
contradict" his direct testimony, as opposed to his
cross-examination testimony. A divided Supreme
Court rejected that argument. It refused to adopt
a "flat rule" that would restrict the impeachment
exception to impeachment of direct testimony, but
it also noted that the extension of that exception to
impeachment of cross-examination testimony was
not without limits. The Court distinguished a pre-
Walder ruling, *Agnello v. U.S.* (1925), in which
impeachment by reference to illegally seized evidence had been disallowed. The *Havens* majority
noted that *Agnello* had been a case in which "the
government had 'smuggled in' the impeaching opportunity in the course of cross-examination." In
Havens, on the other hand, the questions asked on
cross-examination "would have been suggested to a
reasonably competent cross-examiner by Havens'
direct examination." Under that circumstance,
prohibiting impeachment by reference to reliable
but illegally obtained evidence would be contrary
to the emphasis in *Harris* and *Walder* on the
"defendant's obligation to speak the truth in response to proper questions."

(b) Fifth Amendment evidence

As noted above, *Harris v. N.Y.* (1971) held that an impeachment exception also applied to the *Miranda* exclusionary rule. The majority there rejected the contention that the exception had been developed in Fourth Amendment cases and should not apply to *Miranda* violations because of *Miranda*'s Fifth Amendment foundation. Viewing *Miranda*'s exclusionary rule as serving a deterrent function similar to the Fourth Amendment exclusionary rule, the *Harris* majority concluded that that function was adequately served by excluding evidence from the prosecution's case-in-chief and did not require providing "a license to use perjury." See also *Ore. v. Hass* (1975) (impeachment use permitted where officer obtained statement, in violation of *Miranda,* by continuing interrogation after defendant asked for a lawyer; "speculative possibility" that this interrogation technique would be employed purposely to gain impeachment evidence was not sufficient to change the "balance * * * struck in *Harris*").

The *Harris* opinion suggested that the ruling there might not apply to involuntary confessions. The Court noted that the case before it did not involve a "coerced confession," and commented that, "of course," the "trustworthiness" of any statement used for impeachment must satisfy "legal standards." In *Mincey v. Ariz.* (1978), the *Harris* suggestion was converted into a direct ruling that involuntary statements could not be used for impeachment purposes. This ruling was later explained as resting on more than the potential untrustworthiness of involuntary confessions. A coerced confession, it was noted, involves the application of the Fifth Amendment privilege "in its most pristine form," while *Miranda* violations involve a rule designed "to deter unlawful police conduct." Because of *Miranda*'s prophylactic function, some balancing was permissible in *Harris,* but not in *Mincey.* See also *N.J. v. Portash* (1979) (holding that grand jury testimony given pursuant to a grant of immunity was coerced testimony, similar to an involuntary confession, and therefore could not be used for impeachment even though it was at least as reliable as the statements used for that purpose in *Harris*).

(c) Sixth Amendment violations

Mich. v. Harvey (1990) overturned a state court ruling that had barred impeachment use of defendant's statement because it had been obtained in violation of the ruling in *Mich. v. Jackson* (§ 4.3(f)). *Jackson* held that any statement given by an accused in a discussion initiated by police after the accused had earlier requested counsel was presumptively based on an invalid waiver of his Sixth Amendment right to counsel. That presumption, the majority in *Harvey* noted, operated simply as a "prophylactic rule" designed to ensure "voluntary, knowing, and intelligent waivers of the Sixth Amendment rights," and "did not mark the exact boundary of the Sixth Amendment right itself." The violation of *Jackson* did not invariably mean that the statement was not in fact based on a voluntary, knowing, and intelligent waiver, just as a violation of *Miranda* did not invariably mean a statement was compelled in violation of the Fifth Amendment. Accordingly, the logic of *Harris* applied, and the "shield provided by the prophylactic rule [would not] be perverted into a license to use perjury by way of a defense, free from the risk of confrontation with prior inconsistent utterances."

The *Harvey* ruling was strictly limited to *Jackson* violations. The Court noted that, since the state court had not decided whether the waiver in this case was knowing and voluntary under "traditional standards," it "need not consider the admissibility for impeachment purposes of a voluntary statement obtained in the absence of a knowing and voluntary waiver of the right to counsel." The majority did state that it had previously "mandated the exclusion of reliable and probative evidence for *all* purposes [i.e., including impeachment] only when it is derived from involuntary statements" (citing *Portash* and *Mincey,* discussed supra), and it obviously assumed, in the question it left open, that Sixth Amendment waivers may be invalid under "traditional standards" and not necessarily produce "involuntary" (i.e., "compelled") statements. However, the *Harvey* dissenters, who viewed the facts there as presenting "a plain violation of respondent's Sixth Amendment rights," cited support for the proposition that the Sixth Amendment operated in much the same way as the Fifth Amendment in barring all use of statements.

Citing some of the cases discussed in § 6.1(b), the dissenters argued that "the exclusion of statements made by a represented and indicted defendant outside the presence of counsel follows not as a remedy for a violation that has preceded trial, but as a necessary incident of the constitutional right itself." The majority in *Harvey* had no need to settle the question as to whether this is the proper characterization of the operation of the Amendment in excluding evidence.

(d) Defendant's silence

In *Doyle v. Ohio* (1976) and several later cases, the Court moved from impeachment by reference to illegally obtained statements to impeachment by reference to defendant's prior silence. *Doyle* rejected the contention that *Harris* should be extended to allow general impeachment by reference to the fact that defendant, in contrast to his exculpatory testimony at trial, had refused to give any statement to the police after receiving his *Miranda* warnings. The Court stressed that "silence in the wake of warnings may be nothing more than the arrestee's exercise of *Miranda* rights." Moreover, it noted, the implicit message of the warnings is that the defendant's exercise of his right of silence will "carry no penalty"; it therefore would be "fundamentally unfair," after giving the warnings, to then use the silence to "impeach an explanation subsequently offered at trial."

Later cases limited *Doyle* to the special element of unfairness presented where the government had induced defendant's silence through the *Miranda* warnings. Thus, *Anderson v. Charles* (1980) allowed impeachment by prior inconsistent statements given after *Miranda* warnings because "a defendant who voluntarily speaks after receiving *Miranda* warnings has not been induced to remain silent." Also distinguishing *Doyle, Jenkins v. Anderson* (1980) held that the constitution did not bar impeachment by reference to the defendant's prearrest silence. When the defendant in *Jenkins* testified at trial that he had killed in self-defense, the prosecutor forced him to acknowledge on cross-examination that he had not reported the killing to the police until two weeks later. Here, unlike *Doyle,* the defendant's silence had not been "induced by governmental action" since "the failure to speak occurred before he had been taken into custody and given *Miranda* warnings." *Fletcher v. Weir* (1982) extended *Jenkins* to allow impeachment by post-arrest silence not preceded by *Miranda* warnings.

Two concurring justices in *Jenkins* contended that the issue presented there was not truly one of a state's attempt to impeach by reference to defendant's exercise of a constitutional right because "the privilege against compulsory self-incrimination is simply irrelevant to a citizen's decision to remain silent when he is under no official compulsion to speak." This view, which presumably would require at least custodial interrogation before silence would be viewed as an exercise of the suspect's self-incrimination privilege, finds support in various cases holding that the Fifth Amendment applies only to "official coercion" directed at producing a statement. See § 4.7(a),(c). The *Jenkins* majority found no reason to reach this issue because even if there had been an exercise of the privilege, *Raffel v. U.S.* (1926) had held that impeachment by reference to the exercise of the privilege in a prior proceeding (in *Raffel*, defendant's silence at an earlier trial on the same charge) did not impose an impermissible burden on the exercise of the privilege. *Doyle*, the *Jenkins* majority noted, did not undermine the *Raffel* ruling. It was based strictly on due process grounds of "fundamental unfairness" that had no bearing when the exercise of the privilege had not been induced by advice such as that contained in the *Miranda* warnings.

(e) Third party impeachment

In *James v. Ill.* (1990), a divided Court refused to extend the impeachment exception to permit the prosecution to introduce unconstitutionally obtained evidence to impeach defense witnesses other than the defendant, even though their testimony was directly contradicted by that evidence. At issue in *James* was the use of an admission obtained from defendant as a fruit of a Fourth Amendment violation, but the Court's rationale was not restricted to the character of the underlying constitutional violation. Expanding the impeachment exception to cover third-party witnesses, the majority reasoned, "would not promote the truth-seeking function to the same extent as did the creation of the original exception, and yet it would significantly undermine the deterrent effect of the general exclusionary rule." The additional contribution to truthfinding would be limited because (1) the threat of subsequent criminal prosecution for false testimony is alone more likely to deter a defense witness than a defendant, and (2) such expansion "likely would chill some defendants from presenting their best defense * * * through the testimony of others," as a variety of factors would make problematic the potential for a defense witness to offer truthful testimony but also "make some statement in sufficient tension with the tainted evidence to allow the prosecution to introduce that evidence for impeachment." On the other side, deterrence through exclusion from the case-in-chief would lose much of its sting, as allowing impeachment use "to *all* witnesses would significantly enhance the expected value to the prosecution of illegally obtained evidence," both by "vastly increas[ing] the number of occasions in which such evidence could be used" and by "deter[ing] defendants from calling witnesses in the first place."

§ 6.8 STANDING

(a) "Personal rights" analysis

In order to raise a constitutional challenge to governmental action, a litigant must have a sufficient interest in the challenged action to be said to have "standing" to present that claim. The standing requirement demands that the objecting party establish at least that "personal stake in the outcome of the controversy" as will "assure that concrete adversariness which sharpens the presentation of issues upon which the Court so largely depends for illumination of difficult constitutional questions." *Baker v. Carr* (1962). In a criminal case, that minimal requirement presumably is met by the defendant's interest in challenging the admissibility of evidence, for his avoidance of a conviction (obviously a significant personal stake) may rest on the success of his challenge.

In many areas of constitutional law, however, the Court has required for standing more than a minimal adverse interest; it has insisted also that the litigant's adverse interest be based upon a violation of his personal rights, rather than the violation of the rights of a third party which indirectly affects the litigant. *Tileston v. Ullman* (1943). As applied to the exclusionary remedy, this principle would deny standing to defendants who are objecting to the prosecution's use of evidence obtained through the violation of the rights of others. The *Wong Sun* case, described in § 6.4(d), is illustrative. Where the illegal arrest of A led to the illegal seizure of narcotics in B's home and that, in turn, led to the subsequent arrest of C at another location, the narcotics could not be introduced in evidence against A, but could be introduced against C. A had standing because the seizure of the narcotics was the fruit of his illegal arrest, although he could not contest the seizure insofar as it violated the rights of B. C, on the other hand, totally lacked standing because neither the arrest of A nor the subsequent seizure of narcotics in B's home violated his constitutional rights.

The requirement that a litigant assert his "personal rights" and not those of third parties "has not been imposed uniformly as a firm constitutional mandate" of standing. *Flast v. Cohen* (1968). Thus, the argument was advanced that an exception to the "personal rights" requirement should be adopted for claims based upon the Fourth Amendment's exclusionary rule, thereby strengthening the rule's deterrent impact. In *Alderman v. U.S.* (1969), the Supreme Court rejected this argument in the context of claimed "third-party" standing to challenge unconstitutional electronic surveillance.

The *Alderman* majority denied the alternative contentions that (i) all defendants should derive standing to challenge evidence obtained from the illegal wiretapping of others, (ii) at least codefendants and coconspirators should have standing to suppress evidence obtained through illegal wiretapping of other codefendants or coconspirators, or (iii) a special standing rule should be recognized to permit a defendant to exclude evidence obtained unlawfully from the wiretapping of another when that wiretapping was "directed at" obtaining evidence for the prosecution of the defendant. Two dissenters supported the latter position, commonly described as "target standing." However, the court majority concluded that there was "no necessity" to depart from "the general rule that Fourth Amendment rights are personal rights which * * * may not be vicariously asserted." It did not follow from the adoption of the exclusionary rule "that anything which deters illegal searches [must] thereby [be] commanded by the Fourth Amendment." The majority was "not convinced that the additional benefits of extending the exclusionary rule to other defendants [i.e., non-victims] would justify further encroachment upon the public interest in prosecuting those accused of crime and having them acquitted or convicted on the basis of all the evidence which exposes the truth."

In reaching the above conclusion, the *Alderman* majority relied in part on the deterrent impact of other sanctions against illegal electronic eavesdropping provided in Title III (see § 3.2(b)). However, in *Rakas v. Ill.* (1978), the Court made it clear that the *Alderman* analysis rejected third party standing for all Fourth Amendment cases. See also *U.S. v. Payner* (1980) (federal lower court lacked authority to use its supervisory power to bypass *Alderman* limits by allowing a defendant to gain suppression of evidence obtained through calculated and deliberate violation of the Fourth Amendment rights of another that had been undertaken specifically to obtain evidence against persons such as defendant).

(b) Identifying the issue

The Court's insistence upon a "personal rights" approach to standing makes the issue of standing a fairly simple one in dealing with challenges based upon the Fifth Amendment, Sixth Amendment, or due process. The nature of the constitutional right involved clearly identifies the person who may be the victim of an alleged violation. In the case of an allegedly coerced confession, for example, the victim is the defendant from whom the confession was obtained, and not those who may have been mentioned in the confession and may now be objecting to use against them of evidence discovered through the confession. In the application of the Fourth Amendment exclusionary rule, however, a determination of whose rights were violated by a particular search or seizure can be much more difficult. A search can invade the justified expectation of privacy of more than one person, and where that is claimed, the Court commonly resolves that issue under the personal rights approach to standing. In *Alderman,* for example, after rejecting third-party standing, the Court had to consider exactly whose rights were violated by an illegal wiretap. The Court concluded that the violation extended not only to the parties to the unlawfully overheard conversations, but also to the owner of the residence in which the tapped phone was located, even though he had not been a party to those conversations.

Although the question of whether the defendant seeking exclusion was himself the victim of the challenged Fourth Amendment violation had traditionally been discussed under the heading of standing, *Rakas* suggested that separate treatment of standing was no longer necessary after the Court's flat rejection of third-party standing in *Alderman*. *Rakas* saw no "useful analytical purpose" in considering the defendant's victim-status as a matter "apart from the merits of the defendant's Fourth Amendment claim." The appropriate question, the Court noted, is whether the "disputed search infringed an interest of the defendant which the Fourth Amendment was designed to protect." Perhaps because the Court foresaw some confusion between the question asked in determining whether there was a search (did the police intrude upon *anyone*'s justified expectation of privacy) and the question traditionally labeled as one of standing (did the police intrude upon *this defendant's* expectation of privacy), its subsequent opinions have not totally discarded the practice of referring to the latter issue as one of standing. See e.g., *Ark. v. Sanders* (1979).

Whether the issue is described as one of standing or one of defining the scope of Fourth Amendment rights, particular attention must be given to the precise police conduct being called into question. It must be recalled that the fruits doctrine can readily give the defendant the right to challenge evidence obtained during a search of the premises of another, even though the defendant has no expectation of privacy in those premises and clearly was not a victim of that search. In *Wong Sun*, for example, defendant A was allowed to object to the prosecution's use of narcotics found in B's house because the search of B's house was the fruit of the illegal entry into A's home and A's illegal arrest. In the cases discussed below in subsections (c), (d) and (e), the challenges generally were directed at the searches that directly produced the seized evidence, rather than reliance upon the fruits doctrine and some earlier violation. Those cases discuss three types of interests that have been advanced, with varying success, to establish standing in search and seizure cases.

(c) Legitimate presence at the site of the search

In *Jones v. U.S.* (1960), an occasional occupant of an apartment was held to have standing to object to a search of that apartment conducted while he was present. The *Jones* opinion rejected the view that a party whose privacy was interrupted by an unlawful search only had standing if he had some recognized property right in the premises. The Court noted that property distinctions such as those between "lessee, licensee, invitee, and guest, often only of gossamer strength, ought not to be determinative in fashioning procedures ultimately referable to constitutional safeguards." It concluded that "anyone legitimately on the premises where a search occurs may challenge its legality * * * when its fruits are proposed to be used against him."

In *Rakas v. Ill.* (1978), the majority reexamined and recast the *Jones* ruling. The Court reaffirmed that the "arcane distinctions" of property law were not controlling. It did not follow, however, that any person legitimately on the premises necessarily had an expectation of privacy in the searched portion of the premises. The defendant in *Jones*, the Court noted, occasionally stayed at the apartment searched in that case and had been given a key to the apartment by the owner. At the time of the search, he was the only occupant of the apartment. Under these circumstances, he had a legitimate expectation of privacy in the apartment, but this did not mean that all persons legitimately on the premises would have such an expectation. The Court offered two illustrations of cases in which legitimate presence would not be sufficient. A "casual visitor who had never seen, or been permitted to visit the basement of another's house" could not object to a search of the basement simply because he happened to be in the kitchen of the house at the time of the search. Likewise, "a casual visitor who walks into a house one minute before the search commences and leaves one minute after the search ends" would not have a reasonable expectation of privacy in the search of the house.

Once the *Rakas* majority had rejected legitimate presence as an "automatic measure" of standing, it had little difficulty with the case before it. The defendants in *Rakas* were two passengers in a car that had been stopped in connection with the investigation of a robbery. After the occupants were ordered out of the car, the police searched it and found a sawed-off rifle under the front passenger seat and a box of rifle shells in the glove compartment. The Court found that the defendants had no protected Fourth Amendment interests in the areas searched. The glove compartment and the area under the seat, "like the trunk of the automobile, are areas in which a passenger qua passenger simply would not have a legitimate expectation of privacy." The *Rakas* majority stressed, however, that it was dealing with defendants whose only claim of privacy rested on their status as passengers in the automobile. It noted that the petitioners "asserted neither a property nor a possessory interest in the automobile, nor an interest in the property seized." A concurring opinion further noted that neither had the defendants challenged the "constitutionality of the police action in stopping the automobile" or in ordering the defendants out of the automobile. Cf. *Wong Sun.*

(d) Possessory interest in the premises

A defendant with a present possessory interest in the premises searched, such as the owner or lessee of a house, thereby commonly has a legitimate expectation of privacy in those premises. That interest gives him standing to challenge the search even though he was not present when the search was made. *Chapman v. U.S.* (1961). The "possessory" interest which provides standing under this analysis ordinarily encompasses any interest which grants the defendant a general right to occupy the premises. That right need not be exclusive. Occupants of hotel rooms have been held to have a sufficient interest, *Stoner v. Cal.* (1964), and *Mancusi v. DeForte* (1968) deemed sufficient the interest of an employee in an office he shared with several other workers. *Mancusi* reasoned that the defendant clearly would have had standing if the office had been his alone, and the joint use of the office had not so diminished his expectation of privacy as to subject it to a search by government officials acting without the permission of his employer or fellow workers.

(e) Property interest in the item seized

Various lower court opinions and a few Supreme Court opinions have suggested that, even though a defendant lacks a possessory interest in the premises searched, he still may challenge a search if he has a property interest in the item seized. In support of this conclusion, reliance is placed upon the language of the Fourth Amendment, which refers to protecting an individual's "effects" as well as his home against unreasonable searches and seizures. However, most personal effects, not being containers, are simply seized, without themselves being searched, after a plain view sighting that provided sufficient grounds to justify the seizure (as in the case of apparent contraband). Thus, the seizure of the item is itself lawful (see § 2.7(d)), provided the officer did not violate the rights of the defendant in obtaining the plain view.

The defendant's property interest in the item therefore becomes important not to contest the seizure as such, but to establish a reasonable expectation of privacy in the place where his effects are found—i.e., in the premises entered or the container opened.

The Supreme Court decision providing the strongest support for standing tied to an interest in the item seized, *U.S. v. Jeffers* (1951), presented a situation in which the defendant clearly had such an expectation of privacy in the place where the item was located. The defendant in *Jeffers* was allowed to challenge the search of his aunts' hotel room, where police found 19 bottles of cocaine that he had stored in the closet. The Court emphasized that the search and seizure were directed at obtaining defendant's "property" (the fact that he had no lawfully recognized interest in the contraband drugs being irrelevant). The *Jeffers* opinion also noted, however, that the "[aunts] had given [defendant] a key to their room, that he had their permission to use the room as well, and that he often entered the room for various purposes." Subsequently, in *Rakas,* the Court noted that *Jeffers* was a case in which defendant's standing was "based on Jeffers' possessory interest in both the premises searched and the property seized."

The *Rakas* description of *Jeffers* was reiterated and given special emphasis in *U.S. v. Salvucci* (1980). *Salvucci* overturned the previously accepted doctrine of "automatic standing" for cases involving possessory offenses (see (f) infra). In reaching that result, the Court rejected the contention that the prosecution was engaged in self-contradiction when it alleged, on the one hand, that the defendant violated a statute prohibiting possession of contraband and, on the other, that he lacked standing to challenge the search of the home of another in which the contraband was seized. The Court noted that the challenge before it was not to the legality of the seizure in itself, but to the legality of the preceding search of the premises. It could not be assumed that "a person in legal possession of the goods seized during an illegal search has * * * necessarily been subject to a Fourth Amendment deprivation" since such possession "does not invariably represent the protected Fourth Amendment interest" violated by the illegal search. While possession is a factor to be considered, the Court noted, it could not be made into a "substitute" or "proxy" for a factual finding that the defendant had a "legitimate expectation of privacy in the area searched."

Rawlings v. Ky. (1980) furnishes an illustration of the point made in *Salvucci* that a possessory interest in the seized goods and an expectation of privacy in the area searched do not invariably coincide. Defendant in *Rawlings* was charged with possession of drugs that he had placed in the purse of an acquaintance [Cox]. Assuming that the search of Cox's purse was illegal, the Court held that the defendant could not challenge the legality of that search. The record below amply supported the lower court's conclusion that Rawlings "had no legitimate expectation of privacy in Cox's purse at the time of the search." When Rawlings "dumped thousands of dollars worth of illegal drugs into Cox's purse," shortly before the police arrived on the scene, he had "known her only a few days" and "had never received access to her purse prior to that sudden bailment." He had no right to exclude others from her purse, and a longtime companion had, in fact, had free access to the purse. While there was some question as to whether Cox had consented to the "bailment," even if she had, "the precipitous nature of the transaction hardly support[ed] a reasonable inference that petitioner took normal precautions to maintain his privacy." Finally, the Court noted, petitioner had "frank[ly] admitt[ed] * * * that he had no subjective expectation that Cox's purse would remain free from government intrusion."

(f) Establishing standing

In *Simmons v. U.S.* (1968), the defendant, seeking to establish standing to challenge the search of a suitcase, testified that he was the owner of the suitcase. His motion to suppress was subsequently denied, and the government used his testimony at trial in establishing guilt. In finding the use of that testimony unconstitutional, the Supreme Court noted that, at least in marginal cases where the defendant is uncertain as to the probable outcome of his motion, the potential use of such testimony at trial obviously would have a deterrent impact upon his assertion of Fourth Amendment rights. Moreover, the placement of this condition upon the assertion of those rights raised self-incrimination difficulties since "the defendant who wishes to establish standing must do so at the risk that the words which he utters may later be used to incriminate him." Accordingly, the Court held, "when a defendant testifies in support of a motion to suppress evidence on Fourth Amendment grounds, his testimony may not thereafter be admitted against him at trial on the issue of guilt unless he makes no objection."

Prior to *Simmons,* in *Jones v. U.S.* (1960), the Court had held that a defendant charged with a crime requiring proof of his possession of seized property automatically had standing to challenge the search that led to the seizure of that property. Without automatic standing, the *Jones* Court noted, the defendant would face the dilemma of either relinquishing his claim or being forced to "allege facts the proof of which would tend * * * to convict him." In *U.S. v. Salvucci* (1980), the Court discarded the *Jones* automatic standing rule, reasoning that *Simmons* had eliminated the defense dilemma that *Jones* had sought to avoid.

§ 6.9   BURDEN OF PROOF

(a) Allocation of the burden

At common law, the burden of establishing the factual basis for suppressing otherwise admissible evidence fell upon the party seeking suppression, and the Supreme Court has never questioned the constitutionality of that rule as carried over to the exclusionary rules. Thus, a state may, if it so desires, place upon the defendant the burdens of going forward and of persuasion as to the factual event (i.e., the seizure, the search, the obtaining of a statement, or the identification) which provides the grounding for an exclusionary rule claim. The Supreme Court has held, however, that the prosecution must bear the burden of proof as to certain elements that determine the applicability of an exclusionary rule. Initially, because waiver of a constitutional right is not lightly to be presumed, the prosecution has the burden of establishing that defendant waived his *Miranda* rights or his right to counsel under *Wade*. See §§ 4.4(b), 5.2(b). So too, *Bumper v. N.C.* (1968) held that the burden of establishing a voluntary consent to an otherwise unconstitutional search falls upon the prosecution. For similar reasons, if a constitutional violation is established, and the state contends its evidence is nonetheless admissible under an independent source or inevitable discovery exception to the fruits doctrine, the state has the burden of proving that those exceptions are in fact applicable. *Nix v. Williams* (§ 6.6(b)). See also *Alderman v. U.S.* (1969) (where there has been an illegal wiretap, government has "ultimate burden of persuasion to show that its evidence is untainted"). A similar burden is placed on the state where defendant had been compelled to testify under an immunity order and the government claims its evidence was not directly or indirectly derived from that immunized testimony. See *Kastigar v. U.S.* (§ 4.10(d)) (government's "affirmative duty" is not limited to a "negation of taint," but requires proof that its evidence "is derived from a legitimate source wholly independent of the compelled testimony").

Without speaking directly to the issue, the Court has indicated that the state may also be required to bear the burden as to certain other elements of an exclusionary rule claim. *Lego v. Twomey* (1972), discussed in the next subsection, certainly raises serious doubts as to whether a state could place upon the defendant the burden of persuasion as to the issue of voluntariness. Language in *Beck v. Ohio* (1964), noting that the government there needed to establish probable cause with "more specificity," suggests that the prosecution may be required to establish the existence of probable cause supporting a warrantless search or seizure. At a minimum, since the defendant in such a case does not know what information the police acted upon (unlike the warrant case, there is no probable cause affidavit), the prosecution should have the burden of going forward, if not the ultimate burden of persuasion.

(b) Quantum of proof

Where the prosecution constitutionally must carry the burden of proof, what is the level of persuasion it must reach? In *U.S. v. Wade*, the Court stated that the prosecution must show by "clear and convincing evidence" that an in-court identification is not the product of an unconstitutional lineup identification. See § 5.2(c). *Wade* stands in contrast, however, to a substantial line of later cases that held satisfactory a preponderance of the evidence standard.

The leading case on the requisite level of proof is *Lego v. Twomey* (1972). The Court there found the preponderance standard constitutionally acceptable as applied to the prosecutor's burden of establishing the voluntariness of a confession. The majority rejected the contention, advanced in the dissent, that proof of admissibility beyond a reasonable doubt was needed "to give adequate protection to those values that the exclusionary rules are designed to serve." The majority found it "very doubtful that escalating the prosecution's burden of proof in Fourth and Fifth Amendment suppression hearings would be sufficiently productive [in implementing the deterrent impact of the exclusionary rules] to outweigh the public interest in placing probative evidence before juries for the purpose of arriving at truthful decisions about guilt or innocence." Moreover, the defendant had "offer[ed] nothing to suggest that admissibility rulings [based upon a preponderance of the evidence standard] have been unreliable or otherwise wanting in quality because not based on some higher standard."

Nix v. Williams (§ 6.6(b)), relying on *Lego,* held that the preponderance standard also was satisfactory in establishing admissibility under the inevitable discovery doctrine. So too, in *U.S. v. Matlock* (1974), the Court commented that the "controlling burden of proof at [Fourth Amendment] suppression hearings should impose no greater burden than proof by a preponderance of evidence." Although *Miranda* spoke of the "heavy burden" that rests on the government to show a knowing and intelligent waiver of *Miranda* rights, *Colo. v. Connelly* (1986) held that here too, the preponderance standard was satisfactory. The Court reasoned: "If, as we held in *Lego v. Twomey,* the voluntariness of a confession need be established only by a preponderance of the evidence, then a waiver of the auxiliary protections established in *Miranda* should require no higher burden of proof."

CHAPTER 7
RIGHT TO COUNSEL

§ 7.1 SIXTH AMENDMENT RIGHT

(a) Right to retained counsel

The Sixth Amendment provides that, "in all criminal prosecutions, the accused shall enjoy the right * * * to have the Assistance of Counsel for his defense." Most of the Supreme Court decisions involving the Sixth Amendment right to counsel have dealt with the state's failure to appoint counsel, at its expense, to assist the indigent defendant, rather than the right of the more affluent defendant to utilize the assistance of privately retained counsel. The latter right is so clearly established by the Sixth Amendment's language and history that it rarely has been the subject of litigation, at least as applied to the formal stages of the criminal prosecution. Indeed, the Supreme Court has characterized the defendant's right to utilize retained counsel in such proceedings as "unqualified." *Chandler v. Fretag* (1954).

(b) Right to appointed counsel

A constitutional right of an indigent defendant to the assistance of court appointed counsel was first recognized by the Supreme Court in *Powell v. Ala.* (1932), but that ruling was based on due process and was carefully limited to situations similar to that before the Court—a "capital case" in which the defendant was "incapable adequately of making his own defense because of ignorance, feeble mindedness, illiteracy or the like." *Powell* concluded that, at least under those circumstances, the appointment of counsel to assist the indigent defendant was a "logical corollary" of the defendant's right to a fair hearing.

Despite its limited holding, the *Powell* opinion strongly suggested that in all but exceptional cases, the appointment of counsel would be necessary to ensure the indigent a fair trial. The opinion stressed the inability of even the "intelligent and educated layman" to properly represent himself, and concluded that there was a need for "the guiding hand of counsel at every step of the proceedings." In *Johnson v. Zerbst* (1938), the Court relied heavily upon *Powell*'s discussion of the general need for counsel in holding that the Sixth Amendment required federal courts to provide indigent defendants with appointed counsel in all felony cases. The Court concluded that the Sixth Amendment, recognizing the "obvious truth that the average defendant does not have the professional legal skill to protect himself," "withholds from * * * courts the power and authority to deprive an accused of his life or liberty unless he has or waives the assistance of counsel." Accordingly, if the accused lacked funds to retain counsel, the state had the responsibility to provide counsel at its expense if it wished to try him.

In *Betts v. Brady* (1942), the Court refused to apply the *Johnson v. Zerbst* ruling to the states via the Fourteenth Amendment's due process clause. The majority held that due process did not necessarily require appointment of counsel in all felony cases, but only in those cases where the particular circumstances indicated that the absence of counsel would result in a trial lacking "fundamental fairness." *Gideon v. Wainwright* (1963), adopting a selective incorporation interpretation of the Sixth Amendment (see § 1.2(d)), overruled *Betts*. *Gideon* held that the Fourteenth Amendment fully incorporated the Sixth Amendment right and accordingly required the state to make appointed counsel available to indigent defendants in all felony cases. The *Gideon* Court deemed it "an obvious truth" that a person denied the assistance of counsel "cannot be assured a fair trial," as evidenced by the fact that "lawyers to prosecute are everywhere deemed essential" and "there are few defendants charged with crime * * * who fail to hire the best lawyers they can get."

(c) The misdemeanor, non-incarceration limitation

Prior to *Argersinger v. Hamlin* (1972), some doubt existed as to whether the constitutional right to appointed counsel applied to any misdemeanor prosecutions. *Gideon* involved a felony case, and later opinions had referred to *Gideon* as simply establishing a right to counsel in "felony prosecutions." *Argersinger,* however, held *Gideon* applicable to all indigent misdemeanor defendants who are sentenced to a jail term. The Court rejected the state's contention that the Sixth Amendment right to counsel, like the Sixth Amendment right to a jury trial, should not apply to "petty offenses" (i.e., offenses punishable by no more than six months imprisonment). While there was "historical support" for the jury trial limitation, "nothing in the history of the right to counsel" suggested a "retraction of the right in petty offenses wherein the common law previously did require that counsel be provided." Moreover, there was no functional basis for drawing the line at petty offenses. The legal questions presented in a misdemeanor trial were no less complex because the jail sentence did not exceed six months. Neither was there less need for the advice of counsel prior to entering a plea of guilty. Indeed, the Court noted, petty misdemeanors may create a special need for counsel's assistance because their great volume "may create an obsession for speedy dispositions, regardless of the fairness of the result."

Since the defendant in *Argersinger* had been sentenced to jail, the Court found it unnecessary to rule on a misdemeanor defendant's right to appointed counsel where "a loss of liberty was not involved." The *Argersinger* opinion laid the foundation, however, for distinguishing between misdemeanor cases involving sentences of imprisonment and those in which only fines are imposed. The

Court stressed the special character of imprisonment, "for however short a time," including its
possible "serious repercussions affecting [defen-
dant's] career and reputation." In *Scott v. Ill.*
(1979), the Court adopted the dividing line of imprisonment, as suggested by *Argersinger*. Defendant there was convicted of shoplifting, a misdemeanor punishable by a maximum sentence of
imprisonment for one year, but was sentenced to
only a fine of $50.00. The Court held that he had
not been entitled to appointed counsel since the
Sixth Amendment, as to misdemeanor charges,
"require[s] only that no indigent criminal defendant be sentenced to a term of imprisonment unless the State has afforded him the right to assistance of appointed counsel." The Court undoubtedly was influenced by the practical problems of
providing counsel for all misdemeanor charges,
typically a caseload ten times as great as the felony
caseload (with only a small percentage resulting in
jail sentences). "*Argersinger*," it noted, "has
proved reasonably workable, whereas any extension would create confusion and impose unpredict-
able, but necessarily substantial cost to 50 quite
diverse states."

Where a magistrate decides not to provide counsel for an indigent misdemeanor defendant, that
ties the hands not only of that magistrate in sentencing (a jail sentence being precluded) but also of
prosecutors and judges who might later want to
utilize defendant's conviction under a recidivist or
enhancement provision. For the Court has held

that the imprisonment dividing line of *Scott–Arger-singer* encompasses imprisonment subsequently imposed through a provision that increases a sentence by reference to the earlier conviction without counsel. *Baldasar v. Ill.* (1980).

(d) Scope of the "criminal prosecution"

The Sixth Amendment right to counsel is by its terms a right that extends only to "the accused" in a "criminal prosecution." The Court has held that the starting point for the criminal prosecution—i.e., the point at which the individual becomes "an accused"—is the initiation of "adversary judicial proceedings." *Kirby v. Ill.* (1972). Precisely what constitutes the initiation of adversary judicial proceedings is a matter commonly raised in connection with pretrial investigative procedures, and it has been discussed previously in that connection. See §§ 4.3(e), 5.1(e). As noted there, an arrest alone, without the filing of charges in court or the presentation of the arrestee before the magistrate, does not constitute the initiation of adversary judicial proceedings. The reasoning underlying this position was explored in a somewhat different context in *U.S. v. Gouveia* (1984).

In *Gouveia,* prison officials, after concluding that several inmates had participated in a prison murder, assigned them to a special detention unit where they remained until finally indicted months later. The inmates claimed that the government's failure to honor their request for appointment of counsel while they were confined in the special

detention unit had been a Sixth Amendment violation. They argued, and the lower court agreed,
that the lack of counsel at that point could impair
their ability to preserve evidence and otherwise
prepare for the eventual charges. Rejecting defendant's contention, the Court noted that just as it
had "never held that the right to counsel attaches
at the time of arrest," it had "never suggested that
the purpose of the right * * * is to provide a
defendant with a preindictment private investigator." On the contrary, the right was limited by its
objective "of protecting the unaided layman at
critical confrontations with his adversary," and it
therefore demanded the initiation of adversary judicial proceedings, which marked the point at
which "the adverse positions of government and
defendant have solidified."

Once started, the criminal prosecution continues
through to the end of the trial stage, including
sentencing. See *Mempa v. Rhay* (§ 7.3(g)). After
that point, however, the criminal prosecution has
come to an end for Sixth Amendment purposes.
Thus, *Douglas v. Cal.* (§ 7.2(d)) and *Evitts v. Lucey*
(§ 7.2(d)), dealing with the right to appointed and
retained counsel on a first level appeal, focus only
on possible equal protection and due process
groundings for those rights. So too, in *Gagnon v.
Scarpelli* (§ 7.3(g)), the Court held that a probation
revocation proceeding not a part of the initial
sentencing (compare *Mempa*) was not a stage in
the "criminal prosecution" for Sixth Amendment
purposes.

(e) The "critical stage" requirement

The Court has held that Sixth Amendment right to counsel does not simply start with the initiation of adversary judicial proceedings and then require counsel's assistance at every step in the criminal prosecution thereafter. Rather, the right demands that the assistance of counsel be available only at the "critical stages" in the criminal prosecution— those steps at which substantial rights of the accused may be affected "by counsel's absence." *Mempa v. Rhay* (1967). Applying that test, the Court has held that all of the following present a critical stage: subjecting the accused to some (but not all) identification procedures (§§ 5.2, 5.3); police or prosecutor attempts to elicit inculpatory statements from the accused (§ 4.3); a first appearance where action taken there (or inaction there) can later be used against the accused (§ 7.3(c)); an arraignment with similar characteristics (§ 7.3(e)); a preliminary hearing (§ 7.3(d)); the trial (§ 7.3(f)); and sentencing, even where imposed in conjunction with a probation revocation (§ 7.3(g)).

§ 7.2 ADDITIONAL CONSTITUTIONAL RIGHTS TO COUNSEL AND OTHER ASSISTANCE

(a) Due process/fair hearing right to counsel

Powell v. Ala. (1932), recognized due process rights to the assistance of appointed and retained counsel at a time when the Sixth Amendment's requirements had not been extended to the states.

Today, both rights continue to have significance for those portions of the criminal justice process that are not part of the criminal prosecution for Sixth Amendment purposes. Where the defendant is entitled, by constitution or state law, to a hearing at a point in the process not encompassed by the Sixth Amendment, the Court will look to due process to determine whether fundamental fairness includes a right to representation by counsel at that hearing.

As noted in *Mathews v. Eldridge* (1976), traditional due process analysis as to whether an additional procedural safeguard is essential to achieving fundamental fairness balances three factors: (1) the significance of "the private interest that will be affected by the [governmental] action"; (2) the "risk of an erroneous deprivation of such interest through the procedures used, and the probable value, if any, of [the] additional * * * procedural safeguard"; and (3) "the Government's interest, including the function involved and the fiscal and administrative burdens that the additional * * * procedural requirement would entail." Since the "private interest" at issue in the context of criminal justice hearings is the liberty of the individual (indeed, often with incarceration at stake), the individual has no difficulty in establishing the importance of the "private interest" involved. The critical factor is how the Court will weigh the second and third considerations noted in *Mathews*. As illustrated by the cases discussed in § 7.3, that balance has been struck differently at different stages in the process. The Court has held that due process includes a right to counsel at the first appeal as of right, sometimes includes a right to counsel in parole and probation violation hearings, and does not include a right to counsel on appeals beyond the first appeal of right and in collateral attack. See §§ 7.3(g)–(i).

Traditional due process analysis, as discussed in § 1.2(b), often employs a case-by-case evaluation, looking to all of the facts of the particular case. That was the approach adopted in the pre-*Gideon* cases dealing with the right to counsel at trial, when that issue was governed by a "fundamental fairness" standard rather than the Sixth Amendment. See *Powell v. Ala.* and *Betts v. Brady,* discussed in § 7.1(b). It was also the approach later applied in *Gagnon v. Scarpelli,* dealing with counsel in probation and parole revocation proceedings. See § 7.3(g). On the other hand, *Evitts v. Lucey* adopted a flat due process requirement of counsel on the first appeal as of right. See § 7.2(d) and § 7.3(h). So too, the cases finding no due process right to counsel as to later appeals and collateral attack also were flat rulings that did not look to possible variations in the circumstances of individual cases (apart, perhaps, from the capital case). See § 7.3(h), (i).

(b) Due process right to retained counsel

In the course of discussing the impact of "the introduction of counsel" upon revocation proceedings, *Gagnon v. Scarpelli* (1973) left open the question of "whether a probationer or parolee has a right to be represented at a revocation hearing by retained counsel in situations other than those where the state would be obliged to furnish counsel for an indigent." Legislation barring counsel from such proceedings would raise the issue of whether there exists a due process right to utilize retained counsel that extends beyond the right to counsel under either the Sixth Amendment or a due process/fair hearing analysis. *Powell* suggested that there might be such an independent right to utilize retained counsel, noting that due process would be denied if a court, even in a civil case, "were arbitrarily to refuse to hear a party by counsel, employed by and appearing for him." The *Powell* opinion also noted the separate grounding of the right to retained counsel based upon the early rejection in this country of the English common law practice of denying defendants the full assistance of retained counsel in felony cases. In accordance with this history, during the period prior to *Gideon,* when due process was held to require appointment of counsel only under special circumstances, the Court nevertheless recognized an absolute due process right to representation by retained counsel in criminal cases. See *Chandler v. Fre⁺ag* (1954). An independent due process right to utilize retained counsel would give constitutional grounding to defendant's right to make full use of his resources in presenting his defense and bar state interference with that right where not based on some overriding state interest. Such a right would not be tied to "critical stages" in the criminal prosecution or the need for counsel's assistance to ensure a fair hearing. It would preclude a state, for example, from barring representation by retained counsel in a misdemeanor trial which did not result in a sentence of incarceration (compare *Scott v. Ill.*, § 7.1(c)), although it presumably would not bar preclusion of retained counsel where the state has a special administrative justification for excluding counsel. *Gagnon* suggested that might be the case for the parole revocation proceeding that does not present issues creating a due process requirement of counsel. Here, the state might justifiably exclude retained counsel because the state is not represented by counsel and the predictive judgment to be made as to rehabilitative potential may gain from hearing an uncounseled prisoner. Consider also *Moran v. Burbine* (§ 4.9(b)).

(c) Derivative right to counsel

A constitutional right to the assistance of counsel also can be derived from other constitutional guarantees besides the due process right to a fair hearing. Thus, *Miranda v. Ariz.* recognized a right to consult with counsel as a measure protecting the self-incrimination privilege of a person subjected to custodial interrogation. See § 4.4. The Court there required that the police inform such a person that "he has a right to consult with a lawyer and to have the lawyer with him during interrogation," and that "if he is indigent, a lawyer will be appointed to present him." This requirement extends beyond the Sixth Amendment right to counsel since custodial interrogation often occurs before the individual is an "accused" in a "criminal prosecution." The *Miranda* approach of requiring an opportunity to consult with counsel as a means of safeguarding another constitutional guarantee has also been advanced, without success, in other contexts. In *Kirby v. Ill.* (1972) that approach was urged unsuccessfully by the dissenters, who argued that a suspect placed in a lineup, even though not yet an accused, should have a right to the presence of retained or appointed counsel as a means of safeguarding the trial right of confrontation. See § 5.2(a),(e). In *U.S. v. Mandujano* (1976), two justices argued that the self-incrimination privilege of a target-witness before a grand jury carried with it a right to consult with a retained or appointed attorney prior to the questioning. While the Court did not find it necessary to rule on that contention, four justices found it unpersuasive. See § 7.3(b).

(d) Equal protection and appointed counsel

Although it did not deal with the right to counsel, *Griffin v. Ill.* (1956) provided the doctrinal foundation for the eventual recognition of an equal protection right to appointed counsel. *Griffin* held that where state law conditioned appellate review upon the availability of a stenographic transcript of the trial proceedings, the state must make such a transcript available without charge to indigent defendants so they would have equal access to appellate review. The plurality opinion stressed that, although the state was not required by due process to afford appellate review, once it did so, it could not condition such review "in a way that discriminates against some convicted defendants on account of their poverty." "There can be no equal justice," the opinion noted, "where the kind of trial a man gets depends on the amount of money he has." In *Douglas v. Cal.* (1963), the Court relied upon the "*Griffin* principle" to hold invalid the California practice of refusing to appoint counsel on an appeal by an indigent when the appellate court, after reviewing the trial record, concluded that "no good whatever could be served" by appointment. The Court noted that the more affluent defendant was not required to run "this gantlet of a preliminary showing of merit" in order to have his appeal presented by counsel. The indigent defendant, it concluded, was entitled to equal treatment, at least on a first appeal granted by the state as a matter of right. The state therefore was required to appoint counsel for all indigent defendants on first appeal, just as it was required by *Gideon* to provide counsel at the trial level.

Construed broadly, the *Griffin-Douglas* concept of equal protection could require the appointment of counsel to assist the indigent at every stage in the administration of criminal justice at which the more affluent defendant is allowed by state law to be represented by privately retained counsel. The question of appointment would rest on the need for providing equal treatment rather than the need for a lawyer's assistance to assure a fair hearing. However, in stressing the importance of the first appeal, and in characterizing a defendant's presentation of that appeal without counsel as a "meaningless ritual," the *Douglas* opinion cited factors that would have been relevant in assessing a due process/fair hearing right to appointed appellate counsel. Subsequently, in *Ross v. Moffitt* (1974), the Court focused on this aspect of the *Douglas* ruling and read the *Griffin* principle as it related to appointed counsel to be closely tied to such a due process right to counsel.

Ross involved a state practice of appointing counsel to assist indigent appellants on their appeals to the state intermediate appellate court, but not on their applications for review by the state supreme court or their petitions for certiorari to the United States Supreme Court. A divided Court held that the failure to appoint counsel at these later stages of the appellate process did not deprive the appellants of equal protection. The Court stressed that the indigent defendant did not need counsel to have "meaningful access" to the higher appellate courts. On application for review, the state supreme court would have before it a transcript, the lower court brief, and, in many cases, an opinion of the state intermediate court. These materials, supplemented by any personal statement of appellant, provided an "adequate basis" for the state court to determine whether to grant review—especially since the "critical issue" for that decision was not whether there had been "a correct adjudication of guilt in every individual case," but whether the appeal presented issues of general legal significance. The same factors, the Court noted, also applied to its own consideration of petitions for writ of certiorari.

The *Ross* majority acknowledged that a lawyer skilled in preparing petitions for review "would * * * prove helpful" to an appellant, but went on to add: "The fact that a particular service might be of benefit to an indigent defendant does not mean that service is constitutionally required. * * * [Equal protection] does not require absolute equality or precisely equal advantages. * * * The duty of the state * * * is not to duplicate the legal arsenal that may be privately retained by a criminal defendant in a continuing effort to reverse his conviction, but only to assure the indigent defendant an adequate opportunity to present his claims fairly in the context of the State's appellate process."

Ross' characterization of the *Douglas* equal protection analysis as ensuring only that the indigent have an "adequate opportunity" to utilize the state process suggests a standard that comes close to demanding under equal protection only what the indigent defendant would otherwise be entitled to under due process. Arguably, *Douglas'* equal protection analysis would extend beyond due process by imposing a flat requirement of appointment of counsel for all first appeals granted as a matter of right, without examining the indigent appellant's need for counsel on the case-by-case basis traditionally employed in due process analysis. See § 7.2(a). However, whether equal protection provides broader coverage than due process even in imposing that flat requirement may be questioned in light of *Evitts v. Lucey* (1985). As discussed in § 7.3(h), *Evitts* held that due process includes a right to representation by competent counsel on a first appeal as of right, and also did so as flat requirement. Still, the practice of the Court remains, as illustrated by *Pa. v. Finley* (see § 7.3(i)), to separately analyze due process and equal protection claims. Of course, as also illustrated by *Finley,* the circumstances that lead the Court to conclude that due process does not require counsel for a fair hearing are equally potent in establishing that "meaningful access" is available to the indigent without counsel at that proceeding.

(e) Assistance other than counsel

Under *Griffin v. Ill.* and its progeny, indigent defendants have been held to have an equal protection right not only to a free trial transcript where needed for appeal, but also to a trial transcript for use in a collateral attack upon a conviction, for a transcript of a habeas proceeding to be used on appeal from a denial of habeas relief, and for a transcript of a preliminary hearing to be used in preparing for trial. See e.g., *Roberts v. LaVallee* (1967). The defendant must, of course, have some need for the transcript, but that is established where the transcript is the common and apparently preferable means of presenting the particular type of claim that defendant desires to advance. See *Draper v. Wash.* (1963). But note *U.S. v. MacCollom* (1976) (free trial transcript for use in collateral attack could be conditioned on judicial certification that petitioner's asserted claim was "not frivolous").

As evidenced by *Mayer v. Chicago* (1971), the right to a free transcript can extend to proceedings which are not part of the "criminal prosecution" for Sixth Amendment purposes nor sufficiently significant to require appointment of counsel under a due process analysis. *Mayer* required that an indigent defendant, fined $500.00 for disorderly conduct and interference with a police officer, be provided a free transcript needed to challenge on appeal the sufficiency of the evidence supporting his conviction. The Court stressed, inter alia, the potential significance of conviction for "even petty offenses" of the "kind involved here." "A fine," it noted, "may bear as heavily upon an indigent accused as forced confinement," and "the collateral consequences may be even more severe, as when (as was apparently a possibility in this case) the impecunious medical student finds himself barred from the practice of medicine because of [the] conviction." Under *Scott v. Ill.* (§ 7.1(c)), the defendant would not have been entitled to the appointment of counsel at his trial on the ordinance violation. Providing a transcript may be distinguished from providing a lawyer, however, on the ground that the lack of the transcript would have effectively denied Mayer all access to the appellate process, while Scott still had access to the trial process, albeit through self-representation.

In *Ake v. Okla.* (1985), the Court relied on due process, rather than equal protection, to hold that, "when a defendant has made a preliminary showing that his insanity at the time of the offense is likely to be a significant factor at trial, * * * the state [must] provide access to a psychiatrist's assistance on this issue if the defendant cannot otherwise afford one." This obligation, the Court stressed, was limited to cases in which the defendant's mental condition was "seriously in question" and did not go beyond providing the defense with assistance of a single psychiatrist selected by the trial court. The *Ake* majority noted that the Court had never held that "a State must purchase for the indigent all the assistance that his wealthier counterpart might buy," but due process did require that the indigent defendant be given the "basic tools" needed to present his defense. Taking into consideration the defendant's interest "in the accuracy of the criminal proceeding," the limited financial burden that would be imposed upon the state under the proposed standard for appointment, and the probable value of psychiatric assistance in presenting an insanity defense, a court appointed psychiatrist clearly was such a "basic tool" where insanity is likely to be a serious issue.

§ 7.3 RIGHT TO COUNSEL: STAGES OF THE PROCESS

(a) Police investigation

Prior to the initiation of adversary judicial proceedings, an individual has no Sixth Amendment right to counsel. However, under *Miranda,* a person subjected to custodial interrogation has a right to consult with counsel (appointed, if the person is indigent) prior to and during such interrogation. Once the adversary judicial proceedings have been initiated, the individual (now an "accused") may not be subjected to police action designed to elicit potentially incriminating statements without an appropriate waiver of counsel. See § 4.3. So too, the accused may not be subjected to eyewitness identification in a lineup or show-up without having counsel present or having waived that right. See § 5.2. On the other hand, that right does not extend to other identification procedures involving an accused (e.g., the taking and analyzing of blood samples). See § 5.3(b).

(b) Grand jury proceedings

The Supreme Court found it unnecessary in *U.S. v. Mandujano* (1976) to determine whether an indigent "target witness" before the grand jury has a constitutional right to appointed counsel. However, a four-justice plurality opinion argued that there was no such right. Relying on the *Kirby* holding that the starting point for the Sixth Amendment is the initiation of adversary judicial proceedings (see § 7.1(d)), the plurality noted that the Sixth Amendment did not apply here since grand jury witnesses, though targets, have not been charged with any offense. The plurality also relied upon the reasoning in *In re Groban's Petition* (1957). In *Groban,* a witness was not allowed to have retained counsel present during his examination by a state fire marshall in a proceeding to determine the cause of a fire. In finding that this denial of counsel did not violate due process, the majority cited as an analogy the grand jury proceeding, noting that "a witness before a grand jury cannot insist, as a matter of constitutional right, on being represented by his counsel." Justice Black's dissent in *Groban,* although disagreeing with the majority's conclusion as to the fire marshall's proceeding, agreed with its statement regarding the grand jury. The key there was the presence of the grand jurors as representatives of the community. "It would be very difficult," the dissent noted, "for officers of the state [i.e., the prosecuting attorney] to seriously abuse or deceive a witness in the presence of the grand jury."

Two dissenters in *Mandujano* contended that the target grand jury witness had a right to counsel (including a right to appointed counsel for the indigent) because the questioning of such a witness "inextricably involves" his privilege against self-incrimination. The *Mandujano* plurality did not speak specifically to a possible Fifth Amendment grounding for a witness' right to counsel, but it did reject an analogy based on *Miranda,* see § 4.10(b).

Accordingly, the plurality opinion, with the support of *Groban,* is generally taken to state the prevailing position that no constitutional right to counsel exists at the grand jury stage. Still, while most jurisdictions do not provide for the appointment of counsel to assist the indigent target witness, all do permit grand jury witnesses to interrupt their testimony for the purpose of consulting with retained counsel located in an adjoining room. The *Mandujano* plurality had no need to consider whether this practice was constitutionally mandated because the witness there had been informed that he could leave the grand jury room to consult with retained counsel (which he did not have).

(c) Initial appearance

With the arrested person's initial appearance (at which the magistrate will set forth the charges, inform the accused of his rights, and set bail), adversary judicial proceedings have been initiated. See *Mich. v. Jackson* (§ 4.3(e)). Where the state requires the defendant to make an election at the initial appearance that may be prejudicial, *White v. Md.* (1963) establishes that the initial appearance also constitutes a "critical stage," requiring the assistance of counsel. In *White,* the state followed a practice, utilized in several jurisdictions, of requesting a felony defendant to enter an initial, non-binding plea before the magistrate. The defendant there, without the assistance of counsel, entered a plea of guilty, and after he shifted his

plea to not guilty at his arraignment, that earlier
plea was used against him at trial. The Supreme
Court reversed the ensuing conviction, holding that
the use of the plea rendered defendant's initial
appearance a critical stage at which counsel should
have been made available to assist the "accused to
* * * plead intelligently."

(d) Preliminary hearing

Coleman v. Ala. (1970) ruled that the preliminary hearing is a "critical stage" under the Sixth
Amendment. While there was no opinion for the
Court, a majority agreed that the failure to appoint
counsel at a typical state preliminary hearing resulted in a constitutional violation, though not
necessarily requiring reversal of a subsequent conviction. The majority stressed the practical importance of the preliminary hearing and noted five
advantages that could result from counsel's assistance at that proceeding: (1) a "lawyer's skilled
examination and cross-examination of witness"
may lead the magistrate to conclude that the state
lacks the probable caused needed for a bindover;
(2) "the skilled interrogation * * * by an experienced lawyer can fashion a valuable impeachment
tool for use in cross-examination" at trial; (3) the
defense counsel may use the preliminary exam to
"preserve [favorable] testimony * * * of a witness
who does not appear at trial"; (4) "trained counsel
can more effectively discover the case the state has
against his client and make possible [better] preparation * * * [for] trial"; and (5) "counsel can also

be influential at the preliminary hearing in making effective arguments * * * on such matters as the necessity for an early psychiatric examination or bail." The majority added, however, that denial of counsel at preliminary hearing could constitute harmless error where the advantages lost through the lack of counsel had no bearing on the subsequent trial.

(e) Arraignment

The formal arraignment occurs after the information or indictment is issued, and involves a reading of the charges contained therein and the entry of a plea in response to those charges. Even where the accused enters a plea of not-guilty, the arraignment may be a critical stage due to the consequences of inaction at that point. In *Hamilton v. Ala.* (1961), local law treated certain defenses, such as insanity, as "irretrievably lost" if not raised at arraignment. Finding a constitutional violation in the state's failure to provide defendant with the assistance of counsel, the Court rejected the contention that the critical nature of the proceeding should depend upon a showing of actual prejudice—i.e., a showing that defendant would have raised one of the "lost" defenses if he had been assisted by counsel. It concluded that the degree of prejudice "can never be known" because only counsel present at the time "could have enabled the accused to know all the defenses available to him and to plead intelligently."

(f) Trial

The earliest right to counsel cases dealt primarily with assistance of counsel at trial, and such assistance is clearly recognized as the "core" of the Sixth Amendment right. Denial of the right to counsel at trial requires the automatic reversal of defendant's conviction, as prejudice is presumed. *Gideon v. Wainwright* (1963). See also *Loper v. Beto* (1972) (where indigent defendant was denied his right to appointed counsel under *Gideon,* the resulting conviction was void and could not be used to impeach his credibility when he testified at a subsequent trial on a different charge); *Burgett v. Tex.* (1967) (conviction void under *Gideon* could not be used as a prior conviction under recidivist statute).

(g) Sentencing, probation and parole

Mempa v. Rhay (1967) confirmed the implications of prior decisions in holding that sentencing was a "critical stage" of a criminal prosecution, therefore requiring the assistance of appointed counsel. *Mempa* held, moreover, that sentencing remained a "critical stage" even though deferred to a probation revocation proceeding. In *Mempa,* the trial judge placed the defendant on probation without fixing the term of imprisonment that would be imposed if probation were later revoked. The Court concluded that the subsequent determination and imposition of a prison sentence at the probation revocation proceeding was as much a part of the "criminal prosecution" as sentencing imposed immediately after trial. Rejecting the state's contention that counsel was not needed since the term of the prison sentence was set by state law, the Court noted that the trial judge was required to submit a recommendation to the parole board and counsel could assist the defendant in presenting his case on that recommendation. Also, certain legal rights (e.g., withdrawal of a guilty plea) could be lost if not raised at the time the prison sentence was imposed, and counsel also was needed to protect those rights.

In *Gagnon v. Scarpelli* (1973), the Court held that *Mempa* did not extend to a probation revocation proceeding that involved only a determination as to revocation, a prison sentence previously having been imposed and suspended in favor of probation. The probation revocation determination is not based on the commission of the original offense and accordingly is not part of the "criminal prosecution" governed by the Sixth Amendment. The same is true of parole revocation, also covered by the *Gagnon* opinion. However, *Gagnon* concluded that due process requires that the state provide appointed counsel under some circumstances.

The loss of liberty resulting from parole or probation revocation had been held prior to *Gagnon* to be a "serious deprivation" requiring the protection of due process. Under that precedent, due process afforded the parolee or probationer substantial hearing rights, including the rights to prevent evidence and confront opposing witnesses. *Gagnon* concluded that due process also requires the state to provide appointed counsel where, under the facts of the particular case, counsel is needed to ensure the "effectiveness of the [hearing] rights guaranteed by [due process]." It refused to attempt to formulate "a precise and detailed set of guidelines" for determining when that need exists, but it did note that counsel ordinarily should be provided where there is a significant factual dispute or the individual relies upon contentions that a layman would have difficulty presenting.

Applying traditional due process analysis (see § 7.2(a)), the *Gagnon* opinion refused to impose, a flat requirement of counsel in all revocation cases. While such a requirement "had the appeal of simplicity, it would impose direct costs and serious collateral disadvantages without regard to the need or the likelihood in a particular case for a constructive contribution by counsel." In most revocation cases, the issue presented simply did not require the expertise of a lawyer. Quite often, "the probationer or parolee has been convicted of committing another crime [which automatically establishes grounds for revocation] or has admitted the charges against him." On the other side, "the introduction of counsel" would "alter significantly the nature of the [revocation] proceeding." The state would respond by retaining its own counsel and the role of the hearing body would become "more akin to that of a judge at trial, and less attuned to the rehabilitative needs of the individual probationer."

(h) Appeals

In *Ross v. Moffitt* (1974), in the course of holding that neither due process nor equal protection requires appointment of counsel to assist a convicted defendant in preparing a petition for second-tier, discretionary appellate review, the Court emphasized the different constitutional status of the trial and the appellate process. While a state could not dispense with the trial stage of criminal proceedings, *McKane v. Durston* (1894) had held it could refuse to provide "any appeal at all." Similarly, while due process requires that the state provide a trial attorney to serve as a "shield to protect [defendant] against being 'haled into court' by the State and stripped of his presumption of innocence," a different interest is presented where defendant seeks an attorney to "serve as a sword to upset the prior determination of guilt." Notwithstanding this lesser grounding, the Court has established a constitutional right to counsel on a first appeal granted of right under state law that is equal in strength to the Sixth Amendment right to counsel at trial. *Douglas v. Cal.,* as discussed in § 7.2(d), established an equal protection right of the indigent defendant to appointed counsel on such an appeal. *Evitts v. Lucey* (1985) held that the *Douglas* ruling also had a due process foundation and therefore established as well a right to representation by retained counsel on first appeal of right.

At issue in *Evitts* was a defendant's claim of incompetent representation by retained counsel on a first appeal of right. Since a constitutional claim based on ineffective assistance applies only where there is a constitutional right to counsel (see § 7.7(a)), the Court had to decide whether due process established a right to counsel on the appeal, as such a right would encompass retained counsel (unlike the equal protection right of Douglas). The *Evitts* Court acknowledged the considerations noted in *Ross,* but held that they should not prevail as to the first appeal of right. While the state had no obligation to create an appellate process, a first appeal of right, once established, became "an integral part of [its] system for finally adjudicating the guilt or innocence of a defendant." Its significance in this regard was quite distinct from the second tier review that was discretionary and came after one appellate court had reviewed the conviction for error.

Where *Douglas* requires appointment of appellate counsel, it also bars the state from adopting a procedure that invites counsel to evade his obligation of advocacy on his client's behalf. Thus, *Anders v. Cal.* (1967) found a denial of defendant's rights under *Douglas* when appointed counsel filed a statement simply noting that the appeal had no merit, and the appellate court, without further briefing, then examined the record and affirmed the judgment. The Court held that, while appointed counsel may request withdrawal when he finds a case to be "wholly frivolous," he cannot do so by simply stating his conclusion that the appeal lacks merit. His request must be accompanied by a brief discussing all points in the record "that might arguably support the appeal," including, if the state court requests, the authority on all sides. *McCoy v. Court of Appeals* (1988). The appellate court may then dismiss the appeal (or affirm the conviction) if it finds that none of the legal points are "arguable." In *Pa. v. Finley* (1987), these requirements were described as a "prophylactic framework" designed to prevent an undermining of *Douglas.*

(i) Collateral proceedings

In *Pa. v. Finley* (1987), the Court noted that it has "never held that prisoners have a constitutional right to counsel when mounting collateral attacks to their convictions and we decline to so hold today." The habeas petitioner in *Finley* had been given court appointed counsel pursuant to local practice, and her complaint was directed at the state's failure to follow the *Anders* requirements in allowing counsel to withdraw. The Court rejected that claim, pointing out that the *Anders* requirements are "relevant when and only when, a litigant has a previously established constitutional right to counsel." Relying on the reasoning of *Ross v. Moffitt,* the Court concluded that "since a defendant has no federal constitutional right to counsel when pursuing a discretionary appeal on direct review of his conviction, *a fortiori* he has no such right when attacking a conviction that has long since become final upon exhaustion of the appellate process."

Finley stressed that on collateral attack, as in seeking discretionary appellate review, the petitioner had "meaningful access" to the process without being provided counsel, and that the state's withdrawal procedure, which fully comported with "fundamental fairness," did not undermine that access. In earlier cases, the Court had imposed certain obligations upon state prison authorities to ensure that access to the federal writ of habeas corpus was available to incarcerated defendants. *Johnson v. Avery* (1969) held that a state regulation prohibiting prisoners from assisting each other in preparing habeas corpus petitions violated the prisoner's right of access to federal habeas corpus in the absence of the state providing some alternative form of assistance. *Bounds v. Smith* (1977) later extended *Johnson v. Avery* to hold that "the fundamental right of access to the courts requires prison authorities to assist inmates in the preparation and filing of meaningful legal papers by providing prisoners with adequate libraries or adequate legal assistance from persons trained in the law."

In *Murray v. Giarratano* (1989), the Court was divided as to what due process required for habeas petitioners who were challenging capital convictions. At issue there was the claim of Virginia's death row inmates that they were entitled to appointed counsel to help them prepare habeas challenges to their convictions and sentences. Four justices (per Stevens, J.) argued that the capital case presented a special circumstance which distinguished *Finley*. They stressed the special needs of capital petitioners, as reflected by a success rate on habeas challenges of 60–70%, as compared to a rate of 0.25–7% in noncapital cases. Four justices (per Rehnquist, C.J.) thought *Finley* controlling. While the Eighth Amendment and the due process clause required additional procedural safeguards for capital cases at trial, the Court had consistently refused to apply special standards on appellate and collateral review. The deciding vote was cast by Justice Kennedy. He initially accepted Justice Stevens' analysis insofar as it established (1) that "collateral proceedings are a central part of the review process for prisoners condemned to death" and (2) that the "complexity of our jurisprudence in this area * * * makes it unlikely that capital defendants will be able to file successful petitions for collateral relief without the assistance of persons learned in the law." He noted, however, that the necessary assistance can be provided in "various ways" and there was no showing that Virginia's approach (which made available the assistance of "unit attorneys") had been unsatisfactory. Accordingly, Justice Kennedy concurred in the rejection of the inmates' claim based "on the facts and record of this case."

§ 7.4 WAIVER OF COUNSEL AND THE RIGHT TO PROCEED PRO SE

(a) The "knowing and intelligent" requirement

The Supreme Court frequently has noted that the defendant may waive his constitutional right to assistance of counsel, but a waiver will be acceptable only if made "knowingly and intelligently." *Johnson v. Zerbst* (1938). At the same time, it has emphasized that waiver will not be "lightly assumed." "Trial courts must indulge every reasonable presumption against waiver." Id. What is necessary to establish a valid waiver will vary with the setting in which the waiver occurred. Previous sections have dealt with the waiver of counsel in connection with police investigative practices. See §§ 4.3(f), 4.9, 5.2(b). Our concern here is with waiver in what the Supreme Court has characterized as a "trial-type situation." *Schneckloth v. Bustamonte* (1973). In that setting, *Carnley v. Cochran* (1962) holds that waiver will not be presumed from a "silent record"; the evidence must show that the defendant was informed specifically of his right to the assistance of appointed or retained counsel and that he clearly rejected such assistance. "No amount of circumstantial evidence that the person may have been aware of his right [and intended to silently relinquish it] will suffice" as a replacement for specific notice and rejection on the record.

Even though the formal prerequisites of *Carnley* are established, the rejection of counsel still may not have been made "knowingly and intelligently"—i.e., it may not have been the product of a reasoned and deliberate choice based upon adequate knowledge of what the assistance of counsel encompasses. In determining whether defendant's rejection reflects such a choice, courts rely upon an analysis of the particular facts of the case, including defendant's age, mental condition, and experience, the particular setting in which the offer of counsel was made, and the manner in which it was explained. Moreover, a valid waiver at one stage of the proceeding (e.g., preliminary examination) does not necessarily indicate an intent to waive at a later stage (e.g., trial), and the prosecution must show that the defendant was given the opportunity to exercise his right to counsel at each separate stage.

Waiver of counsel builds upon, and should be distinguished from, the general level of mental competency that a defendant must possess to stand trial. Due process prohibits proceeding against a defendant unless he has "sufficient present ability to consult with his lawyer with a reasonable degree of rational understanding and has a rational as well as factual understanding of the proceedings against him," *Godinez v. Moran* (1993), and under certain circumstances, will require a psychiatric evaluation in order to assess whether defendant has that level of competency, *Drope v. Mo.* (1975). But once competency is established, no "higher standard" of mental capacity is required for waiving counsel or pleading guilty, although those waivers require separate inquiries to ensure that the defendant has the specific understanding needed for a "knowing and voluntary" of the particular rights being waived. *Godinez,* supra.

(b) Waiver prior to the entry of a guilty plea

Very frequently the defendant at arraignment will seek to waive counsel with the obvious intention of entering a plea of guilty. The constitutional limitation upon waiver in this circumstance is supplemented by the due process requirement that the guilty plea be voluntary. See § 8.5(a),(b). But as to the waiver of counsel itself, the Court has insisted that the trial judge, in addition to specifically advising defendant of his right to counsel, also make a careful inquiry to ensure that defendant appreciates the type of decision he is making on his own. In *Von Moltke v. Gillies* (1948), four justices suggested that the trial court must seek to ensure that that waiver is made "with an apprehension of the nature of the charges, the statutory offenses included within them, the range of allowable punishments thereunder, possible defenses to the charges and circumstances in mitigation thereof, and all other facts essential to a broad understanding of the whole matter." Lower courts generally view this standard as a basic guideline, rather than a precise formula, and will not hold a waiver invalid, for example, merely because the trial court failed to inform the defendant of something he obviously knew or something that would have been of no importance in the context of the case.

(c) The right to proceed pro se

Faretta v. Cal. (1975) held that the Sixth Amendment also guarantees to the defendant the right to proceed *pro se* (i.e., to represent himself without counsel). *Faretta* relied upon the "structure of the Sixth Amendment, as well as * * * the English and colonial jurisprudence from which the Amendment emerged." The Court noted that, while the Sixth Amendment does not specifically refer to the right of self-representation, that right is "necessarily implied" by the Amendment's references to the accused's presentation of his defense. The Sixth Amendment, it noted, refers to the rights of confrontation, compulsory process, and notice as rights of "the accused." Similarly, the counsel provision speaks only of the "assistance" of counsel, and suggests thereby that "counsel, like the other defense tools guaranteed * * * shall be an aid to a willing defendant—not an organ of the State interposed between an unwilling defendant and his right to defend himself personally."

Faretta recognized that a constitutional right to proceed *pro se* "seems to cut against the grain" of decisions, like *Gideon,* that are based on the premise that "the help of a lawyer is essential to assure a fair trial." It rejected, however, the dissent's contention that the state's interest in providing a fair trial permitted it to insist upon representation by counsel. An analysis of the historical roots of the Sixth Amendment suggested that the founders had placed on a higher level the right of "free choice." Moreover, where the defendant opposes representation by counsel, "the potential advantage of a lawyer * * * can be realized, if at all, only imperfectly. To force a lawyer on a defendant can only lead him to believe that the law contrives against him."

(d) Waiver in the pro se situation

Faretta stressed that the defendant who proceeds *pro se* must act "knowingly and intelligently" in giving up those "traditional benefits associated with the right to counsel." Thus, "he should be made aware of the dangers and disadvantages of self-representation, so that the record will establish that 'he knows what he is doing and his choice is made with eyes open.' " The Court also noted that the right to self-representation "is not a license to abuse the dignity of the courtroom." Under *Ill. v. Allen* (§ 8.8(b)), the judge may terminate self-representation by a defendant "who deliberately engages in serious and obstructionist misconduct." Similarly, self-representation is "not a license" for failure to comply with "relevant rules of procedural and substantive law." Thus, "whatever else may or may not be open to him on appeal, a defendant who elects to represent himself cannot thereafter complain that the quality of his own defense amounted to a denial of 'effective assistance of counsel.' "

Once the trial court is assured that the defendant is knowingly and intelligently giving up the benefits of counsel, it must accept his decision. It matters not that defendant lacks "technical legal knowledge." A person need not "have the skill and experience of a lawyer in order to competently and intelligently choose self-representation." If the defendant is improperly denied a request to proceed pro se (which must be timely), the state cannot argue that the error was "harmless" because counsel gave defendant better representation than he could have given himself. "Since the right of representation is a right that when exercised usually increases the likelihood of a trial outcome unfavorable to the defendant, its denial is not amenable to 'harmless error' analysis." *McKaskle v. Wiggins* (1984).

(e) Standby counsel

Faretta had noted that "a state may—even over objection by the accused—appoint a 'standby counsel' to aid the accused if and when the accused requests help and to be available to represent the accused in the event that termination of the defendant's self-representation is necessary." *McKaskle v. Wiggins* (1984) added that the standby counsel appointed over defendant's objection was not necessarily limited to a "seen but not heard" role. The trial court could properly direct counsel to "steer the defendant through the basic procedures of trial," thereby relieving the court of that responsibility. In *McKaskle,* however, standby counsel had engaged in unsolicited participation that involved more than "routine clerical or procedural matters." Nonetheless, such action was deemed not to violate defendant's right to proceed pro se because (i) it did not interfere with defendant's own actions in such a way as to deprive him of "actual control over the case he chose to present to the jury," and

(ii) it did not "destroy the jury's perception that the defendant [was] representing himself."

§ 7.5　LAWYER–CLIENT RELATIONSHIP

(a) Selection of appointed client

Morris v. Slappy (1983) concluded that the record there did not actually present the issue considered by the appellate court below—whether a defendant whose originally appointed public defender had been hospitalized for emergency surgery was entitled to a timely requested delay until that defender could return to the case, even though a substitute defender was prepared for the trial as originally scheduled. The Court nevertheless went on to criticize the lower appellate court's conclusion that the refusal to grant such a continuance would deprive defendant of a "meaningful attorney-client relationship and therefore violate his Sixth Amendment right to appointed counsel." Flatly rejecting that "novel idea," the Court noted that the Sixth Amendment hardly guaranteed defendant "the kind of rapport with his attorney" that the court below envisaged. It was sufficient that counsel was competent and prepared, and when that was the case, an appellate court must keep in mind "the broad discretion that must be granted trial courts on matters of continuances." The Sixth Amendment, *Slappy* indicates, mandates only that appointed counsel be capable of effective representation, not that she or he be the counsel in whom the indigent defendant has the most confidence.

(b) Choice of retained counsel

A defendant's right to retained counsel obviously includes the right to select counsel of his choice, but that right is not absolute. In *Wheat v. U.S.,* discussed in § 7.7(f), the Court stressed that the right to counsel of choice was an aspect of a general right to counsel designed to "guarantee an effective advocate" in an adversary system, and that choice therefore could be limited consistent with the fundamental tenets of the adversary system. Thus, a trial court may insist that counsel "be qualified to practice law" under applicable standards, and may, as in *Wheat,* refuse to accept counsel whose joint representation of codefendants presents a potential conflict of interest.

Other concerns of judicial administration also may prevail over the right to counsel of choice, although here a trial court may have a greater obligation to seek to accommodate defendant's choice. *Powell v. Ala.* (1932) established that the right to retained counsel included as a "necessary corollary" the right to a reasonable delay to employ retained counsel, but the trial court may, under appropriate circumstances, restrict defendant's choice through its imposition of scheduling requirements. The right to counsel of one's choice, it frequently is noted, may not be insisted upon at the expense of the trial court's power to ensure that there is an orderly disposition of its docket.

See *Ungar v. Sarafite* (1964) (rejecting a constitutional challenge to a continuance denial that resulted in the withdrawal of defense counsel and self-representation by defendant, who was a lawyer, and citing such factors as defendant's delay in seeking the continuance, ample time for counsel's preparation in light of the evidence and clearly identified issues, and the need to give deference to the trial judge's judgment).

In *Caplin & Drysdale Chartered v. U.S.* (1989), the Court sustained a restriction on defendant's ability to retain counsel of choice flowing from a governmental interest totally unrelated to judicial administration. At issue there was the asset forfeiture provisions of a federal statute which subjected to forfeiture all properties "constituting or derived from" the "proceeds" of any drug distribution enterprise. With the forfeiture provisions allowing for both a governmental recapture of all such properties transferred to third parties (including lawyers) and a pretrial freeze on their transfer, the Court assumed that their impact in particular cases would be to render defendants unable to hire any counsel, forcing them to accept court appointed counsel. The dissenters saw these provisions as giving the prosecution an "intolerable degree of power over any private attorney" through the use of a "fictive property law concept." The majority, however, characterized the government's property interest and the petitioner's claim quite differently. The defendant, it noted, certainly "has no Sixth Amendment right to spend another person's money for services rendered by an attorney," and that is what was at stake here. Under the well accepted "taint theory" of forfeiture law, the defendant never had "good title" to the property, as the government obtained a "vested property interest" in the proceeds at the point at which the illegal transactions occurred. The government was fully entitled through the exercise of that interest to "separate a criminal from his ill gotten gains" (which were either returned to defrauded rightful owners or devoted to law enforcement) and thereby to strip the drug enterprise of "undeserved economic power," including "the ability to command high priced legal talent."

(c) Counsel's control over defense strategy

Although a defendant has a right to proceed pro se, if the defendant proceeds with counsel, the defendant will have no constitutional complaint if counsel makes strategic decisions contrary to defendant's wishes. Thus, *Jones v. Barnes* (1983) held that a defendant was not denied the effective assistance of counsel where appellate counsel refused to brief a nonfrivolous claim that his client wished to press. Counsel was free to make a strategic choice of contentions, following the time tested advice of advocates that inclusion of "every colorable claim" will "dilute and weaken a good case and will not save a bad one." So too, in *Taylor v. Ill.* (1988), the defendant was stuck with the consequences of counsel's strategy, apparently adopted without consultation with the client, which risked exclusion of evidence rather than give the prosecution advance notice (and time to investigate) as required by the state's discovery rules.

Certain decisions, however, though they may have a strategic element, are so "personal" that counsel must abide by his client's wishes. These include decisions that involve actions by the defendant and basic issues as to the structure of the proceeding. Thus, the Supreme Court has stated, in dictum or holding, that it is for the defendant to decide whether to take each of the following steps: plead guilty or take action tantamount to entering a plea, as in *Brookhart v. Janis* (1966) (where the defense counsel argued that the state need only produce a prima facie case which the defense would not contest); waive the right to jury trial; waive the right to be present at trial; testify on his own behalf; or forego an appeal. See *Jones,* supra; *Taylor,* supra.

§ 7.6 STATE INTERFERENCE WITH COUNSEL

(a) Restrictions upon counsel's assistance

The "right to the assistance of counsel," the Supreme Court noted in *Herring v. N.Y.* (1975), "has been understood to mean that there can be no restrictions upon the function of counsel in defending a criminal prosecution in accord with the traditions of the adversary factfinding process." Accordingly, state action, whether by statute or trial court ruling, that prohibits counsel from making full use of traditional trial procedures may be viewed as denying defendant the effective assistance of counsel. In considering the constitutionality of such "state interference," courts are directed to look to whether the interference denied counsel "the opportunity to participate fully and fairly in the adversary factfinding process." If the interference had that effect, then the overall performance of counsel apart from the interference, and the lack of any showing of actual prejudice, are both irrelevant.

Three Supreme Court cases illustrate the type of state imposed restriction upon counsel's performance that will be held to violate the Sixth Amendment. In *Geders v. U.S.* (1976), the Court found unconstitutional interference when the trial court ordered the defendant not to consult with his attorney during an overnight recess which separated the direct-examination and the cross-examination of the defendant. But note *Perry v. Leeke* (§ 8.8(f)). In *Herring v. N.Y.* (1975), the Court held that defendant's Sixth Amendment right to counsel was violated by a statute under which the trial court could refuse to permit a closing argument in a bench trial. The Court reasoned that a final summation by counsel was as basic an element of the adversary process in a bench trial as it was in a jury trial. In *Brooks v. Tenn.* (1972), a statute requiring the defendant to testify as the first defense witness or not at all was held to deprive the defendant of the " 'guiding hand of counsel' in the timing of this critical element of the defense." In each of these cases, it should be noted, the Court might also have found the particular restriction unconstitutional on the ground that it imposed an undue burden on the exercise of a constitutionally protected trial right. See § 8.8(e) (discussing the alternative grounding of *Brooks*).

(b) Defective appointment

In *U.S. v. Cronic* (1984), the Court noted that there could be situations in which the appointment of counsel was so deficient as to be treated as an automatic violation of the Sixth Amendment, in much the same fashion as a failure to appoint counsel (as in *Gideon*) or a state action that "prevented [counsel] from assisting the accused during a critical stage of the proceeding" (as in the cases discussed in (a) supra). In those two situations, a "breakdown of the adversarial process [is] presumed"; the "circumstances * * * [are] so likely to prejudice the accused that the cost of litigating their effect in a particular case is unjustified." A similar breakdown could be presented by the manner and setting in which counsel is appointed. There may be "occasions when, although counsel is available to assist the accused during trial, the likelihood that any lawyer, even a fully competent one, could provide effective assistance is so small that a presumption of prejudice is appropriate without inquiry into the actual conduct of the trial." In such instances, the Court would not determine whether counsel's performance was in

fact defective under the standard specified in
Strickland v. Washington (§ 7.7(b)), but would, instead, presume an "adverse effect on the reliability
of the trial process" resulting in a denial of defendant's Sixth Amendment right.

Cronic offered one illustration of a case involving
an appointment so defective as to be treated as a
per se Sixth Amendment violation. That case was
Powell v. Ala. (1932). The trial court there had
utilized such a haphazard process of appointment—ordering admittedly unprepared outstate
counsel to proceed with whatever help the local
bar, appointed en masse, might provide—that
there was no need to look at the actual performance of counsel in determining that defendant's
constitutional rights had been violated. *Cronic*
rejected the contention, however, that the case
before it fell in the same category.

The lower appellate court in *Cronic*, without
referring to any specific error or inadequacy in
counsel's performance, had found that counsel
could not have been able to "discharge his duties"
in light of five factors: "(1) [T]he [limited] time
afforded for investigation and preparation; (2) the
[in]experience of counsel; (3) the gravity of the
charge; (4) the complexity of possible defenses;
and (5) the [in]accessibility of witnesses to counsel."
The *Cronic* majority acknowledged that these five
factors were "relevant to an evaluation of a lawyer's ineffectiveness in a particular case, but neither separately nor in combination [did] they pro-

vide a basis for concluding that competent counsel was not able to provide * * * the guiding hand that the Constitution guarantees." The Court had previously refused to "fashion a per se rule requiring reversal of every conviction following tardy appointment of counsel," *Chambers v. Maroney* (1970), and neither would it find per se ineffectiveness because counsel was young and conducting his first jury trial in a serious, complex case.

(c) State invasion of the lawyer-client relationship

In *Weatherford v. Bursey,* discussed in § 6.2(b), the Court recognized that a state invasion of a lawyer-client relationship (there an informant's participation in a conference between defendant and his lawyer) could constitute a Sixth Amendment violation, but only if the situation posed a realistic likelihood of the state having gained some advantage. The approach here, like that in *Cronic,* was to look to the actual impact upon the adversarial system. *U.S. v. Morrison* (1981) raised the question of whether a showing of actual adverse impact should also be required where the government had absolutely no justification for the invasion (in comparison to *Weatherford,* where the informant participated in the conference to avoid revealing his true status). In *Morrison,* D.E.A. agents met with the accused in the absence of her retained attorney and disparaged his likely performance. The Court found it unnecessary to rule on the government's contention that a Sixth Amendment violation could not be established without "some [defense] showing of prejudice," because the court below had gone too far in ordering dismissal of the prosecution, a remedy in no way "tailored" to the injury that may have been suffered.

§ 7.7 EFFECTIVE ASSISTANCE OF COUNSEL

(a) Constitutional foundation

The Supreme Court has long recognized, with respect to the due process/fair hearing right to counsel, the Sixth Amendment right to counsel, and the equal protection right to counsel, that these rights are not fulfilled if counsel fails to provide effective assistance to the defendant. See e.g., *Powell v. Ala.* (1932); *Jones v. Barnes* (1983). In *U.S. v. Cronic* (1984), the Court explained both the relationship of the effective assistance requirement to the constitutional right to counsel and the general nature of the quality of assistance it demands. *Cronic* noted that the function of the right to counsel, "assur[ing] fairness in the adversary process," necessarily requires that accused have a counsel who acts as his advocate and subjects the prosecution's case to the "crucible of meaningful adversary testing." Accordingly, "when a true adversarial criminal trial has been conducted—even if defense counsel may have made demonstrable errors—the kind of testing envisioned by the Sixth Amendment has occurred." A violation of the right to counsel flows only from a deficiency in counsel that causes "the process [to] lose * * * its character as a confrontation between adversaries."

Consistent with the analysis of *Cronic,* the Court has held that defendant does not have a constitutional basis for complaining about even the most clearly deficient performance of counsel where he lacked an underlying constitutional right to counsel that was tied to ensuring a fair proceeding. Thus, *Wainwright v. Torna* (1982) found that no constitutional right of the defendant had been violated by the negligence of his retained attorney in failing to file a timely application for discretionary review at the state's second level of appeal. At that stage of the proceedings, a defendant has neither a Sixth Amendment, equal protection, nor due process/fair hearing right to the assistance of counsel. See *Ross v. Moffitt* (§ 7.3(h)). While defendant arguably might have a due process right not to have the state interfere with his full deployment of his resources by presenting his case through retained counsel (see § 7.2(b)), there is no such state interference where retained counsel has simply been negligent.

The defendant in a case like *Torna* must bear the consequences of his unwise choice of counsel. The same is not true, however, when defendant has a constitutional right to counsel tied to ensuring a fair proceeding. At one time, it was thought that a deficient trial performance by retained counsel did not present a constitutional violation unless that deficiency was so obvious that the trial judge should have known that the adversarial process was breaking down. This was distinguished from incompetency by appointed counsel, where the state was thought to have greater responsibility since the court had selected counsel. Such a distinction in judging the performance of retained and appointed counsel was rejected in *Cuyler v. Sullivan* (1980), where the Court noted: "Since the State's conduct of a criminal trial itself implicates the State in the defendant's conviction, we see no basis for drawing a distinction between retained and appointed counsel that would deny equal justice to defendants who must choose their own lawyers." While *Cuyler* dealt with the Sixth Amendment right to counsel, the state's responsibility would be similar in those proceedings not a part of the criminal prosecution where the due process/fair hearing rationale, equal protection, or a derivative right analysis guarantees a right to the assistance of counsel. See *Evitts v. Lucey* (§ 7.3(h)).

(b) The *Strickland* standards

Strickland v. Washington (1984) set forth a two-pronged standard for determining whether counsel's performance was so defective as to deny defendant his constitutional right to counsel. Under *Strickland,* to establish constitutionally ineffective representation, the defendant must prove both incompetence and prejudice. Incompetency is to be judged by an "objective standard of reasonableness": "Whether in light of all the circumstances, the identified acts or omissions [of counsel] were outside the range of professionally competent assistance." The standard for the element of prejudice is whether "there is a reasonable probability that, but for counsel's unprofessional errors, the result of the proceeding would have been different." A "reasonable probability" in this regard is "a probability sufficient to undermine confidence in the outcome."

Prior to *Strickland,* several lower courts had relied heavily upon generally accepted guidelines for counsel's performance, such as the A.B.A. Standards, in judging competency. Indeed, some had suggested that any substantial deviation from those guidelines automatically established incompetency. The *Strickland* majority flatly rejected this approach in explaining its standard of reasonableness. The "performance inquiry" the Court noted, "must be whether counsel's assistance was reasonable under all the circumstances" and "more specific guidelines are not appropriate." Utilizing specific guidelines as a per se test for competent performance was inappropriate because (i) "no particular set of detailed rules for counsel's conduct can satisfactorily take account of the variety of circumstances faced by defense counsel or the range of legitimate decisions regarding how best to represent a criminal defendant," and (ii) "reliance on such guidelines * * * could distract counsel from the overriding mission of vigorous advocacy of the defendant's cause." Of course, prevailing norms of practice help to define reasonableness, but the ultimate point of reference is whether counsel's performance met a level consistent with "the proper functioning of the adversarial process"—for that is what sets "the range of competence demanded of attorneys in criminal cases."

Consistent with its emphasis upon a fact-sensitized judgment respecting "the wide latitude counsel must have in making tactical decisions," the *Strickland* majority also warned lower courts against "second-guess[ing]" counsel's performance: "Judicial scrutiny * * * must be highly differential. * * * A fair assessment of attorney performance requires that every effort be made to eliminate the distorting effects of hindsight, to reconstruct the circumstances of counsel's challenged conduct, and to evaluate the conduct from counsel's perspective at the time. Because of the difficulties inherent in making the evaluation, a court must indulge a strong presumption that counsel's conduct falls within the wide range of reasonable professional assistance; that is, the defendant must overcome the presumption that, under the circumstances, the challenged action 'might be considered sound trial strategy.' "

Prior to *Strickland,* lower courts had taken a wide variety of positions on the element of prejudice in an ineffective assistance claim, ranging from presuming prejudice upon a finding of incompetency to placing a heavy burden on defendant to show prejudice. *Strickland* sought to resolve those differences in its explanation of its prejudice prong.

The Court initially noted that, since the underlying function of the constitutional right to counsel is to "ensure * * * the assistance necessary to justify reliance on the outcome of the proceeding," any deficiency in counsel's performance "must be prejudicial to the defense in order to constitute ineffective assistance."

Moreover, here, unlike the situation in the state interference cases (see § 7.6(a)), or conflict of interest cases (see (c) infra), such prejudice could not be presumed: "Attorney errors come in an infinite variety and are as likely to be utterly harmless in a particular case as they are to be prejudicial." As for the requisite likelihood of prejudice, the Court described its "reasonable probability" standard as falling between the overly lenient "some conceivable effect" standard (which would invariably lead to a finding of prejudice) and the overly rigorous "more likely than not" test (which would ignore the constitutional grounding of defendant's claim by placing upon it the same burden applied to newly discovered evidence).

In light of the function of the prejudice requirement, the Court has warned against "an analysis focusing solely on mere outcome determination, without attention to whether the result of the proceeding was fundamentally unfair or unreliable." *Lockhart v. Fretwell* (1993). Prejudice does not automatically follow from a reasonable probability of a different result had counsel been competent. Thus, *Nix v. Whiteside* (1986) held that defendant, "as a matter of law," could not establish prejudice where he claimed that his counsel had improperly prevented him from presenting perjured testimony which could have swayed the jury. So too, in *Lockhart,* supra, the Court held that there was "no 'prejudice' within the meaning of *Strickland*" where counsel's incompetence consisted of failing to present an objection that was supported by precedent at the time of trial, but later was rejected with the overturning of that precedent. In *Kimmelman v. Morrison* (1986), counsel's incompetence was in failing to present a Fourth Amendment exclusionary rule claim, and the Court remanded for consideration of the prejudice issue. Arguably implicit in the remand was the assumption that prejudice would be established if there was a reasonable likelihood that the exclusion of the illegally seized evidence would have altered the outcome. However, three concurring justices argued that the failure to gain exclusion of evidence that clearly was reliable, though illegally seized, did not lead to "an unjust or fundamentally unfair result" and therefore could not constitute prejudice.

(c) Application of the *Strickland* standards

A series of post-*Strickland* Supreme Court rulings illustrate the application of the *Strickland* standards. *Nix v. Whiteside* (1986) and *Smith v. Murray* (1986) present examples of ineffective assistance claims easily rejected under the *Strickland* standards, *Kimmelman v. Morrison* (1986) a claim easily sustained as to incompetence, and *Burger v. Kemp* (1987) a claim that sharply divided the Court as to incompetence.

The defendant in *Whiteside* alleged ineffectiveness based on counsel's threat to withdraw and reveal defendant's perjury if defendant persisted in his plans to testify falsely, a threat which led defendant to delete false statements from his actual testimony. The Court unanimously concluded that defendant failed to meet the prejudice prong of *Strickland.* Five justices added that defendant had failed as well to meet the incompetency prong of *Strickland.* While the *Strickland* opinion had warned against viewing the breach of an ethical standard or other guideline as incompetency per se, where counsel's action was fully consistent with universally accepted ethical standards (here, those relating to client perjury), that action could hardly be deemed to fall below prevailing professional norms.

The defendant in *Smith* based his ineffectiveness claim on counsel's failure to raise on appeal a Fifth Amendment contention that had been presented at trial and that was later found to have merit. Although defendant alleged that it was "inconceivable" that counsel would have discarded the claim as lacking merit if he had "investigated [it] more fully," the Court viewed the surrounding circumstances as painting a different picture of counsel's performance. Counsel had conducted a vigorous defense, had researched a wide range of claims prior to filing an appeal, and had obviously sought to "winnow out" those he viewed as weaker, a "hallmark of effective advocacy." "Often," the Court noted, "even the most informed counsel will fail to anticipate" a new ruling overturning an "established state rule," which was what had happened here.

In *Kimmelman,* the incompetency claim was based on counsel's failure to file in a timely fashion a defense motion to suppress items obtained through an allegedly unconstitutional search, an error which led to the trial court's refusal to consider the merits of the untimely motion. Counsel's explanation for his failure to make the motion before trial (as required) was that he hadn't previously known that the state had seized those items. Although he would have learned of the seizure through readily available pretrial discovery, counsel hadn't sought such discovery because (i) he had assumed the state had a legal obligation to inform him of its evidence and (ii) he had not expected the case to go to trial because the complainant was reluctant to testify (although there had been no court order needed to justify a dismissal on that ground). These answers, the Court noted, reflected a "startling ignorance" of state law and practice that clearly placed counsel's actions outside "prevailing professional norms." There was no suggestion counsel's decision was tactical, and his error could not be excused by otherwise competent performance during the remainder of the trial.

The claim of incompetency in *Burger* was based on counsel's failure to both develop and present in a capital sentencing hearing substantial mitigating evidence relating to defendant's background. Finding that this omission did not fall outside "the wide range of professionally competent assistance," the majority noted that counsel had learned of some of the mitigating evidence in the course of interviewing defendant and the persons closest to him, but had concluded that introducing such material would open the door to cross-examination that might be especially harmful. Having made a "reasonable professional judgment" after interviewing "all potential witnesses who had been called to his attention," counsel's failure to conduct an "all out investigation into petitioner's background" did not constitute incompetency. The dissenters argued that with background information playing such a crucial role in capital sentencing hearings, counsel could not make a "reasonable professional judgment" not to present such information based on his limited investigation. Thus, as the majority saw the case, counsel had made a tactical judgment based on a reasonable though not thorough investigation, and as the dissenters saw it, counsel had simply jumped to a conclusion, using some very feeble excuses for failing to explore adequately an issue of obvious importance.

(d) Multiple representation and conflicts of interest

One requirement of effective assistance is that counsel's actions stem from his "undivided loyalty" to his client rather than from an attempt to balance his client's interests against the interests of another. While various situations can subject counsel to a conflict of interest, the decisions of the Supreme Court have dealt primarily with the conflict potential in joint representation of codefendants by a single attorney. Although acknowledging that the possibility of prejudice "inheres in almost every instance of multiple representation," the Court has refused to treat joint representation as "per se violative of constitutional guarantees of effective assistance of counsel." *Holloway v. Ark.* (1978). While the obligations of representing codefendants may lead counsel to take action that favors one over the other, there are instances where joint representation may benefit both defendants, as where "a common defense * * * gives strength against a common attack." *Holloway.*

To establish incompetency based upon counsel's performance in a multiple representation situation, defendant must show "an actual conflict of interest [that] adversely affected his lawyer's performance." *Cuyler v. Sullivan* (1980). *Glasser v. U.S.* (1942) is illustrative. The record there showed that counsel had failed to cross-examine a key witness against Glasser and had failed to object to "arguably inadmissible evidence." Both omissions then were found to "have resulted from counsel's desire to diminish the jury's perception of a codefendant's guilt," which established an actual, acted upon conflict. That such a conflict existed is not always evident, as it was in *Glasser*, from the fact that counsel failed to adopt a particular strategy that might have helped defendant while working to the disadvantage of a codefendant. Depending upon the available evidence (including counsel's own testimony at any post-trial inquiry), a court may conclude that counsel in fact acted in what he believed to be the defendant's best interests in deciding against that strategy (i.e., he did not act to protect the jointly represented codefendant). If that is the case, and counsel's decision otherwise was an acceptable professional judgment, then incompetency has not been established. See *Burger v. Kemp* (1987).

Once the defendant establishes that "a conflict of interest actually affected the adequacy of his representation," he is automatically entitled to relief. *Holloway.* Here, an exception is drawn to the proof-of-prejudice requirement of *Strickland.* A showing of likely prejudicial impact upon the outcome of the proceeding is not needed even though the constitutional violation is based on counsel's actual performance. Rather, a "presumption of prejudice" is drawn, as in the state interference cases. Adoption of such a presumption is deemed appropriate because (i) "the duty of loyalty to a client is 'perhaps the most basic' responsibility of counsel," (ii) " 'it is difficult to measure the precise effect on the defense of representation corrupted by conflicting interests', * * * due in part to the fact that the conflict may affect almost any aspect of the lawyer's preparation and presentation of the case," (iii) lawyers "are charged with knowledge that they are obliged to avoid such conflict," and (iv) a "judge can avoid the problem by questioning the defendant, in any case presenting a situation that may give rise to a conflict, in order to determine whether the defendant is aware of the possible conflict and whether he has waived his right to conflict-free representation." *Burger v. Kemp* (1987) (Blackmun, J. dis.).

(e) Trial court duty to inquire

Holloway v. Ark. (1978) established that, under some circumstances, the trial court has a constitutional obligation to inquire into the existence of an actual conflict, and that violation of that duty will constitute in itself an abridgment of the defendant's constitutional right to counsel. In *Holloway,* a public defender made a timely objection to his joint representation of three codefendants. The defender informed the trial court that one or two of the defendants might testify, and he would not be able to cross-examine a testifying defendant on behalf of the other defendants because of "confidential information" he had received from each of the codefendants. The trial court pushed aside counsel's concern, directing him simply to let each defendant testify "to what he wants." This was done and each of the defendants testified (in narrative form) that he was not at the scene of the crime. Reversing the convictions of the three codefendants, the Supreme Court held that "in the face of the representations made by counsel," the trial court failed to safeguard the defendant's constitutional right to the assistance of counsel and thereby committed reversible error. Even if counsel had not provided the trial court with sufficient information to establish the constitutional necessity for separate representation, that court had the obligation to make sufficient inquiry to ensure that the "risk [of conflict] was too remote to warrant separate counsel." The trial court's failure to take that step relieved the defendants of the obligation of showing that an actual conflict had existed.

The *Holloway* opinion specifically left open the scope of the trial court's responsibility "where the trial counsel did nothing to advise the trial court as to the actuality or possibility of a conflict." In the subsequent decision of *Cuyler v. Sullivan* (1980), the Court held that a considerably different standard applied to that situation. *Cuyler* initially rejected the contention that a trial court had a constitutional duty to make some inquiry as to a possible conflict in all cases of multiple representation. Ordinarily, the Court noted, the trial judge could rely upon the absence of any objection by counsel, since counsel has "an ethical obligation to avoid conflicting representations and to advise the court promptly when a conflict arises during the course of the trial." Thus, "absent special circumstances," where counsel has raised no objection, the trial court "may assume either that multiple representation entails no conflict or that the lawyer and his clients knowingly accept such a risk of conflict as may exist." The Court noted, however, that there may be cases where the trial court "reasonably should know" from the surrounding circumstances that a particular conflict exists and then it would have an obligation to make an inquiry on its own initiative. Such circumstances were not present in *Cuyler,* where the defense attorneys' presentation was consistent on its face with the protection of the interests of all the codefendants they represented.

(f) Disqualification of potentially conflicted counsel

Wheat v. U.S. (1988) sets forth the constitutional standards governing a trial court's disqualification of counsel whose multiple representation creates a potential conflict of interest. The Court there found that the trial court had not violated defendant's Sixth Amendment right to counsel of choice when it rejected defendant's motion, "made close to trial," to allow him to be represented by the same lawyer who represented two other codefendants in a complex drug conspiracy, one of whom the government intended to call as a prosecution witness at defendant's trial. The *Wheat* majority initially rejected the defense contention that "the provision of waivers by all affected defendants cures any problems created by multiple representation." A trial court could appropriately prefer not to rely on such a waiver. It could take cognizance of inherent weaknesses in such waivers that could lead to later challenges—recognizing that potential conflicts often reflect "imponderables" that "are difficult enough for a lawyer to assess, and even more difficult to convey by way of explanation to a criminal defendant untutored by the niceties of legal ethics," and that "the willingness of an attorney to obtain such waivers from his clients may bear an inverse relation to the case with which he conveys all the necessary information to them." Moreover, the trial courts also may give weight to the institutional interest of "ensuring that criminal trials are conducted within the ethical standards of the profession and that the legal proceedings appear fair to all who observe them."

The Court stressed, however, that while the trial court must be given "substantial latitude in refusing waivers," that authority was not unlimited. The trial court's findings must establish a sufficient likelihood of conflicted representation to overcome the Sixth Amendment presumption favoring defendant's choice of counsel. Because the likely materialization and dimensions of a conflict are "notoriously hard to predict" in the "murkier pretrial context when relationships between parties are seen through a glass darkly," the authority to disqualify would not be limited to cases in which an actual conflict was apparent. The trial court could properly override the presumption also upon a finding of "a serious potential for conflict", and in making that finding, it could look to its "instinct and judgment based on experience" in evaluating those factors that could produce an actual conflict.

CHAPTER 8

THE POST-INVESTIGATORY PROCESS: FROM BAIL TO APPELLATE REVIEW

§ 8.1 PRETRIAL RELEASE

(a) Eighth Amendment

The Eighth Amendment provides in part: "Excessive bail shall not be required." Although the Court has not had occasion to rule on whether this prohibition is incorporated in the Fourteenth Amendment, *Schilb v. Kuebel* (1971) stated that it "has been assumed to have application to the States through the Fourteenth Amendment." The traditional purpose for setting "bail"—whether it be in the form of a bail bond, property deposit, third-party supervision, or some other condition of release—is to assure that the accused will appear at subsequent proceedings. *Stack v. Boyle* (1951). In this context, the prohibition against excessive bail bars imposing conditions for release beyond what is "reasonably calculated" to provide "adequate assurance" of the "presence of the accused" at those proceedings. *Stack.* Setting bail that provides such assurance requires an assessment of the facts of the particular case, and not simply looking to the character of the offense charged. Id.

U.S. v. Salerno (1987) rejected the contention that preclusion of flight is the only constitutionally acceptable grounding for setting conditions of bail. The Court there denied a challenge to the constitutionality on its face of a "preventive detention" statute. That statute directed that the setting of bail also take into account the protection of community safety, and authorized denial of release where no set of conditions would "reasonably assure the safety of any other person or the community." The Court found no need to rule on the suggestion, advanced in dictum in *Carlson v. Landon* (1952), that the Eighth Amendment serves only to bar judicial setting of excessive bail and does not limit Congress' authority to make nonbailable particular classes of offenses or offenders. For even if it were "to conclude that the Eighth Amendment imposes some substantive limitation on the National Legislature's powers in this area," the "only arguable substantive limitation of the Bail Clause is that the government's proposed conditions of release or detention not be 'excessive' in light of the perceived evil." "Nothing in the text of the Bail Clause," the Court noted, "limits permissible government considerations solely to questions of flight." The history of the clause, allowing the refusal of bail in capital cases and as to defendants who present a threat to witnesses, was also cited as supporting Congress' authority to take account of other "compelling interests" beyond flight, as it did in the preventive detention statute.

(b) Due process

As noted in *Salerno,* denial of pretrial release also may raise substantive and procedural due process difficulties. While the presumption of innocence is viewed solely as "a doctrine that allocates the burden of proof" at trial and therefore has "no application * * * before trial has even begun," *Bell v. Wolfish* (1979), substantive due process would bar a pretrial detention provision aimed at punishing individuals thought to be dangerous but not yet found guilty of crimes. *Salerno* concluded that the pretrial detention provision upheld there was not aimed at punishment, but designed to serve the "legitimate regulatory goal" of "preventing danger to the community." The "incidents of pretrial detention" under the statute both clearly reflected that objective and avoided excessive detention. These included limiting "the circumstances under which detention may be sought to the most serious crimes," providing a "prompt detention hearing" at which "the government must convince a neutral decisionmaker by clear and convincing evidence that no conditions of release can reasonably assure the safety of the community," the limitation of the length of detention by the "stringent time limitations of the Speedy Trial Act," and the requirement that detainees be housed separately from convicted defendants insofar as that is feasible. As for procedural due process, that standard was met by the statutory mandate of a detention hearing. Although the rules of evidence were not applicable at that hearing, the defendant was entitled to be represented by counsel, to present information "by proffer or otherwise", and to cross examine witnesses called by the prosecution. Also, the judicial officer had to provide written findings of fact and a written statement of reasons for a decision to detain, which was then subject to immediate appellate review.

§ 8.2   DECISION TO CHARGE

(a) Limitations upon the charging decision

The American prosecutor traditionally has had broad discretion in determining whether to initiate formal charges and in selecting among possible charges. The Supreme Court has frequently recognized the freedom of individual jurisdictions to grant immense charging discretion to the prosecutor. See e.g., *U.S. v. Batchelder* (1979) (holding constitutional a statutory scheme that allowed a prosecutor to choose between two offenses, carrying substantially different punishments, but prohibiting the same conduct). Nonetheless, the Court has also noted that the prosecutor's charging discretion must be exercised consistent with the equal protection guarantee and the due process prohibition against "vindictiveness."

As noted in *Oyler v. Boles* (1962), the prosecutor's "conscious exercise of * * * selectivity in law enforcement" may not be "deliberately based" upon grounds that would violate equal protection, "such as race, religion, or other arbitrary classification." However, a defendant claiming that selective prosecution under a particular statute violates this standard carries a heavy burden, in "recognition of the fact that the decision to prosecute is particularly ill-suited to judicial review." *Wayte v. U.S.* (1985). That burden includes establishing both "discriminatory effect" and "discriminatory purpose." Thus, *Wayte,* a case involving a government policy of enforcing the offense of failing to register for the draft only against those who self-reported their violation or were reported by others, held that defendants' equal protection claim failed on two grounds: (i) this "passive" enforcement policy had not in fact resulted in imposing a "special burden" on a single, suspect class (alleged by defendants' to be those vocal opponents of the draft who had failed to register); and (ii) even if the government's policy had a discriminatory impact upon that class, the defendants had not shown that the government intended such a result, as opposed to merely being aware that such an impact would follow from a policy seeking to serve other ends (e.g., administrative convenience in allocating limited prosecutorial resources).

A due process prohibition against prosecutorial vindictiveness in charge selection was first recognized in *Blackledge v. Perry* (1974), a case in which defendant was originally convicted of a misdemeanor assault, exercised his right under local law to a trial de novo, and then was charged before the de novo court with a felony assault based on the same conduct. Striking down the prosecutor's raising of the charge to a felony, the Court noted that defendant was "entitled to pursue his statutory right to a trial de novo without apprehension that the State will retaliate by substituting a more serious charge for the original one." In *Blackledge,* the prosecution initially had gone to trial on the misdemeanor charge, and the Court was willing to assume that the subsequent raising of the charge was vindictive. *U.S. v. Goodwin* (1982) held, however, that a presumption of vindictiveness would not be applied in a pretrial setting because at that stage changes in the charge were so much more likely to be based on non-vindictive grounds. Thus, for the defendant to establish vindictiveness under the facts of *Goodwin* (where defendant, originally charged with a petty offense, sought a jury trial, resulting in the transfer of the case to another court, where a new prosecutor obtained a felony indictment), he would have to show that the raising of the charge against him stemmed from an "actual retaliatory motive" rather than some other factor (e.g., differences in the perspectives of the two prosecutors).

(b) Grand jury or preliminary hearing review of the charge

Under the Sixth Amendment, a federal prosecutor cannot proceed on a decision to charge for a felony offense ("an infamous crime") unless a grand jury affirms that charging decision by indicting the defendant for that offense or the defendant waives his right to be proceeded against only by indictment. *Hurtado v. Cal.* (1884) held that this Sixth Amendment requirement did not reflect a "fundamental principle of liberty" and therefore was not imposed upon the states by the Fourteenth Amendment. The state in the *Hurtado* case had substituted a preliminary hearing as a screening alternative to the grand jury, but *Lem Woon v. Ore.* (1913) held that due process was not violated where a state eliminated all independent screening procedures, allowing the prosecution to file felony charges directly in the trial court upon a prosecutorial oath that the charge was fairly grounded. Although *Hurtado* and *Lem Woon* were decided during the early stages of the application of the Fourteenth Amendment to state criminal justice systems, the Court has continued to cite those decisions with approval. See *Gerstein v. Pugh* (1975).

Although states are not constitutionally required to provide for independent screening of the prosecution's decision to charge by grand jury or preliminary hearing, once such a procedure is imposed under local law, it cannot be conducted in a manner that denies equal protection. Thus, the Supreme Court has long held that an indictment is subject to constitutional challenge if the grand jury selection procedure operated to discriminate on racial grounds. See *Ex parte Va.* (1879). Indeed, since racial discrimination "strikes at the fundamental values of our judicial system and our society as a whole," such a challenge is cognizable on appeal or postconviction review even though a fairly selected petit jury subsequently convicted defendant on the charges presented in the grand jury indictment. *Rose v. Mitchell* (1979). See also *Vasquez v. Hillery* (1986) (even though the petit jury's conviction establishes sufficient evidence to indict, a grand jury of a different racial composition may have been willing to exercise its power to "charge a lesser offense than evidence might support").

Additionally, while the Court has not faced the issue in the context of a challenge to a state indictment, it has suggested that selecting grand jurors from a venire that fails to reflect a fair cross-section of the community would violate due process. *Hobby v. U.S.* (1984). Cf. *Beck v. Wash.* (1962) (raising, but not deciding, the question of whether a state grand jury indictment is subject to a due process challenge on the ground of juror bias).

§ 8.3 SCOPE AND TIMING OF THE PROSECUTION

(a) Joinder of offenses

A defendant's actions in the course of a single criminal episode may result in several violations of the law. Where local law gives the prosecutor the option of prosecuting each of those violations in a separate trial, two aspects of the Fifth Amendment's prohibition against double jeopardy may impose restraints upon the prosecutor's exercise of such discretion. While the double jeopardy clause does not directly mandate that different charges be joined in the same prosecution, it may prohibit the prosecutor from presenting in a second trial those charges that are not joined in the initial prosecution.

Initially, successive prosecutions may be barred by the Fifth Amendment's basic prohibition against repeated jeopardy for the "same offense." Even though there has been a violation of two distinct state criminal provisions, those provisions may nevertheless be considered part of the "same offense" for double jeopardy purposes. "[T]o determine whether there are two offenses or only one," the Court applies the "same-elements" test of *Blockburger v. U.S.* (1932): "whether each [criminal] provision requires proof of an additional fact which the other does not." An obvious illustration of separate provisions that are part of the same offense under this test are the higher and lower degrees of the same crime (e.g., first degree and second degree homicide). However, the two provisions need not be part of a formal degree classification in order to constitute one offense under the *Blockburger* test. Thus *Brown v. Ohio* (1977) found that the crimes of theft of a vehicle and joyriding in that vehicle were part of the same offense since, as defined by state law, theft was simply joyriding with an additional element (an intent to permanently deprive the owner of the property). Since the defendant was charged in the initial prosecution only as to joyriding, a second prosecution for theft of the vehicle was barred by the double jeopardy clause.

Application of the *Blockburger* test becomes more complex where an offense includes several alternative elements, each of which also constitutes an offense. *Harris v. Okla.* (1977) presented such a case. Defendant there initially was prosecuted for felony murder in the perpetration of a robbery with a firearm, the state homicide statute making all felonies predicate offenses for felony murder. A second prosecution was later brought for the robbery with a firearm. Although commission of that particular felony was not a necessary element of a felony murder, the Court looked to the theory of the earlier prosecution as establishing the relevant statutory elements. Accordingly, it held that this second prosecution for what was basically a lesser-included offense was barred by *Blockburger*. In *Grady v. Corbin* (1990), the Court went beyond *Harris* to hold that a defendant who had been prosecuted for driving while intoxicated and crossing the median could not subsequently be prosecuted for negligent homicide where the element of negligence was to be proven by the same conduct. However, *U.S. v. Dixon* (1993) overruled the "same conduct" standard of *Grady,* and held that double jeopardy protection did not go beyond the *Harris* application of *Blockburger*. Illustrating the limits of this standard, the *Dixon* Court noted that *Harris* would have been decided differently if the felony murder statute there had a specified predicate offense simply of robbery and the second prosecution had been for robbery with a firearm. Then, the two prosecutions each would have required proof of a different element (the killing in the felony-murder prosecution and the firearm in the armed robbery prosecution).

The "same offense" double jeopardy objection may be lost if the defendant is responsible for splitting the two charges into separate trials. *Jeffers v. U.S.* (1977) (defense successfully opposed government motion to consolidate). Similarly, the government will not be held responsible for failing to bring the two charges together when the elements of the second offense charged did not exist or could not have been known at the time the first charge was resolved (a situation that would be presented in a felony-murder situation if the charge on the predicate offense was resolved before the victim died). See also *Garrett v. U.S.* (1985) (separate continuing enterprise charge not barred because that offense was still ongoing when defendant pled guilty to included narcotics transaction).

A second double jeopardy doctrine—the collateral estoppel doctrine—primarily affects joinder of violations arising from the same criminal episode that are separate offenses under *Blockburger* and *Grady*. Recognized as an aspect of double jeopardy in *Ashe v. Swenson* (1970), the collateral estoppel doctrine bars prosecution for a second offense where the defendant was previously acquitted on a factually related offense and that acquittal was based on a factual element that is also an essential element of the second offense. Thus, in *Ashe*, a defendant charged with robbing the initial victim in a single, multi-victim robbery, and acquitted by the jury on the ground that he had not been present at the robbery, could not subsequently be prosecuted on a charge of robbing the next victim. Under the collateral estoppel doctrine, the earlier acquittal only bars use on same critical facts as an element of another offense; it does not preclude use of the same evidence for another purpose requiring a lesser standard of proof, such as a civil forfeiture or showing similar past behavior in a prosecution for an unconnected offense. *Dowling v. U.S.* (1990). Also, it applies only to the ultimate fact on which the jury acquitted and not as to some subsidiary issue. Id.

(b) Joinder of parties

Where several persons have participated in a single offense or a series of related offenses, state law ordinarily grants the prosecutor discretion to prosecute them jointly or separately. In at least one situation, where the prosecutor desires to use a confession of one of the participants, the prosecutor's exercise of discretion to try the defendants jointly is subject to a significant constitutional restraint. *Bruton v. U.S.* (1968) held that where the confession of one codefendant contains references to a second codefendant, and the confessor refuses to take the stand, the use of that confession in a joint trial violates the second codefendant's Sixth Amendment right of confrontation; it is not sufficient simply to inform the jury that the confession constitutes admissible evidence only against the confessor. While *Bruton* does not bar joinder of accomplices where the prosecution intends to use a confession, it imposes as a significant price the deletion of the confession's prejudicial references to the other accomplice, which often will substantially undercut the effectiveness of the confession as evidence against the confessor. This restriction applies even though the prosecution uses interlocking confessions of each of the non-testifying codefendants. *Cruz v. N.Y.* (1987). Where, however, the non-testifying codefendant's statement is attributable to the other codefendants under the hearsay exception for coconspirators' statements made during the course of and in furtherance of the conspiracy, the confrontation clause will not require that the statement be redacted to delete references to the other codefendants. Cf. *Dutton v. Evans* (1970). Where *Bruton* does apply and the confession is redacted, the presence of some "evidentiary linkage" of the other defendants to the confession will not bar joinder. Here, because there exists only the risk of "inferrential incrimination," an instruction to the jury to treat the confession as evidence against only the confessor will constitute sufficient protection. *Richardson v. Marsh* (1987).

(c) Timing of the prosecution

State discretion as to the timing of a trial is limited by the Sixth Amendment requirement that "the accused shall enjoy the right to a speedy trial." Denial of this right automatically requires dismissal of the delayed prosecution with prejudice; the impact of the denial is too diffuse to permit trial courts to seek to tailor the remedy (e.g., by reducing defendant's sentence) to the hardship that may have been caused in the particular case. *Strunk v. U.S.* (1973). Flexibility has been the governing philosophy, however, in determining whether delay constitutes a denial of the right. Thus, the leading speedy trial decision, *Barker v. Wingo* (1972), rejected what it described as "inflexible approaches" (e.g., imposing a specific time limitation) in favor of "a balancing test, in which the conduct of both the prosecution and the defendant are weighed." *Barker* listed four factors to be weighed in determining whether there had been a denial of the speedy trial right: (1) length of the delay; (2) the government's justification for the delay; (3) whether the defendant asserted his right to a speedy trial; and (4) prejudice caused by the delay, such as lengthened pretrial incarceration, lengthened anxiety, and possible impairment of the presentation of a defense. In discussing those factors, the Court indicated that though a defense demand for a speedy trial is not essential, the absence of a demand will work strongly against the defendant who had counsel. The speedy trial right, it noted, was unlike most other constitutional rights in that the "deprivation of the right may work to the accused's advantage," and it could not be assumed that defendant wanted a speedy trial, delay being a "not uncommon defense tactic." The absence of a defense demand played a large role in sustaining much of a five year delay in *Barker*, where defendant had been at large on bail through most of that period and pursued the strategy of awaiting the outcome of the ongoing prosecution of his accomplice.

Where the Court has had before it a lengthy delay following a defense demand for a prompt trial, its primary focus has been on evaluating the cause for the delay. While each ruling has been tied to the facts of the particular case, the decisions clearly indicate that the state must offer some affirmative justification, not merely the absence of a deliberate attempt to gain advantage by postponing the trial. Thus, *Smith v. Hooey* (1969) and *Dickey v. Fla.* (1970) found speedy trial violations where the state failed to make any effort to respond to the demand of a defendant, then serving a federal sentence, for a prompt trial on pending state charges. The state's failure to even request that federal officials make the defendant available for trial could not be justified by its lack of authority to compel such cooperation. Neither could its failure be justified on the ground that the cost of transporting the prisoner would have had to be borne by the state.

The lack of an affirmative justification also was critical in the unusual case of *Doggett v. U.S.* (1992), where there was no demand, but defendant was not in a position to make a demand because he did not know charges were pending against him. The government there indicted defendant while he was out of the country, but then was negligent in failing to note his return, so that nearly six years elapsed between his return and his arrest. The Court noted that two of the *Barker* prejudice elements obviously were not present—the accused was not subjected to pretrial incarceration and he had no anxiety and concern as to charges of which he was unaware—and the only evidence of the third element was the length of the delay in itself, there being no affirmative proof of particularized prejudice. Accordingly, if the government had pursued the accused with reasonable diligence, his speedy trial claim would have failed. However, "when, the government's negligence * * * causes delay six times as long as that generally sufficient to trigger judicial review [i.e. six years], and when the presumption of prejudice, albeit unspecified, is neither extenuated, as by the defendant's acquiescence, nor persuasively rebutted, the defendant is entitled to relief."

Of course, the speedy trial guarantee, like other Sixth Amendment rights, applies only to the "accused." Thus, as suggested in *MacDonald,* discussed infra, if the government had dismissed the indictment in *Doggett* after failing to locate the defendant, that would have tolled the running of the Sixth Amendment time period without regard to whether a court later concluded that the government had exercised due diligence in looking for him.

While *Klopfer v. N.C.* (1967) held unconstitutional a state practice that, in effect, suspended a prosecution with automatic leave to reinstate, *U.S. v. MacDonald* (1982) viewed an outright dismissal as quite different. Once the charges are dismissed, the individual is no longer a subject of public accusation and has no restraints on his liberty, leaving him in a situation analogous to that in *U.S. v. Lovasco,* discussed infra. See also *U.S. v. Loud Hawk* (1986) (*MacDonald* controlling as to period of pending government appeal from a lower court's dismissal of an indictment, the defendant no longer being subject to restraint, although government's desire to reinstitute the prosecution if successful on appeal was a "matter of public record"). Undue delay between the dismissal and the reinstitution of charges remains subject to constitutional control, but only under the due process clause. *MacDonald.*

The speedy trial guarantee protects the defendant only against undue delay between the initiation of prosecution and trial, *U.S. v. Marion* (1971), and prosecution is initiated for this purpose with either the filing of formal charges or the arrest and holding of the defendant for the purpose of filing charges, *Dillingham v. U.S.* (1975). However, undue delay between the completion of the crime and the institution of prosecution can constitute a violation of due process. *U.S. v. Lovasco* (1977). To establish such a due process violation, defense must show initially that the prosecution had sufficient evidence to institute prosecution at an earlier point, and that the delay resulted in actual trial prejudice (e.g., the loss of favorable witnesses). In addition, the court must find that the reasons for the delay were so unjustified as to "deviate from 'fundamental conceptions of justice.'" *Lovasco* cited as legitimate justifications such administrative needs as "await[ing] the results of additional investigation" to possibly identify other offenders and bringing charges together so as to avoid "multiple trials involving a single set of facts." A clearly impermissible grounding for delay would be the prosecution's gain through the hoped for loss of defense evidence over the period of the delay. *Marion.*

§ 8.4   NOTICE, DISCOVERY AND DISCLOSURE

(a) Notice

The Sixth Amendment requires that the defendant "be informed of the nature and cause of the accusation" against him. This requirement has application primarily to the indictment or information, which must identify the offense charged and "sufficiently apprise the defendant of what he must be prepared to meet." *Russell v. U.S.* (1962). That standard commonly is met by a concise statement in the indictment or information of the essential facts constituting the offense charged. *U.S. v. Debrow* (1953). Having charged the defendant with a particular offense, a state shift to another offense during the course of the proceedings may present a notice violation, depending upon the circumstance surrounding that shift. See *Cole v. Ark.* (1948) (state appellate court violated due process when it affirmed the conviction of the defendants, charged and tried for one offense, on the ground that defendants had actually committed another offense, which was "separate, distinct, and substantially different").

(b) Defense discovery

The Constitution allows the states considerable flexibility in determining the extent to which they will grant to the defense a right to pretrial discovery of the evidence that the prosecution intends to use at trial. As will be seen in § 8.8(d), the prosecution does have a constitutional duty under the *Brady* doctrine to disclose material exculpatory evidence in its possession, and to allow the defense to make effective use of that evidence, such disclosure sometimes may have to be made before trial. However, the evidence that the prosecution intends itself to use at trial ordinarily will be incriminating, rather than *Brady*-encompassed exculpatory evidence, leading the Court to state: "There is no general constitutional right to discovery in a criminal case, and *Brady* did not create one." *Weatherford v. Bursey* (1977). Similarly, the Court has noted that while broad pretrial discovery is the "better practice," the state does not violate due process by refusing to grant pretrial discovery even if the prosecution's evidence will almost certainly take the defendant by surprise. See e.g., *Weather-*

ford (failure to inform the defendant that an asso-ciate was an undercover agent and would testify against him at trial).

Where a state provides for prosecution pretrial discovery from the defense, it thereby assumes a constitutional obligation to provide reciprocal dis-covery for the defense. *Wardius v. Ore.* (1973) (due process violated by an alibi-notice provision that required defense disclosure of its alibi witnesses without requiring the prosecution to make recipro-cal disclosure of its alibi rebuttal witnesses). While the "due process clause has little to say regarding the amount of discovery which the par-ties must be afforded," it "does speak to the bal-ance of forces between the accused and his accus-er." The state "may not insist that trials be run as 'a search for truth' so far as defense witnesses are concerned, while maintaining 'poker game secrecy for its own witnesses.' " Id.

(c) Prosecution discovery

Many jurisdictions make pretrial discovery, to some extent, a "two way street." They require not only that the prosecution grant discovery to the defense, but that the defense grant similar discov-ery to the prosecution. In *Williams v. Fla.* (1970), a divided Court held constitutional a Florida re-quirement that defendant give advance notice of an alibi defense (including the names and address-es of alibi witnesses) did not violate defendant's privilege against self-incrimination. The majority stressed that the Florida rule only required the defendant to disclose evidence that he intended to produce subsequently at trial, and, if he changed his mind, the rule permitted the defendant to abandon the alibi defense without any harm to his case. It rejected the defendant's contention that forcing him to disclose his alibi-defense and witnesses prior to trial violated his self-incrimination privilege by compelling him to furnish information that might lead the state to incriminating rebuttal evidence. The Court noted that the "dilemma demanding a choice between complete silence and presenting a defense" had never been viewed as compelling self-incrimination when posed at the end of the prosecution's case-in-chief, and "[n]othing in the Fifth Amendment privilege entitles a defendant as a matter of constitutional right to await the end of the state's case before announcing the nature of his defense." This concept of allowing the state to "accelerate disclosure" presumably could be applied to all types of pretrial discovery requirements that require the defendant to reveal in advance witnesses and defenses that he intends to present at trial. However, *Williams* involved a situation in which there was no suggestion that the disclosure might assist the state in building a case-in-chief that it would not otherwise obtain, a situation where the defendant might be facing before trial the dilemma of choice that would not later be presented at trial. Whether *Williams* will be extended to prosecutor discovery that poses a serious threat of assisting the state in its case-in-chief (as in identifying self-defense witness, who could testify as to defendant's commission of the crime), remains to be seen.

Where the prosecution is aware of the identity of persons providing information to the defense, requiring production of written statements submitted by the witness does not require testimony from the defendant except insofar as the act of production is testimonial. See § 4.10(c): *U.S. v. Nobles* (1975) (where a defense investigator testified at trial as to statements made to him by prosecution witnesses, permitting prosecution inspection of the investigator's report, for possible impeachment use, did not violate defendant's Fifth Amendment rights since no portion of the report reflected information supplied to the investigator by the defendant). On the other hand, where the defense does not intend to use those persons as its witnesses, requiring disclosure of their recorded statements may be viewed as an infringement upon defendant's right to counsel. Such a requirement readily could deter counsel's full exploration of possible sources of information for fear that such information would then become discoverable to the prosecution.

Where the defense fails pretrial to disclose witness names, in contravention of a valid state discovery requirement, the authorized sanctions typically include excluding the testimony of the unlisted witness. *Taylor v. Ill.* (1988) upheld that sanction as applied to a nondisclosure that was "deliberate", "aimed at seeking a tactical advantage" and in "the category of willful misconduct [for] which the severest sanction is appropriate." The Court rejected the contention that exclusion was automatically banned by the Sixth Amendment's compulsory process clause, noting that the pretrial discovery rules are intended to serve "the same high purpose" in "full and truthful disclosure of the facts" as the compulsory process clause and other Sixth Amendment rights. Also rejected was the contention that exclusion should be barred because alternative and more appropriate sanctions (e.g. allowing the state a continuance to respond to the surprise evidence) were always available. In some instances, those alternatives "would be less effective than the preclusion sanction" and in some instances, they would actually "perpetuate rather than limit the prejudice to the State and [the] harm to the adversary process."

§ 8.5   GUILTY PLEAS

(a) Voluntariness requirement

A guilty plea is not a constitutionally acceptable basis for a conviction unless that plea is "voluntary." This voluntariness requirement has been imposed pursuant to the due process clause. It has been likened by the Court to the prohibition against admission of involuntary confessions, *Waley v. Johnston* (1942), although its content also is shaped in part by the traditional "knowing and intelligent" standard for waivers of trial rights, *Boykin v. Ala.* (1969). See § 7.4(a). In *Brady v. U.S.* (1970), the Supreme Court noted that "the standard as to voluntariness of guilty pleas must be essentially that defined by * * * [a leading lower court opinion]: '[A] plea of guilty entered by one fully aware of the direct consequences, including the actual value of any commitments made to him by the court, prosecutor, or his own counsel, must stand unless induced by threats (or promises to discontinue improper harassment), misrepresentation (including unfulfilled or unfulfillable promises), or perhaps by promises that are by their nature improper as having no proper relationship to the prosecutor's business (e.g., bribes).' "

(b) Acceptance of a guilty plea

The voluntariness requirement imposes a duty upon the trial judge to ensure that the guilty plea is made knowingly and without coercion. The Court has emphasized that the scope of that duty, like the definition of voluntariness itself, is governed by constitutional standards. However, the leading cases dealing with the scope of that duty are quite limited in their holdings. *Boykin v. Ala.* (1969) is illustrative. In that case, "so far as the record shows, the judge asked no questions of the [defendant] concerning his plea and [defendant] did not address the court." The Court concluded that this established "error, plain on the face of the record," due to the trial judge's acceptance of a guilty plea "without an affirmative showing that it was intelligent and voluntary." The Court added that a guilty plea involves a relinquishment of the rights to a jury trial, to confront one's accusers, and to refuse to testify at trial, and it could not "presume a waiver of these important federal rights from a silent record." Whether this means that the defendant must be specifically advised as to those three rights (and if so, only as to those rights) remains unclear. All jurisdictions today require that the trial judge inform the defendant of the three rights and most include other rights as well. Moreover, *N.C. v. Alford* (1970) later suggested that the state could also establish a knowing waiver by counsel's testimony in a subsequent proceeding that counsel had fully informed defendant of the rights relinquished by pleading guilty.

Henderson v. Morgan (1976) dealt with the voluntariness requirement that the defendant be aware of the "true nature of the charge against him." *Henderson* did not go so far as to require that the judge inform the defendant of the major elements of the offense charged, although many trial courts follow that practice. The Court held only that the record did not establish an understanding plea to second degree murder where the elements of that offense were not charged in the indictment, neither the defense lawyers nor the trial court explained to defendant that the offense required an intent to kill, and the defendant's version of the offense, as explained to the court by counsel, implicitly negated that element.

Most jurisdictions also require that the trial court determine that there is a "factual basis" for the plea before accepting it. *N.C. v. Alford* (1970) suggests that a finding of a factual basis may be necessary constitutionally, but the Court there was dealing only with the situation in which the defendant desires to plead guilty, but claims that he is innocent. *Alford* found no constitutional violation in the acceptance of a plea from a defendant who claimed to be innocent where (i) the defendant desired to enter the plea to a lesser offense to avoid the possibility of a substantially harsher penalty (the death sentence) on a higher offense and (ii) the trial court had received a summary of the state's case which contained "strong evidence of actual guilt." The defendant's position as to his innocence was not substantially different from that of a defendant who pleads nolo contendere, and the "strong factual basis" indicated that the "plea was being intelligently entered."

(c) Negotiated pleas

Prior to the decision in *Brady v. U.S.* (1970), some uncertainty existed as to the voluntariness of a guilty plea that was the product of "plea bargaining"—i.e., a negotiated arrangement under which the defendant pleads guilty in return for certain concessions, such as the reduction of charges or the promise of a more lenient sentence. *Brady* did not itself involve a negotiated plea, but the Court, in discussing the voluntariness of Brady's plea, drew an analogy between that plea (which allowed Brady to avoid the possibility of a death sentence) and a negotiated plea. The *Brady* opinion stressed in particular what it described as the "mutuality of advantage" in plea bargaining. From the state's view, the granting of concessions to those pleading guilty was consistent with the administrative as well as the rehabilitative goals of the criminal justice system. The state was "extend[ing] a benefit to a defendant who in turn extends a substantial benefit to the state and who demonstrates by his plea that he is ready and willing to admit his crime and to enter the correctional system in a frame of mind which affords hope for success in rehabilitation over a shorter period of time than might otherwise be necessary." Guilty pleas could not be treated as involuntary simply because they were "motivated by the defendant's desire to accept the certainty * * * of a lesser penalty rather than * * * [a trial that might result in] conviction and a higher penalty." Indeed, to reject all pleas induced by promises of more lenient treatment would be, in large part, to "forbid guilty pleas altogether."

Corbitt v. N.J. (1978) explored the implications of the *Brady* analysis for what might be characterized as a "legislative plea bargain." A state statute there presented defendants charged with first degree murder with the option of going to trial and receiving a mandatory life sentence if convicted, or entering a guilty plea which allowed the trial court to impose a sentence of either life imprisonment or the lesser sentence utilized for second degree murder convictions. In *U.S. v. Jackson* (1968), the Court had struck down a sentencing provision that allowed the imposition of the death penalty if defendant proceeded to a trial by a jury but not if he received a bench trial or pleaded guilty. *Jackson* held this statutory scheme "needlessly penalized" the exercise of jury and other trial rights, as the state's objective of having capital sentences imposed only by jurors could be achieved by use of advisory sentencing juries in connection with guilty pleas and bench trials. *Corbitt* distinguished *Jackson,* holding that the statutory scheme before it merely sought to achieve, in the potentially lighter sentence for a guilty plea, the mutuality of advantage noted in *Brady.* Of course, the discussion in *Brady* had referred to bargaining by the prosecutor, and the *Corbitt* dissent argued that the legislature performed a quite different role and offered none of the flexible "give and take" involved in traditional plea negotiation. But the majority declared that the Court could hardly permit bargaining by the prosecutor, "and yet hold that the legislature may not openly provide for the possibility of leniency in return for a plea."

Bordenkircher v. Hayes (1978) explored the relationship between *Brady*'s approval of plea bargaining and the prohibition against prosecutorial vindictiveness in charge selection (see § 8.2(a)). The prosecutor there charged defendant with a crime that carried a sentence of five years imprisonment, but noted at the outset that a recidivist charge, carrying a mandatory sentence of life imprisonment, would be added if the defendant did not plead guilty to the initial charge. The Court held that this was not a situation suggesting a vindictive attempt by the prosecutor to punish the defendant for exercising his right to demand a trial. Rather, it reflected the "give and take" of plea bargaining, with the prosecutor agreeing to forego a legitimate recidivist charge to produce the "mutuality of advantage" of a negotiated plea. The recidivist charge fell within the legitimate scope of prosecutorial discretion, being supported by probable cause. "To hold that the prosecutor's desire to induce a guilty plea is an 'unjustifiable standard,' which like race or religion, may play no part in his charging decision, would contradict the very premises that underlie the concept of plea bargaining." The *Bordenkircher* opinion also stressed that the prosecutor's intention was known to the defendant before he decided to go to trial, and that defendant, represented by counsel, was "presumptively capable of intelligent choice in response to prosecutor persuasion."

(d) Broken bargains

As was noted in *Brady*'s definition of voluntariness ((a) supra), an "unfulfilled or unfulfillable promise" renders a guilty plea involuntary. Thus, if as part of the plea agreement the prosecutor has promised to recommend a particular disposition, the plea becomes subject to challenge if the prosecutor fails to make that recommendation or makes a contrary recommendation. *Santobello v. N.Y.* (1971). The Court left open in *Santobello,* however, the possibility that the prosecutor could resurrect the bargain by now performing as promised (i.e., going before a new sentencing judge and making the promised recommendation) even though the defendant insists upon the withdrawal of the plea. The Court also has not had occasion to discuss the opposite side of that question, whether the defendant can insist upon specific performance of an unfulfilled bargain where the prosecution takes the position that only withdrawal should be permitted. Where the defendant has broken the bargain after entry of the plea (e.g., by failing to give testimony against codefendants as promised), the prosecution can insist upon invalidation of the plea, permitting it to start over again with a prosecution on the original charge. *Ricketts v. Adamson* (1987) (invalidation upheld where defendant refused to testify against accomplices, believing that was not part of the bargain; defendant took the risk that (as occurred) the state appellate court would adopt a contrary interpretation and find the bargain breached).

Whether there has in fact been a breach of the plea bargain is an issue for the courts to decide, but the Court has warned against "imply[ing] as a matter of law a term which the parties themselves did not agree upon." *U.S. v. Benchimol* (1985) (lower court erred in finding a breach where the prosecutor simply made the promised recommendation of probation without comment, as the government had not made an express commitment either to make the recommendation enthusiastically or to state reasons for it). *Mabry v. Johnson* (1984) held that there was no breached agreement where the prosecution made an initial offer of a 21 year concurrent sentence, withdrew that offer when defense counsel sought to accept it three days later, and then submitted a second offer of a 21 year consecutive sentence that the defense eventually accepted. In the absence of detrimental reliance by the defense, due process did not preclude the prosecution from withdrawing its original offer, nor could such withdrawal be successfully challenged as having "undermined [defendant's] confidence in his defense counsel."

(e) Collateral challenges

In general, "a voluntary and intelligent plea of guilty made by an accused person, who has been advised by competent counsel, may not be collaterally attacked" by reference to procedural errors that occurred prior to the entry of the plea. *Mabry v. Johnson* (1984). This is true even though such errors were constitutionally grounded. See e.g., *McMann v. Richardson* (§ 6.6(h)) (coerced confession); *Tollett v. Henderson* (1973) (racial discrimination in grand jury selection). Where a defendant chooses to take "the benefit, if any, of a guilty plea," he "accepts the inherent risk that good-faith evaluations of a reasonably competent attorney will turn out to be mistaken either as to the facts or as to what a court's judgment might be on given facts." *McMann*. In determining whether the defendant actually received the competent assistance of counsel in entering his guilty plea, *Strickland*'s two-pronged ineffective assistance of counsel standard is applied (see § 7.7(b)). *Hill v. Lockhart* (1985).

Notwithstanding the general rule prohibiting collateral attacks where the defendant had the competent assistance of counsel, a voluntary guilty plea may be challenged collaterally where defendant's constitutional claim rests on a "right not to be hailed into court at all" as to the offense to which he pleaded. *Blackledge v. Perry* (1974) (plea did not bar collateral challenge where the prosecution acted vindictively in bringing the charge). While a voluntary guilty plea admits "factual guilt" and thereby "renders irrelevant those constitutional violations not logically inconsistent with the valid establishment of factual guilt," that is not the case for a claim that argues "that the State may not convict petitioner no matter how validly his factual guilt is established." *Menna v. N.Y.* (1975) (guilty plea did not preclude collateral challenge based on double jeopardy bar to the prosecution). Where the claim goes to "the very power of the State to bring the defendant into court to answer the charge," the error is not one which the state might have "cured" except for its reliance upon the guilty plea. *Blackledge.* This stands in contrast to the *Tollett* and *McMann* errors, which could have been "cured" through new pretrial proceedings (*Tollett*) or a prosecution without use of the tainted evidence (*McMann*). It applies, however, only where the state's lack of authority to bring the charge is apparent on the face of the record. *U.S. v. Broce* (1989) (guilty plea to two counts facially indicating separate offenses cannot be challenged as violating double jeopardy because both counts were, in fact, for the same offense).

§ 8.6 IMPARTIAL JURY AND JUDGE

(a) Right to a jury trial

While the Sixth Amendment declares that an accused shall have the right to a jury trial "in all criminal prosecutions," that provision has always been read in light of the common law tradition which did not provide juries for "petty offenses." *D.C. v. Clawans* (1937). The Court has held that the most "relevant criteria" in characterizing a crime as "petty" is the "severity of the maximum authorized penalty", as it reflects a legislative judgement about the relative seriousness of the offense. *Blanton v. North Las Vegas* (1989). An authorized punishment of more than six months establishes per se that the offense is outside the petty offense category, *Baldwin v. N.Y.* (1970), and while an authorized punishment of six months imprisonment or less does not automatically place the offense in the petty offense category, it is "presum[ed] for purposes of the Sixth Amendment that society views such an offense as 'petty'." *Blanton*. The offense can then be taken out of that category only if "additional statutory penalties, viewed in conjunction with the maximum authorized period of incarceration, are so severe that they clearly reflect a legislative determination that the offense *** is a serious one." *Blanton* (additional penalties for DUI offense, including license suspension and community service, did not take it out of the petty category).

In the case of criminal contempts, which ordinarily are not governed by a statutorily prescribed penalty, the contempt falls within the petty offense category when the penalty actually imposed does not exceed six months imprisonment. *Frank v. U.S.* (1969). See also *Muniz v. Hoffman* (1975) ($10,000 fine imposed on labor union in a criminal contempt bench trial was "not of such magnitude" as to deprive union "of whatever right to jury trial it might have under the Sixth Amendment"). The defendant's Sixth Amendment right to a jury trial does not carry with it a correlative right to insist upon a trial before a judge alone, so a jurisdiction may grant the prosecutor or trial court the right to insist upon a jury trial even where defendant desires a bench trial. *Singer v. U.S.* (1965).

Although most jurisdictions provide for a 12 person jury in felony cases, that is not a constitutional requirement. *Williams v. Fla.* (1970) upheld the use of a six person jury for non-capital felony cases. The key to constitutional acceptance, the Court noted, was that the jury be large enough to fulfill its traditional functions, i.e., "to promote group deliberation, free from outside attempts at intimidation, and to provide a fair possibility for obtaining a representative cross section of the community." In *Ballew v. Ga.* (1978), the Court held that a 5–member jury was too small to serve these functions and therefore was not allowable for a non-petty offense. Placing a similar emphasis on the jury's function, the Court has sustained state acceptance of less-than-unanimous verdicts for both acquittal and conviction where the state required sufficient supporting votes to assure adequate deliberations. See *Apodaca v. Ore.* (§ 1.2(e)); *Johnson v. La.* (1972) (upholding a 9–3 felony conviction); *Burch v. La.* (1979) (rejecting a 5–1 vote for non-petty offenses).

The right to a jury trial, like other trial rights, cannot be subjected to a "needless" burden that has a "chilling effect" on the exercise of that right. See *U.S. v. Jackson* discussed in § 8.5(c). In *Ludwig v. Mass.* (1976), the Court held that the right to a jury trial was not unconstitutionally burdened by a state's "two-tier" trial system under which a defendant was not entitled to a jury in his initial trial before a magistrate's court, but then, if convicted, received a trial de novo with a jury before a higher trial court. The Court emphasized that the particular two-tier system before it permitted the defendant to rapidly reach the trial de novo stage, by "admitting sufficient findings of fact" before the magistrate court, and thus did not require defendant to "pursue, in any real sense, a defense at the lower tier."

(b) Equal protection

Long before the Sixth Amendment guarantee was applied to the states, the Court relied on the equal protection guarantee to reject racial discrimination in jury selection. *Strauder v. W. Va.* (1879). A long line of cases since then have dealt with the troublesome problem of establishing proof of discrimination where the jury selection system does not, on its face, authorize exclusion on racial grounds. Under these cases, a prima facie case of discrimination is established by showing that only a small percentage of blacks have been called to jury duty despite a much larger percentage in the community. The burden then shifts to the state to prove that this pattern did not result from discrimination. *Turner v. Fouche* (1970). The same standards for establishing presumed discrimination apply to alleged discrimination based on ethnicity. *Castaneda v. Partida* (1977).

In allowing for statistical showings to establish presumed discrimination, the Supreme Court has acknowledged the potential for manipulation and discrimination in juror selection processes that do not rely on automatic selection systems (e.g., random selection from voter registration lists). Nonetheless, the Court has refused to require states to abandon relevant selection criteria simply because they are susceptible to manipulation and have been used in the past to achieve racial discrimination, at least where there is "no suggestion" those criteria were "originally adopted or subsequently carried forward for the purpose of fostering racial discrimination." *Carter v. Jury Comm.* (1970) (finding unconstitutional discrimination in the individual case, but refusing to hold invalid a statute limiting jury service to persons "esteemed in the community for their integrity, good character, and sound judgment").

Batson v. Ky. (1986) and *Ga. v. McCollum* (1992) hold that the prohibition against racial and ethnic discrimination applies not only to the selection of the jury venire, but also to the selection of individual jurors through the exercise of peremptory challenges. *Batson* held that the prosecutor could not use peremptory challenges to exclude prospective jurors because of their race. That applied not only where the prosecutor did so generally, in the belief persons of a particular race should not sit as jurors, but also where the prosecutor acted in the particular case "on the assumption—as his intuitive judgment—that they would be partial to the defendant because of their shared race." *McCollum* held that the defense's exercise of peremptory challenges to strike black jurors on the basis of their race was equally forbidden. *McCollum* reasoned that: (i) the "State action" requirement of the Fourteenth Amendment is met because a defendant exercising peremptories "is performing a traditional judicial function", cf. *Edmonson v. Leesville Concrete Co.* (1991) (*Batson* applies to civil cases); (ii) the "State has standing to challenge a defendant's discriminatory use of peremptory challenges," as "its own judicial process is undermined" thereby and there are significant obstacles to the excluded jurors themselves obtaining relief; and (iii) the interest served by *Batson* need not "give way to the rights of a criminal defendant," as the right to a fair trial, assistance of counsel, and

impartial jury do not include "the right to discriminate against a group of citizens based upon their
race."

The equal protection claim under *Batson* and
McCollum, as with other equal protection claims,
applies only to a purposeful discrimination on racial grounds. However, *Batson,* following the lead
of the cases dealing with discrimination in the
selection of the venire, recognized a process of
establishing a "prima facie case of purposeful discrimination" based on the manner in which the
peremptories were exercised. *Batson* described the
elements of such a prima facie case in the context
of the prosecution's use of peremptories to "remove
from the venire members of the defendant's race"
where the defendant was a member of a "cognizable racial group" historically discriminated
against. The Court noted that the defense must
show "that these facts and other relevant circumstances raise an inference that the prosecutor
* * * excluded veniremen on account of their
races". In determining whether a prima facie case
is established, the trial court must consider "all
relevant circumstances," such as any pattern of
strikes on the basis of race and the nature of the
prosecutor's questions and statements on voir dire.
If a prima facie case is established, then "the
burden shifts to the State to come forward with a
neutral explanation for challenging black jurors."
In *Hernandez v. N.Y.* (1991), the plurality emphasized that a "neutral explanation" means simply
an "explanation based on something other than

the race of the juror," and that the issue is whether "a discriminatory intent" was present, not whether there was a "racially disproportionate impact." Such a neutral reason existed where the prosecutor's peremptory challenges "rested neither in the intention to exclude Latino or bilingual jurors, nor in stereotypical assumptions about Latinos or bilinguals," but rather in an intent to exclude only those bilinguals who "might have difficulty in accepting the translator's rendition of Spanish-language testimony."

For over a century, equal protection objections were thought to be available only to defendants who were of the same race as the excluded prospective jurors. *Powers v. Ohio,* in 1991, rejected any such limitation. The Court reasoned that the guarantee of equal protection was designed to preclude not merely the potential unfairness to a defendant tried by a jury from which members of his race are excluded, but also the harm to the community at large and to the excluded prospective jurors kept "solely by reason of their race" from a "significant opportunity to participate in civil life." Accordingly, defendants in criminal cases, whether or not members of the group discriminated against, had standing to raise the equal protection rights of excluded jurors, who would themselves confront "considerable practical barriers" to challenging their exclusion. *Powers* involved "a white defendant * * * object[ing] to the prosecution's peremptory challenges of black venire persons," and Court did note that, as a practical matter, establishing a claim in such a case could be more difficult than in *Batson,* where "racial identity between the defendant and the excused person" may assist in establishing "both a prima case and a conclusive showing that wrongful discrimination has occurred."

(c) The "fair cross-section" requirement

Relying on the Sixth Amendment, the Court had gone beyond racial discrimination to hold that a jury's representative function requires that it be selected from a "fair cross-section of the community." *Taylor v. La.* (1975). Since all defendants are entitled to this representative potential of the jury, the cross-section objection can be raised whether or not the defendant is a member of the distinctive class allegedly excluded. *Taylor* (male may object to exclusion of women). The objection is limited, however, to the selection of the venire; it does not encompass the use of peremptory challenges or challenges for cause. *Lockhart v. McCree* (1986) (challenges for cause in death penalty issue); *Holland v. Ill.* (1990) (peremptory challenges on alleged racial grounds). Its purpose, noted the Court in *Holland,* is to "deprive the State of ability to 'stack the deck in its favor' " in that part of the jury selection process it alone controls, and that function does not run counter to allowing each side, "once a fair hand is dealt, [to] use peremptory challenges to eliminate prospective jurors belonging to groups it believes would unduly favor the other side." Limits on the latter practice stem solely from *Batson* and its progeny.

The fair cross-section requirement does not give the defendant a right to a jury venire of any particular composition, but only to one drawn from the community in a manner that does not systematically exclude or substantially reduce the representative of a particular class of possible jurors. However, even that restriction does not go so far as to protect every possible group in the community, and while it extends to a discriminatory impact that is not the product of purposeful discrimination, the government is given a certain degree of administrative latitude in justifying that impact.

The leading case, *Taylor,* held that the cross-section requirement was violated by a state practice of excluding females unless they volunteered for jury service. See also *Duren v. Mo.* (1979) (*Taylor* applied to a state granting an automatic exemption to women when all but a small portion of the women claimed the exemption). The Court in *Taylor* referred to the exclusion of "large, distinctive groups" and "identifiable segments playing major roles in the community." In *Hamling v. U.S.* (1974), the Court ruled that, even if "the young" should be "an identifiable group entitled to a group-based protection under * * * prior decisions," the defendant had not been denied a representative jury simply because the jury selection list was compiled every four years and therefore excluded young persons who had become eligible dur-

ing the interim period. The cross-section requirement, the Court noted, does not deny the government sufficient "play in the joints of the jury
selection process" to accommodate "the practical
problems of judicial administration."

In *Lockhart v. McCree* (1986), the Court held that
the cross-section requirement did not apply to challenges for cause, but also noted that the group at
issue there—jurors firmly opposed to the death
penalty—would not fall within the protection of
the requirement in any event. The Court described the requirement as relating only to distinctive groups in the community (e.g., "blacks, wom-
en, or Mexican-Americans") and not to groups,
such as the death-penalty excluded jurors, "defined
solely in terms of shared attitudes that would
prevent or substantially impair members of the
group from performing or substantially performing
one of their duties as jurors." The Court also
stressed the three purposes of the cross-section
requirement: (1) avoiding "the possibility that the
composition of juries would be arbitrarily skewed
in such a way as to deny criminal defendants the
benefit of the common-sense judgment of the community"; (2) avoiding an "appearance of unfairness"; and (3) ensuring against deprivation of "often historically disadvantaged groups of their right
as citizens to serve on juries in criminal cases."

(d) Jury impartiality

The Sixth Amendment guarantees a right to
trial by an "impartial" jury. The primary proce-

dures used to ensure jury impartiality are the voir dire of the prospective jurors and the exercise of challenges for cause and peremptory challenges. The constitutional regulation of the voir dire is quite limited, being directed primarily at racial bias. In *Ham v. S.C.* (1973), the Court held that a bearded civil rights worker, convicted of marijuana possession, had no constitutional right to insist that the trial judge allow voir dire questions concerning defendant's wearing of a beard. The Court acknowledged that it was possible that one or more potential jurors may have been prejudiced against bearded persons, but it stressed that the state must be allowed to give trial courts "broad discretion" in conducting the voir dire. *Ham* also ruled, however, that possible racial prejudice presented a special problem because, inter alia, a principal purpose of the Fourteenth Amendment was to bar racial discrimination. Here, voir dire questioning directed to possible prejudice would be mandated constitutionally on a proper defense showing. Consider also *Morgan v. Ill.,* discussed infra (requiring voir dire on death penalty qualifications).

Even as to racial prejudice, the court has noted, there is no constitutional right to voir dire questioning unless "special circumstances" create a "significant likelihood that racial prejudice might affect [the] trial." *Ristaino v. Ross* (1976). Those circumstances were present in *Ham,* where the defendant, who was black, claimed that he had been "framed because of his civil rights activities." *Ristaino* (involving a black defendant and white victim in a robbery case) held that the fact that the crime is interracial does not in itself establish such special circumstances. But *Turner v. Murray* (1986) held that, because of the jury's special role in capital sentencing, "a capital defendant accused of an interracial crime * * * [is] entitled to have prospective jurors * * * questioned on the issue of racial bias" (although the plurality also concluded that denial of such voir dire required reversal only of the death sentence, not the conviction). See also *Rosales-Lopez v. U.S.* (1981) (a defendant of Mexican descent, charged with aiding members of his own ethnic group in gaining illegal entry into the United States, was not entitled constitutionally to requested questions aimed at racial or ethnic prejudice).

The constitutional regulation of peremptory challenges also is limited primarily to prohibiting racial discrimination, as reflected in *Batson* and its progeny. See § 8.6(a). *Batson* characterized the peremptory challenge as "one of the most important of the rights reserved to the accused," and stressed its value in "facilitat[ing] the exercise of challenges for cause by removing the fear of incurring a juror's hostility through examination and challenge for cause." Nevertheless, *Batson* also stated that "nothing in the Constitution requires the Congress [or the States] to grant peremptory challenges."

Apart from the pretrial publicity cases discussed in subsection (e) infra, the leading Supreme Court cases on challenges for cause have dealt with the possibility of imputing bias without regard to the voir dire responses of the juror. *Dennis v. U.S.* (1950) rejected the contention that federal employees should be challengeable solely by reason of their employment where the defendant was charged with an offense involving a "direct affront" to federal governmental authority (there contempt of a legislative committee investigating allegedly disloyal groups). *Smith v. Phillips* (1982) held that bias could not be imputed to a juror because the juror had a currently pending application with the District Attorney's office for a position as an investigator. The prosecutor there had failed to disclose immediately to the trial court his midtrial discovery of the juror's employment application, but the Supreme Court concluded that the defense had not been prejudiced since the trial court had carefully examined the juror in a posttrial inquiry and had determined that the juror had not entertained the assumption that a vote for conviction would favorably affect the evaluation of his job application.

Witherspoon v. Ill. (1968) concluded that the defendant had been denied his Sixth Amendment right to an impartial jury because the trial court had been too generous in granting the prosecution's challenges for cause, but that ruling was limited to the special aspects of capital sentencing. When the state "swept from the jury all who expressed conscientious or religious scruples against capital punishment or all who opposed it in principle," the result was not a jury simply "neutral" as to penalty, but one "uncommonly willing to condemn a man to die." As subsequently interpreted in *Wainwright v. Witt* (1985), the *Witherspoon* principle does allow exclusion of jurors even though they might not "automatically" vote against the death penalty. The critical question is "whether the juror's views would 'prevent or substantially impair the performance of his duties in accordance with his instructions and his oath.'"

A lengthy line of cases have dealt with the application of the *Witherspoon–Witt* standard. *Gray v. Miss.* (1987) found that a death penalty was nullified by a single juror excluded improperly by the prosecution. *Lockhart v. McCree* (1986) held that a state could apply *Witherspoon–Witt* to remove jurors for cause for both the guilty and sentencing determinations even though it utilized a bifurcated capital trial. *Buchanan v. Ky.* (1987) found that the defendant there was not deprived of any Sixth Amendment rights when the prosecution death-qualified the jury, in accordance with *Witherspoon–Witt,* at the joint trial of the defendant, who did not face the death penalty, and his codefendant against whom the penalty was sought. In *Ross v. Okla.* (1988), the trial judge erred in denying a reverse-*Witherspoon* motion of the defense to exclude a juror unwilling to consider any penalty short of death, but defense's striking of that juror with one of nine peremptories cured that error and loss of the peremptory did not produce a constitutional violation since such challenges "are not of constitutional dimension." *Morgan v. Ill.* (1992) held, however, that a defendant in a capital case did have a constitutionally mandated right to voir dire to determine if prospective jurors were subject to disqualification on a reverse-*Witherspoon* motion.

(e) Prejudicial publicity and jury selection

Where a pending prosecution has received considerable newspaper or television publicity, the selection of an impartial jury requires extra care. The Court has never insisted that prospective jurors be totally unaware of all adverse publicity. Such a standard, it has noted, would be impossible "in these days of swift, widespread, and diverse methods of communications." On the other hand, the jurors must not have been so influenced by the publicity that they cannot put aside any "preconceived notions" and "render a verdict based on the evidence presented in court." *Irvin v. Dowd* (1961). The Court's rulings on the impact of prejudicial publicity have tended to be tied to the facts of the particular case. *Irvin* found that extensive and highly prejudicial pretrial publicity had resulted in the selection of a tainted jury. The Court stressed, in particular, the voir dire examination at which several jurors had acknowledged that they were firmly convinced of defendant's guilt. *Murphy v. Fla.* (1975), on the other hand, held that defendant had not been denied a fair jury (although several jurors had learned from news accounts of his prior crimes) where (i) the news

articles appeared several months before jury selection and the community atmosphere was not "inflammatory," (ii) only one-fourth of the potential
jurors examined had to be excused because of firmly set opinions, and (iii) the voir dire statements of
the jurors who were seated revealed no hostility
that would cause one to doubt their assurances of
impartiality. See also *Patton v. Yount* (1984) (passage of time since critical publicity "clearly rebut[ted] any presumption of partiality" and voir
dire "resulted in selecting those who had forgotten
or would need to be persuaded again" with respect
to any previous opinions).

In *Mu'Min v. Va.* (1991), the Court considered
the bearing of the *Irvin* line of cases on the scope
of voir dire in pretrial publicity cases. After a
substantial percentage of prospective jurors acknowledged knowing something about the case
from media coverage, the trial judge questioned
the jurors in small groups and asked whether such
information would affect their impartiality, but
refused to allow questioning of each juror out of
the presence of the others so that they could be
asked specific questions as to what they learned
from the media coverage. Sustaining that procedure against constitutional challenge, Chief Justice
Rehnquist's majority opinion stressed that a trial
judge must be given "great latitude" in voir dire
questioning, that the ultimate question was whether the trial court was so lacking in its basis for
finding credible the seated jurors' claims of impartiality as to constitute "fundamental unfairness",

and that the depth and extent of the publicity in this case was not of the extreme type found in *Irvin*, which "might well have required more extensive examination of potential jurors than [was] under[taken] here." Justice O'Connor's concurring opinion, providing the majority's critical fifth vote, noted that the trial judge was in a position to conclude that, even if it was assumed that each seated juror was aware of all of the publicity, their statements that they had not formed opinions and would be impartial were credible.

In an exceptional case, the Court in *Rideau v. La.* (1963) adopted an approach quite different from the above rulings, as it found a constitutional violation without looking to the voir dire and the responses of the jurors. The *Rideau* Court found that "it was a denial of due process * * * to refuse a request for a change in venue" when the entire community has been "exposed repeatedly and in depth" to the "spectacle" of defendant confessing to the crime in a police interview broadcast on local television. See also *Groppi v. Wis.* (1971) (holding unconstitutional a state statute barring change of venue in misdemeanor cases as applied to a misdemeanor case receiving extensive pretrial publicity).

(f) The right to an impartial judge

Just as the Sixth Amendment requires an impartial jury, due process requires an impartial judge, particularly in cases involving a bench trial. *Ward v. Village of Monroeville* (1972). However, a judge ordinarily is subject to a due process challenge only if he has a financial interest or some other "personal involvement" in the case. It is not objectionable, for example, that the trial judge presided at a pretrial proceeding and therefore has already considered some of the evidence in the case. *Withrow v. Larkin* (1975). It is objectionable, however, that the judge's salary will depend upon the fines he assesses. *Tumey v. Ohio* (1927). Similarly, where a contempt charge is based upon defendant's highly personal attack against the trial judge, that judge is constitutionally precluded from presiding at a subsequent non-summary contempt proceeding. *Mayberry v. Pa.* (1971). In neither case is it necessary to establish that the judge is in fact prejudiced. The guiding standard on personal involvement, the Court has emphasized, must be the "likelihood or appearance of bias" rather than "proof of actual bias." *Taylor v. Hayes* (1974).

§ 8.7 FAIR TRIAL AND FREE PRESS

(a) "Gag orders"

In *Sheppard v. Maxwell* (1966), the Court, commenting upon a trial court's failure to control publicity prejudicial to defendant's right to a fair trial, noted that "the trial court might well have proscribed extra-judicial statements by any lawyer, party, witness, or court official." There was no mention of the media, and in *Nebraska Press Ass'n v. Stuart* (1976) the court flatly rejected a "gag order" directed at the press. Barring the reporting of what occurred at an open preliminary hearing violated the "settled principle" that "once a public hearing has been held, what transpired there could not be subject to prior restraint." As for prohibiting media publication of information received from other sources (e.g., police or counsel), the heavy First Amendment presumption against prior restraints made such an order virtually impossible to sustain in light of numerous other measures (e.g., change of venue) that might be taken to ensure that defendant receives a fair trial notwithstanding adverse pretrial publicity.

Gentile v. State Bar of Nevada (1991) held that the potential for eliminating prejudice through these other alternatives did not require a state to impose a "clear and present danger" standard upon its prohibition of certain public statements by counsel in pending cases. Because counsel have "a fiduciary responsibility not to engage in public debate that will redound to the detriment of the accused or that will obstruct the fair administration of justice," and because their statements pose a special threat in this regard, since "they are likely to be received as especially authoritative" in light of the lawyer's "special access to information through discovery and client communication", the First Amendment was not violated by a standard prohibiting those statements that posed a "substantial likelihood of material prejudice." However, in the case before the Court, the state's prohibition was held to be void for vagueness because it also included a vague "safe harbor" provision (allowing defense counsel to set forth in a media statement, "without elaboration", the "general nature" of the client's "defense"), upon which the defense counsel had relied.

(b) Public right of access

Gannett Co. v. DePasquale (1979) held that the Sixth Amendment right to a public trial was the personal right of the accused, but *Richmond Newspapers, Inc. v. Va.* (1980) recognized a press/public constitutional right of access to the criminal trial based upon the First Amendment interest in "ensur[ing] that the individual citizen can effectively participate in and contribute to our republican system of government." Although also dealing with the trial, *Globe Newspaper Co. v. Superior Court* (1982) established the foundation for extending the reach of this public access right. The Court there noted that the keys to defining the reach of the right were an historic tradition of openness for the particular proceeding and the contribution of public access to the functioning of the proceeding. Relying on these two factors *Press-Enterprise Co. v. Superior Court (Press Enterprise I)* (1984) held that the right of access extended to the voir dire examination of jurors, and *Press-Enterprise Co. v. Superior Court (Press Enterprise II)* (1986) held the right applicable to the preliminary hearing. The same conclusion would seem to follow for a wide range of pretrial hearings (e.g., bail and suppression hearings), with the one excep-

tion being the historically closed grand jury proceeding (recognized as such in *Press Enterprise II*).

As noted in *Globe Newspaper,* the First Amendment right of access "is not absolute." Closure of a
proceeding subject to the right can be justified
upon a showing that closure is "necessitated by a
compelling government interest, and is narrowly
tailored to serve that interest." *Globe* held that
protecting minor victims of sex crimes "from further trauma" was such an interest, but it would
not justify a general statutory prohibition requiring exclusion whenever a victim under 18 testified.
To ensure that closure is narrowly tailored to that
interest, the state procedure must require that the
trial court "determine on a case-by-case basis
whether closure is necessary" to protect the particular minor. So too, *Press Enterprise I* acknowledged that a prospective juror's privacy interests
regarding personal matters might justify closing a
very limited segment of the voir dire.

As for closure in order to avoid prejudicial publicity, *Press Enterprise II* set forth the governing
standard: "If the [compelling] interest asserted is
the right of the accused to a fair trial, the * * *
[proceeding] shall be closed only if specific findings
are made that first, there is substantial probability
that the defendant's right to a fair trial will be
prejudiced by publicity that the closure would prevent and second, reasonable alternatives to closure
cannot adequately protect the defendant's free trial rights." For pretrial proceedings that would

produce prejudicial publicity (e.g., a suppression hearing), the relevant alternatives to closure would include extensive voir dire to identify biased petit jurors, continuances, and change of venue; as to publicity during the trial, the key alternatives would be admonitions to the jurors and sequestration.

(c) Media interference

Sheppard v. Maxwell (1966) found a denial of due process in the trial judge's failure both to respond adequately to massive publicity and to prevent certain media interference with the trial. As to the element of interference, the Court cited the judge's failure to provide privacy for the jury, to insulate witnesses from newsmen, and to control various media activities that contributed substantially to the carnival atmosphere of the trial. In *Estes v. Tex.* (1965), a divided Court held that defendant had been denied due process by the televising of his trial over his objection. Relying on *Rideau* (§ 8.6(e)), the majority found that the likely prejudicial impact upon the jury of a cumbersome and conspicuous televising procedure eliminated the need for a showing of specific instances of "isolatable prejudice." Indeed, four members of the majority expressed the view that public television of a trial was inherently prejudicial, but the fifth justice limited his concurrence to "criminal trial[s] of great notoriety" such as that involved in *Estes*. Subsequently, in *Chandler v. Fla.* (1981), the Court relied upon that concurrence to hold that a state may permit televising and still photographing, over the objection of the accused, under the restricted conditions prescribed there by state rule. Those restrictions included placing on the trial judges "positive obligations to be on guard to protect the fundamental right of the accused to a fair trial." Moreover, it would remain open to the particular defendant "to show that the media's coverage of his case * * * compromised the ability of the jury to judge him fairly," or to "show that broadcast coverage of his particular case had an adverse impact on the trial participants sufficient to constitute a denial of due process."

§ 8.8 THE TRIAL

(a) Right to a public trial

The defendant's Sixth Amendment right to a public trial exists apart from the press/public right of access discussed in § 8.7(b). Whether it has a broader reach than the First Amendment right of access has not been considered by the Court. It has been held to apply to criminal contempt proceedings, *In re Oliver* (1948), and to certain pretrial proceedings, such as a suppression hearing, which bear a resemblance to a trial, *Waller v. Ga.* (1984). In *Waller,* the Court held that the standards adopted in *Press-Enterprise I* for overriding the right of access also governed the closure of a suppression hearing over defendant's objection. See § 8.7(b). The defendant's constitutional right to a public trial has been characterized as serving the defendant's interest by (i) providing "a safeguard against an attempt to employ our courts as instruments of persecution" (the knowledge that the trial "is subject to contemporaneous review in the form of public opinion" serving as "an effective restraint on possible abuse of judicial power"), (ii) assuring testimonial trustworthiness by inducing a fear in witnesses that false testimony will be detected, and (iii) making the proceedings known to possible material witnesses who might otherwise be unknown to the defense. *Oliver.* As these interests, particularly the first, overlap substantially with those underlying the right of access, the weighing of claimed "compelling interests" for closure is likely to be similar in both settings.

(b) Right of presence

While "rooted to a large extent in the confrontation clause of the Sixth Amendment," the defendant's constitutional right to be present also has a due process component. *U.S. v. Gagnon* (1985). Accordingly, it is not restricted to those parts of the trial in which the defendant is "actually confronting witnesses or evidence against him," but encompasses all trial-related proceedings at which defendant's presence "has a relation, reasonably substantial, to the fullness of his opportunity to defend against the charge." *Gagnon.* In determining whether the right extends to a particular proceeding apart from the trial itself, the Court has looked to the function of the right as it relates to the context of the particular case. Thus, while an in-chambers inquiry into a juror's possible prejudice would generally require defendant's presence, *Gagnon* held that was not the case where the trial judge (with counsel for the defendant present) did no more than first explain to the juror that defendant's continuous sketching during trial was innocuous and then receive from the juror an assurance of continued impartiality. See also *Ky. v. Stincer* (1987) (in-chamber examination of two young victims of alleged sex offense, to determine solely whether they were competent to testify, did not constitutionally require defendant's presence, where defense counsel participated and further questions concerning competency could be raised at trial with defendant present).

The state cannot unnecessarily condition defendant's presence at trial in such a way as to create possible juror bias against him. Thus, it cannot insist that he stand trial in prison garb, *Estelle v. Williams* (1976), but it can insist upon reasonable security precautions, *Holbrook v. Flynn* (1986). Also, defendant can forfeit his right to be present by his disruptive misconduct. See *Ill. v. Allen* (1970) (where defendant had continued in his disruptive behavior despite due warning, the trial court acted appropriately in banishing him from the courtroom rather than resorting to less desirable remedies (e.g., binding and gagging him) simply to ensure his physical presence during the remainder of the trial).

(c) Right of confrontation

Although the Sixth Amendment's confrontation clause also contributes to other rights—consider e.g., the defendant's right of presence ((b) supra) and *Parker v. Gladden* (1966) (holding the confrontation clause violated by a bailiff's expression of personal opinion to the jury)—the Supreme Court has characterized the right to cross-examine prosecution witnesses as the "primary interest" secured by that clause. *Douglas v. Ala.* (1965). The Court has characterized its cases dealing with that right as falling into "two broad, albeit not exclusive categories, 'cases involving the admission of out-of-court statements and cases involving restrictions imposed by law or by the trial court on the scope of cross-examination.'" *Ky. v. Stincer* (1987).

As to the first category of cases, the Court has recognized that "hearsay rules and the confrontation clause are generally designed to protect similar values" and has therefore accepted "firmly rooted" hearsay "exceptions" which allow its use. *White v. Ill.* (1992). Apart from those exceptions, out of court statements will also be accepted as consistent with the confrontation clause where supported by a "showing of particularized guarantees of trustworthiness", judged in light of the circumstances "that surround the making of the statement and that render the declarant particularly worthy of belief." *Idaho v. Wright* (1990). As for the second group of cases, involving state restriction of the scope of cross-examination, the Court has held that relevant cross-examination can be restricted, if at all, only by a showing of some compelling state need. Thus, *Davis v. Alaska* (1974) found that the trial judge committed constitutional error in denying defense the opportunity to raise on cross-examination a key witness' juvenile delinquent probationary status. The Court noted that the state has a legitimate interest in protecting the anonymity of juvenile offenders, but that interest could not be utilized to bar cross-examination as to a factor obviously relevant to the witness' possible motivation for testifying.

In *Coy v. Iowa* (1988), the Court held that the right of confrontation extends beyond cross-examination and encompasses also the right to a "face to face meeting with the witnesses appearing before the trier of fact". *Coy* found that right infringed where a state trial court, on the grounding of no more than a legislatively imposed presumption of trauma (contained in a statute aimed at protecting youthful victims of sexual abuse), allowed two 15–year–old female complainants to testify from behind screens. Subsequently, *Md. v. Craig* (1990) upheld a statute allowing a child witness in a sex abuse case to testify via closed circuit television where the trial court made a specific determination that requiring the child to give courtroom testimony in the presence of the defendant would result in the child "suffering serious emotional distress, such that the child cannot reasonably communicate." The Court held that the state interest in protecting the child from trauma caused by defendant's physical presence, "at least where such trauma would impair the child's ability to communicate," as supported by a case-specific finding of necessity, justified dispensing with the element of face-to-face confrontation.

(d) Access to Evidence

The Supreme Court has characterized a series of constitutional rulings as combining to create "what might loosely be called the area of constitutionally-guaranteed access to evidence." *Ariz. v. Youngblood* (1988) The primary components of this guarantee of access are: (1) the prosecution's duty to disclose evidence within its possession or control that is exculpatory and material; (2) the prohibition against governmental bad faith destruction of evidence within its possession; (3) the state's duty to provide the defense with subpoena authority to gain the production of witnesses and physical evidence; (4) the prohibition against governmental actions that interfere with the defense's utilization of its subpoena power.

The prosecution's duty to disclose exculpatory evidence stems from the ruling in *Brady v. Md.* (1963). The Court there held that due process was violated when the prosecution, in responding to a defense request for recorded statements of a codefendant, failed (perhaps inadvertently) to disclose the statement in which the codefendant admitted that he had done the actual killing. While defendant admitted participation in the crime and was thus guilty of murder in any event, the statement would have lent considerable support to his plea to avoid capital punishment. *Brady* established a constitutional obligation of the prosecution to disclose defense requested evidence that is within the prosecution's possession where that evidence is "favorable to [the] accused" and "material either to guilt or punishment." This obligation was viewed as a logical extension of a line of earlier cases holding that due process was violated where the prosecutor failed to correct perjured testimony which it knew or should have known to be false. See § 8.8(h). Here, by failing to disclose evidence that was material and exculpatory, there was a similar deception of the jury and the trial court. Moreover, the deception existed even though, the failure to disclose "was not the result of guile." The focus of due process was "not punishment of society for misdeeds of a prosecutor, but avoidance of an unfair trial" and therefore the suppression constituted a due process violation "irrespective of the good faith or bad faith of the prosecutor."

A line of cases interpreting *Brady* culminated in *U.S. v. Bagley* (1985) in the announcement of the basic guidelines governing the prosecutor's duty to disclose. The *Brady* obligation of the prosecutor now applies both where the defense makes a specific request for potentially exculpatory evidence, as in *Brady,* and where it fails to make such a request. Moreover, a single standard of materiality applies to both types of cases: "[E]vidence is material * * * if there is a reasonable probability that, had the evidence been disclosed to the defense, the result of the proceeding would have been different.

A 'reasonable probability' is a probability sufficient to undermine confidence in the outcome." A plurality opinion in Bagley added, however, that specific request cases are likely to present special considerations in applying this "reasonable probability" standard. A negative response to a specific request not only denies the defense the evidence requested but suggests that it "does not exist," a misrepresentation that might cause greater prejudice by leading the defense to "abandon lines of independent investigation, defenses, or trial strategies."

Where the defendant claims that evidence lost or destroyed by the prosecution would have been exculpatory and material, application of the *Brady* doctrine presents obvious difficulties. Not only must the "courts face the treacherous task of divining the import of materials whose contents is unknown and often disputed," but "when evidence has been destroyed in violation of the Constitution", the only available remedies are "barring further prosecution or suppressing * * * the State's most probative evidence." *Cal. v. Trombetta* (1984). Unlike the *Brady* situation, the court cannot simply order a new trial in which the nondisclosed evidence will now be available. Accordingly, the Court has imposed two rigorous standards for such claims. Initially, the defendant cannot gain relief if the lost or destroyed evidence was of such nature that the defendant can replace it with "comparable evidence by other reasonably available means". See *Trombetta* (possible malfunctions in Intoxilyzer test could be raised without resort to the destroyed breath samples). Second, where the defense cannot obtain comparable evidence, the defense must show "bad faith" by the police or prosecution in their failure to preserve the evidence. "Requiring a defendant to show bad faith," the Court has noted, appropriately restricts the constitutional obligation to preserve evidence to "that class of cases where the interests of justice most clearly require it, i.e. those cases in which the police themselves by their conduct indicate that the evidence would form a basis for exonerating the defendant." *Ariz. v. Youngblood* (1988).

The leading case on the state's obligation to make the subpoena power available to obtain evidence is *Pa. v. Ritchie* (1987). The defendant there, charged with sexual assault of his daughter, sought through subpoena to obtain pretrial inspection of the records of a state protective service agency. Although the records had a confidential status, the state intermediate court held that defendant was entitled constitutionally to obtain any verbatim recorded statements of the daughter made to the agency's counselors in her reporting of the alleged sexual assault, and the state high court took the further step of requiring that the full file be made available to defense so that it could determine whether any other portions were also relevant. The Supreme Court held that the constitution required only that the trial court review the agency file in camera to ensure defendant received all evidence that would fit the *Brady* standard of being both exculpatory and material. It rejected the contention, apparently adopted by the state high court, that right of compulsory process includes a defense right to itself review the evidence for possible relevance even where it enjoyed confidential status. Noting that it had "never squarely held that the Compulsory Process guarantees the right to discover the *identity* of witnesses or to require the Government to produce exculpating evidence," the Court concluded that if it did exist, any such compulsory process right would provide "no *greater* protections in this area than those afforded by due process," which traditionally allowed in camera review. A plurality opinion added that the Sixth Amendment's confrontation clause should have no bearing because it was strictly a trial right, not a "constitutionally-compelled rule of pretrial discovery". The "ability to question adverse witnesses," the plurality noted, "does not include the power to require the pretrial disclosure of any and all information that might be useful to contradicting unfavorable testimony."

A series of cases have dealt with potential constitutional violations in governmental action that undermines the defense's ability to utilize the subpoena authority to gain access to witnesses. The basic approach here has been to weigh the importance of the lost witness to the defense, the strength of the governmental interest underlying the action that precluded access, and the possibility of serving that interest without posing that obstacle to access. The end result has been rulings that vary with the circumstances of the case. See e.g., *Webb v. Tex.* (1972) (due process violated where trial judge used such "unnecessarily strong terms in warning a key defense witness about perjury that he effectively drove the witness from the stand"); *U.S. v. Valenzuela–Bernal* (1982) (while it was proper for the government to promptly deport illegal alien witnesses upon its determination that they possessed no evidence favorable to a defendant charged with transporting them, defendant must be given the opportunity to establish a due process violation by showing "that the evidence lost would be both material and favorable"); *Roviaro v. U.S.* (1957) (relying on federal supervisory power, but suggesting basic prosecution obligation to reveal name of informer where informer was the "sole participant, other than the accused, in the transaction charged," and thus "was the only witness in a position to amplify or contradict the testimony of government witnesses").

(e) Right to present evidence

Although the defense, in general, is limited by the rules of evidence, under exceptional circumstances those rules may operate to violate the defendant's constitutional rights. This is most likely to occur where the rules have their primary impact in restricting the defense. Thus, *Washington v. Tex.* (1967) held that the defendant's right to compulsory process was violated by a state statute prohibiting one coparticipant in an alleged offense from testifying on behalf of the other participant (although allowing him to testify against the other participant). However, rules neutral on their face may operate in a particular case so arbitrarily as to be unconstitutional. Thus, *Chambers v. Miss.* (1973) similarly relied upon due process in finding, under the "totality of the circumstances," constitutional error in preventing the defendant from showing that another had confessed to the crime with which defendant was charged. *Chambers* found insufficient the state's reliance upon (i) an "adverse witness exception" that prevented defense from cross-examining the confessor (who had been called to testify by the defense) and (ii) a restrictive hearsay ruling that barred the testimony of witnesses who had heard the confession.

(f) Defendant's right not to testify

The Fifth Amendment privilege against self-incrimination recognizes the defendant's right to refuse to take the stand at trial. Most of the Supreme Court cases concerning this right have dealt with incidental aspects of its administration. *Griffin v. Cal.* (1965) held that the privilege barred any adverse comment by court or prosecutor on the defendant's failure to take the stand. The privilege would be undermined, the Court noted, if the jury was, in effect, invited to draw an adverse conclusion from the defendant's failure to testify. Where a prosecutor's statement does not refer specifically to defendant's silence, but might be so interpreted, courts commonly ask whether the language used was such that the jury would naturally take it as a comment on silence. However, the prosecutor's comment must be examined in light of the defense's own presentation. See *Lockett v. Ohio* (1978) (where defense had drawn attention to defendant's failure to testify, prosecutor's reference to state's case as "unrefuted" and "uncontradicted" did not violate *Griffin*); *U.S. v. Robinson* (1988) (where defense counsel argued that the government had never allowed defendant to tell his side of the story, prosecutor's statement that defendant could have "taken the stand" was a "fair response").

Consistent with *Griffin*, the trial court may give a "protective instruction" advising the jury that defendant's silence must be disregarded, and *Lakeside v. Ore.* (1978) held that such an instruction may be given even over the objection of defense counsel. *Brooks v. Tenn.* (1972) held that a state practice imposed an unconstitutional burden on the defendant's exercise of his right not to testify when it required the defendant, if he desired to testify, to do so "before any other testimony for the defense is heard." The effect of the statute was to force the defendant to make his choice as to exercising his right not to testify before he had heard the testimony of his witnesses.

(g) Defendant's right to testify

The constitutional right of the defendant to testify stems from three sources: (1) the guarantee of due process (which ensures a "fair adversary process," including a "right to be heard and to offer testimony"); (2) the Sixth Amendment's compulsory process clause (which "logically include[s]" defendant's "right to testify himself"); and (3) the Fifth Amendment's guarantee against compulsory self-incrimination (a "necessary corollary" of which is the defendant's right to testify "in the unfettered exercise of his own will"). *Rock v. Ark.* (1987). The right to testify may be restricted to accommodate other "legitimate interests in the criminal trial process," but those restrictions, as *Rock* noted, "may not be arbitrary or disproportionate to the purposes they are designed to serve." Thus, *Rock* held that, though the state has a legitimate interest in imposing evidentiary restrictions designed to exclude unreliable evidence, that interest could not justify a per se exclusion of a defendant's hypnotically refreshed testimony. Such a rule was excessive because it operated without regard either to procedural safeguards employed in the hypnosis process to reduce inaccuracies or to the availability of corroborating evidence and other traditional means of assessing the accuracy of the particular testimony. *Perry v. Leeke* (1989), on the other hand, held that it was permissible to treat a testifying defendant like any other witness and bar consultation with counsel during a short recess prior to the start of cross-examination. Distinguishable was the constitutional violation in *Geders v. U.S.,* (see § 7.6(a)), for the defendant/witness there was barred from consultation during an overnight recess, where general matters of defense strategy (rather than simply witness testimony) would have been discussed.

(h) Prosecutorial misconduct

Apart from limitations imposed by the specific constitutional guarantees, the prosecution is subject at trial to due process requirements relating to its role as the representative of the state "whose interest in a criminal prosecution is not that it shall win a case, but that justice shall be done." *Berger v. U.S.* (1935). Building upon this obligation, a series of cases hold the prosecution must correct any material perjured testimony of its witnesses when it knows, or should know from information that it has received, that the testimony is false. See e.g., *Giglio v. U.S.* (1972) (due process violated when the prosecutor, not realizing that promises had been made by his predecessor, failed to correct a witness' statement that no promises had been made in return for his testimony). The test of "materiality" for this purpose is more rigorous than that applied to the prosecution's duty to disclose exculpatory testimony. See § 8.4(d). False testimony is material if there is "any reasonable likelihood * * * [it] could have affected the judgment of the jury"—a standard compared by the Court to the "harmless beyond a reasonable doubt" standard of *Chapman v. Cal.* (§ 8.10(b)). See *U.S. v. Bagley* (1985).

In presenting argument to the jury, particularly closing argument, the prosecutor is also subject to due process limitations. Here due process prohibits statements so prejudicial and inflammatory as to produce a "fundamentally unfair" trial. *Darden v. Wainwright* (1986). In making this assessment, the Court will consider a variety of factors, including the presence or absence of trial court instructions advising the jury to disregard the prosecutor's improper remarks, the frequency of those remarks, the general tenor of the trial, and the likely impact of the remarks in light of the strength of the evidence against the accused.

§ 8.9 POST–TRIAL PROCEDURES

(a) Sentencing

Apart from the area of capital sentencing, where the Eighth Amendment introduces special considerations, the Supreme Court consistently has held that the sentencing process, while not "immune" from the restrictions of due process, is subject to considerably less extensive procedural requirements than the trial process. That conclusion is based, in part, on the historical separation of the trial and sentencing stages, as reflected in the many constitutional guarantees that clearly refer only to the trial. It also has been justified on the ground that fulfillment of the basic objectives of sentencing, particularly the emphasis on relating punishment to the individual as well as the crime, often requires more flexible procedures than those applied to the determination of guilt. Thus, *Williams v. Okla.* (1959) held that a sentencing judge could "consider responsible unsworn or 'out-of-court' information relative to the circumstances of the crime and to the convicted person's life and characteristics." And, in *Williams v. N.Y.* (1949), the Court held that the defendant had no constitutional right to an adversary sentencing proceeding in which he could cross-examine persons who had supplied information to the sentencing court. Consider also *U.S. v. Grayson* (1978) (in considering "the defendant's whole person and personality," the sentencing judge may give consideration to defendant's untruthfulness in his trial testimony, notwithstanding defendant's complaint that he has never been indicted, tried, or convicted for the alleged perjury); *U.S. v. Dunnigan* (1993) (sentence enhancement for obstruction of justice based on defendant's perjured testimony at her trial does not impose an undue burden on defendant's right to testify where the trial court must make specific findings as to the perjury and cannot rely simply on the fact that the jury disbelieved her testimony and found her guilty of the crime charged).

While recognizing that sentencing is different, the Court has not automatically assumed that basic procedural rights are inconsistent with sentencing objectives. It has analyzed separately the role of each right and the particular context in which it is raised. Thus, *Mempa v. Rhay* (§ 7.3(g)) established that the indigent defendant's Sixth Amendment right to appointed counsel applies to the sentencing proceeding. *Townsend v. Burke* (1948) recognized a due process right "not to be sentenced on the basis of materially untrue information", found to be violated there when the trial judge simply pushed aside an uncounseled defendant's protestations (later found to be accurate) that the judge had incorrect information on his prior record. Also, where the sentencing statute simply is triggered by the commission of an offense, and imposing the sentence requires a finding as to some additional condition, the Court has held that due process requires a hearing on the presence of that condition. See *Specht v. Patterson* (1967) (dangerous sex offender statute). Note also *Morrissey v. Brewer* (1972) (hearing required for probation or parole violation determination). The Court has noted, however, that at least as to those additional factors that merely "up the ante in sentencing" for the offense (i.e., enhancement factors), the state can appropriately require only proof by a preponderance of the evidence. *McMillan v. Pa.* (1986).

The double jeopardy clause also has been held to bear upon sentencing. The Court has frequently noted that double jeopardy "protects against multiple punishment for the same offense". *N.C. v. Pearce* (1969). At the same time, however, it has held that the *Blockburger* definition of "same offense" (see § 8.3(a)) does not limit sentencing, so the state may authorize a separate punishment for two crimes even though all the elements of the one are included in the other. *Mo. v. Hunter* (1983). Thus, the prohibition against multiple punishment serves primarily to preclude a sentencing judge from imposing a sentence and then later altering the sentence to the prejudice of defendant. The leading case applying this protection is *Ex parte Lange* (1873), which invalidated a trial judge's attempt to correct an original sentence of both prison and a fine to simply prison (the statute not allowing both) after the defendant had already paid his fine.

Lange was sharply limited in *Jones v. Thomas* (1989). *Jones* found no double jeopardy bar where a trial court originally sentenced defendant to consecutive terms on two offenses, the defendant fully served the shorter term on the lesser offense, an appellate court then ruled that separate sentences were not permissible on both offenses, and the trial judge then vacated the sentence on the lesser offense and gave the defendant credit for the time served against the longer term remaining on the greater offense. By giving credit for the time served, the trial court here, unlike the trial court in *Lange,* had made certain that the total punishment imposed was not beyond that legislatively authorized. *U.S. v. DiFrancesco* (1980) held that *Lange* has no bearing on prosecution appeals of sentences claimed to be illegal, even though the result of the appeal may be to impose a new, higher sentence. *Pearce,* supra, similarly held that where a defendant's conviction is overturned, he starts anew and double jeopardy does not prohibit a higher sentence on reconviction—although he must be given credit for time previously served (and the higher sentence, under due process, cannot be vindictive).

(b) Appeals

The Supreme Court continues to recognize the ruling in *McKane v. Durston* (1894) that a state is not constitutionally required to provide appellate review of criminal convictions. See also *Ross v. Moffitt* (§ 7.2(d)). All states now provide for appellate review, however, and the Court has held that, once established, appellate review cannot be restricted or burdened on arbitrary grounds. Thus, *Griffin v. Ill.* (§ 7.2(d)) held that the availability of review cannot be conditioned on the convicted defendant's financial status, and *Douglas v. Cal.* (§ 7.2(d)) required the appointment of counsel on a first appeal that is granted as a matter of right.

N.C. v. Pearce (1969) granted further protection to the appellate process in barring vindictiveness against those who use the process. *Pearce* involved defendants who appealed their initial convictions, obtained reversals, were retried and convicted on the same charges, and then were sentenced to more severe sentences than on the first conviction. *Pearce* held that due process prohibited the imposition of a more severe sentence for the purpose of discouraging defendants from exercising their statutory right to appeal. Moreover, to facilitate attack on such improper motivation, the Court imposed a "prophylactic" safeguard of requiring the trial judge to set forth reasons for a higher sentence, with these reasons based on factors that refute vindictiveness. Subsequent decisions, however, have limited this aspect of the *Pearce* ruling. The Court has held that the statement of reasons for the higher sentence is not required as to: (i) a second sentence by a jury, *Chaffin v. Stynchcombe* (1973); (ii) a second sentence imposed following a trial de novo, *Colten v. Ky.* (1972); and (iii) a second sentence imposed by a judge who granted the new trial order that resulted in the retrial, *Tex. v. McCullough* (1986). Moreover, *McCullough* strongly suggests that a second sentence imposed by a different judge would fall in the same category. In all of these situations the likelihood of vindictiveness is viewed as not sufficient to justify a presumption of vindictiveness that the sentencer must rebut by setting forth grounds for the higher sentence.

As for the grounds that will justify a higher sentence when reasons must be set forth, *Pearce* suggested these might be limited to specific conduct of the defendant occurring since the first sentence, so as to eliminate grounds that might be manipulated. *Wasman v. U.S.* (1984) held, however, that a higher sentence also could be justified by reference to an intervening conviction on a different offense that had been at the indictment stage at the time of original sentence (and specifically excluded from consideration at that time because the sentencing judge refused to give weight to charges not yet proven). *McCullough* went a step beyond *Wasman* in allowing a higher sentence to be justified on the basis of new testimony which had "a direct effect on the strength of the state's case" and new information revealing that defendant's background was worse than previously assumed.

(c) Retrials

The Fifth Amendment's double jeopardy clause provides that no person shall be "twice put in jeopardy" for the "same offense." See § 8.3(a) (defining the "same offense" for this purpose). Jeopardy attaches in jury trials once the jury is "empaneled and sworn," and it attaches in bench trials when "the first witness is sworn." *Crist v. Bretz* (1978). Once the trial has reached the point where jeopardy attached, any retrial on the same charge presents potential constitutional difficulties. The prohibition against twice putting a person in jeopardy is not absolute, however, and not every retrial for the same offense is constitutionally prohibited.

The double jeopardy prohibition is most flexible as applied to retrials following a mistrial (i.e., a court order dismissing the jury before a verdict is reached). A trial judge granting a mistrial ordinarily contemplates that a new trial will be permitted, but there are situations in which those double jeopardy concerns applicable even before a verdict has been reached—the "minimization of harassing exposure to the harrowing experiences of a criminal trial, and the valued right [of the defendant] to continue with the chosen jury"—will bar a new trial. *Crist v. Bretz*. If the mistrial was ordered at the request of the defense, a new trial will not be barred unless the defense acted in response to prosecutorial or judicial overreaching that was "intended to 'goad' the defendant into moving for a mistrial." *Ore. v. Kennedy* (1982). Where the mistrial was ordered over defense objection (or without giving the defense an opportunity to object), a retrial will be barred unless the "declaration of the mistrial was dictated by 'manifest necessity' or the 'ends of public justice.' " *Ill. v. Somerville* (1973). If the mistrial was due to an uncontrollable event (e.g., the illness of a juror, or a jury that could not agree on a verdict), that ordinarily will meet this "manifest necessity" standard and a retrial will be permitted. Where the mistrial was due to some error by counsel or the trial judge, the Court will look to several factors in applying the "manifest necessity" standard. These include: (i) if the error was by the prosecutor, whether it was the type of error that might be intentionally manipulated to gain a new trial at which the prosecution could strengthen its case, *Downum v. U.S.* (1963); (ii) whether the trial court could have utilized alternative remedies for the error that would have permitted the trial to continue to an impartial verdict that could be sustained on appeal, *U.S. v. Jorn* (1971); and (iii) whether the trial judge's rejection of alternatives to a mistrial involved the assessment of factors (e.g., jury reaction to a prejudicial remark) that are not particularly "amenable to appellate scrutiny." *Ariz. v. Washington* (1978).

Along with the mistrial, a trial court also may keep a case from reaching a verdict by dismissing the prosecution on grounds that do not contemplate a retrial. When such a dismissal is issued after jeopardy has attached, the primary concern is whether it amounts, in effect, to an acquittal. If the trial court's ruling is based on its conclusion that the evidence is insufficient to establish the offense charged, it is treated like a jury verdict of acquittal and further proceedings are not allowed. See *Sanabria v. U.S.* (1978). If the dismissal is based on other grounds, not involving a resolution of the factual elements of the offense, then the state can provide for a prosecution appeal and a retrial if the prosecution is successful in overturning the dismissal. Thus, *U.S. v. Scott* (1978) upheld a government appeal from a mid-trial dismissal that had been issued on the theory that preindictment delay had resulted in a denial of due process.

As suggested above, if the trial reaches a verdict and the jury acquits, reprosecution is barred. The state cannot gain reversal of that acquittal even if the acquittal probably was based on some error in the instructions or the admission of evidence. *Sanabria*. As the Court noted in *Scott* "to permit a second trial after an acquittal, however mistaken the acquittal may have been, would present an unacceptably high risk that the Government, with its vastly superior resources, might wear down the defendant so that 'even though innocent he may be found guilty.'" A special exception exists where the defendant was originally convicted and the trial judge subsequently entered a judgment of acquittal. Here an appeal is possible because reversal of the trial judge's ruling would not result in a retrial, but simply in reinstituting the initial jury conviction. *U.S. v. Wilson* (1975).

Where the trial ends in a verdict of guilty, re-prosecution also is barred unless the defendant successfully challenges that verdict. If he chooses, the defendant may accept the guilty verdict and thereby prevent the government from subjecting him to the "embarrassment, expense, and ordeal" of another trial. *Wilson*. If the defendant appeals the guilty verdict, and gains a reversal, he then may be retried, unless the reversal was grounded on the insufficiency of the evidence to support the verdict. *Burks v. U.S.* (1978). The double jeopardy principle allowing retrials following appellate reversals is often described as the "*Ball* principle," after *Ball v. U.S.* (1896). It is justified as serving "defendant's rights as well as society interests," since a contrary position would obviously discourage appellate courts from granting reversals. *U.S. v. Tateo* (1964). The *Ball* principle does not allow retrial following a reversal based on the insufficiency of the prosecution's evidence since that appellate ruling is equivalent to a directed verdict of acquittal at trial. *Burks*. However, this only applies when all of the evidence before the trial court is insufficient to sustain a conviction, not where the trial court erred in admitting certain evidence and the insufficiency only exists without that evidence. *Lockhart v. Nelson* (1988).

The acquittal concept also enters the picture, when defendant is charged with a higher offense, but is convicted on a lesser charge. Here, the jury's refusal to convict on the higher charge is an implied acquittal on that higher charge. Thus, if the defendant appeals the conviction and obtains a reversal, the *Ball* principle permits a retrial only on the lower charge. *Green v. U.S.* (1957).

Finally, the double jeopardy clause only bars reprosecution by the same sovereign. Thus, if the defendant is tried for bank robbery at the federal level, even if acquitted, he may be prosecuted by the state for the same activity under state law. *Bartkus v. Ill.* (1959). See also *Abbate v. U.S.* (1959) (federal prosecution following state prosecution); *Heath v. Ala.* (1985) (successive prosecutions by different states). Of course, a jurisdiction may relinquish its authority to take advantage of this "dual sovereignty" doctrine, as many states have done. Moreover, the doctrine does not apply to separate prosecutions under state laws and local ordinances. Since local units of government receive their ordinance authority from the states, they are not considered separate sovereignties. *Waller v. Fla.* (1970).

§ 8.10   HARMLESS ERROR

(a) Application to constitutional errors

All jurisdictions have "harmless error" provisions that prohibit appellate reversal based upon errors that did not "affect the substantial rights" of the convicted defendants. Prior to *Chapman v. Cal.* (1967), it frequently was assumed that the harmless error principle did not apply to the review of constitutional errors because such errors were "per se injurious." *Chapman,* however, rejected that position. The *Chapman* opinion acknowledged that a rule of automatic reversal had been applied to certain constitutional errors (see (c) infra), but concluded that there was no basis in theory or past precedent for granting all constitutional errors a blanket exemption from the traditional requirements of appellate review. The Court noted in this respect that harmless error statutes serve "a very useful purpose insofar as they block setting aside convictions for small errors or defects that have little, if any, likelihood of having changed the result of the trial." That purpose was equally served where, "in the setting of a particular case," constitutional errors are "so unimportant or insignificant" as to fall within a narrowly confined harmless error standard.

The harmless error standard serves to determine whether the possible influence of a constitutional violation is so unlikely that a new trial need not be ordered. Thus, the harmless error standard has no bearing on constitutional violations that are not remedied by a new trial, but call for a remedy of precluding prosecution (e.g. double jeopardy or speedy trial violations). Where a new trial is the remedy, there is no need to consider the possible application of the *Chapman* standard if the finding of a constitutional violation rests on a showing of specific prejudice to defense in the outcome of the case. Thus, harmless error analysis also is not applied to a constitutional violation that requires a finding that the challenged behavior presented a "reasonable probability" of having affected the outcome of the proceeding—as in ineffective assistance of counsel claims under *Strickland* (§ 7.7), and due process claims for the nondisclosure of exculpatory evidence under *Brady–Bagley* (§ 8.4(d)). The presence of the violation in itself establishes that the likely impact was more than enough to meet *Chapman's* reasonable double standard ((b) infra).

As to those constitutional violations that are remedied by a new trial and that do not require a showing of prejudicial impact in establishing the violation, application of the *Chapman* standard has become the general rule. As discussed in subsection (c), there remain a group of such errors that require automatic reversal without applying *Chapman,* but "they are the exception and not the rule". *Rose v. Clark* (1986). Thus *Chapman* has been held applicable to all of the violations involved in the use of unconstitutionally obtained evidence: the improper admission of evidence obtained in violation of the Fourth Amendment, including unconstitutional electronic surveillance (chs. 2 and 3); the admission of statements obtained in violation of the Sixth Amendment right to counsel, in violation of *Miranda,* and statements that are involuntary (ch. 4); and the admission of identification evidence that was obtained in violation of the Sixth Amendment right to counsel or that is excludable under due process (ch. 5). So too, *Chapman* applies to most of the constitutional errors discussed in this chapter, such as comment on defendant's failure to testify (the constitutional violation in *Chapman* itself). As to the constitutional violations discussed in ch. 7, *Chapman* generally does not apply to those right to counsel violations that do not relate to the acquisition of evidence, as they tend to fall either in the automatic reversal category discussed in subsection (c) or to require a finding of prejudicial impact in establishing the violation. Consider, however, *Coleman v. Ala.* (§ 7.3(d)), where the harmless error standard of *Chapman* was held applicable to the denial of a Sixth Amendment right to counsel at a preliminary hearing.

(b) The reasonable doubt standard

Chapman also held that the substantive standard for determining whether an error was harmless, as applied to constitutional errors, was a matter of federal rather than state law: "Whether a conviction for crime should stand when a state has failed to accord federal constitutionally guaranteed rights is every bit as much a matter of a federal question as what particular constitutional provisions themselves mean, what they guarantee and whether they had been denied." The state court in *Chapman* had applied a harmless error standard that placed primary emphasis upon the presence of evidence that rendered the proof of guilt "overwhelming," but the Supreme Court stressed that the standard should emphasize the impact of the error upon the "substantial rights" of the defendant. Accordingly, the Court ruled that a constitutional error could be viewed as harmless only if the "beneficiary" of the error (i.e., the prosecution) could "prove beyond a reasonable doubt that the error * * * did not contribute to the verdict obtained."

The *Chapman* opinion clearly indicated that its harmless error standard looked not to whether a jury could have convicted without regard to constitutional error, or whether the appellate court judges would have convicted without the error, but to whether the error had influenced the jury in reaching its verdict. The Court did not clearly indicate, however, precisely what weight could be given to properly admitted, "overwhelming evidence" of guilt in making that determination. *Harrington v. Cal.* (1969) and *Milton v. Wainwright* (1972) subsequently indicated that significant weight could be given to that factor. In *Harrington,* the prosecution had utilized at trial, in violation of the *Bruton* case (§ 8.3(b)), the confession of a nontestifying codefendant that placed the defendant at the scene of the crime; however, the defendant's own statement and the testimony of several eyewitnesses also placed him there, and a testifying codefendant placed him at the scene with a gun in hand. Concluding that the *Bruton* violation was harmless, *Harrington* noted that the improperly admitted statement of the nontestifying codefendant was "merely cumulative" and that the untainted evidence of guilt was "so overwhelming" that to refuse to hold the error harmless would, in effect, exclude *Bruton* violations from the *Chapman* standard. *Milton,* holding harmless the admission of a confession assumed arguendo to have been obtained in violation of the Sixth Amendment, indicated that consideration of untainted evidence would not be limited to a situation in which the inadmissible evidence was precisely matched by the untainted evidence. Although the Court noted that the challenged confession contained "incriminating statements * * * essentially the same as those given in prior [admissible] confessions," it stressed the strength of all the remaining evidence and did not bother to characterize the challenged confession as "cumulative." Indeed, the *Milton* opinion contained language suggesting that where the incriminating evidence is so strong that the jury undoubtedly would have convicted in any event, it can therefore be said beyond a reasonable doubt that the error did not contribute to the jury's verdict. See also *Schneble v. Fla.* (1972) (noting the need to assess the "probable impact" of the inadmissible confession "on the minds of the average jury," and also noting that it was certain that the jury "would not have found the state's case significantly less persuasive had the [confession] been excluded").

(c) Automatic reversal

Chapman noted that "there are some constitutional rights so basic to a fair trial that their infraction can never be treated as harmless error."

Included in this category are: violation of the right
to trial before an impartial judge, *Tumey v. Ohio*
(§ 8.6(f)); denial of the constitutional rights to appointed counsel at trial and on first appeal of right,
Gideon v. Wainwright (§ 7.1(b)), *Penson v. Ohio*
(1988); ineffective assistance claims based on presumed prejudice, i.e., conflict of interest and state
interference with counsel, *Holloway v. Ark.*
(§ 7.7(e)), *Geders v. U.S.* (§ 7.6(a)); denial of a defendant's right to public trial, *Waller v. Ga.*
(§ 8.8(a)); denial of defendant's right to proceed to
pro se, *McKaskle v. Wiggins* (§ 7.4(d)); constitutional violations in the selection of the petit jury,
Gray v. Miss. (§ 8.6(d)); constitutionally deficient
jury instructions on the need for proof beyond a
reasonable doubt, *Sullivan v. La.* (1993); and racial
discrimination in the selection of a grand jury,
Rose v. Mitchell (§ 8.2(b)).

McKaskle, supra, explained the refusal to apply
a harmless error analysis there as flowing logically
from the nature of the right to proceed pro se,
which allows the defendant to control his own
destiny even if it works to his disadvantage. See
§ 7.4(d). *Rose v. Mitchell* "reasoned that racial
discrimination in the selection of the grand jury is
so pernicious, and other remedies so impracticable,
that the remedy of automatic reversal was necessary as a prophylactic means of deterring grand
jury discrimination in the future." *U.S. v. Me-
chanik* (1986). Explaining automatic reversal for
Tumey and *Gideon* violations, *Rose v. Clark* (1986)
noted that such violations deprive defendants of

"basic protections" without which "a criminal trial cannot reliably serve its function as a vehicle for determination of guilt or innocence." *Gray* characterized a constitutional violation in jury selection, even where it involves only one juror, as falling in the same general category as *Tumey* and *Gideon* violations. Since jury selection standards are "rooted in the constitutional right to an impartial jury, and because the impartiality of the adjudicator goes to the very integrity of the legal system, the *Chapman* harmless error standard cannot apply." *Sullivan*, supra, reasoned that a deficient reasonable doubt instruction deprived the defendant of his Sixth Amendment right to a jury finding of guilt beyond a resonable doubt, and an appellate court holding such error harmless would be substituting its judgment for the constitutionally required judgment of a jury. Justice Harlan, in his *Chapman* dissent, characterized many such errors as requiring automatic reversal because of their "inherently indeterminate impact" upon the outcome of the proceeding.

In *Ariz. v. Fulminante* (1991), the Court combined several of the characteristics noted in previous cases in offering a general description of what distinguishes automatic-reversal violations from violations subject to *Chapman*. The automatic-reversal category was reserved for "structural defect[s] affecting the framework within which the trial proceeds." Violations subject to *Chapman* were tied together by the "common thread" of "involv[ing] 'trial error'—error which occurred during the presentation of the case to the jury and which therefore may be quantitatively assessed in the context of other evidence presented in order to determine whether its admission was harmless beyond a reasonable doubt." The *Fulminante* majority therefore rejected earlier precedent suggesting that the admissibility of a coerced confession should be in the automatic-reversal category. The dissent argued that the distinction offered by the majority failed to explain all of the rulings, that placement in one category or the other depended on the nature of the right involved, and that admission of a coerced confession was so fundamentally inconsistent with "the thesis that ours is not an inquisitorial system of criminal justice" that no conviction should ever be sustained where that prohibition was violated.

†